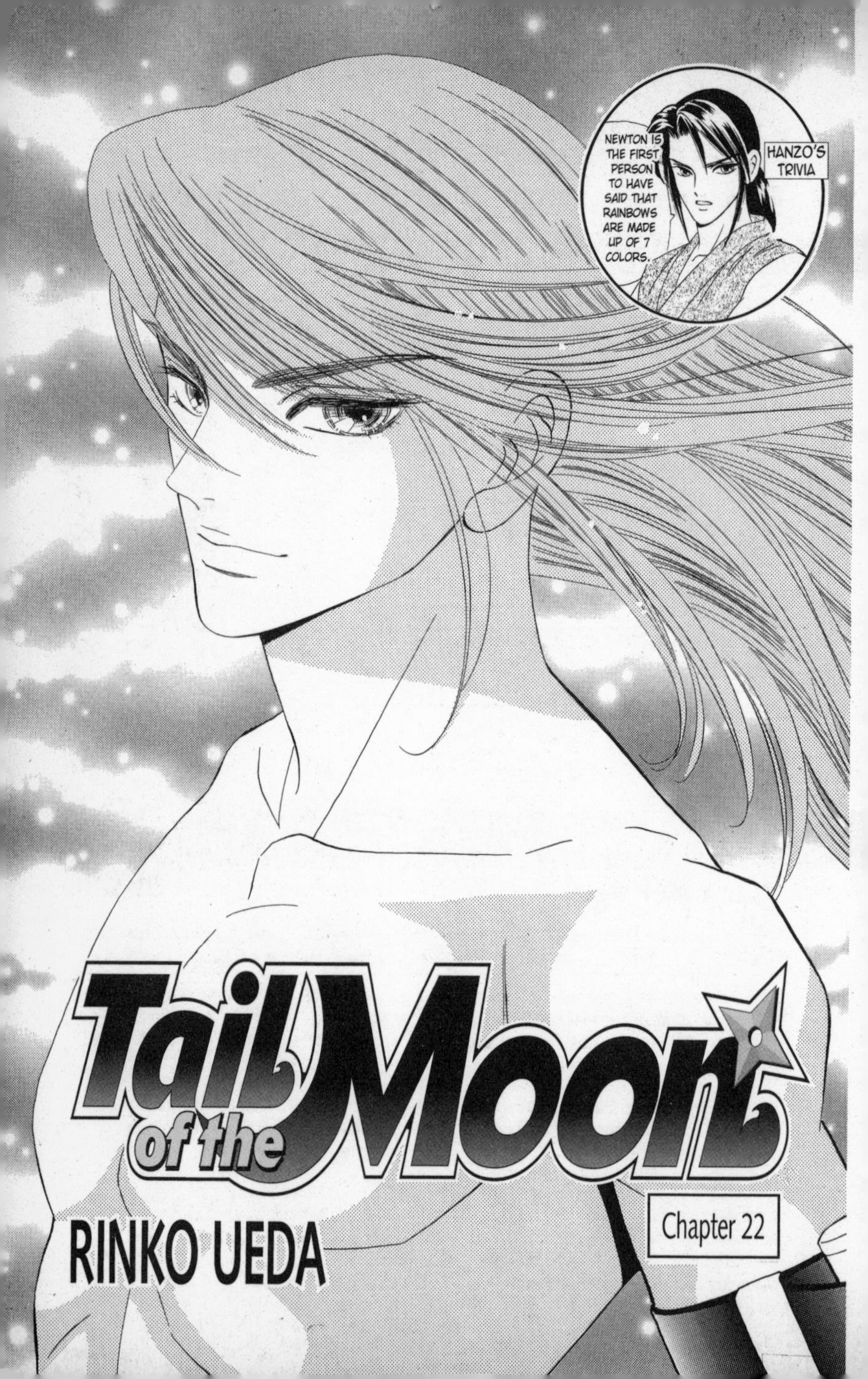
NEWTON IS THE FIRST PERSON TO HAVE SAID THAT RAINBOWS ARE MADE UP OF 7 COLORS.
HANZO'S TRIVIA
Tail of the Moon
Chapter 22
RINKO UEDA

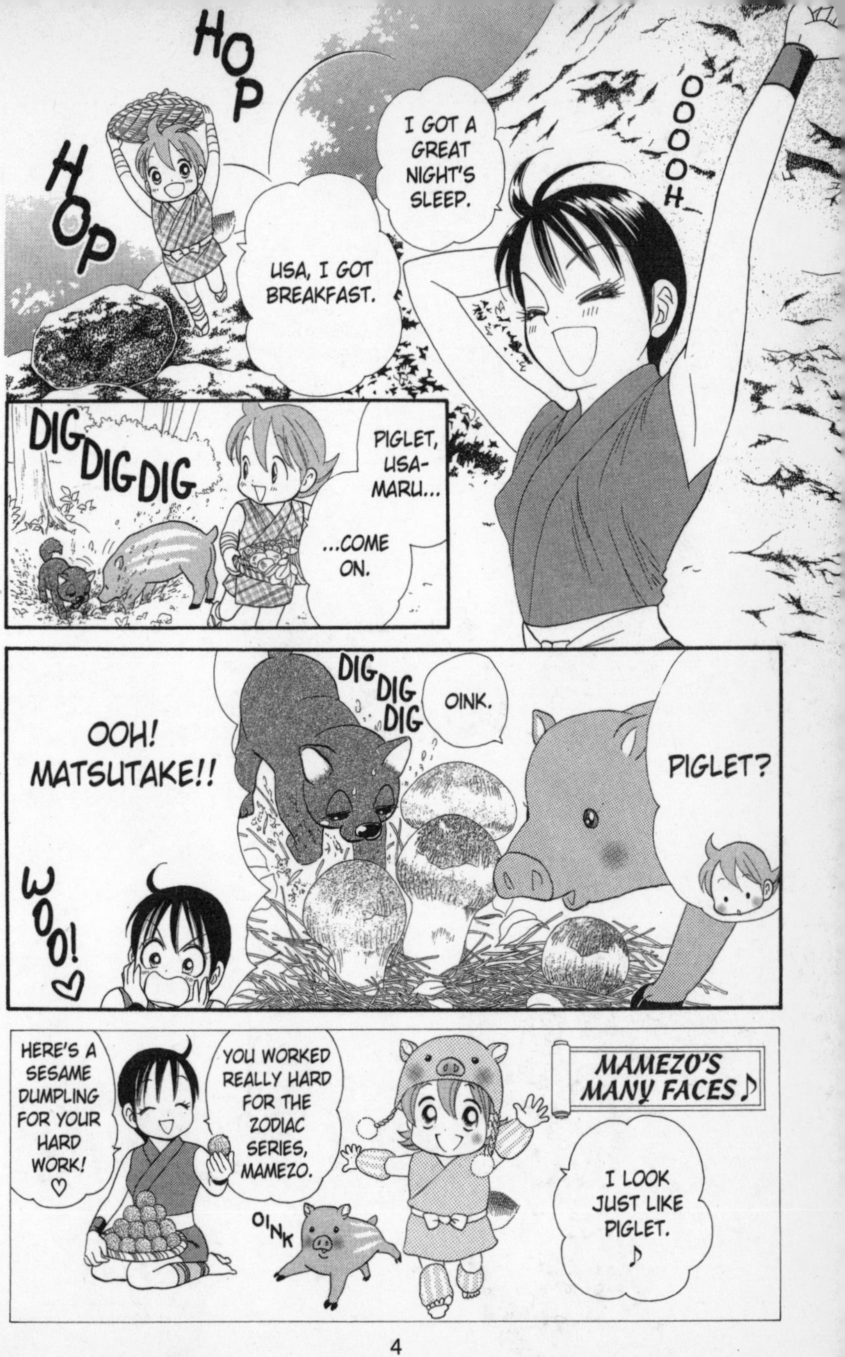
OOOOOH
I GOT A GREAT NIGHT'S SLEEP.
HOP HOP
USA, I GOT BREAKFAST.
DIG DIG DIG
PIGLET, USA-MARU...
...COME ON.
PIGLET?
OINK.
DIG DIG DIG
OOH! MATSUTAKE!!
WOO! ♡
MAMEZO'S MANY FACES♪
I LOOK JUST LIKE PIGLET. ♪
OINK
YOU WORKED REALLY HARD FOR THE ZODIAC SERIES, MAMEZO.
HERE'S A SESAME DUMPLING FOR YOUR HARD WORK! ♡

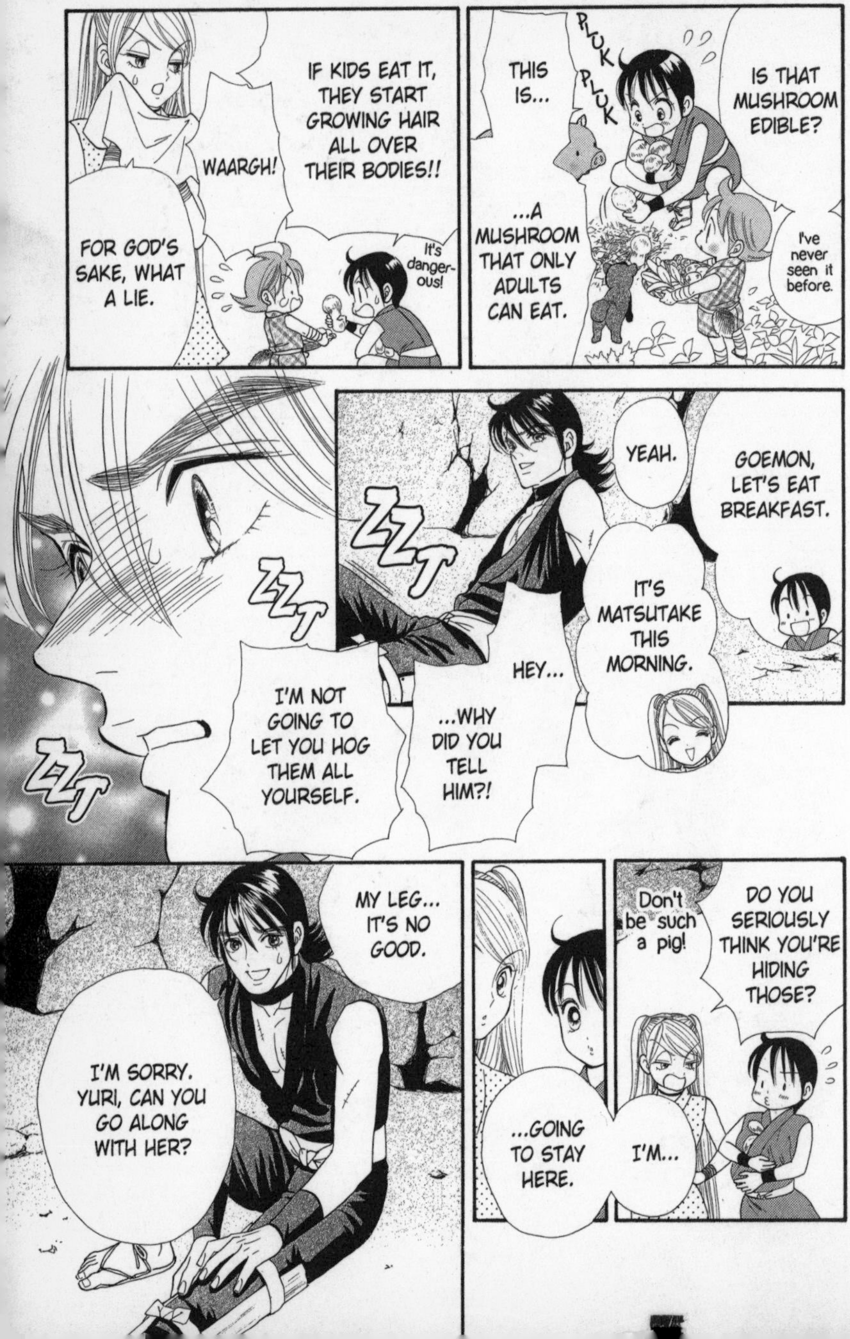
IS THAT MUSHROOM EDIBLE?
I've never seen it before.
PLUK PLUK
THIS IS...
...A MUSHROOM THAT ONLY ADULTS CAN EAT.
IF KIDS EAT IT, THEY START GROWING HAIR ALL OVER THEIR BODIES!!
WAARGH!
It's danger-ous!
FOR GOD'S SAKE, WHAT A LIE.
GOEMON, LET'S EAT BREAKFAST.
YEAH.
IT'S MATSUTAKE THIS MORNING.
ZZT
HEY...
...WHY DID YOU TELL HIM?!
I'M NOT GOING TO LET YOU HOG THEM ALL YOURSELF.
ZZT
ZZT
DO YOU SERIOUSLY THINK YOU'RE HIDING THOSE?
Don't be such a pig!
I'M...
...GOING TO STAY HERE.
MY LEG... IT'S NO GOOD.
I'M SORRY. YURI, CAN YOU GO ALONG WITH HER?

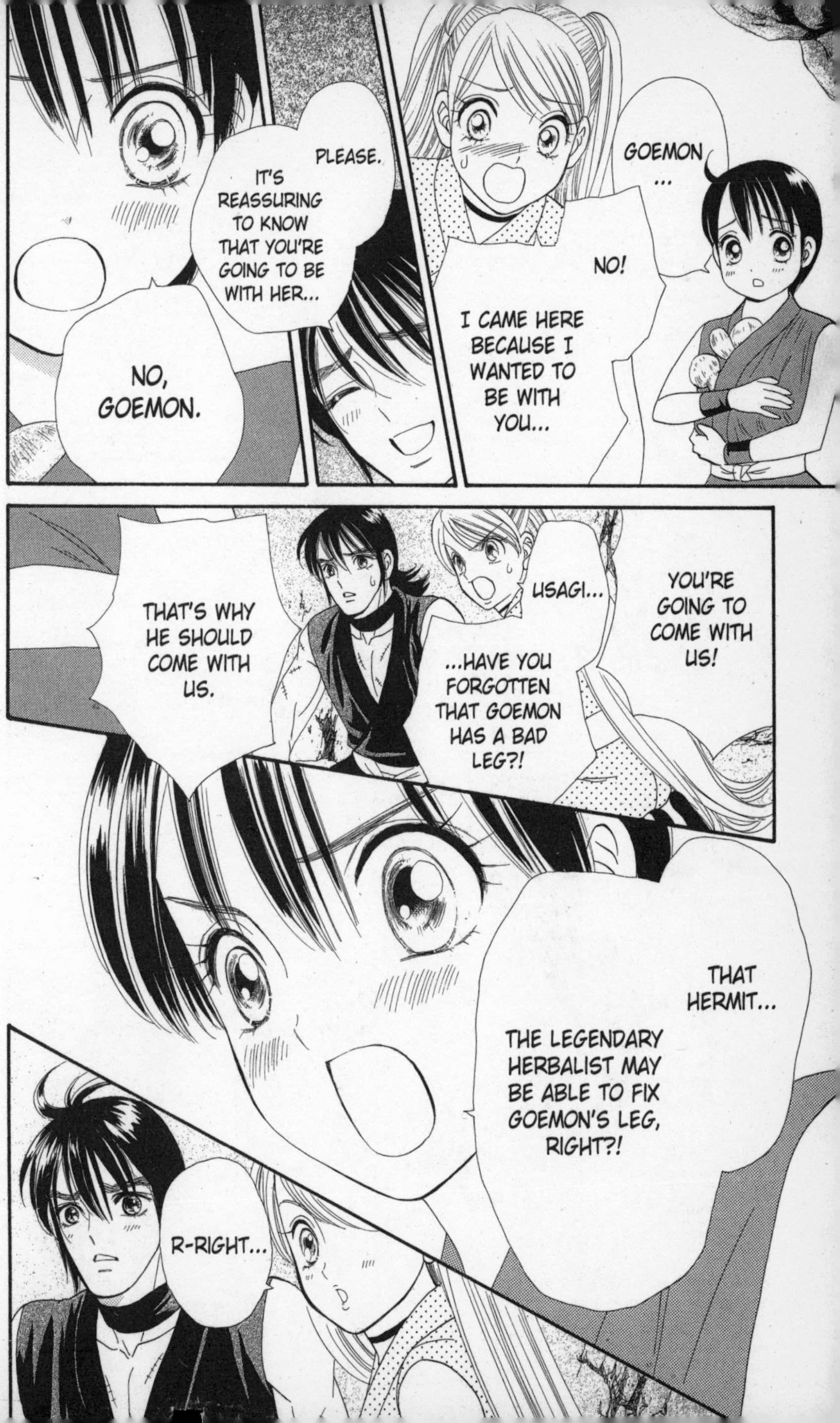
GOEMON ...
NO!
I CAME HERE BECAUSE I WANTED TO BE WITH YOU...
PLEASE.
IT'S REASSURING TO KNOW THAT YOU'RE GOING TO BE WITH HER...
NO, GOEMON.
YOU'RE GOING TO COME WITH US!
USAGI...
...HAVE YOU FORGOTTEN THAT GOEMON HAS A BAD LEG?!
THAT'S WHY HE SHOULD COME WITH US.
THAT HERMIT...
THE LEGENDARY HERBALIST MAY BE ABLE TO FIX GOEMON'S LEG, RIGHT?!
R-RIGHT...

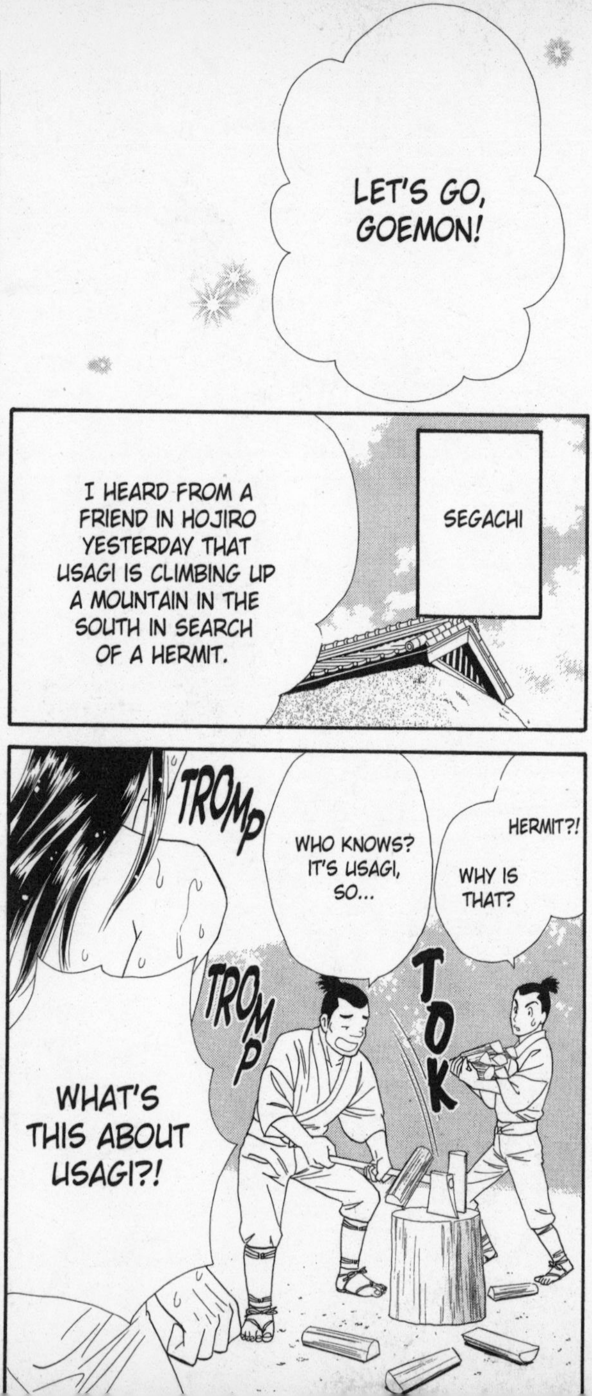
LET'S GO, GOEMON!
SEGACHI
I HEARD FROM A FRIEND IN HOJIRO YESTERDAY THAT USAGI IS CLIMBING UP A MOUNTAIN IN THE SOUTH IN SEARCH OF A HERMIT.
HERMIT?!
WHY IS THAT?
WHO KNOWS? IT'S USAGI, SO...
TROMP
TOK
TROMP
WHAT'S THIS ABOUT USAGI?!

Hello, Ue-Rin here! Continuing on from the last volume, I'd like to write about my research trip to Kouga this time. ♪

I was very happy to receive fan letters for volume 3, as well as letters from people interested in visiting Iga after reading about my research trip.

Fans from Iga wrote letters, saying, "Please visit Iga again." ♡

THANK YOU! ♪

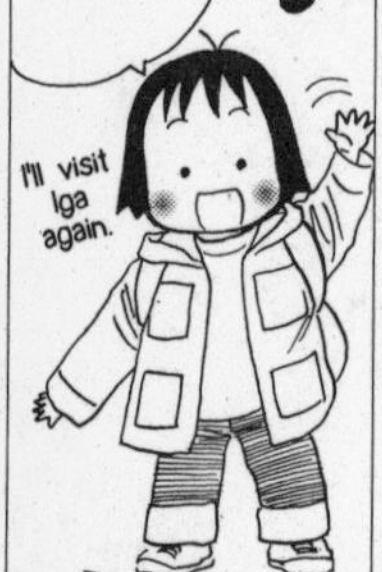
I'll visit Iga again.

standard fieldtrip outfit

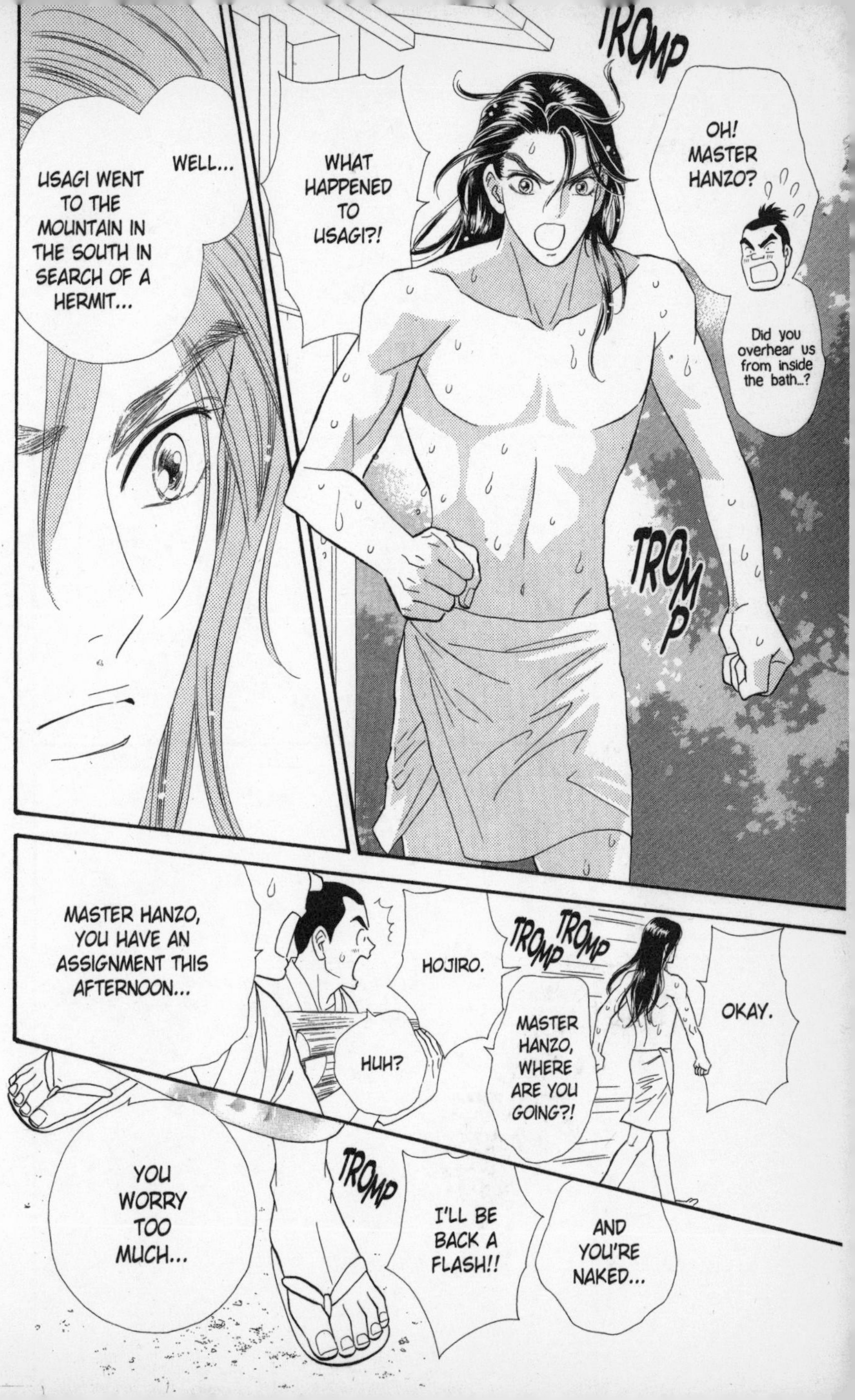
TROMP
OH! MASTER HANZO?
Did you overhear us from inside the bath..?
WHAT HAPPENED TO USAGI?!
TROMP
WELL...
USAGI WENT TO THE MOUNTAIN IN THE SOUTH IN SEARCH OF A HERMIT...
OKAY.
TROMP TROMP
MASTER HANZO, WHERE ARE YOU GOING?!
HOJIRO.
MASTER HANZO, YOU HAVE AN ASSIGNMENT THIS AFTERNOON...
HUH?
AND YOU'RE NAKED...
I'LL BE BACK A FLASH!!
TROMP
YOU WORRY TOO MUCH...

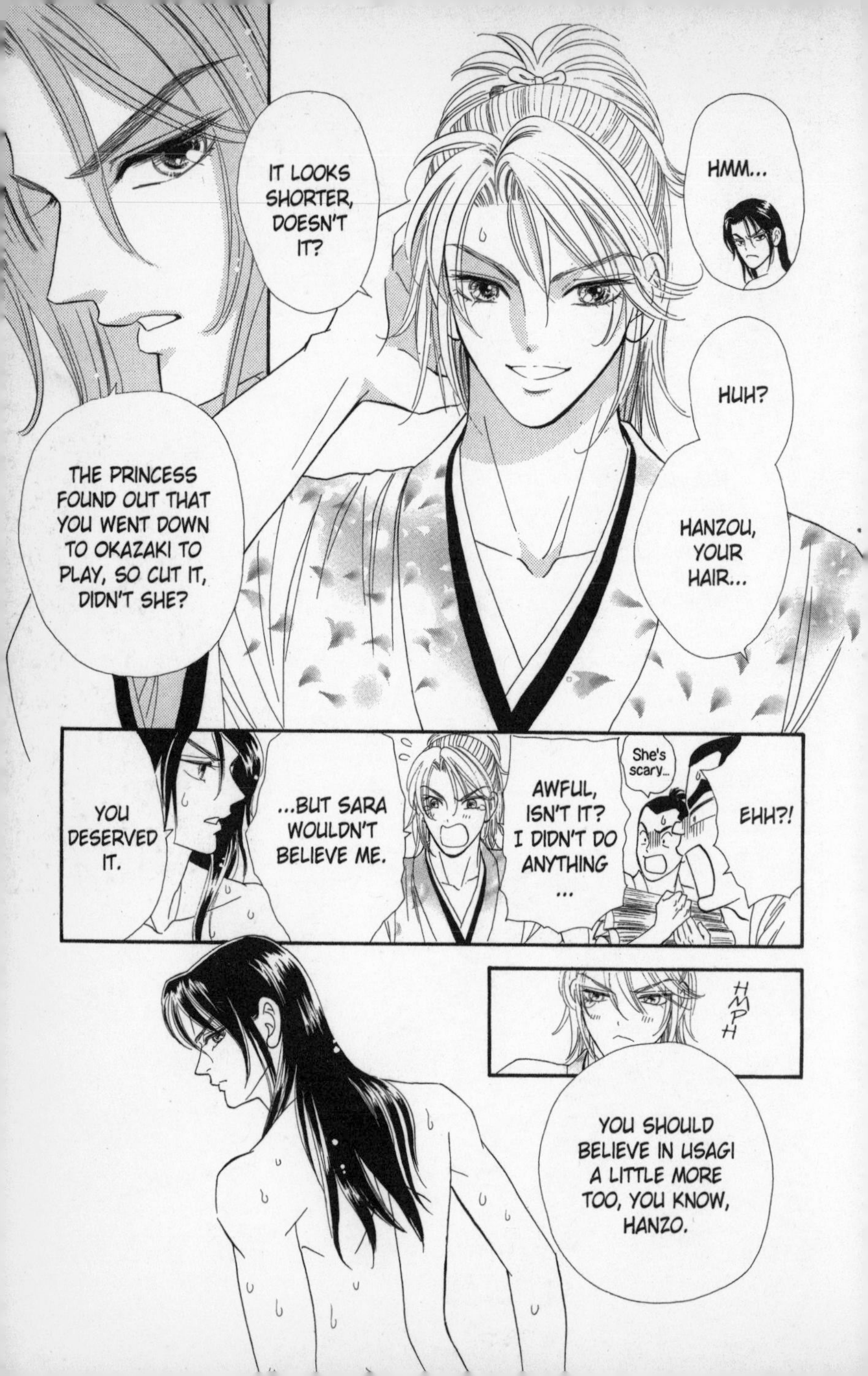
HMM...
HUH?
HANZOU, YOUR HAIR...
IT LOOKS SHORTER, DOESN'T IT?
THE PRINCESS FOUND OUT THAT YOU WENT DOWN TO OKAZAKI TO PLAY, SO CUT IT, DIDN'T SHE?
EHH?!
She's scary...
AWFUL, ISN'T IT? I DIDN'T DO ANYTHING ...
...BUT SARA WOULDN'T BELIEVE ME.
YOU DESERVED IT.
HMPH
YOU SHOULD BELIEVE IN USAGI A LITTLE MORE TOO, YOU KNOW, HANZO.

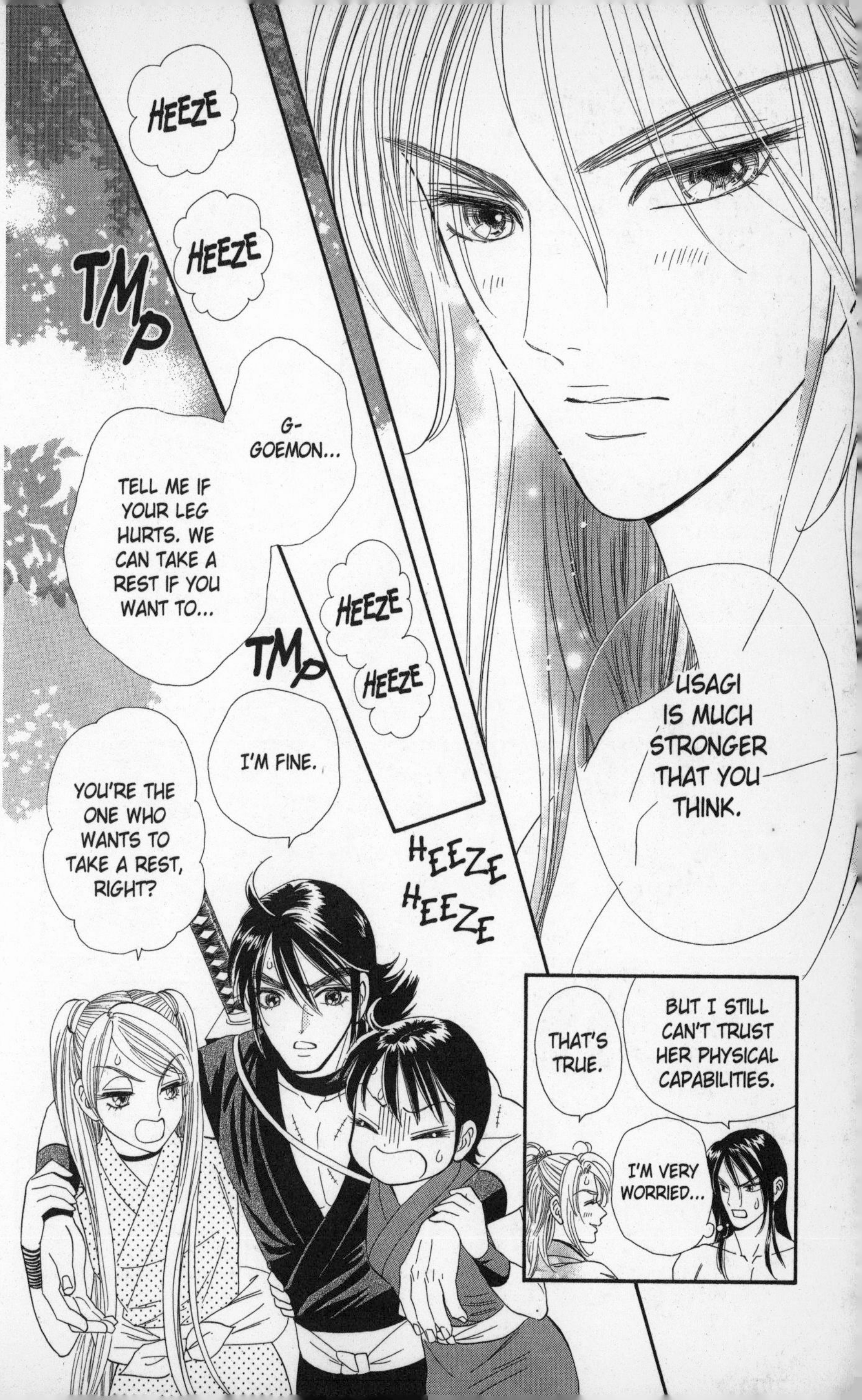
USAGI IS MUCH STRONGER THAT YOU THINK.
BUT I STILL CAN'T TRUST HER PHYSICAL CAPABILITIES.
THAT'S TRUE.
I'M VERY WORRIED...
HEEZE
HEEZE
TMP
G-GOEMON...
TELL ME IF YOUR LEG HURTS. WE CAN TAKE A REST IF YOU WANT TO...
HEEZE
HEEZE
TMP
I'M FINE.
YOU'RE THE ONE WHO WANTS TO TAKE A REST, RIGHT?
HEEZE HEEZE

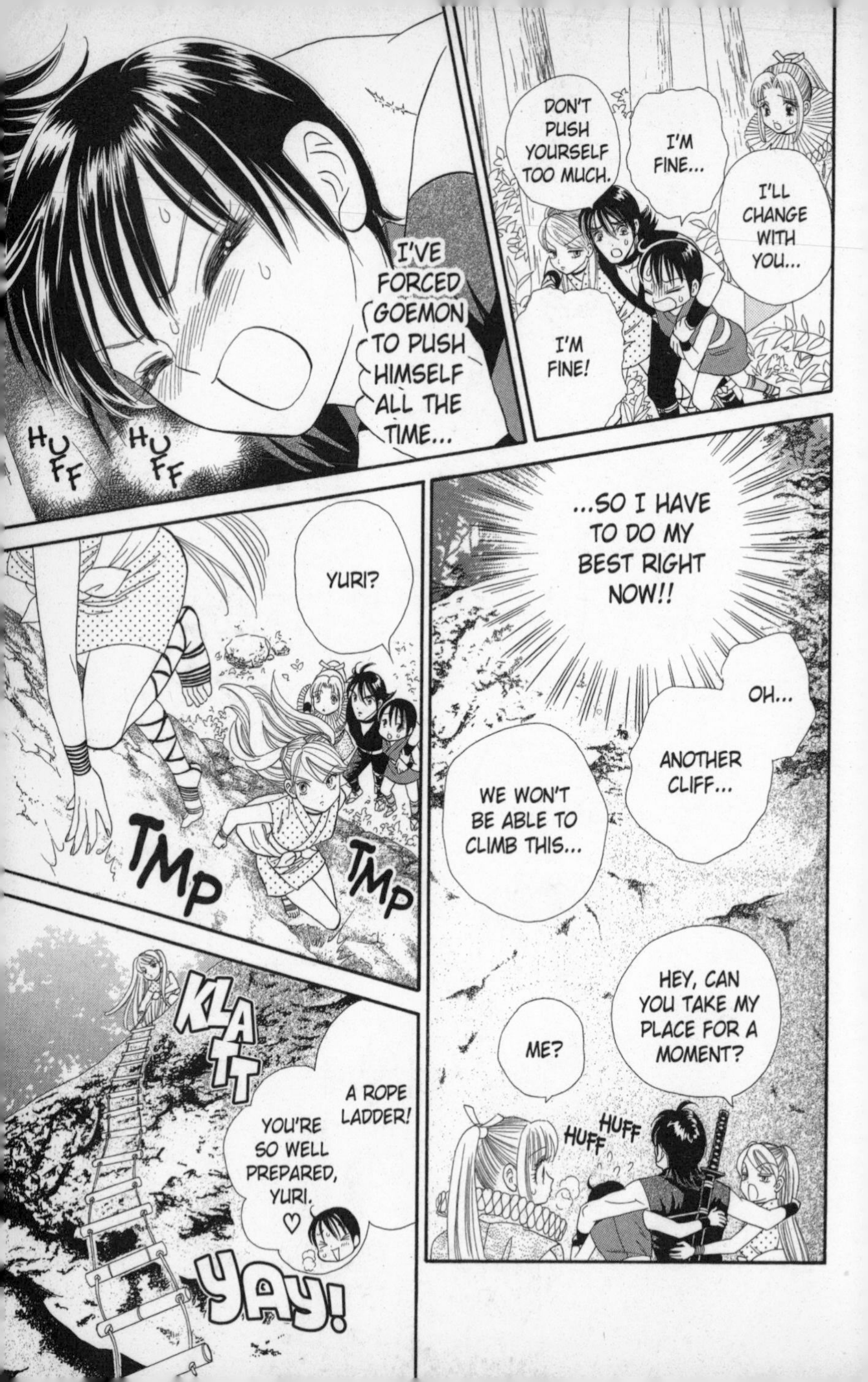
I'LL CHANGE WITH YOU...
I'M FINE...
DON'T PUSH YOURSELF TOO MUCH.
I'M FINE!
I'VE FORCED GOEMON TO PUSH HIMSELF ALL THE TIME...
HUFF
HUFF
...SO I HAVE TO DO MY BEST RIGHT NOW!!
OH...
ANOTHER CLIFF...
WE WON'T BE ABLE TO CLIMB THIS...
HEY, CAN YOU TAKE MY PLACE FOR A MOMENT?
ME?
HUFF
HUFF
YURI?
TMP
TMP
KLATT
A ROPE LADDER!
YOU'RE SO WELL PREPARED, YURI. ♡
YAY!

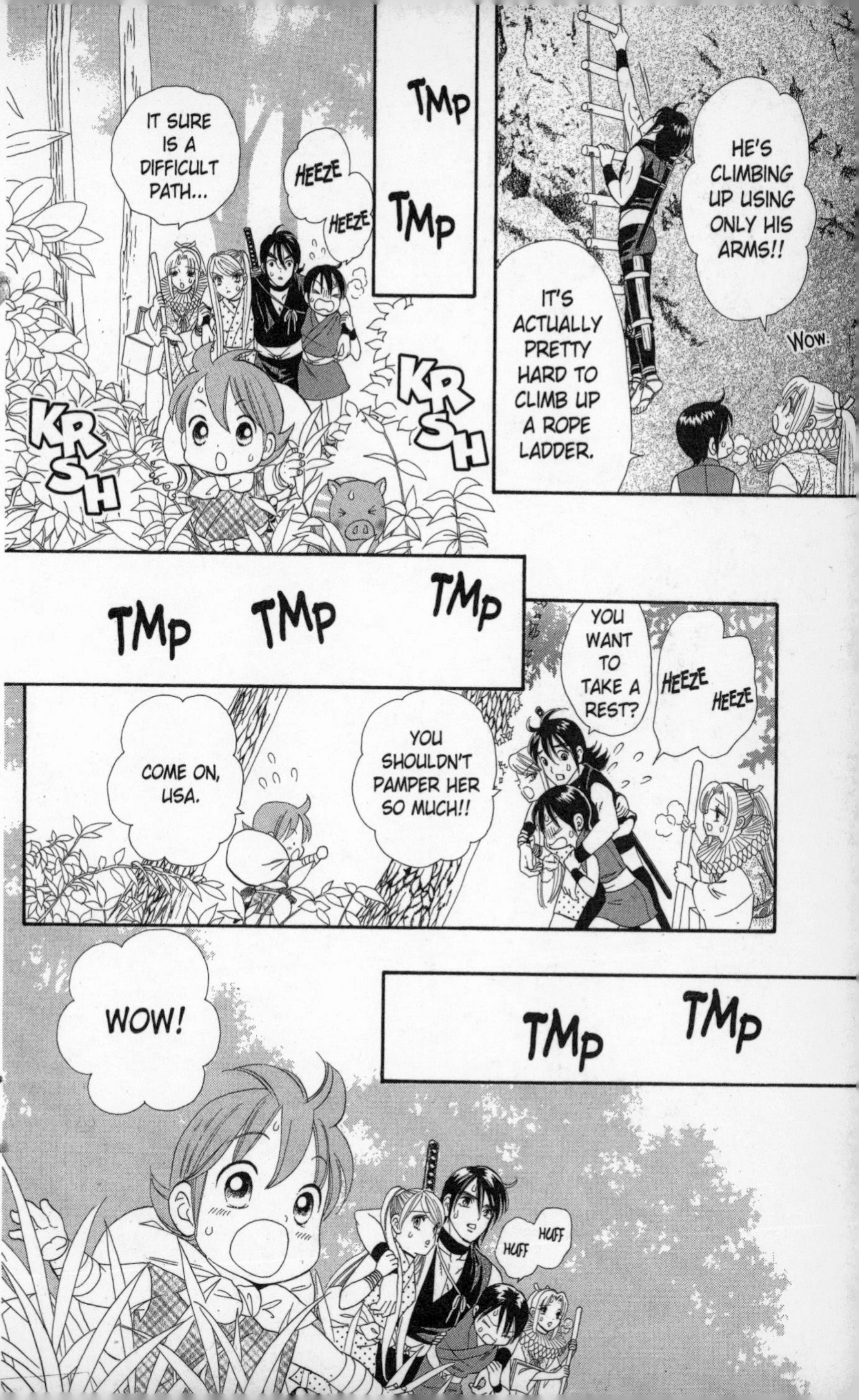

HE'S CLIMBING UP USING ONLY HIS ARMS!!
IT'S ACTUALLY PRETTY HARD TO CLIMB UP A ROPE LADDER.
WOW.
TMP
TMP
IT SURE IS A DIFFICULT PATH...
HEEZE
HEEZE
KRSH
KRSH
TMP
TMP
TMP
YOU WANT TO TAKE A REST?
HEEZE
HEEZE
YOU SHOULDN'T PAMPER HER SO MUCH!!
COME ON, USA.
TMP
TMP
WOW!
HUFF
HUFF

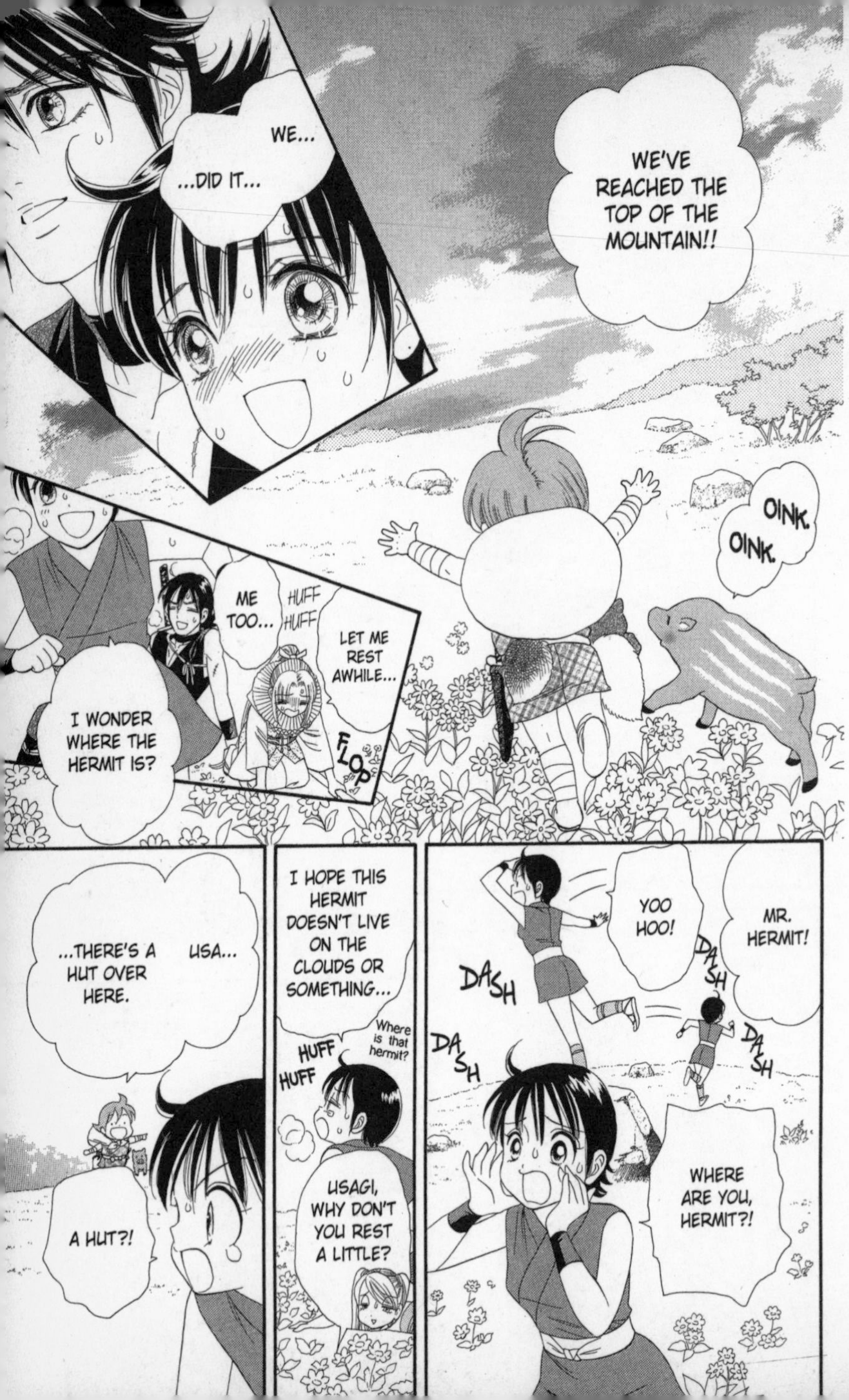
WE'VE REACHED THE TOP OF THE MOUNTAIN!!
OINK.
OINK.
WE...
...DID IT...
ME TOO...
HUFF HUFF
LET ME REST AWHILE...
FLOP
I WONDER WHERE THE HERMIT IS?
MR. HERMIT!
YOO HOO!
DASH
DASH
DASH
DASH
WHERE ARE YOU, HERMIT?!
I HOPE THIS HERMIT DOESN'T LIVE ON THE CLOUDS OR SOMETHING...
Where is that hermit?
HUFF HUFF
USAGI, WHY DON'T YOU REST A LITTLE?
USA...
...THERE'S A HUT OVER HERE.
A HUT?!

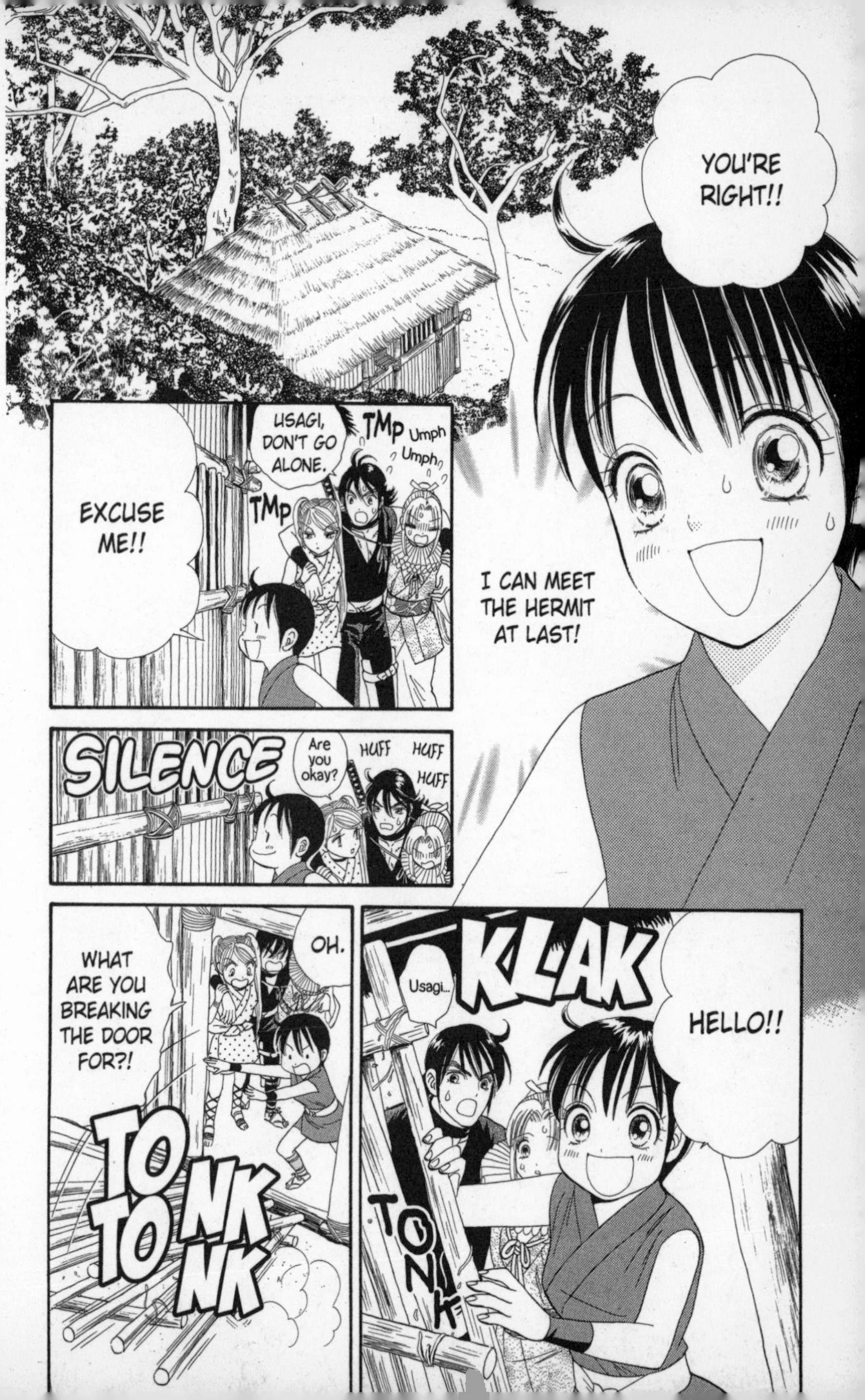
YOU'RE RIGHT!!
I CAN MEET THE HERMIT AT LAST!
Umph Umph
TMp
USAGI, DON'T GO ALONE.
TMp
EXCUSE ME!!
HUFF HUFF HUFF
Are you okay?
SILENCE
KLAK
HELLO!!
Usagi...
TONK
OH.
WHAT ARE YOU BREAKING THE DOOR FOR?!
TONK TONK

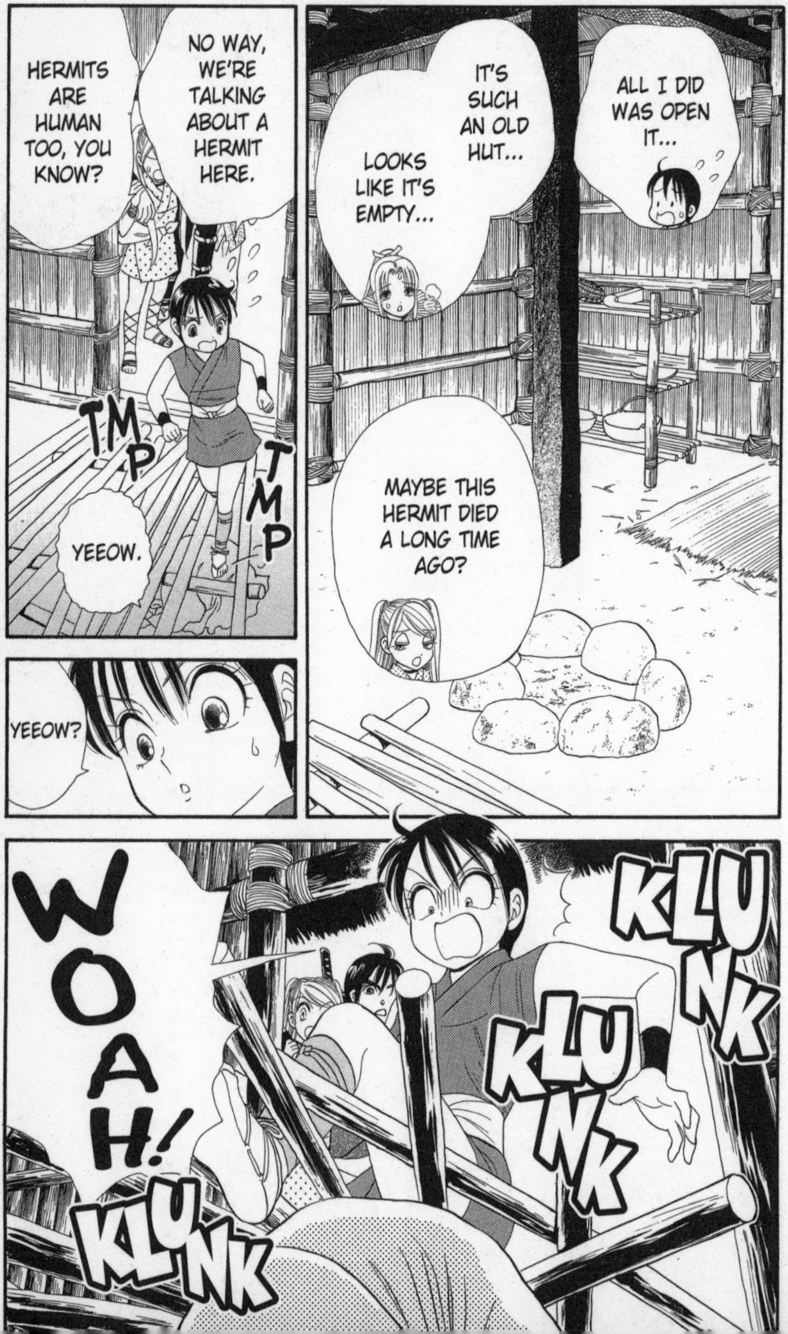
ALL I DID WAS OPEN IT...
IT'S SUCH AN OLD HUT...
LOOKS LIKE IT'S EMPTY...
MAYBE THIS HERMIT DIED A LONG TIME AGO?
NO WAY, WE'RE TALKING ABOUT A HERMIT HERE.
HERMITS ARE HUMAN TOO, YOU KNOW?
TMP
TMP
TMP
YEEOW.
YEEOW?
KLUNK
KLUNK
WOAH!
KLUNK

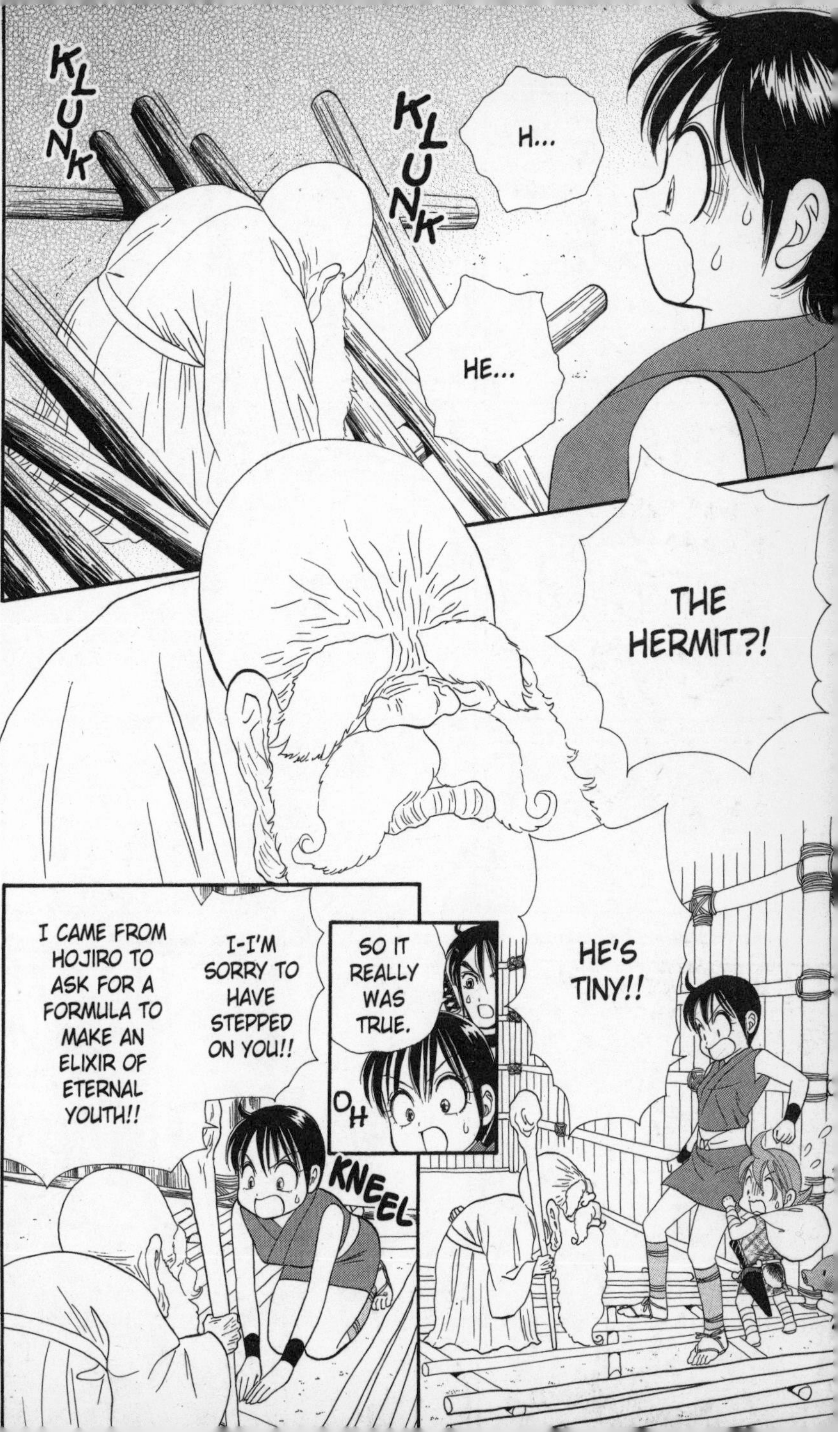
H...
HE...
KLUNK
KLUNK
THE HERMIT?!
HE'S TINY!!
SO IT REALLY WAS TRUE.
OH
I-I'M SORRY TO HAVE STEPPED ON YOU!!
I CAME FROM HOJIRO TO ASK FOR A FORMULA TO MAKE AN ELIXIR OF ETERNAL YOUTH!!
KNEEL

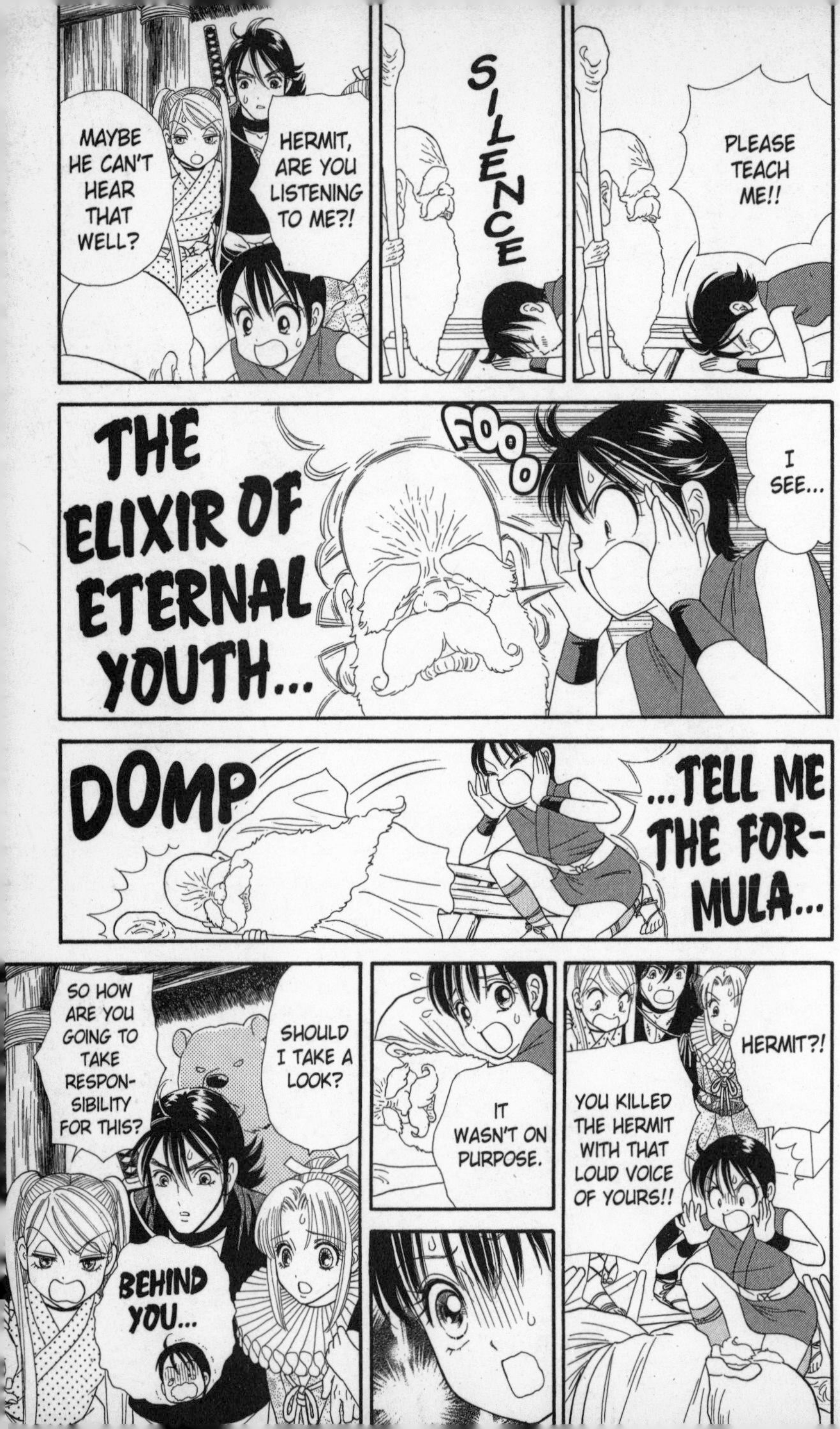
PLEASE TEACH ME!!
SILENCE
HERMIT, ARE YOU LISTENING TO ME?!
MAYBE HE CAN'T HEAR THAT WELL?
I SEE...
FOOO
THE ELIXIR OF ETERNAL YOUTH...
...TELL ME THE FOR-MULA...
DOMP
HERMIT?!
YOU KILLED THE HERMIT WITH THAT LOUD VOICE OF YOURS!!
IT WASN'T ON PURPOSE.
SHOULD I TAKE A LOOK?
SO HOW ARE YOU GOING TO TAKE RESPON-SIBILITY FOR THIS?
BEHIND YOU...

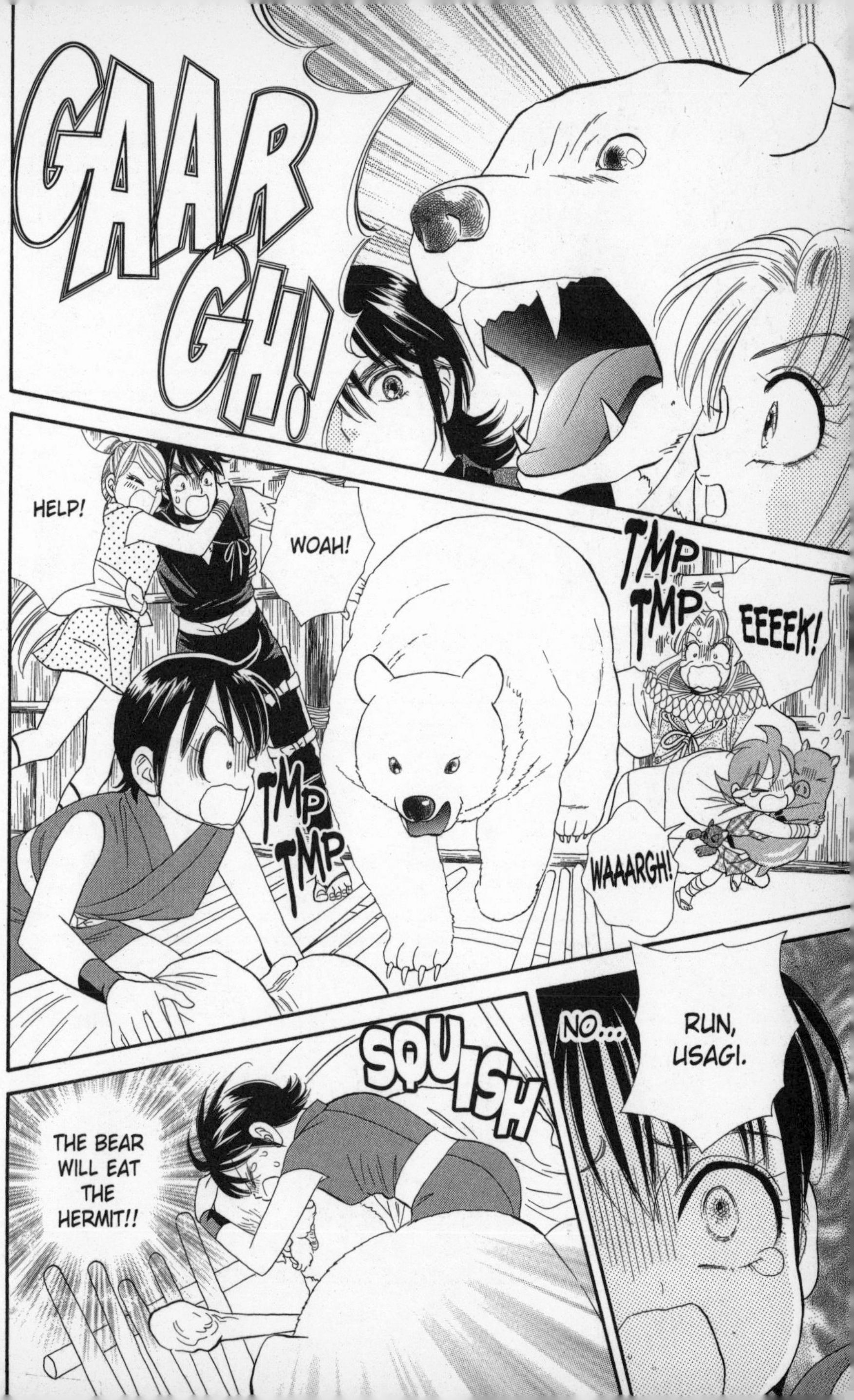
GAARGH!
TMP TMP
EEEEK!
WAAARGH!
WOAH!
HELP!
TMP TMP
RUN, USAGI.
NO...
SQUISH
THE BEAR WILL EAT THE HERMIT!!

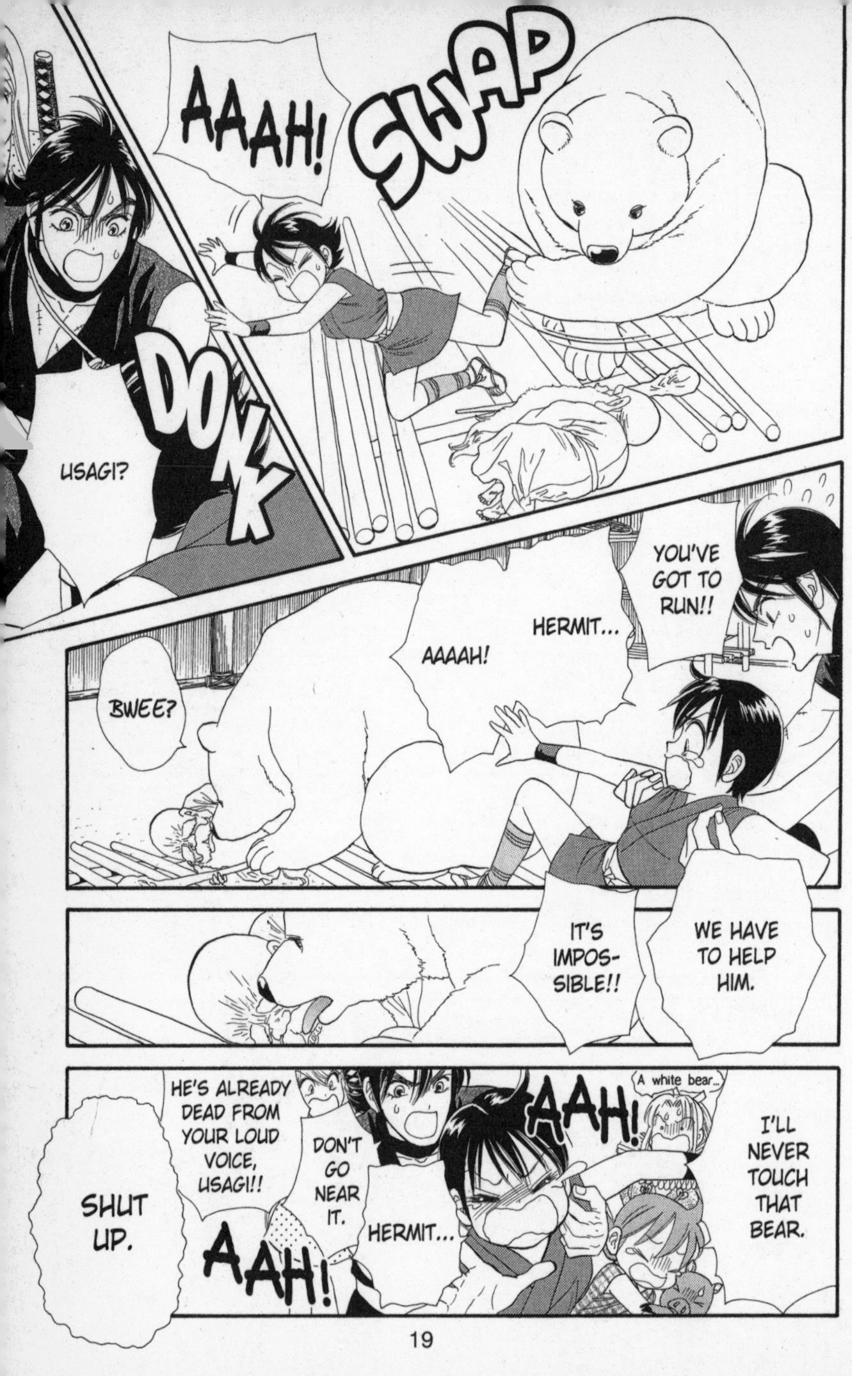
SWAP
AAAH!
DONK
USAGI?
YOU'VE GOT TO RUN!!
HERMIT...
AAAAH!
BWEE?
WE HAVE TO HELP HIM.
IT'S IMPOS-SIBLE!!
I'LL NEVER TOUCH THAT BEAR.
A white bear...
AAH!
HERMIT...
DON'T GO NEAR IT.
HE'S ALREADY DEAD FROM YOUR LOUD VOICE, USAGI!!
AAH!
SHUT UP.

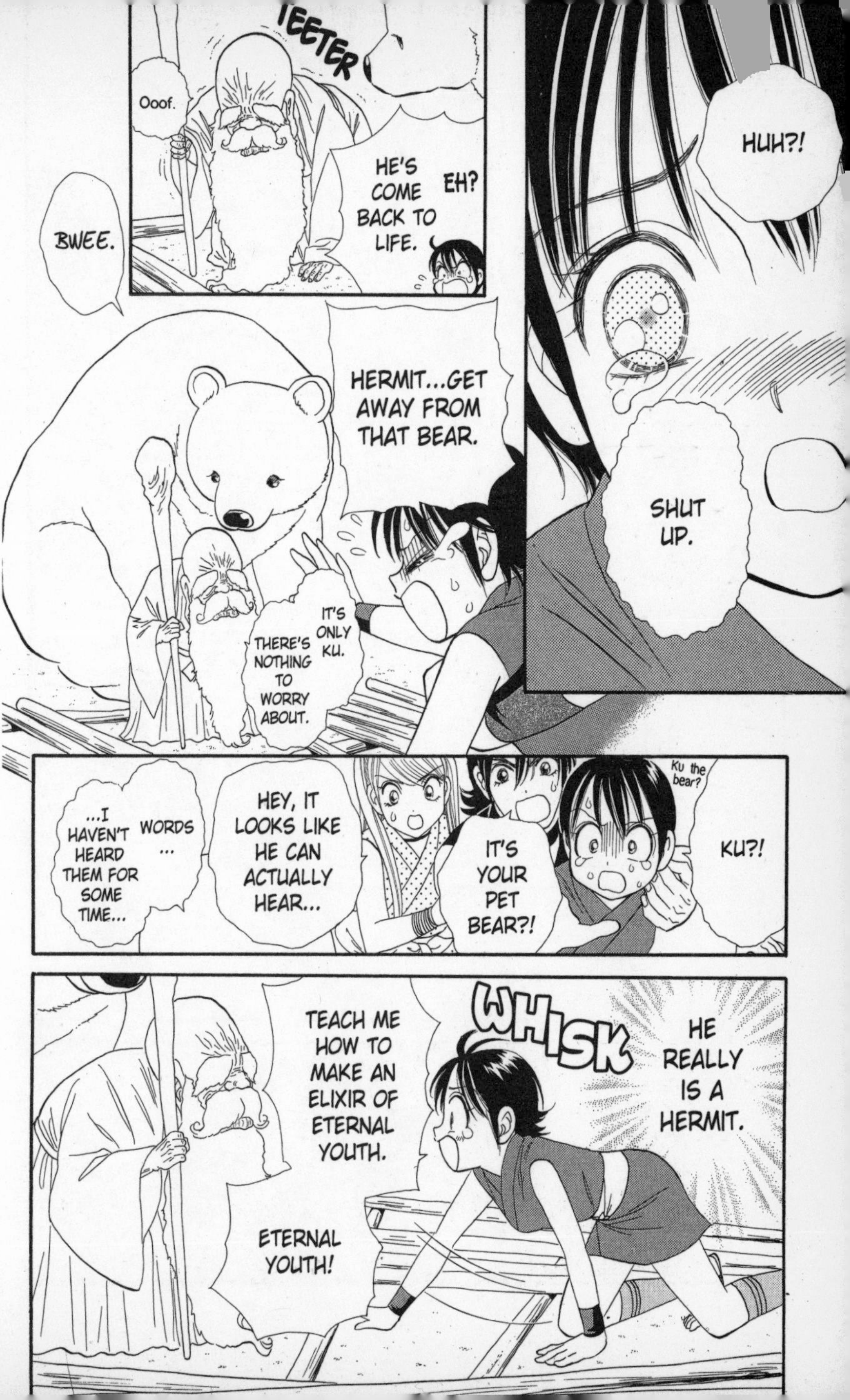
HUH?!
SHUT UP.
IEETER
Ooof.
EH?
HE'S COME BACK TO LIFE.
BWEE.
HERMIT...GET AWAY FROM THAT BEAR.
IT'S ONLY KU.
THERE'S NOTHING TO WORRY ABOUT.
Ku the bear?
KU?!
IT'S YOUR PET BEAR?!
HEY, IT LOOKS LIKE HE CAN ACTUALLY HEAR...
WORDS...
...I HAVEN'T HEARD THEM FOR SOME TIME...
HE REALLY IS A HERMIT.
WHISK
TEACH ME HOW TO MAKE AN ELIXIR OF ETERNAL YOUTH.
ETERNAL YOUTH!

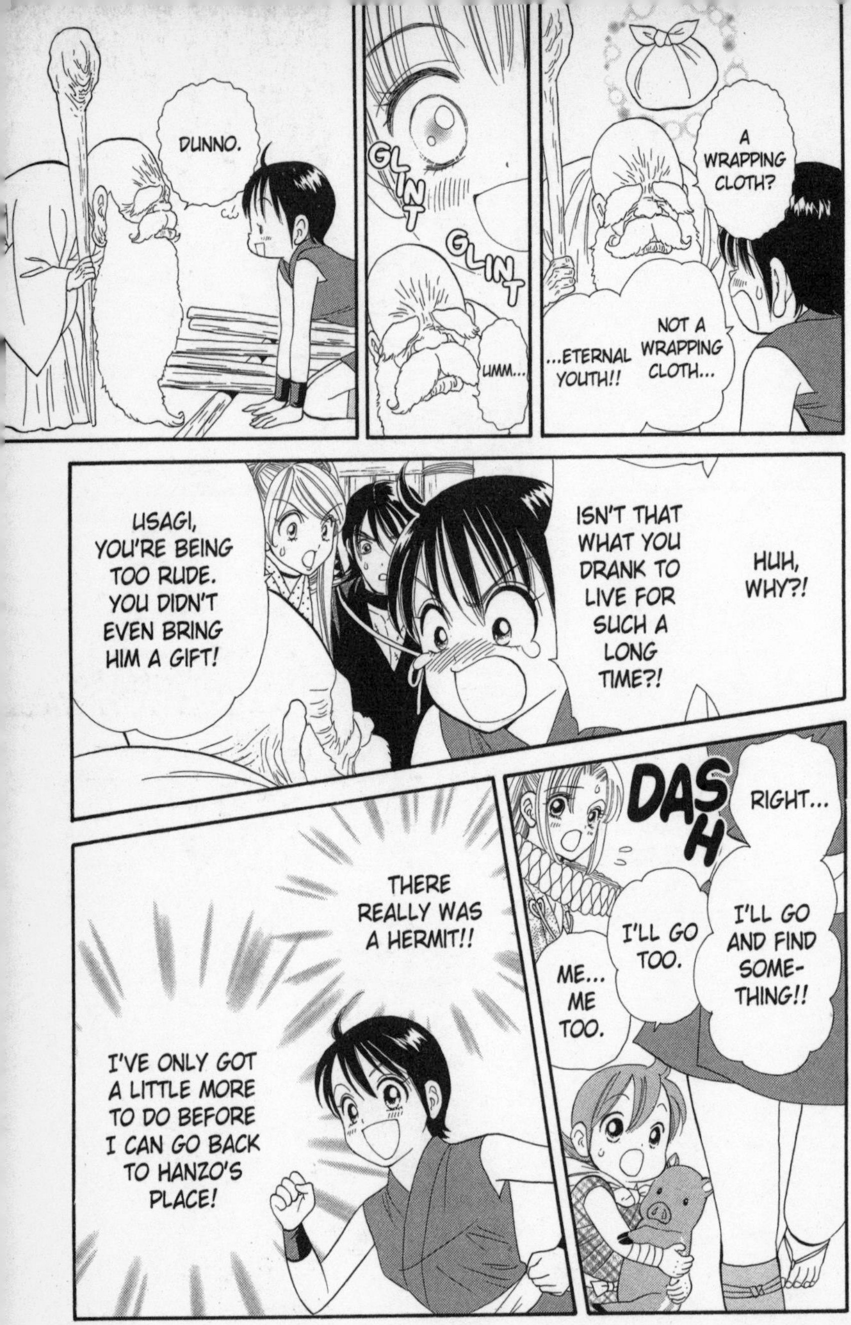
A WRAPPING CLOTH?
NOT A WRAPPING CLOTH...
...ETERNAL YOUTH!!
GLINT
GLINT
UMM...
DUNNO.
HUH, WHY?!
ISN'T THAT WHAT YOU DRANK TO LIVE FOR SUCH A LONG TIME?!
USAGI, YOU'RE BEING TOO RUDE. YOU DIDN'T EVEN BRING HIM A GIFT!
RIGHT...
DASH
I'LL GO AND FIND SOME-THING!!
I'LL GO TOO.
ME... ME TOO.
THERE REALLY WAS A HERMIT!!
I'VE ONLY GOT A LITTLE MORE TO DO BEFORE I CAN GO BACK TO HANZO'S PLACE!

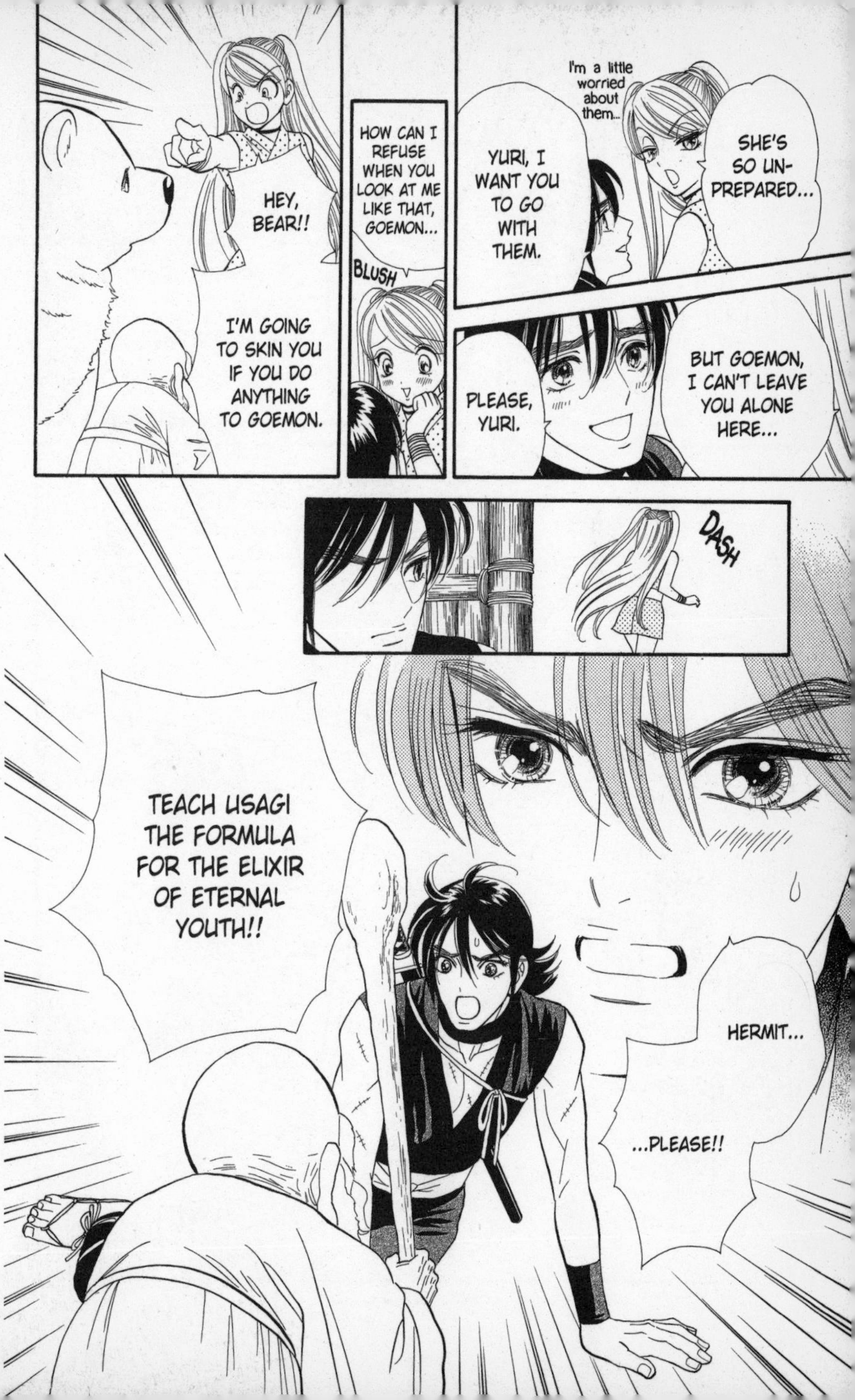
SHE'S SO UN-PREPARED...
I'm a little worried about them...
YURI, I WANT YOU TO GO WITH THEM.
BUT GOEMON, I CAN'T LEAVE YOU ALONE HERE...
PLEASE, YURI.
HOW CAN I REFUSE WHEN YOU LOOK AT ME LIKE THAT, GOEMON...
BLUSH
HEY, BEAR!!
I'M GOING TO SKIN YOU IF YOU DO ANYTHING TO GOEMON.
DASH
HERMIT...
...PLEASE!!
TEACH USAGI THE FORMULA FOR THE ELIXIR OF ETERNAL YOUTH!!

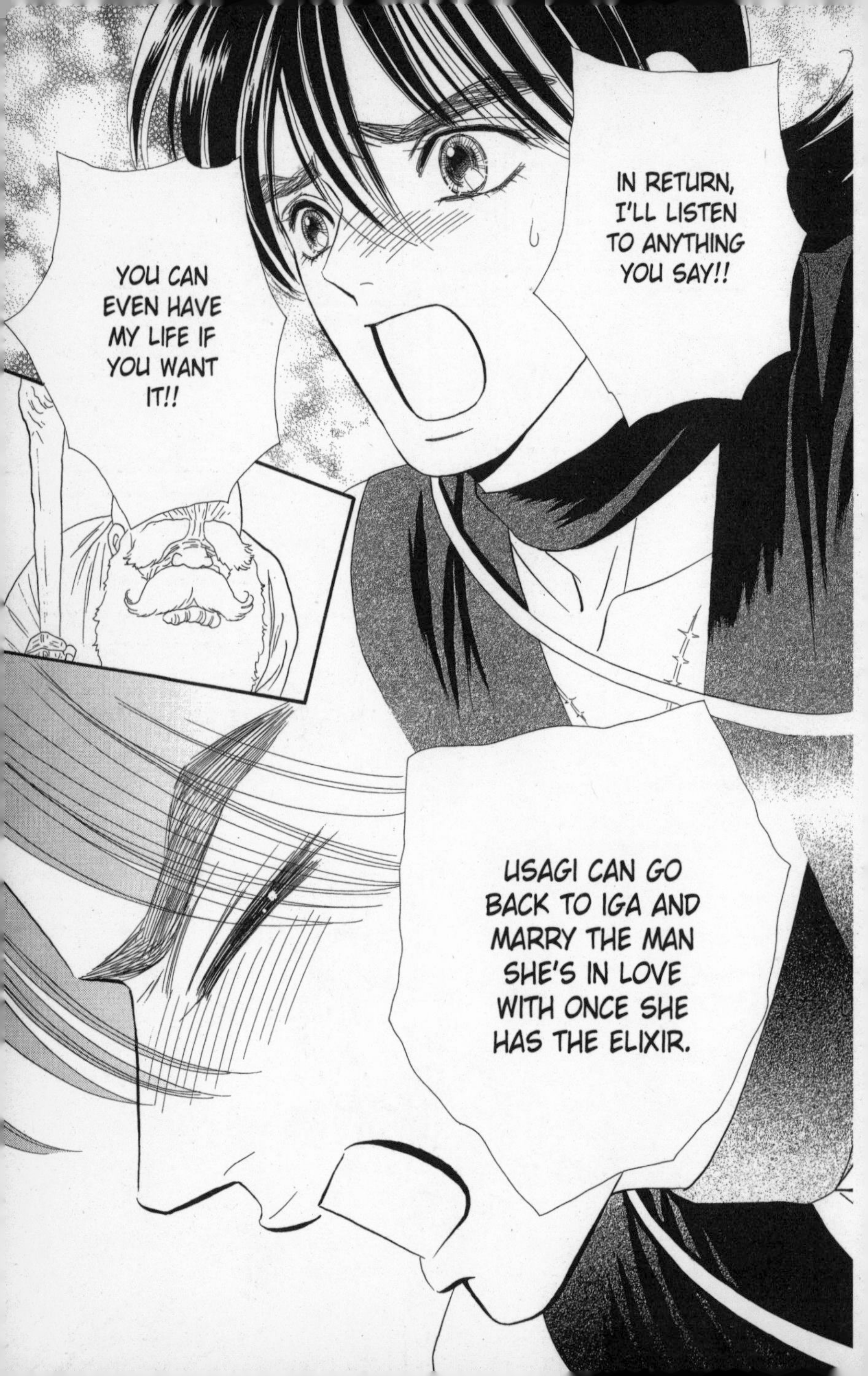
IN RETURN, I'LL LISTEN TO ANYTHING YOU SAY!!
YOU CAN EVEN HAVE MY LIFE IF YOU WANT IT!!
USAGI CAN GO BACK TO IGA AND MARRY THE MAN SHE'S IN LOVE WITH ONCE SHE HAS THE ELIXIR.

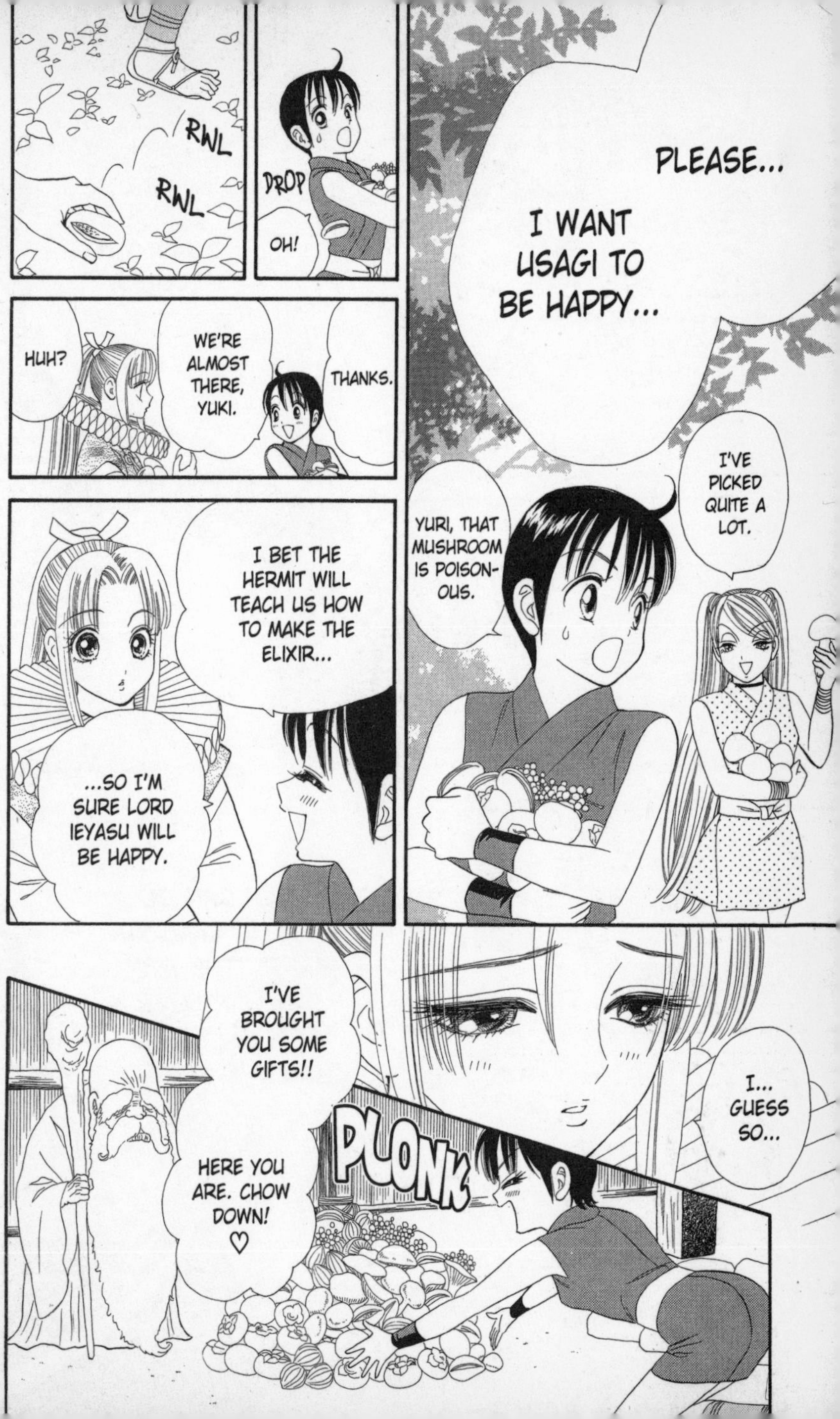
PLEASE...
I WANT USAGI TO BE HAPPY...
I'VE PICKED QUITE A LOT.
YURI, THAT MUSHROOM IS POISONOUS.
DROP
OH!
RWL
RWL
THANKS.
WE'RE ALMOST THERE, YUKI.
HUH?
I BET THE HERMIT WILL TEACH US HOW TO MAKE THE ELIXIR...
...SO I'M SURE LORD IEYASU WILL BE HAPPY.
I... GUESS SO...
I'VE BROUGHT YOU SOME GIFTS!!
PLONK
HERE YOU ARE. CHOW DOWN! ♡

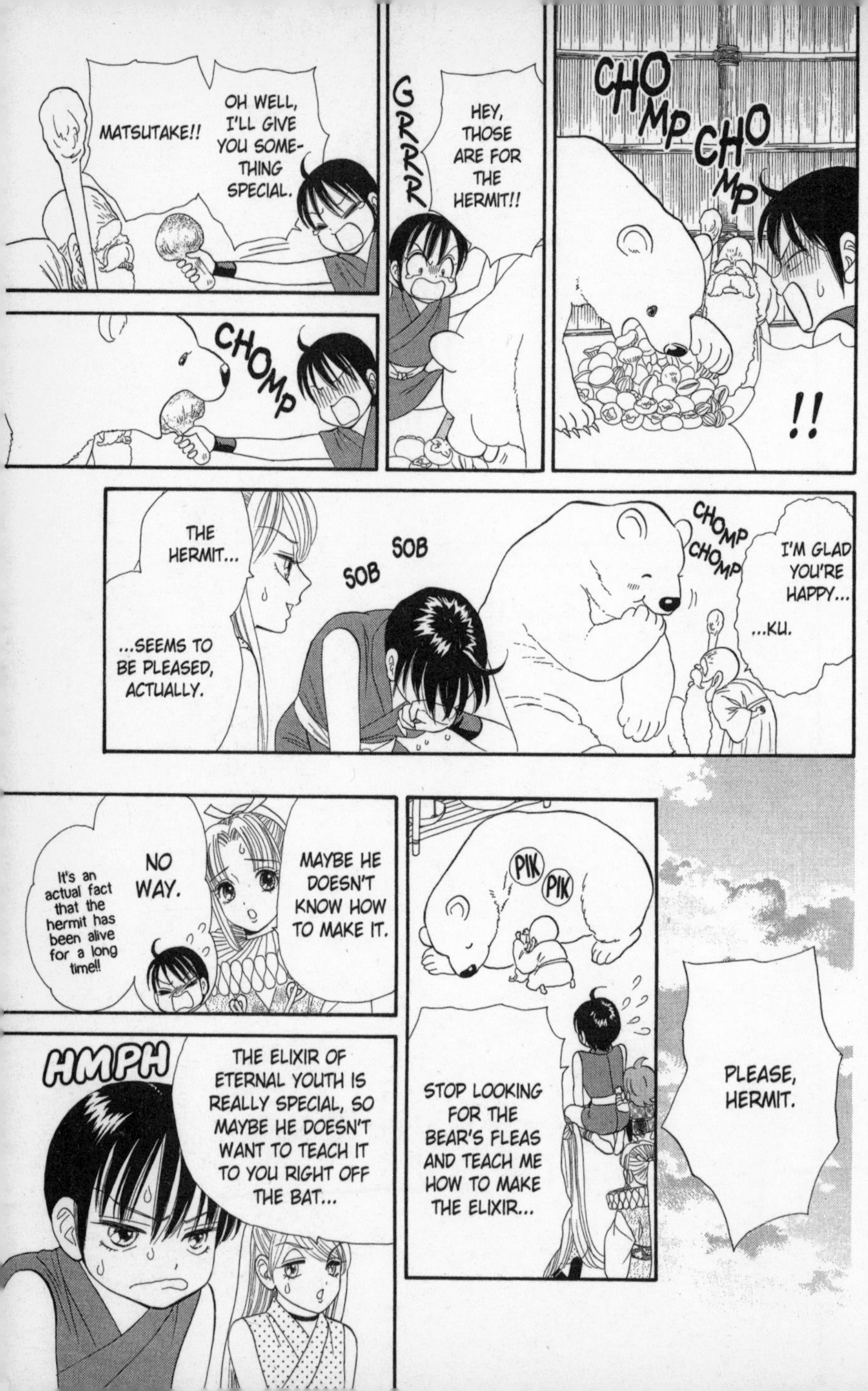
CHOMP CHOMP
!!
HEY, THOSE ARE FOR THE HERMIT!!
GRRRR
OH WELL, I'LL GIVE YOU SOME-THING SPECIAL.
MATSUTAKE!!
CHOMP
I'M GLAD YOU'RE HAPPY...
...KU.
CHOMP CHOMP
SOB SOB
THE HERMIT...
...SEEMS TO BE PLEASED, ACTUALLY.
PLEASE, HERMIT.
PIK PIK
STOP LOOKING FOR THE BEAR'S FLEAS AND TEACH ME HOW TO MAKE THE ELIXIR...
MAYBE HE DOESN'T KNOW HOW TO MAKE IT.
NO WAY.
It's an actual fact that the hermit has been alive for a long time!!
THE ELIXIR OF ETERNAL YOUTH IS REALLY SPECIAL, SO MAYBE HE DOESN'T WANT TO TEACH IT TO YOU RIGHT OFF THE BAT...
HMPH

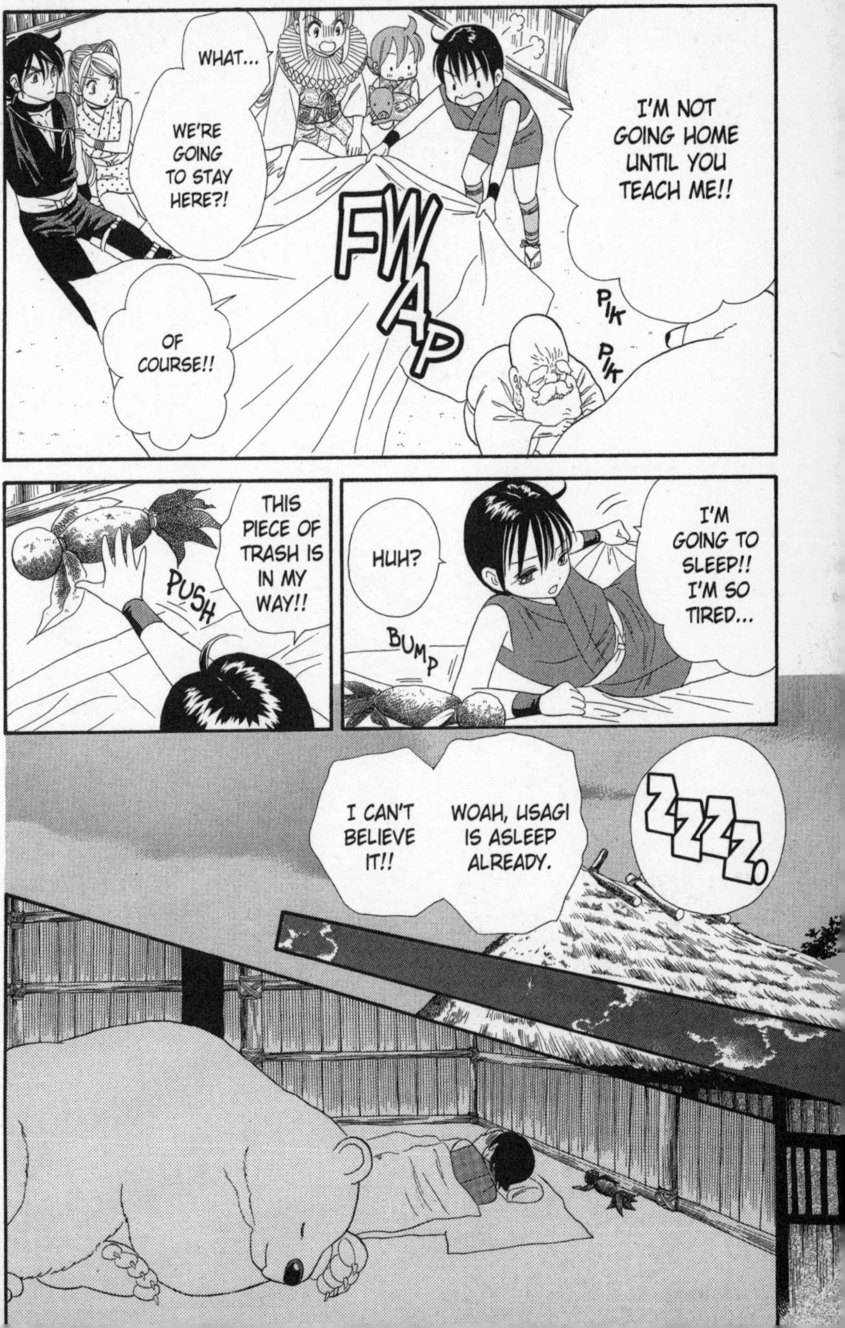
I'M NOT GOING HOME UNTIL YOU TEACH ME!!
WHAT... WE'RE GOING TO STAY HERE?!
FWAP
PIK PIK
OF COURSE!!
I'M GOING TO SLEEP!! I'M SO TIRED...
HUH?
BUMP
THIS PIECE OF TRASH IS IN MY WAY!!
PUSH
ZZZZ
WOAH, USAGI IS ASLEEP ALREADY.
I CAN'T BELIEVE IT!!

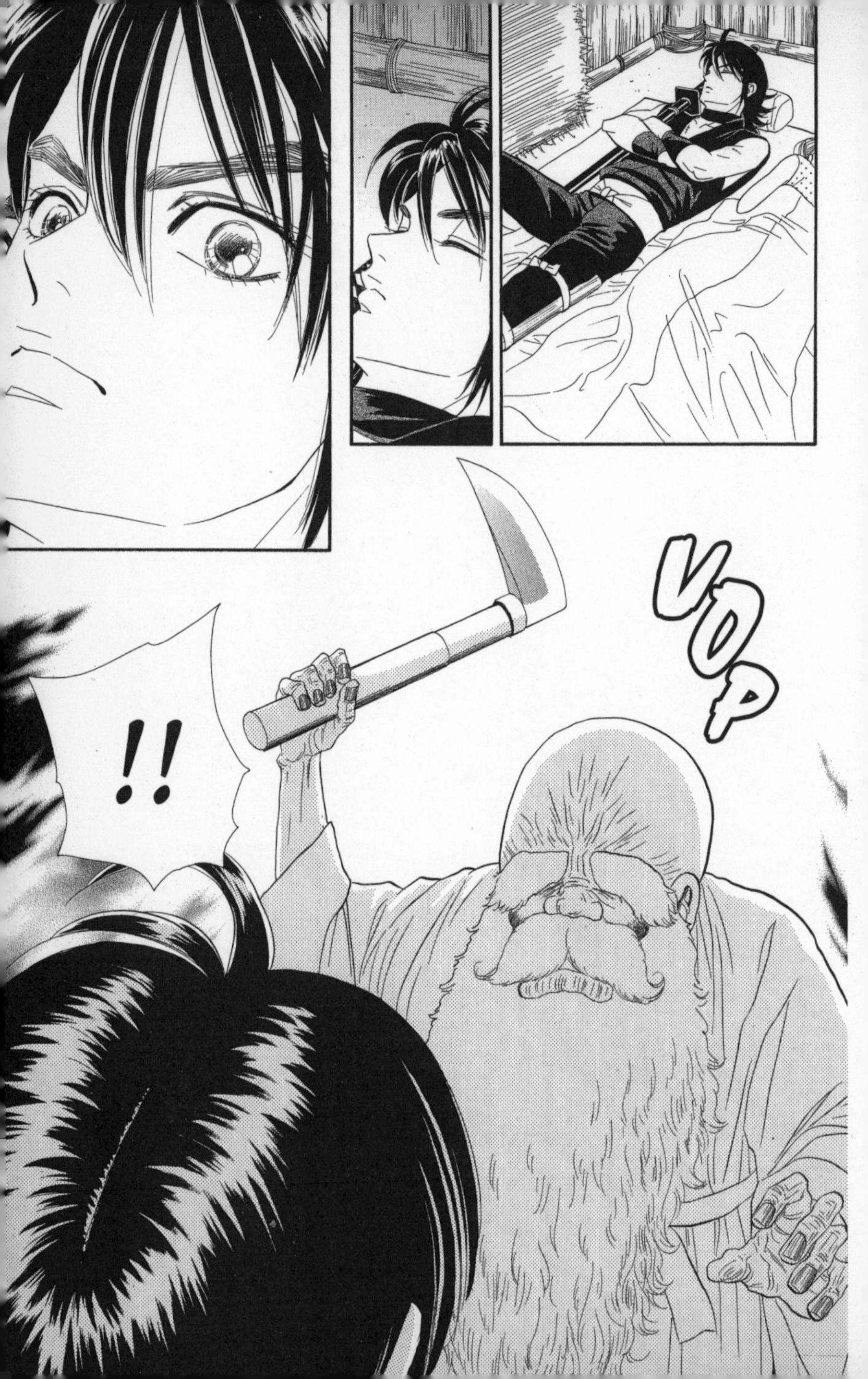
VOOP
!!

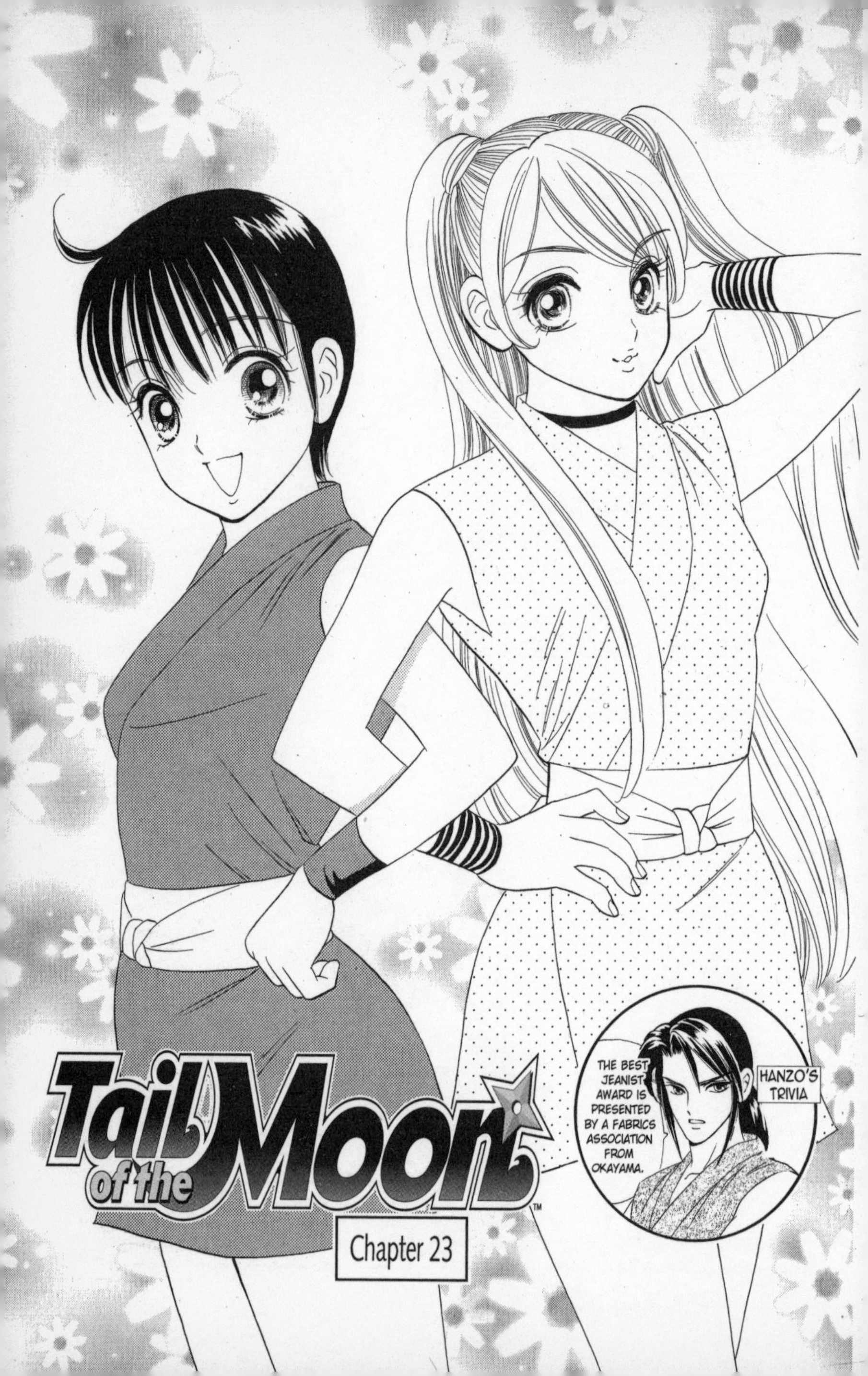
Tail of the Moon™
Chapter 23
HANZO'S TRIVIA
THE BEST JEANIST AWARD IS PRESENTED BY A FABRICS ASSOCIATION FROM OKAYAMA.

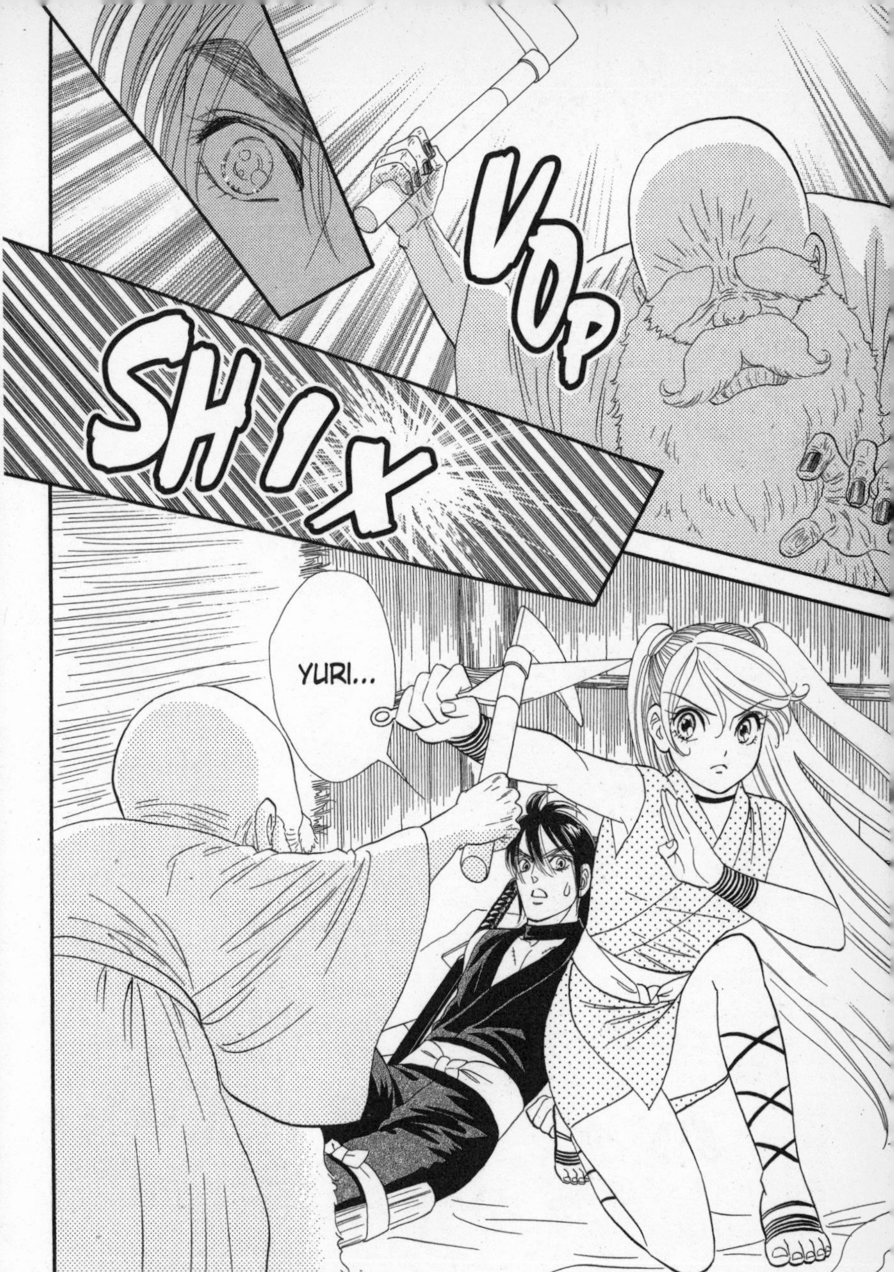
VOP
SHIX
YURI...

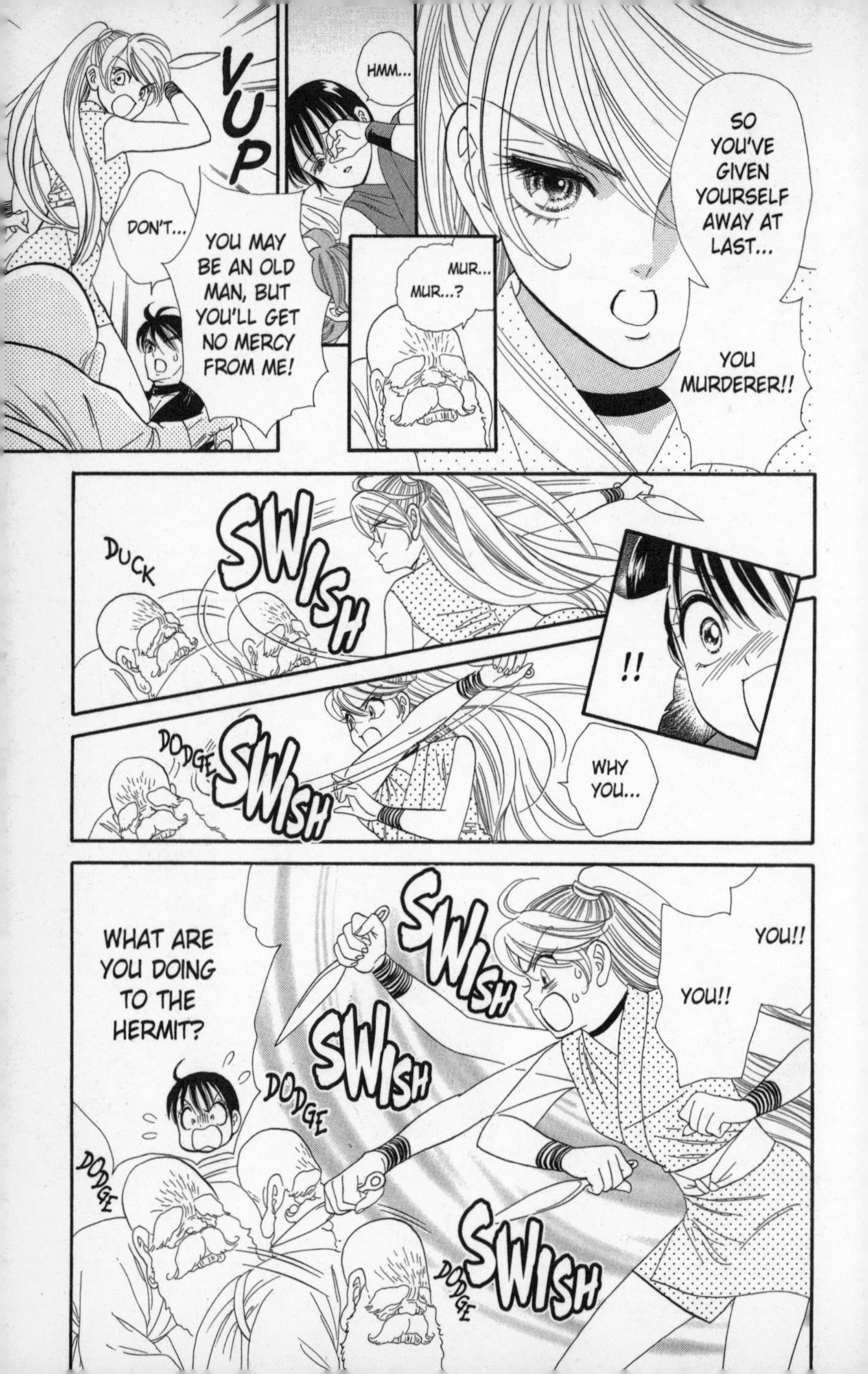
SO YOU'VE GIVEN YOURSELF AWAY AT LAST...
YOU MURDERER!!
HMM...
MUR... MUR...?
VUP
YOU MAY BE AN OLD MAN, BUT YOU'LL GET NO MERCY FROM ME!
DON'T...
!!
WHY YOU...
SWISH
DUCK
SWISH
DODGE
YOU!!
YOU!!
SWISH
WHAT ARE YOU DOING TO THE HERMIT?
SWISH
DODGE
DODGE
SWISH
DODGE

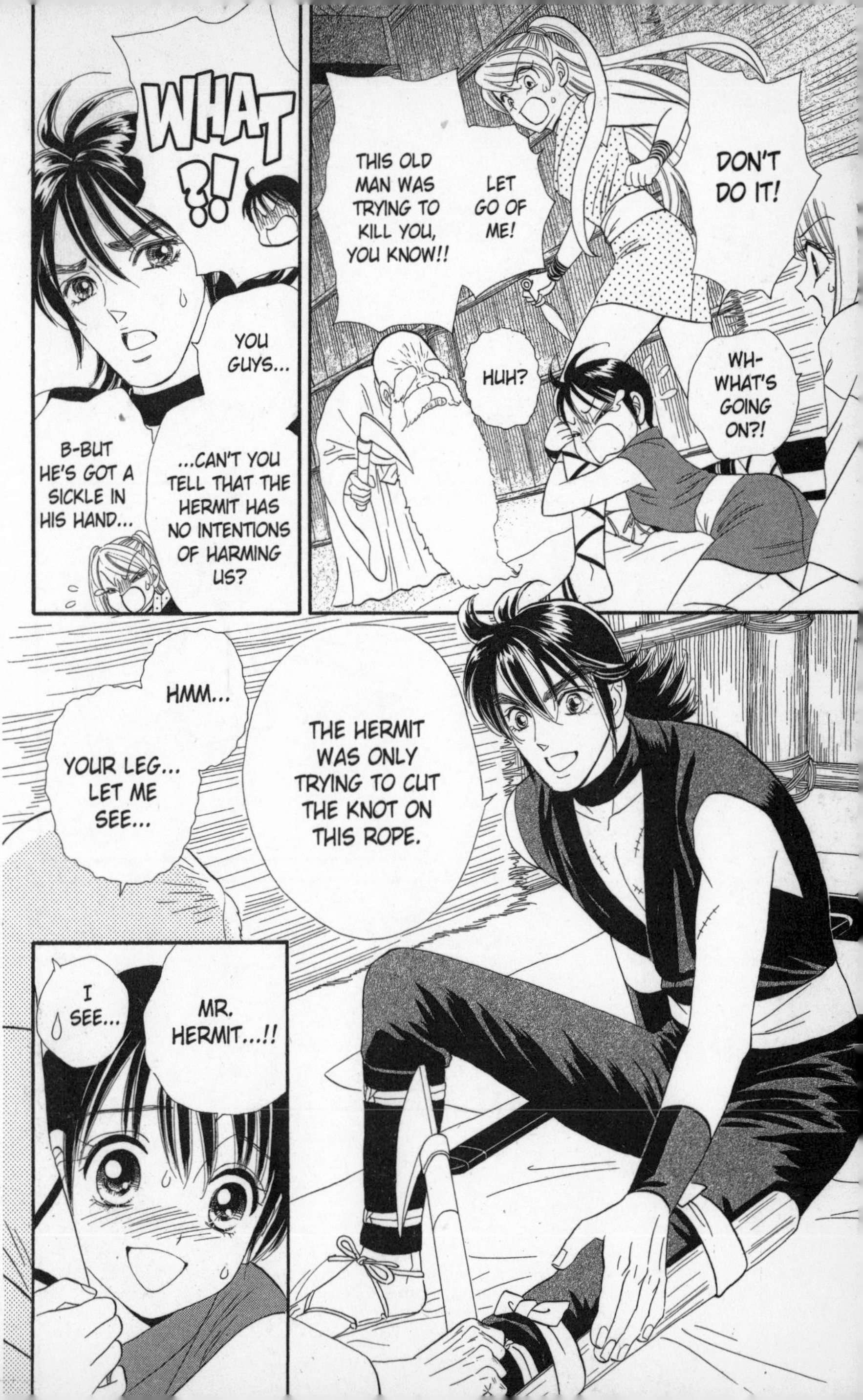
DON'T DO IT!
LET GO OF ME!
THIS OLD MAN WAS TRYING TO KILL YOU, YOU KNOW!!
WH-WHAT'S GOING ON?!
HUH?
WHAT ?!
YOU GUYS...
...CAN'T YOU TELL THAT THE HERMIT HAS NO INTENTIONS OF HARMING US?
B-BUT HE'S GOT A SICKLE IN HIS HAND...
THE HERMIT WAS ONLY TRYING TO CUT THE KNOT ON THIS ROPE.
HMM...
YOUR LEG... LET ME SEE...
MR. HERMIT...!!
I SEE...

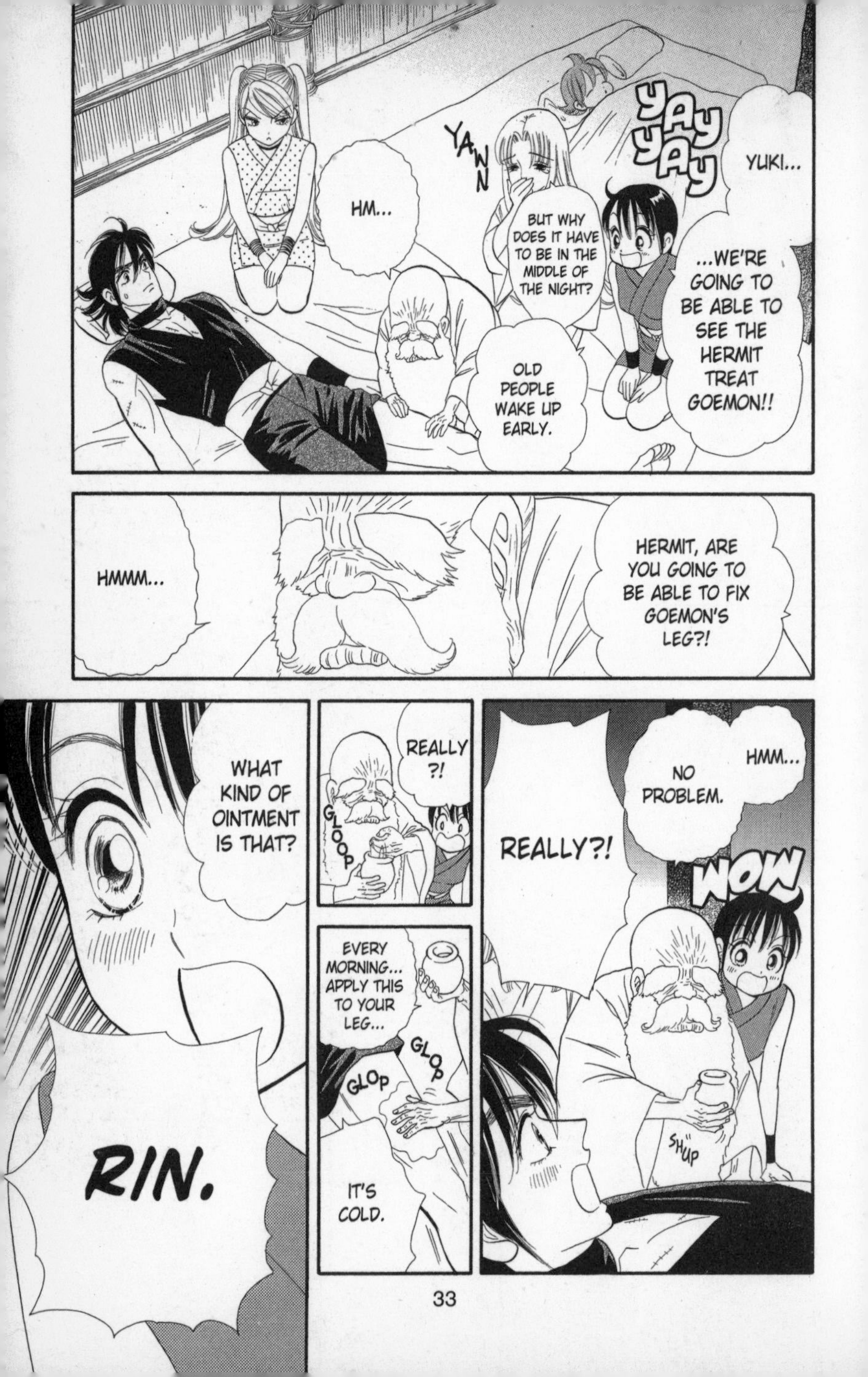
YAY YAY
YUKI...
...WE'RE GOING TO BE ABLE TO SEE THE HERMIT TREAT GOEMON!!
YAWN
BUT WHY DOES IT HAVE TO BE IN THE MIDDLE OF THE NIGHT?
OLD PEOPLE WAKE UP EARLY.
HM...
HERMIT, ARE YOU GOING TO BE ABLE TO FIX GOEMON'S LEG?!
HMMM...
HMM...
NO PROBLEM.
WOW
REALLY?!
SHUP
REALLY?!
GLOOP
EVERY MORNING... APPLY THIS TO YOUR LEG...
GLOP
GLOP
IT'S COLD.
WHAT KIND OF OINTMENT IS THAT?
RIN.

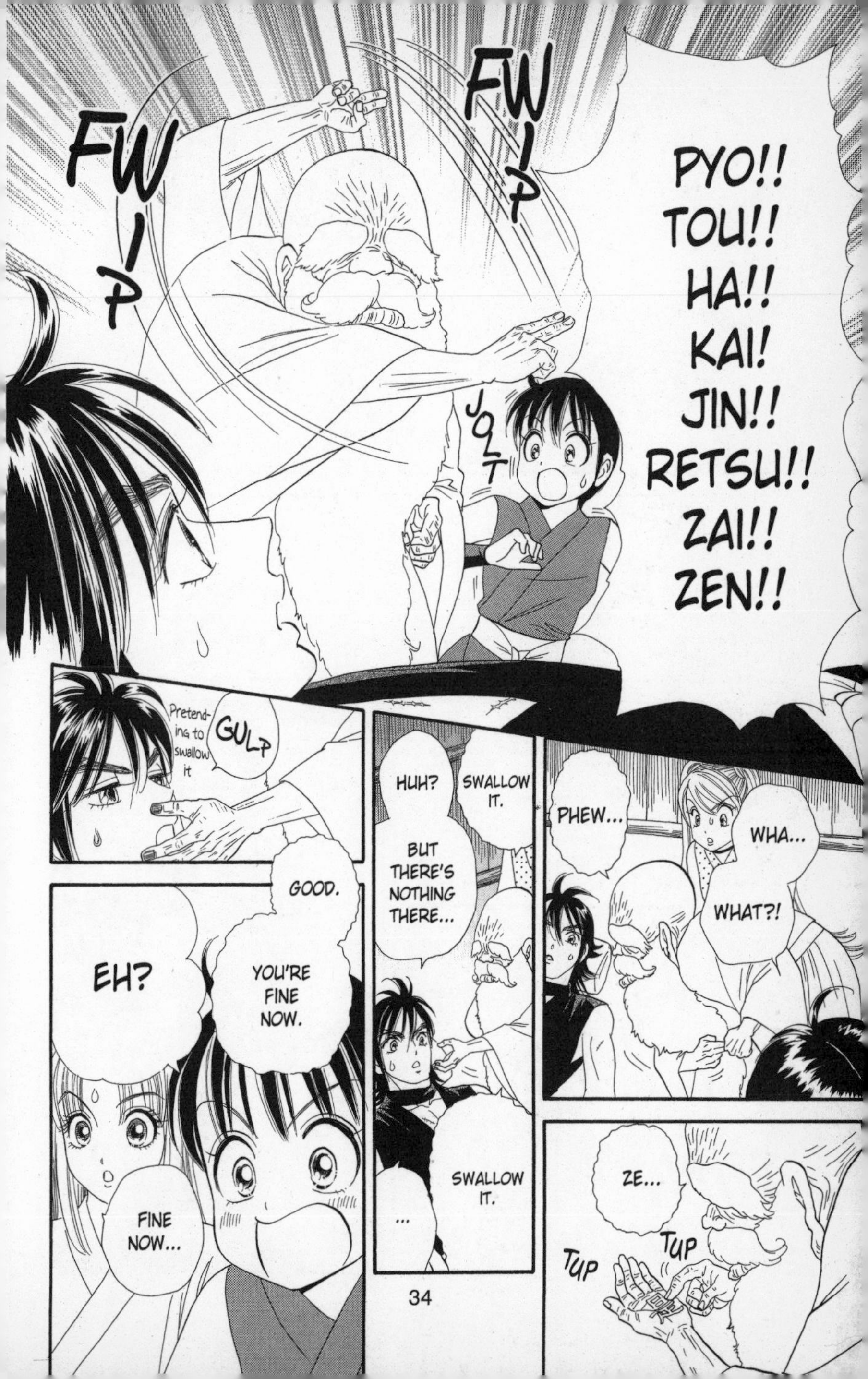
PYO!! TOU!! HA!! KAI! JIN!! RETSU!! ZAI!! ZEN!!
FWIP
FWIP
JOLT
WHA...
PHEW...
WHAT?!
ZE...
TUP
TUP
SWALLOW IT.
HUH?
BUT THERE'S NOTHING THERE...
SWALLOW IT.
...
GULP
Pretending to swallow it
GOOD.
YOU'RE FINE NOW.
EH?
FINE NOW...

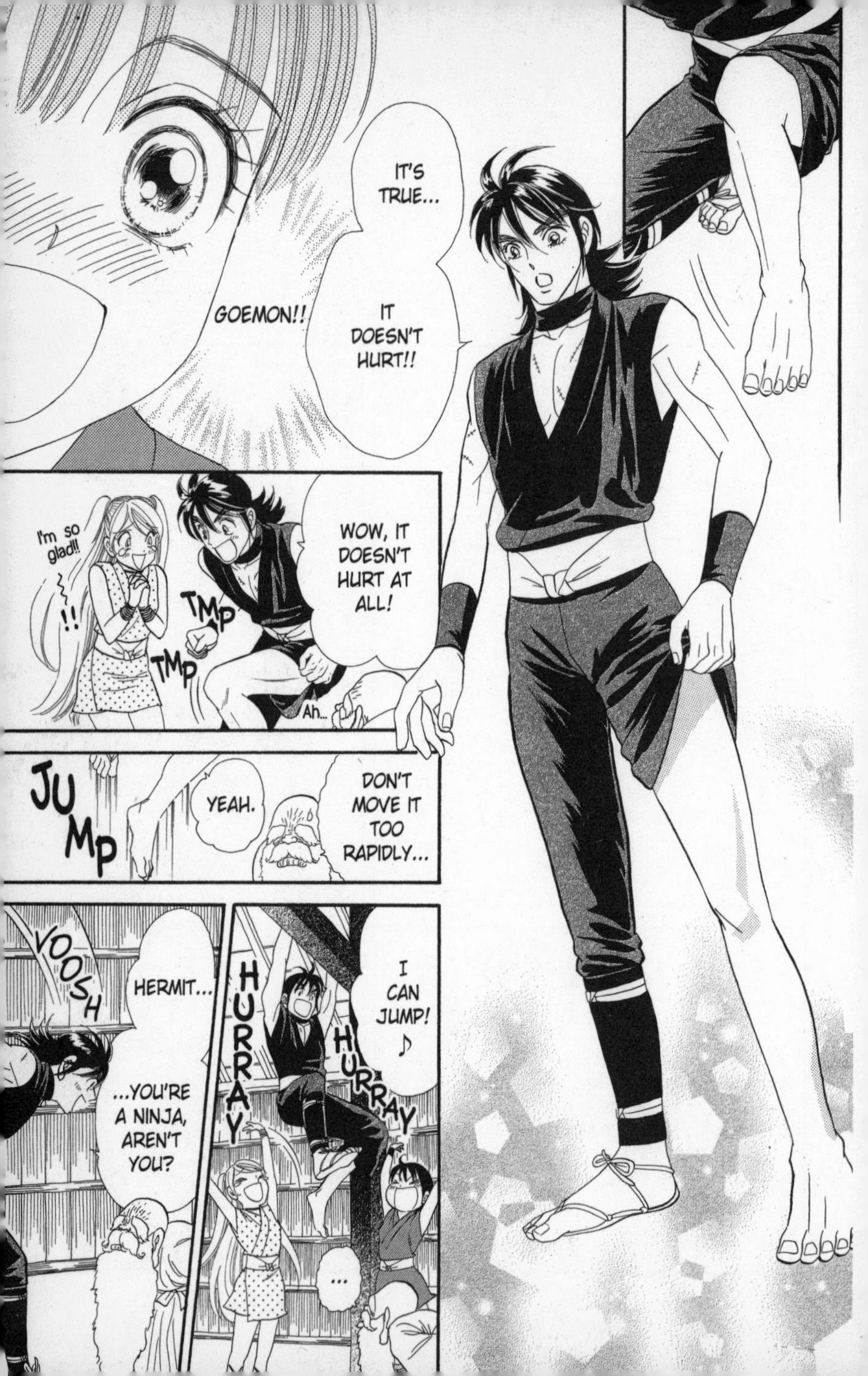
IT'S TRUE...
IT DOESN'T HURT!!
GOEMON!!
WOW, IT DOESN'T HURT AT ALL!
TMP
TMP
I'm so glad!!
!!
Ah...
DON'T MOVE IT TOO RAPIDLY...
YEAH.
JUMP
I CAN JUMP! ♪
HURRAY
HURRAY
HERMIT...
...YOU'RE A NINJA, AREN'T YOU?
VOOSH
...

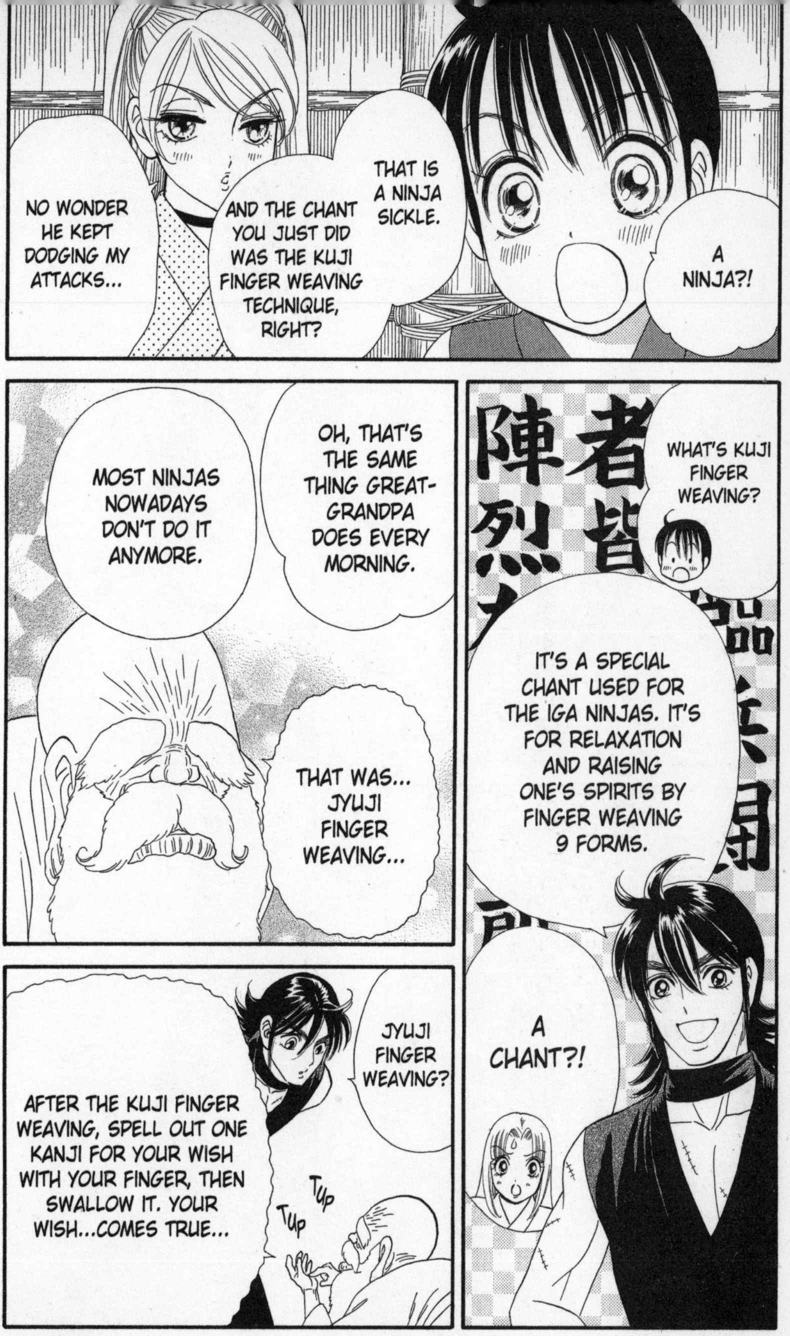
A NINJA?!
THAT IS A NINJA SICKLE.
AND THE CHANT YOU JUST DID WAS THE KUJI FINGER WEAVING TECHNIQUE, RIGHT?
NO WONDER HE KEPT DODGING MY ATTACKS...
者皆
陣烈
WHAT'S KUJI FINGER WEAVING?
IT'S A SPECIAL CHANT USED FOR THE IGA NINJAS. IT'S FOR RELAXATION AND RAISING ONE'S SPIRITS BY FINGER WEAVING 9 FORMS.
A CHANT?!
OH, THAT'S THE SAME THING GREAT-GRANDPA DOES EVERY MORNING.
MOST NINJAS NOWADAYS DON'T DO IT ANYMORE.
THAT WAS... JYUJI FINGER WEAVING...
JYUJI FINGER WEAVING?
AFTER THE KUJI FINGER WEAVING, SPELL OUT ONE KANJI FOR YOUR WISH WITH YOUR FINGER, THEN SWALLOW IT. YOUR WISH...COMES TRUE...
TUP
TUP

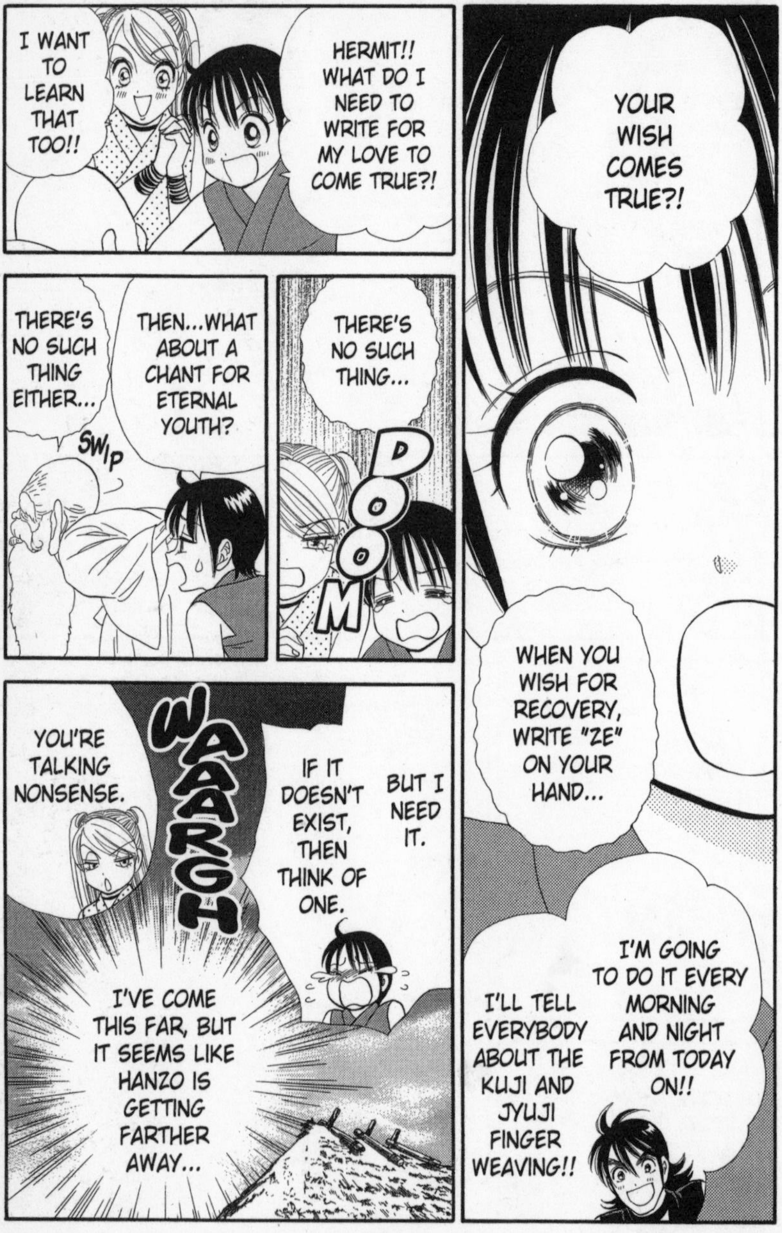
YOUR WISH COMES TRUE?!
WHEN YOU WISH FOR RECOVERY, WRITE "ZE" ON YOUR HAND...
I'M GOING TO DO IT EVERY MORNING AND NIGHT FROM TODAY ON!!
I'LL TELL EVERYBODY ABOUT THE KUJI AND JYUJI FINGER WEAVING!!
HERMIT!! WHAT DO I NEED TO WRITE FOR MY LOVE TO COME TRUE?!
I WANT TO LEARN THAT TOO!!
THERE'S NO SUCH THING...
DOOOM
THEN...WHAT ABOUT A CHANT FOR ETERNAL YOUTH?
THERE'S NO SUCH THING EITHER...
SWIP
BUT I NEED IT.
IF IT DOESN'T EXIST, THEN THINK OF ONE.
WAAARGH
YOU'RE TALKING NONSENSE.
I'VE COME THIS FAR, BUT IT SEEMS LIKE HANZO IS GETTING FARTHER AWAY...

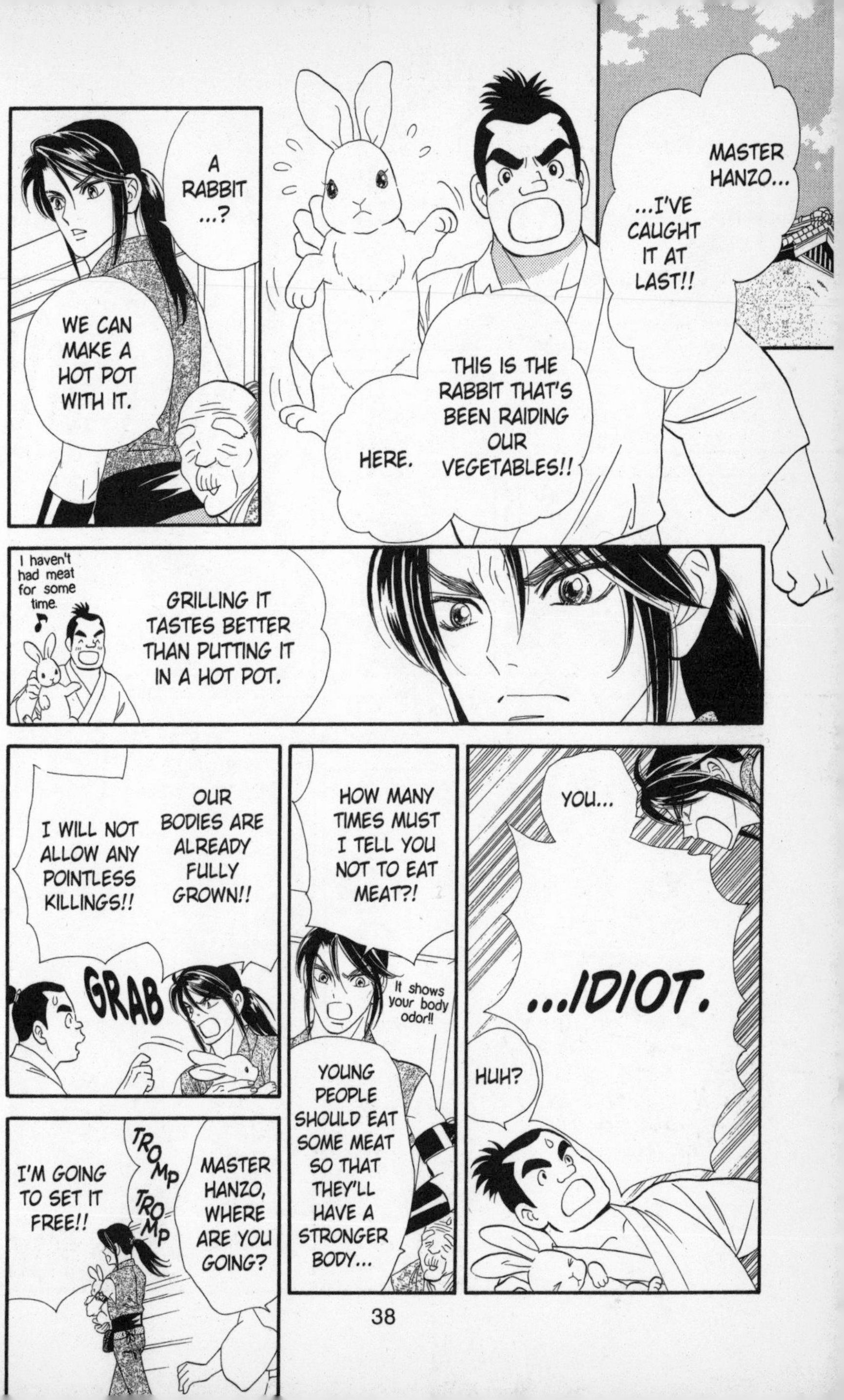
MASTER HANZO...
...I'VE CAUGHT IT AT LAST!!
THIS IS THE RABBIT THAT'S BEEN RAIDING OUR VEGETABLES!!
HERE.
A RABBIT ...?
WE CAN MAKE A HOT POT WITH IT.
GRILLING IT TASTES BETTER THAN PUTTING IT IN A HOT POT.
I haven't had meat for some time.
YOU...
...IDIOT.
HUH?
HOW MANY TIMES MUST I TELL YOU NOT TO EAT MEAT?!
It shows your body odor!!
YOUNG PEOPLE SHOULD EAT SOME MEAT SO THAT THEY'LL HAVE A STRONGER BODY...
OUR BODIES ARE ALREADY FULLY GROWN!!
I WILL NOT ALLOW ANY POINTLESS KILLINGS!!
GRAB
MASTER HANZO, WHERE ARE YOU GOING?
TROMP TROMP
I'M GOING TO SET IT FREE!!

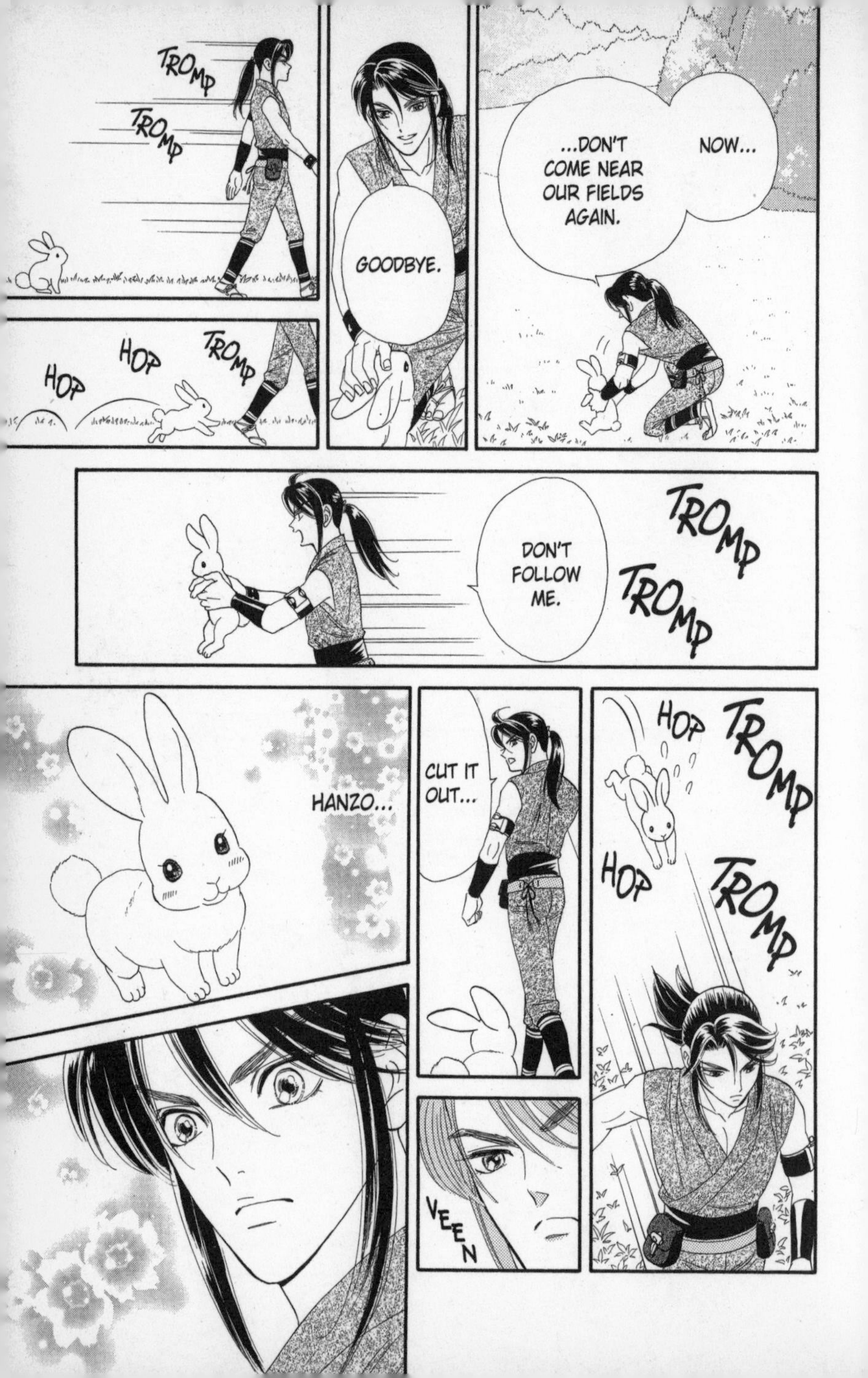
NOW...
...DON'T COME NEAR OUR FIELDS AGAIN.
GOODBYE.
TROMP
TROMP
TROMP
HOP
HOP
TROMP
TROMP
DON'T FOLLOW ME.
TROMP
HOP
TROMP
HOP
CUT IT OUT...
VEEN
HANZO...

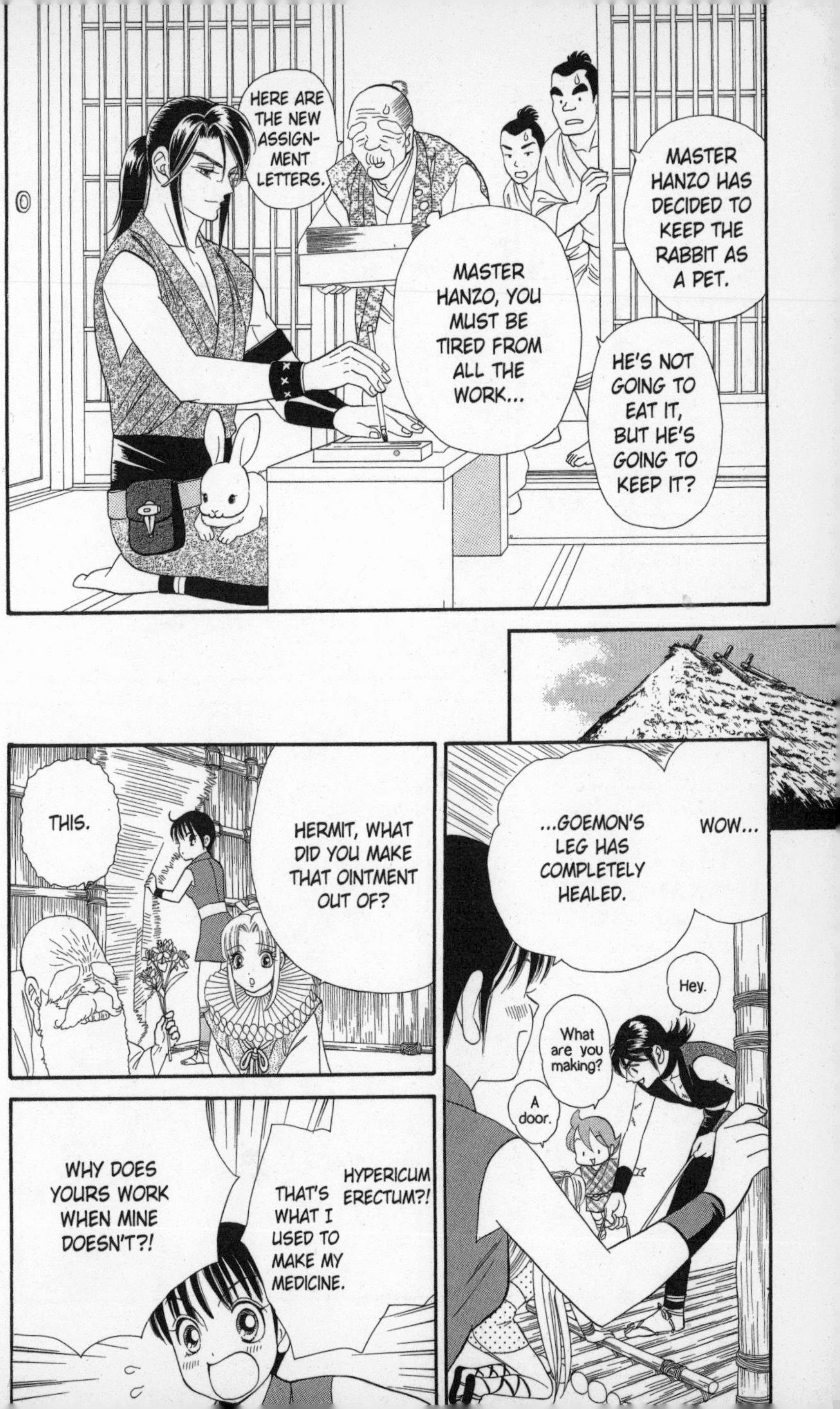
MASTER HANZO HAS DECIDED TO KEEP THE RABBIT AS A PET.
HE'S NOT GOING TO EAT IT, BUT HE'S GOING TO KEEP IT?
HERE ARE THE NEW ASSIGNMENT LETTERS.
MASTER HANZO, YOU MUST BE TIRED FROM ALL THE WORK...
WOW...
...GOEMON'S LEG HAS COMPLETELY HEALED.
Hey.
What are you making?
A door.
HERMIT, WHAT DID YOU MAKE THAT OINTMENT OUT OF?
THIS.
HYPERICUM ERECTUM?!
THAT'S WHAT I USED TO MAKE MY MEDICINE.
WHY DOES YOURS WORK WHEN MINE DOESN'T?!

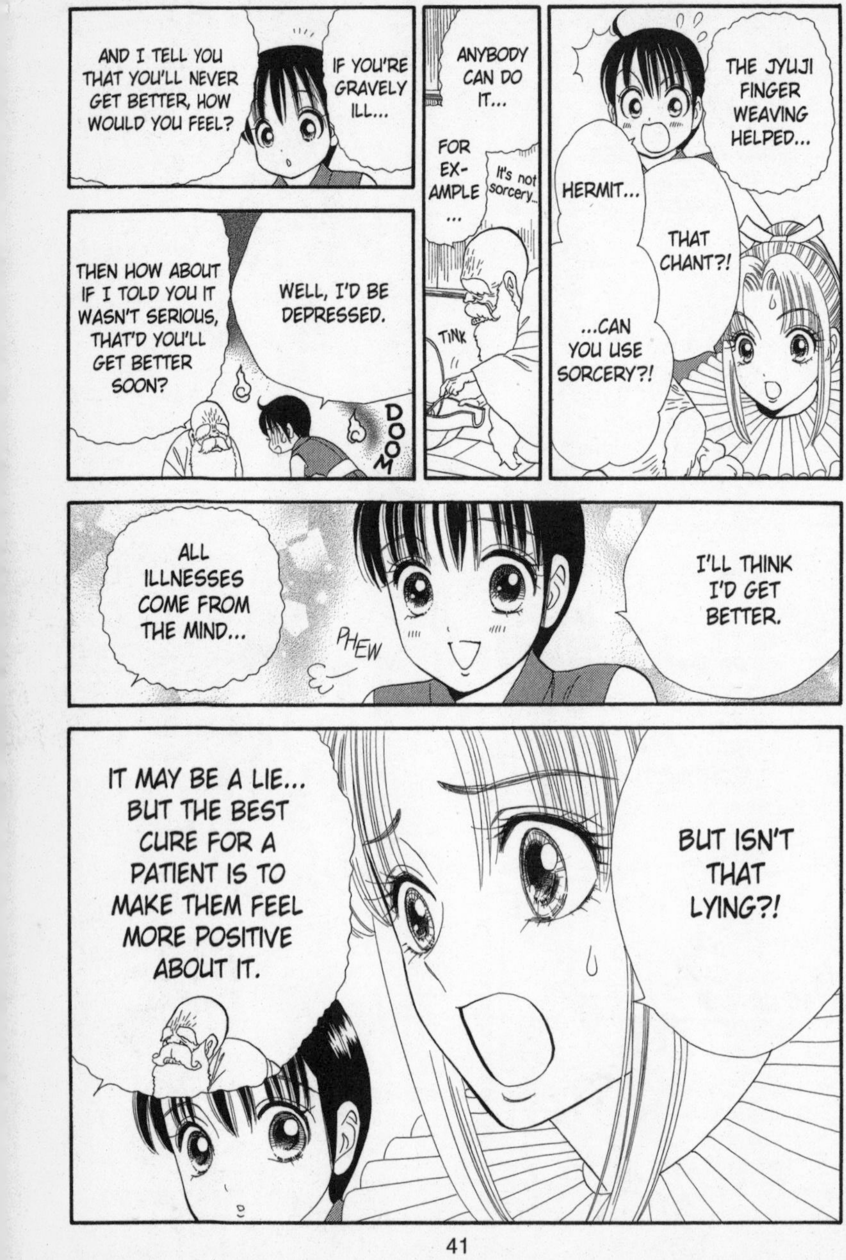
THE JYUJI FINGER WEAVING HELPED...
THAT CHANT?!
HERMIT...
...CAN YOU USE SORCERY?!
It's not sorcery...
ANYBODY CAN DO IT...
FOR EX-AMPLE...
TINK
IF YOU'RE GRAVELY ILL...
AND I TELL YOU THAT YOU'LL NEVER GET BETTER, HOW WOULD YOU FEEL?
WELL, I'D BE DEPRESSED.
THEN HOW ABOUT IF I TOLD YOU IT WASN'T SERIOUS, THAT'D YOU'LL GET BETTER SOON?
DOOM
I'LL THINK I'D GET BETTER.
PHEW
ALL ILLNESSES COME FROM THE MIND...
BUT ISN'T THAT LYING?!
IT MAY BE A LIE... BUT THE BEST CURE FOR A PATIENT IS TO MAKE THEM FEEL MORE POSITIVE ABOUT IT.

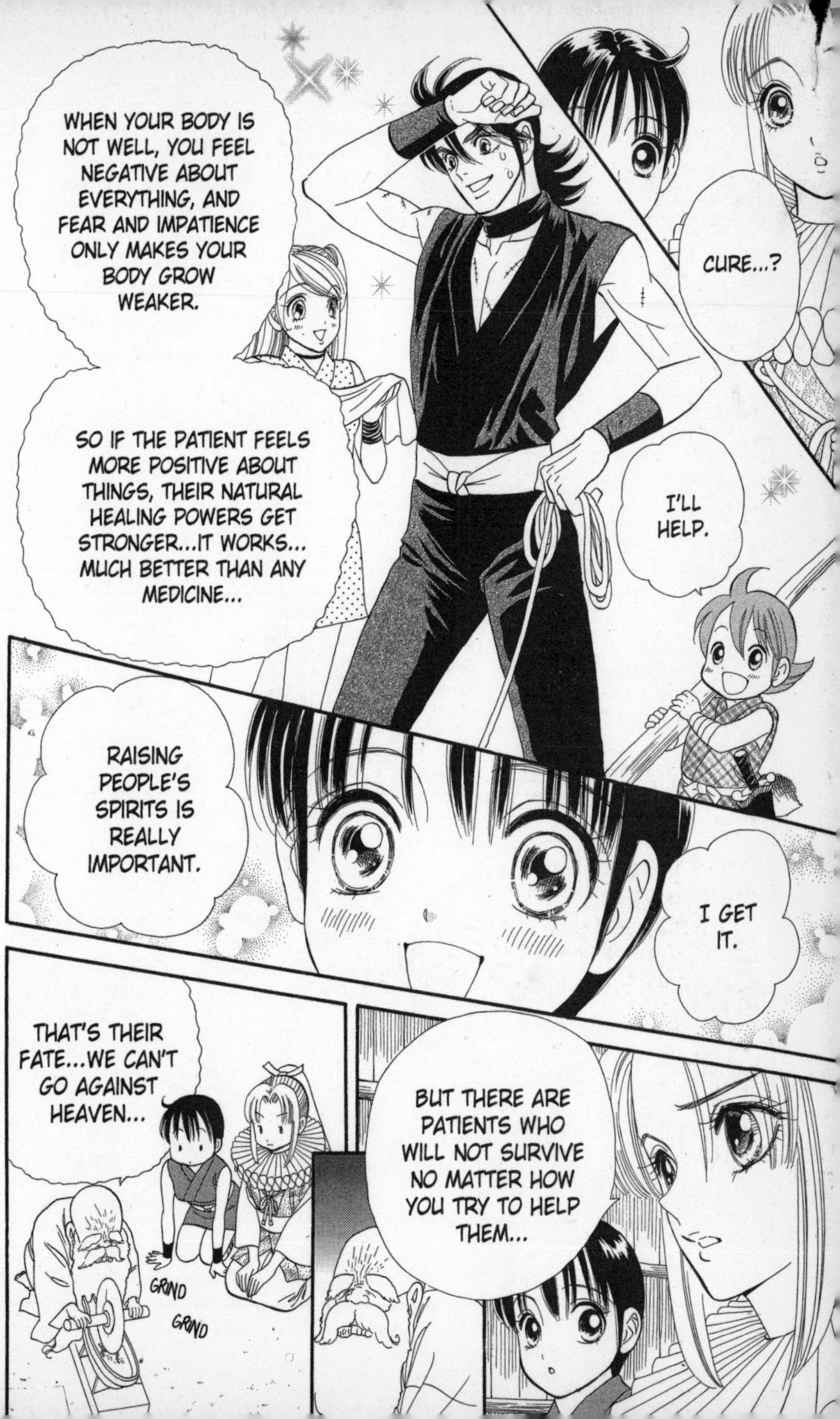
CURE...?
WHEN YOUR BODY IS NOT WELL, YOU FEEL NEGATIVE ABOUT EVERYTHING, AND FEAR AND IMPATIENCE ONLY MAKES YOUR BODY GROW WEAKER.
SO IF THE PATIENT FEELS MORE POSITIVE ABOUT THINGS, THEIR NATURAL HEALING POWERS GET STRONGER...IT WORKS... MUCH BETTER THAN ANY MEDICINE...
I'LL HELP.
RAISING PEOPLE'S SPIRITS IS REALLY IMPORTANT.
I GET IT.
BUT THERE ARE PATIENTS WHO WILL NOT SURVIVE NO MATTER HOW YOU TRY TO HELP THEM...
THAT'S THEIR FATE...WE CAN'T GO AGAINST HEAVEN...
GRIND
GRIND

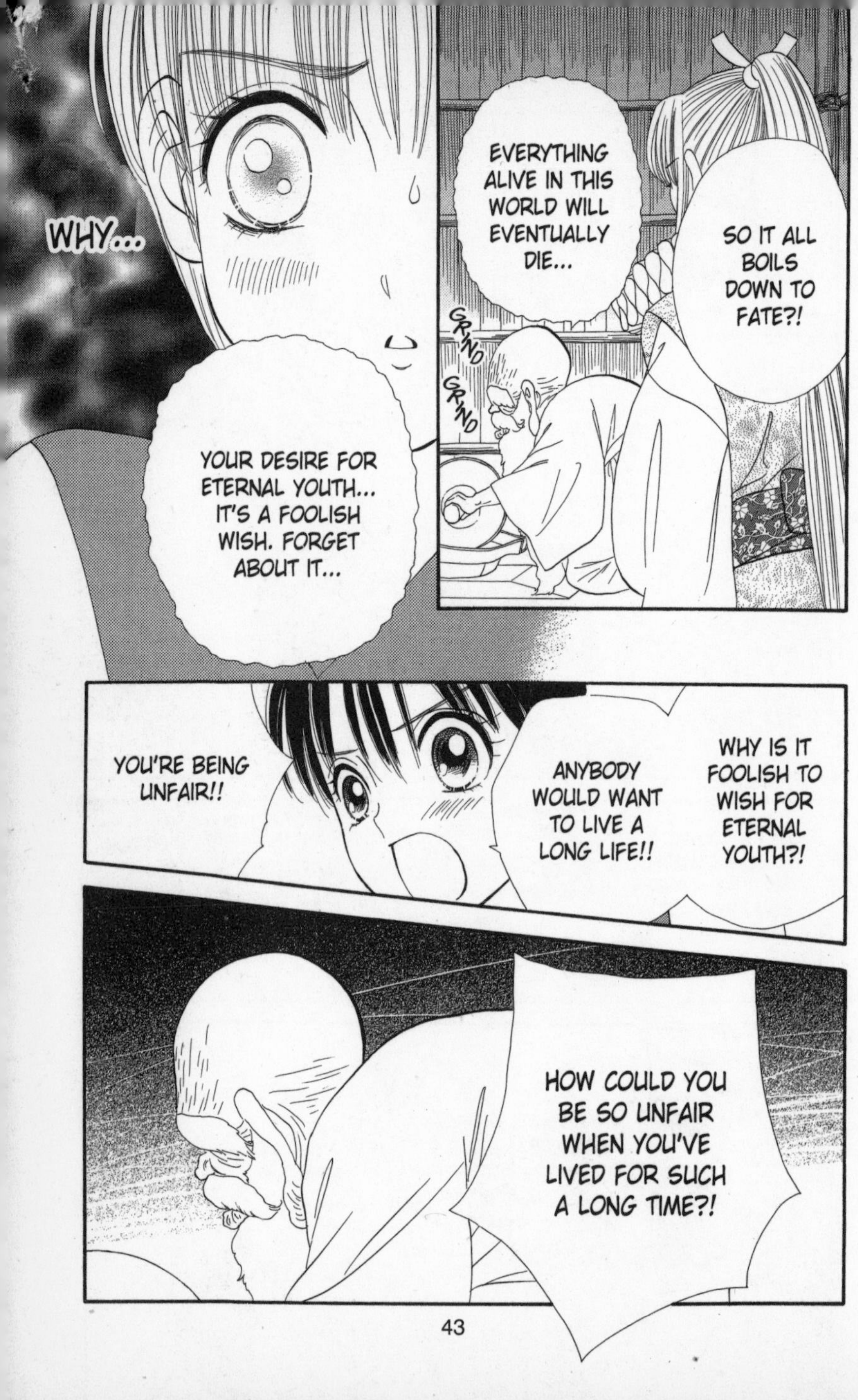
EVERYTHING ALIVE IN THIS WORLD WILL EVENTUALLY DIE...
SO IT ALL BOILS DOWN TO FATE?!
GRIND GRIND
WHY...
YOUR DESIRE FOR ETERNAL YOUTH... IT'S A FOOLISH WISH. FORGET ABOUT IT...
WHY IS IT FOOLISH TO WISH FOR ETERNAL YOUTH?!
ANYBODY WOULD WANT TO LIVE A LONG LIFE!!
YOU'RE BEING UNFAIR!!
HOW COULD YOU BE SO UNFAIR WHEN YOU'VE LIVED FOR SUCH A LONG TIME?!

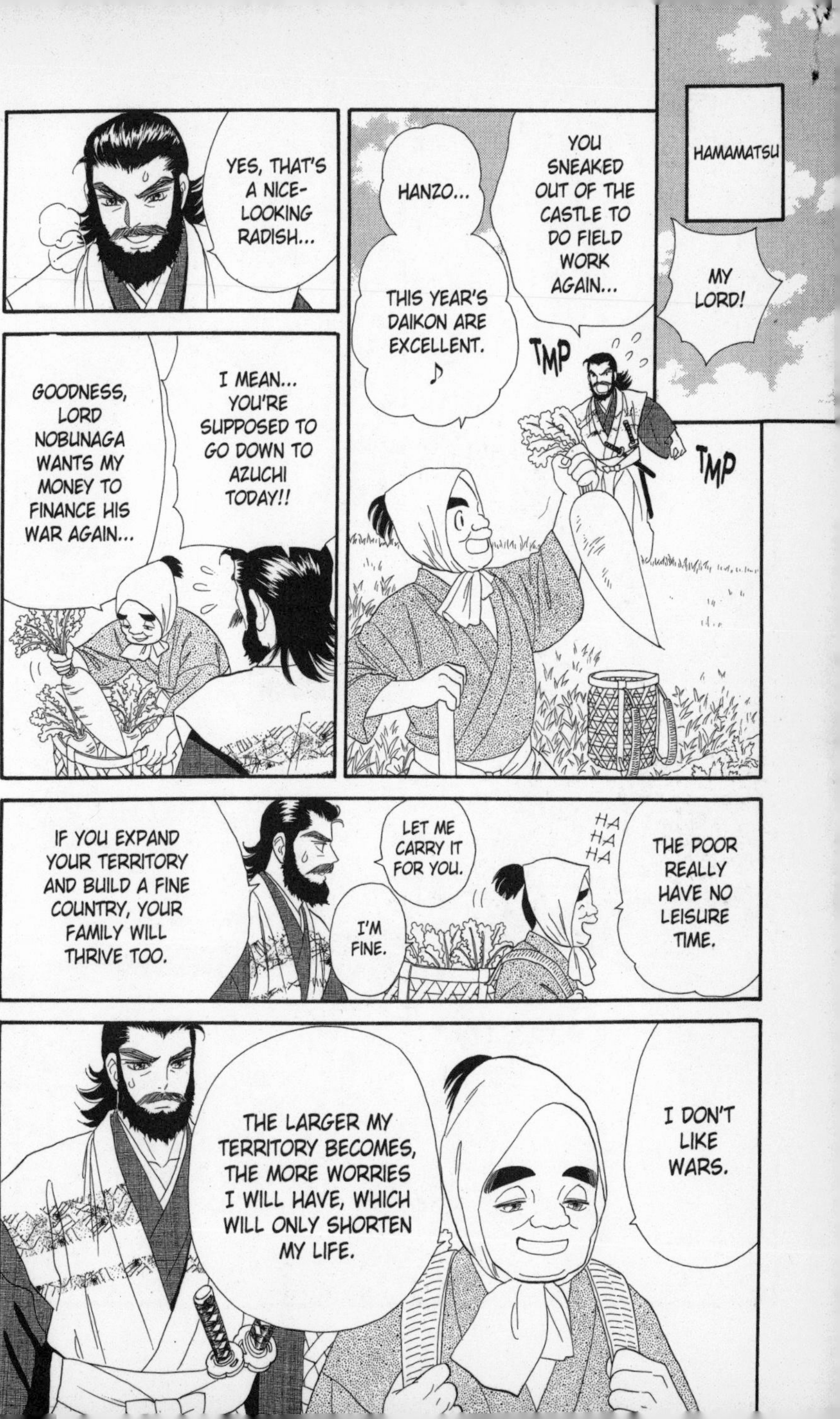
HAMAMATSU
MY LORD!
TMP
TMP
YOU SNEAKED OUT OF THE CASTLE TO DO FIELD WORK AGAIN...
HANZO...
THIS YEAR'S DAIKON ARE EXCELLENT. ♪
YES, THAT'S A NICE-LOOKING RADISH...
I MEAN... YOU'RE SUPPOSED TO GO DOWN TO AZUCHI TODAY!!
GOODNESS, LORD NOBUNAGA WANTS MY MONEY TO FINANCE HIS WAR AGAIN...
THE POOR REALLY HAVE NO LEISURE TIME.
HA HA HA
LET ME CARRY IT FOR YOU.
I'M FINE.
IF YOU EXPAND YOUR TERRITORY AND BUILD A FINE COUNTRY, YOUR FAMILY WILL THRIVE TOO.
I DON'T LIKE WARS.
THE LARGER MY TERRITORY BECOMES, THE MORE WORRIES I WILL HAVE, WHICH WILL ONLY SHORTEN MY LIFE.

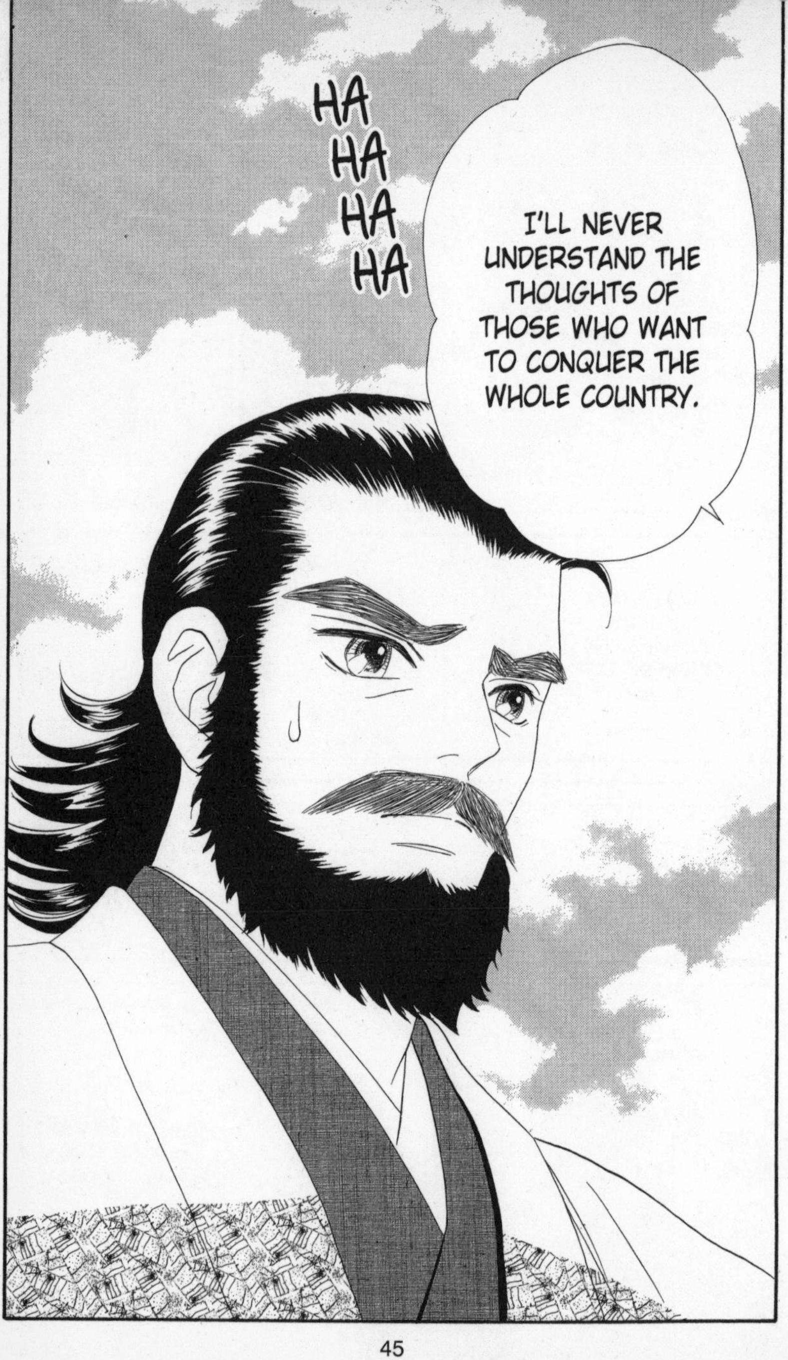
I'LL NEVER UNDERSTAND THE THOUGHTS OF THOSE WHO WANT TO CONQUER THE WHOLE COUNTRY.
HA HA HA HA

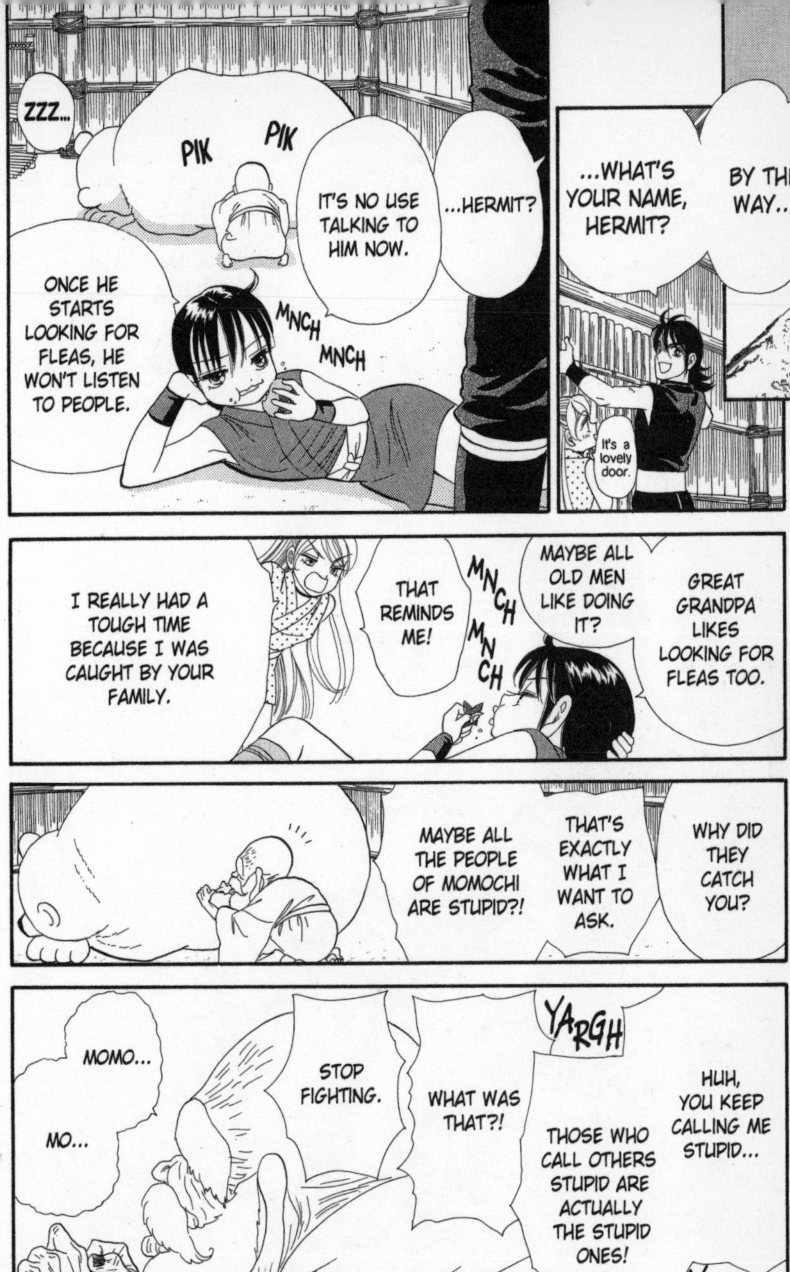
BY THE WAY...
...WHAT'S YOUR NAME, HERMIT?
It's a lovely door.
...HERMIT?
IT'S NO USE TALKING TO HIM NOW.
PIK PIK
ZZZ...
ONCE HE STARTS LOOKING FOR FLEAS, HE WON'T LISTEN TO PEOPLE.
MNCH MNCH
GREAT GRANDPA LIKES LOOKING FOR FLEAS TOO.
MAYBE ALL OLD MEN LIKE DOING IT?
MNCH MNCH
THAT REMINDS ME!
I REALLY HAD A TOUGH TIME BECAUSE I WAS CAUGHT BY YOUR FAMILY.
WHY DID THEY CATCH YOU?
THAT'S EXACTLY WHAT I WANT TO ASK.
MAYBE ALL THE PEOPLE OF MOMOCHI ARE STUPID?!
HUH, YOU KEEP CALLING ME STUPID...
YARGH
THOSE WHO CALL OTHERS STUPID ARE ACTUALLY THE STUPID ONES!
YARGH
WHAT WAS THAT?!
STOP FIGHTING.
MOMO...
MO...

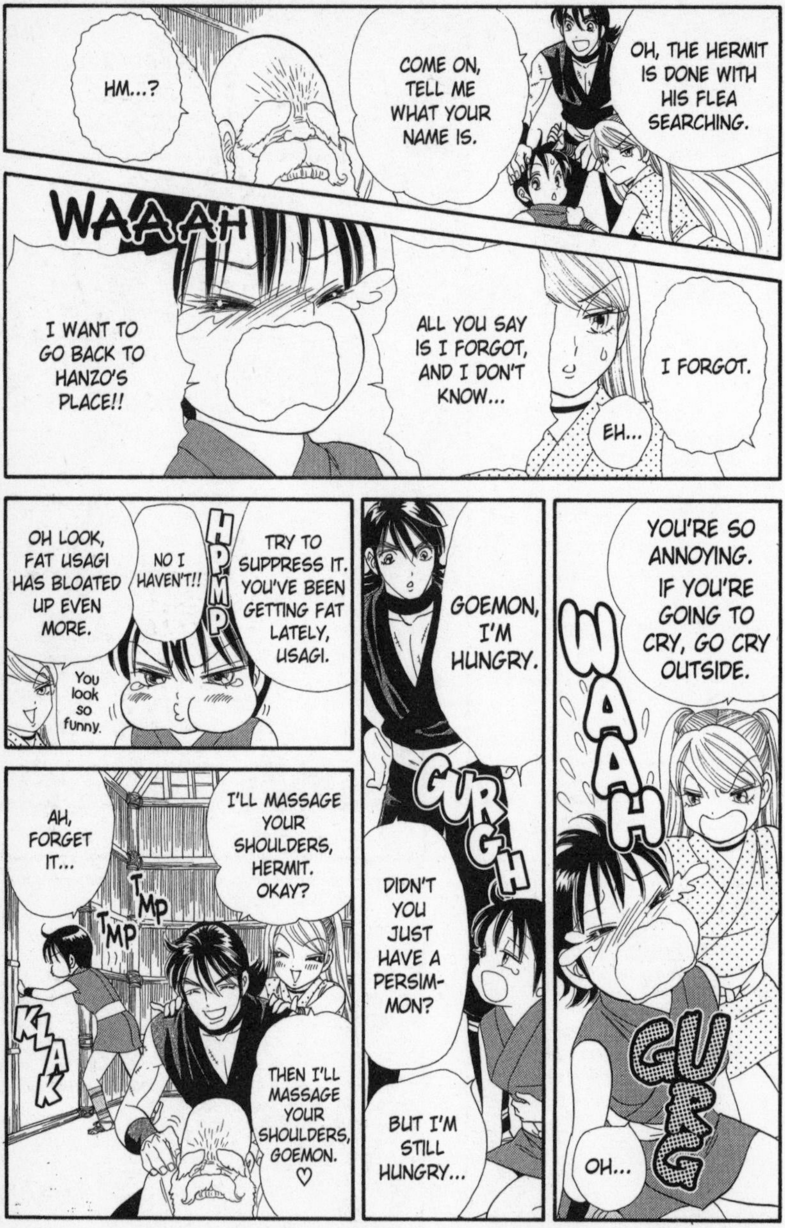
OH, THE HERMIT IS DONE WITH HIS FLEA SEARCHING.
COME ON, TELL ME WHAT YOUR NAME IS.
HM...?
I FORGOT.
EH...
ALL YOU SAY IS I FORGOT, AND I DON'T KNOW...
WAAAH
I WANT TO GO BACK TO HANZO'S PLACE!!
YOU'RE SO ANNOYING. IF YOU'RE GOING TO CRY, GO CRY OUTSIDE.
WAAAH
GURG
OH...
GOEMON, I'M HUNGRY.
GURGH
DIDN'T YOU JUST HAVE A PERSIMMON?
BUT I'M STILL HUNGRY...
TRY TO SUPPRESS IT. YOU'VE BEEN GETTING FAT LATELY, USAGI.
HPMP
NO I HAVEN'T!!
OH LOOK, FAT USAGI HAS BLOATED UP EVEN MORE.
You look so funny.
I'LL MASSAGE YOUR SHOULDERS, HERMIT. OKAY?
AH, FORGET IT...
TMP TMP
KLAK
THEN I'LL MASSAGE YOUR SHOULDERS, GOEMON. ♡

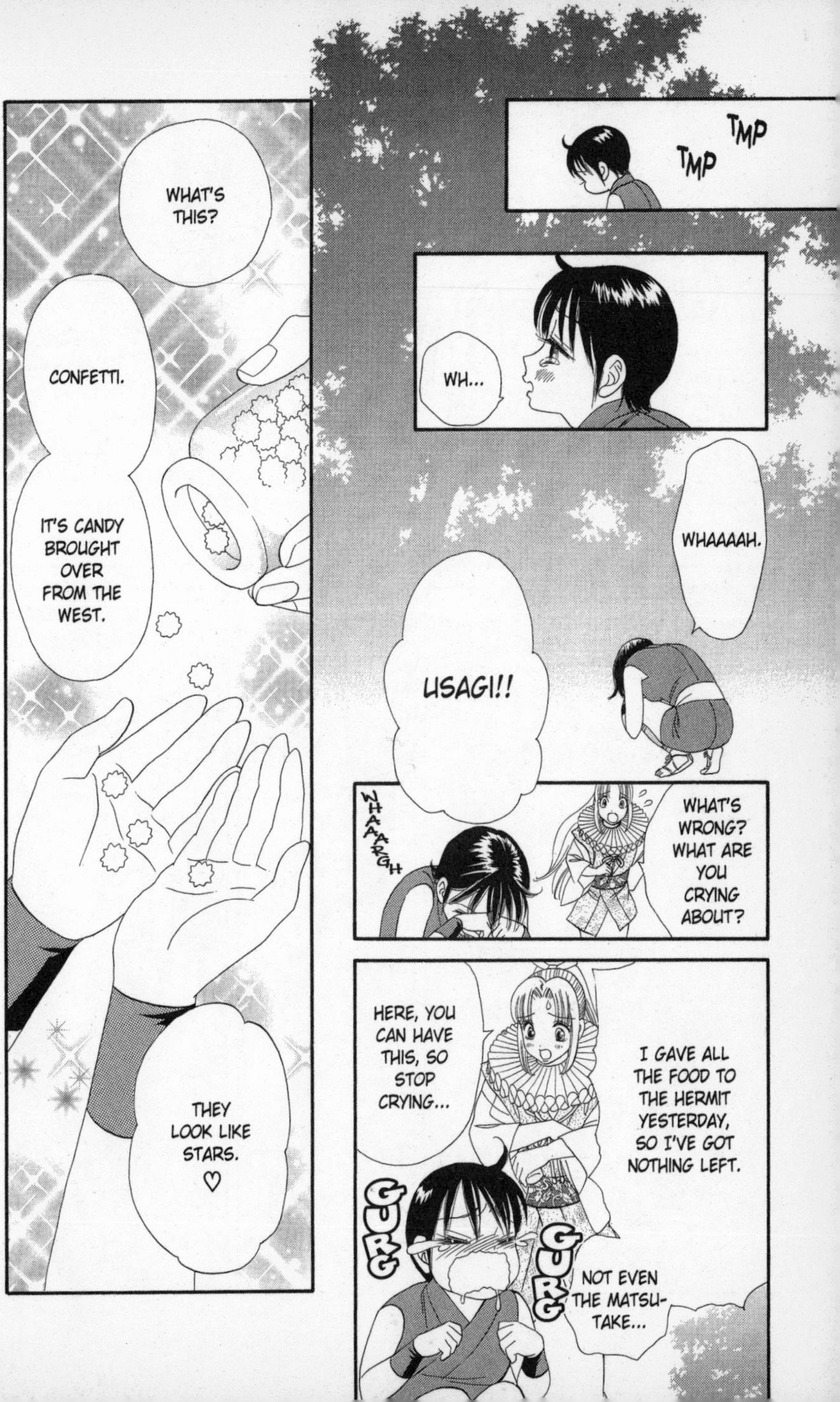
TMP
TMP
WH...
WHAAAAH.
USAGI!!
WHAAARGH
WHAT'S WRONG? WHAT ARE YOU CRYING ABOUT?
I GAVE ALL THE FOOD TO THE HERMIT YESTERDAY, SO I'VE GOT NOTHING LEFT.
GURG
GURG
NOT EVEN THE MATSU-TAKE...
HERE, YOU CAN HAVE THIS, SO STOP CRYING...
WHAT'S THIS?
CONFETTI.
IT'S CANDY BROUGHT OVER FROM THE WEST.
THEY LOOK LIKE STARS. ♡

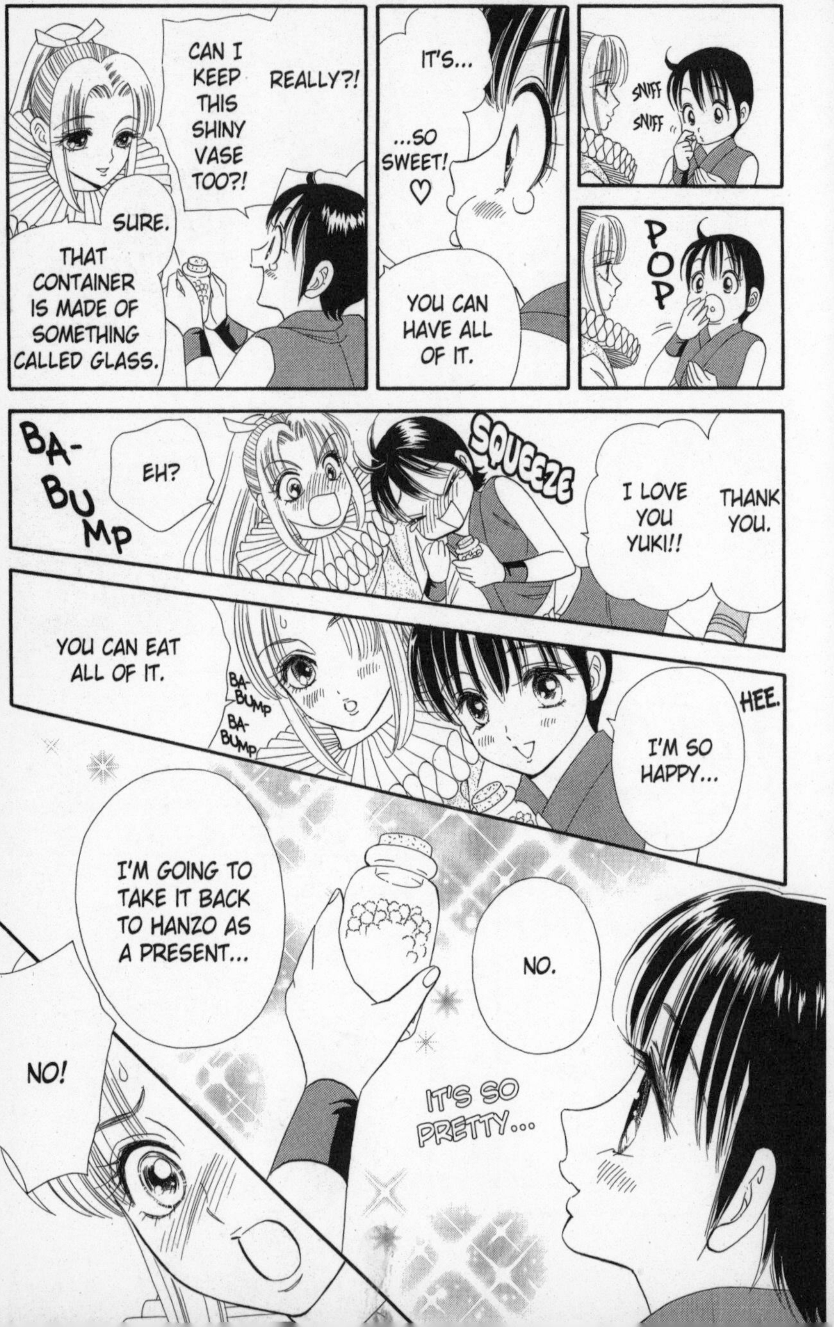
SNIFF
SNIFF
POP
IT'S...
...SO SWEET! ♡
YOU CAN HAVE ALL OF IT.
REALLY?!
CAN I KEEP THIS SHINY VASE TOO?!
SURE.
THAT CONTAINER IS MADE OF SOMETHING CALLED GLASS.
THANK YOU.
I LOVE YOU YUKI!!
SQUEEZE
EH?
BA-BUMP
HEE.
I'M SO HAPPY...
BA-BUMP
BA-BUMP
YOU CAN EAT ALL OF IT.
NO.
IT'S SO PRETTY...
I'M GOING TO TAKE IT BACK TO HANZO AS A PRESENT...
NO!

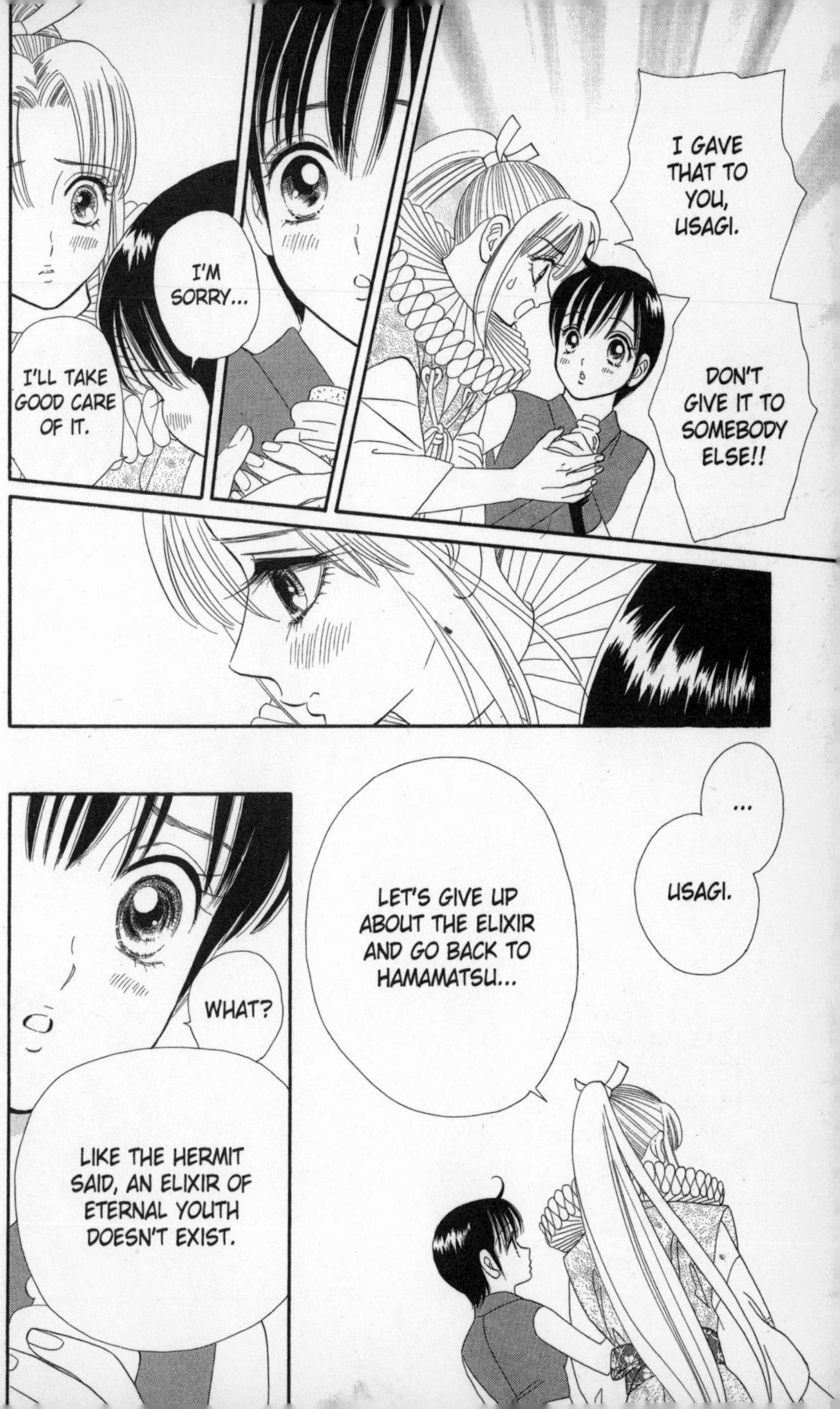
I GAVE THAT TO YOU, USAGI.
DON'T GIVE IT TO SOMEBODY ELSE!!
I'M SORRY...
I'LL TAKE GOOD CARE OF IT.
...
USAGI.
LET'S GIVE UP ABOUT THE ELIXIR AND GO BACK TO HAMAMATSU...
WHAT?
LIKE THE HERMIT SAID, AN ELIXIR OF ETERNAL YOUTH DOESN'T EXIST.

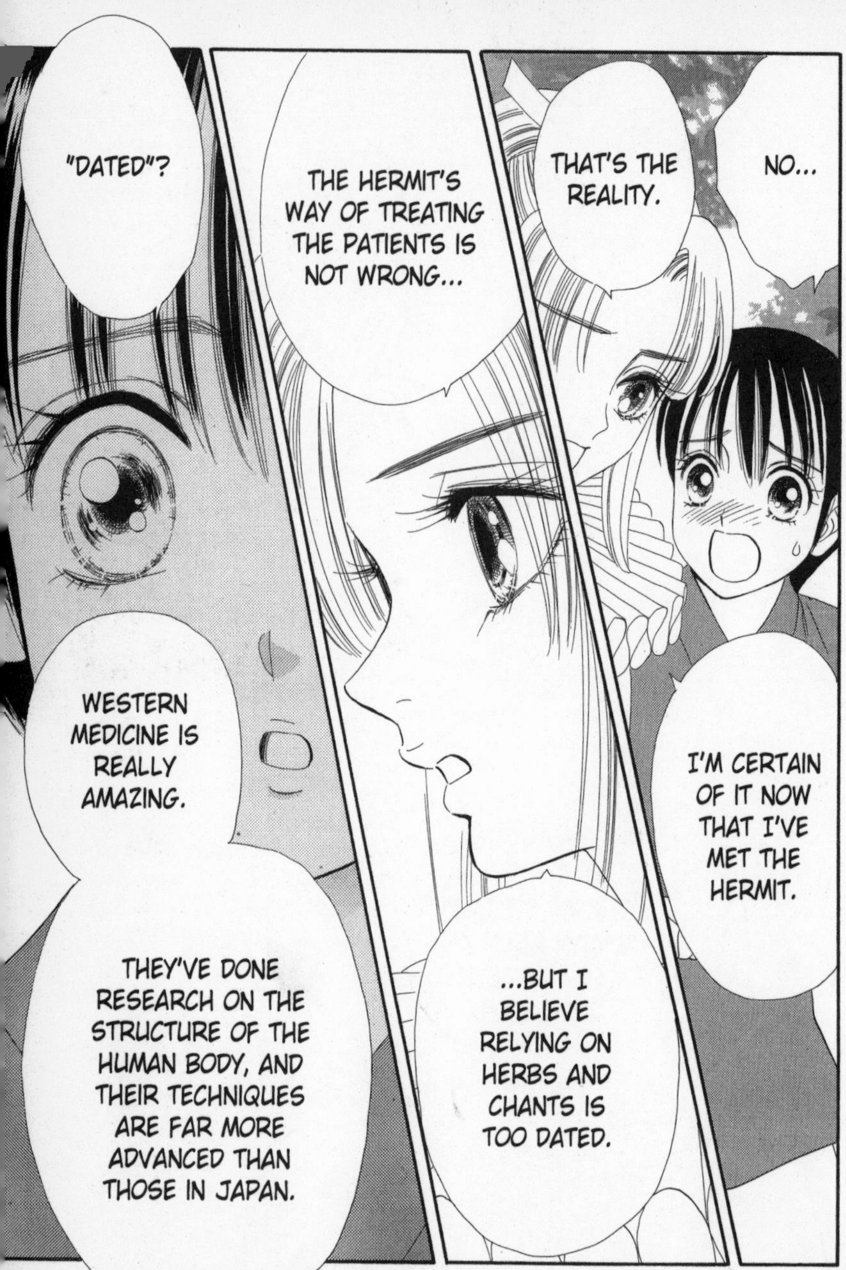
NO...
THAT'S THE REALITY.
I'M CERTAIN OF IT NOW THAT I'VE MET THE HERMIT.
THE HERMIT'S WAY OF TREATING THE PATIENTS IS NOT WRONG...
...BUT I BELIEVE RELYING ON HERBS AND CHANTS IS TOO DATED.
"DATED"?
WESTERN MEDICINE IS REALLY AMAZING.
THEY'VE DONE RESEARCH ON THE STRUCTURE OF THE HUMAN BODY, AND THEIR TECHNIQUES ARE FAR MORE ADVANCED THAN THOSE IN JAPAN.

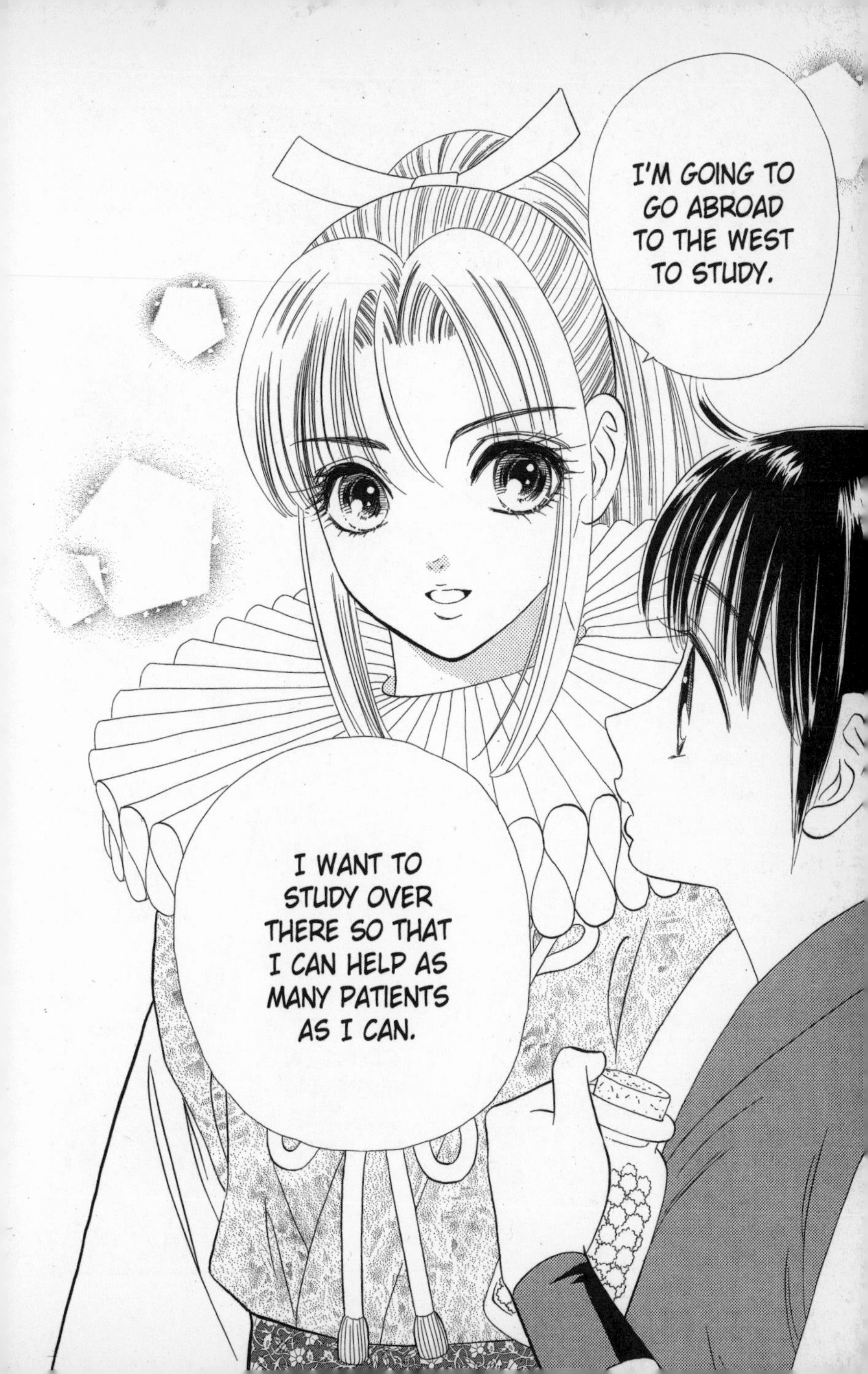
I'M GOING TO GO ABROAD TO THE WEST TO STUDY.
I WANT TO STUDY OVER THERE SO THAT I CAN HELP AS MANY PATIENTS AS I CAN.

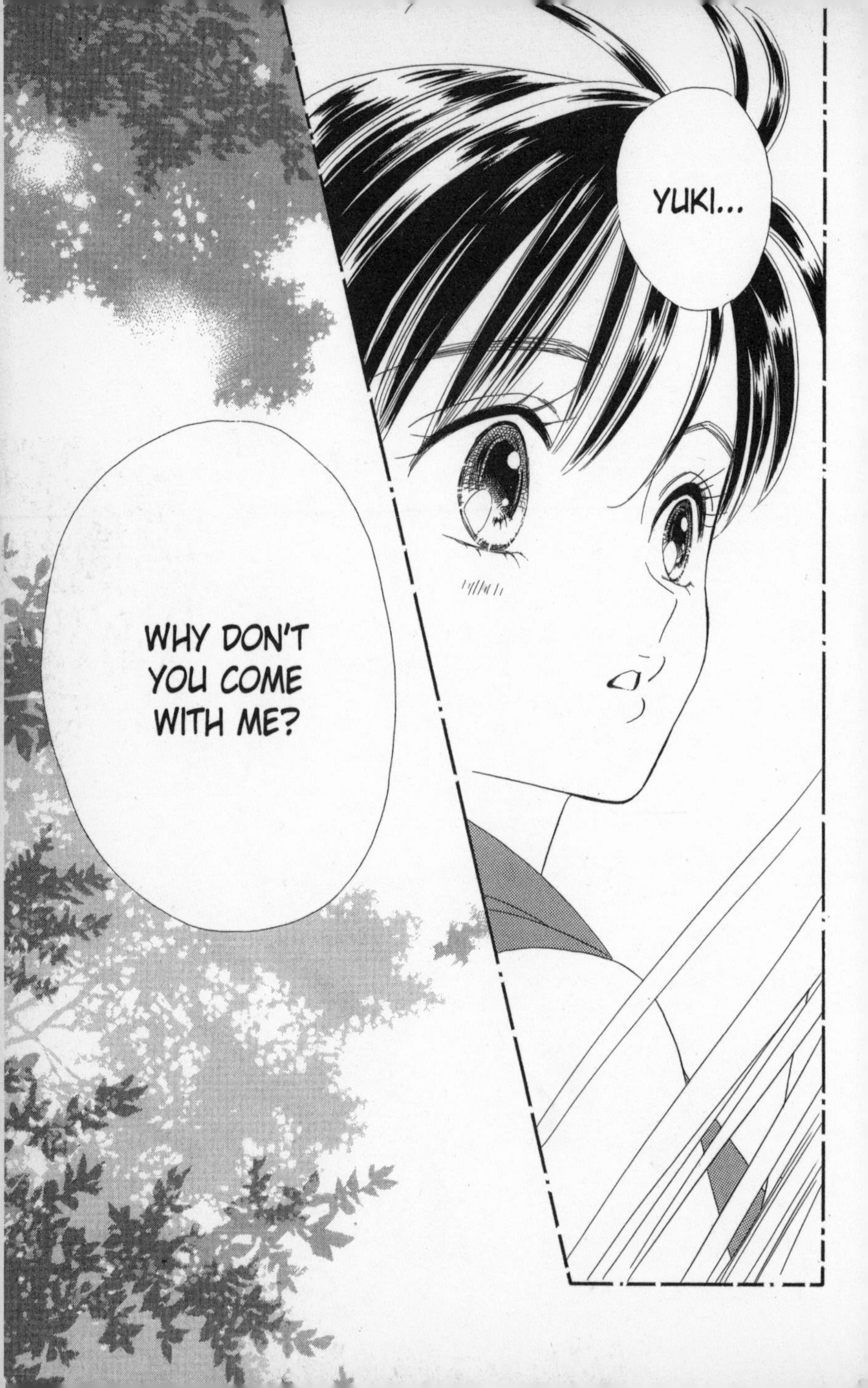
YUKI...
WHY DON'T YOU COME WITH ME?

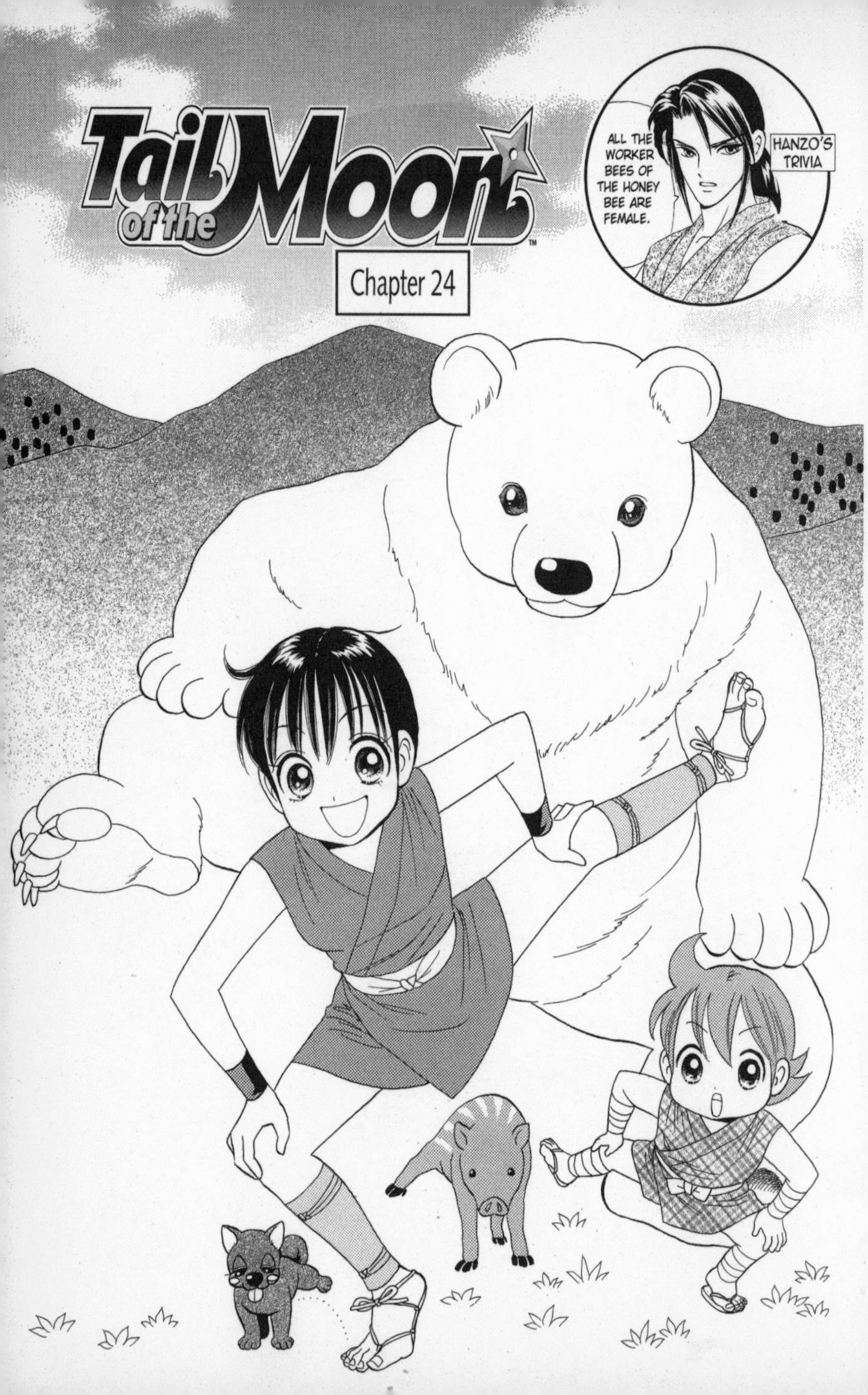

Tail of the Moon™
Chapter 24
HANZO'S TRIVIA
ALL THE WORKER BEES OF THE HONEY BEE ARE FEMALE.

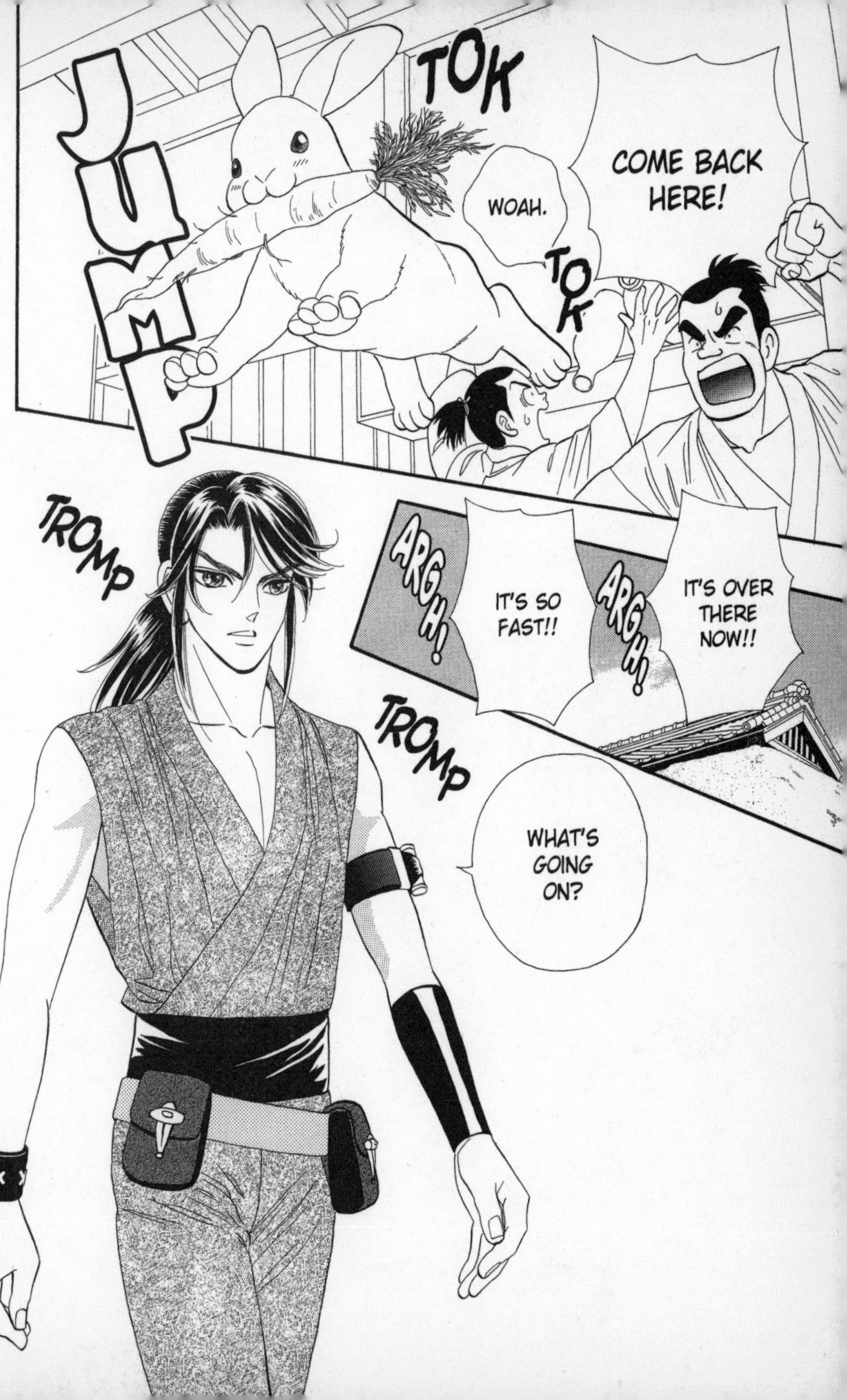
TOK
COME BACK HERE!
WOAH.
TOK
JUMP
IT'S OVER THERE NOW!!
ARGH!
IT'S SO FAST!!
ARGH!
TROMP
WHAT'S GOING ON?
TROMP

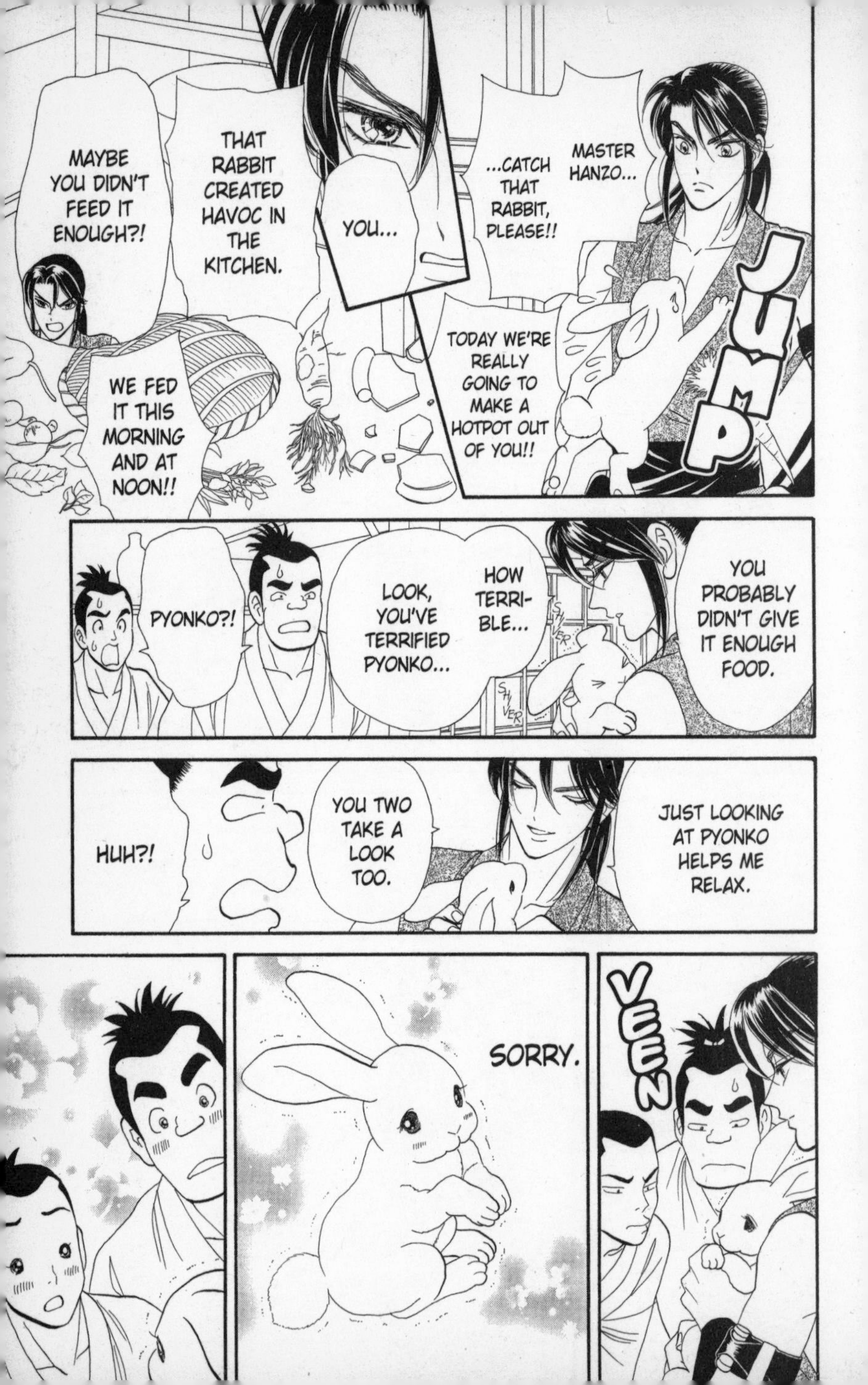
MASTER HANZO...
...CATCH THAT RABBIT, PLEASE!!
JUMP
TODAY WE'RE REALLY GOING TO MAKE A HOTPOT OUT OF YOU!!
YOU...
THAT RABBIT CREATED HAVOC IN THE KITCHEN.
MAYBE YOU DIDN'T FEED IT ENOUGH?!
WE FED IT THIS MORNING AND AT NOON!!
YOU PROBABLY DIDN'T GIVE IT ENOUGH FOOD.
SHIVER
SHIVER
HOW TERRI-BLE...
LOOK, YOU'VE TERRIFIED PYONKO...
PYONKO?!
JUST LOOKING AT PYONKO HELPS ME RELAX.
YOU TWO TAKE A LOOK TOO.
HUH?!
VEEN
SORRY.

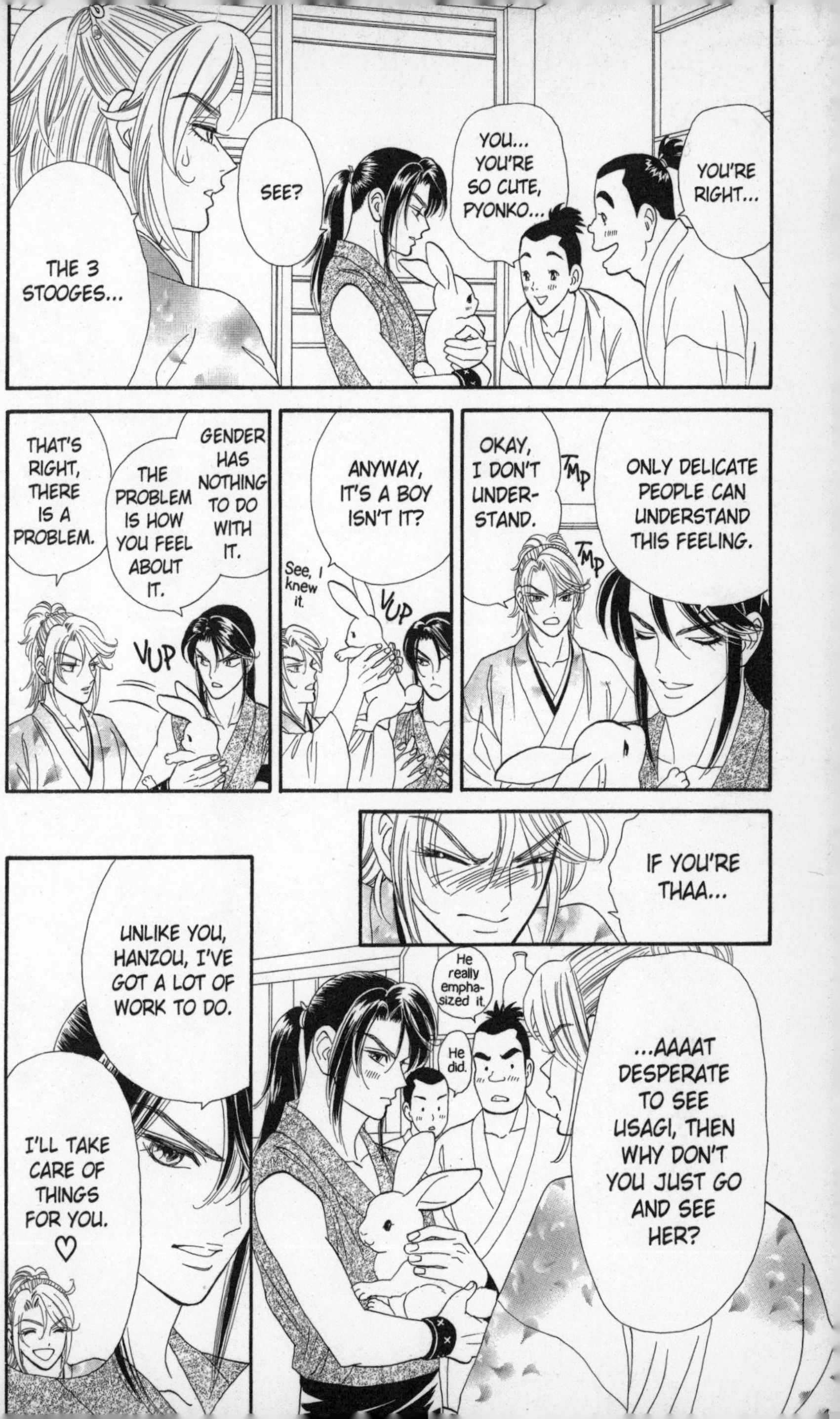
YOU'RE RIGHT...
YOU... YOU'RE SO CUTE, PYONKO...
SEE?
THE 3 STOOGES...
ONLY DELICATE PEOPLE CAN UNDERSTAND THIS FEELING.
TMP
TMP
OKAY, I DON'T UNDER-STAND.
ANYWAY, IT'S A BOY ISN'T IT?
VUP
See, I knew it.
GENDER HAS NOTHING TO DO WITH IT.
THE PROBLEM IS HOW YOU FEEL ABOUT IT.
THAT'S RIGHT, THERE IS A PROBLEM.
VUP
IF YOU'RE THAA...
...AAAAT DESPERATE TO SEE USAGI, THEN WHY DON'T YOU JUST GO AND SEE HER?
He really empha-sized it.
He did.
UNLIKE YOU, HANZOU, I'VE GOT A LOT OF WORK TO DO.
I'LL TAKE CARE OF THINGS FOR YOU. ♡

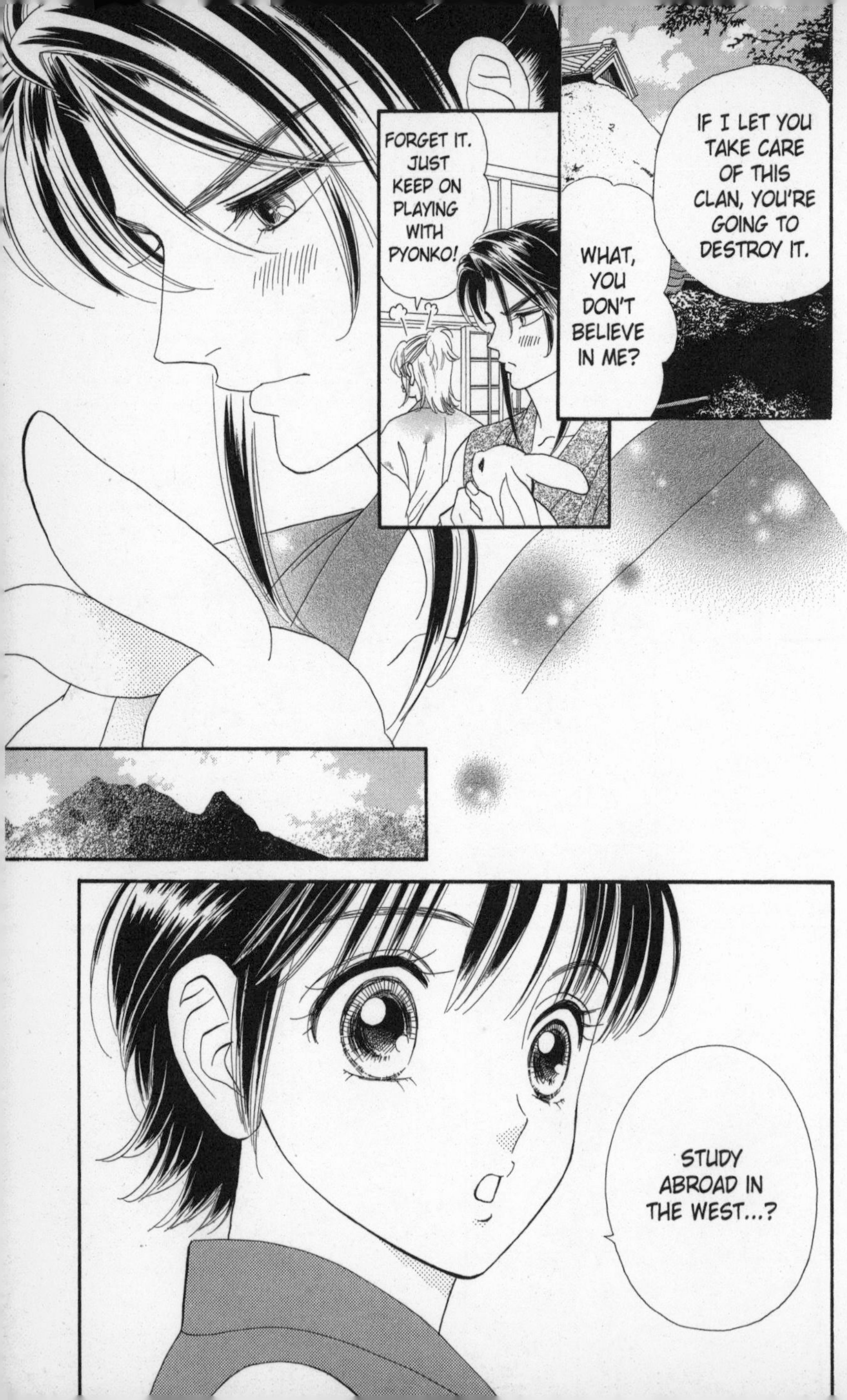
IF I LET YOU TAKE CARE OF THIS CLAN, YOU'RE GOING TO DESTROY IT.
WHAT, YOU DON'T BELIEVE IN ME?
FORGET IT. JUST KEEP ON PLAYING WITH PYONKO!
STUDY ABROAD IN THE WEST...?

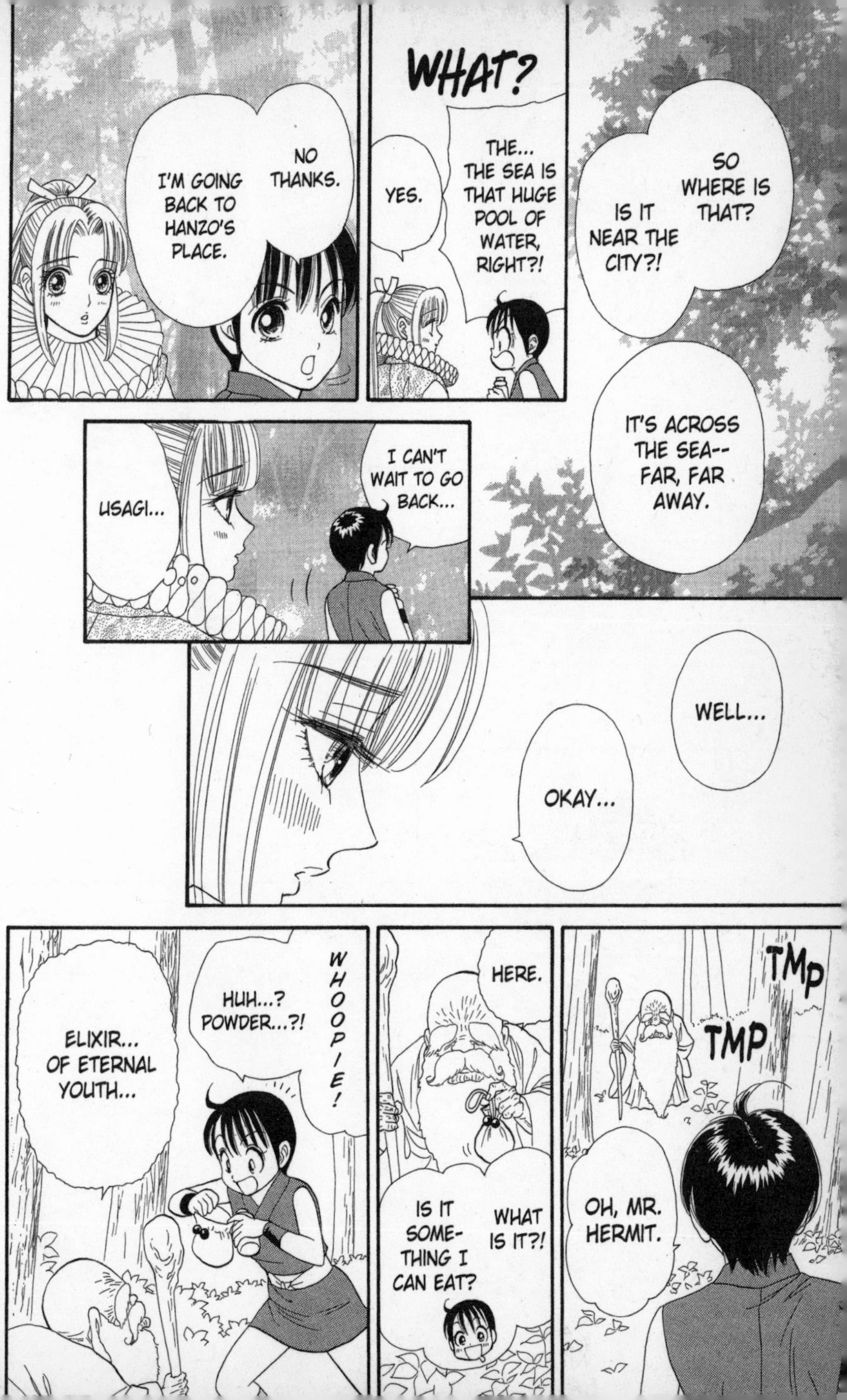
SO WHERE IS THAT?
IS IT NEAR THE CITY?!
IT'S ACROSS THE SEA-- FAR, FAR AWAY.
WHAT?
THE... THE SEA IS THAT HUGE POOL OF WATER, RIGHT?!
YES.
NO THANKS.
I'M GOING BACK TO HANZO'S PLACE.
I CAN'T WAIT TO GO BACK...
USAGI...
WELL...
OKAY...
TMp
TMP
OH, MR. HERMIT.
HERE.
WHAT IS IT?!
IS IT SOME-THING I CAN EAT?
WHOOPIE!
HUH...? POWDER...?!
ELIXIR... OF ETERNAL YOUTH...

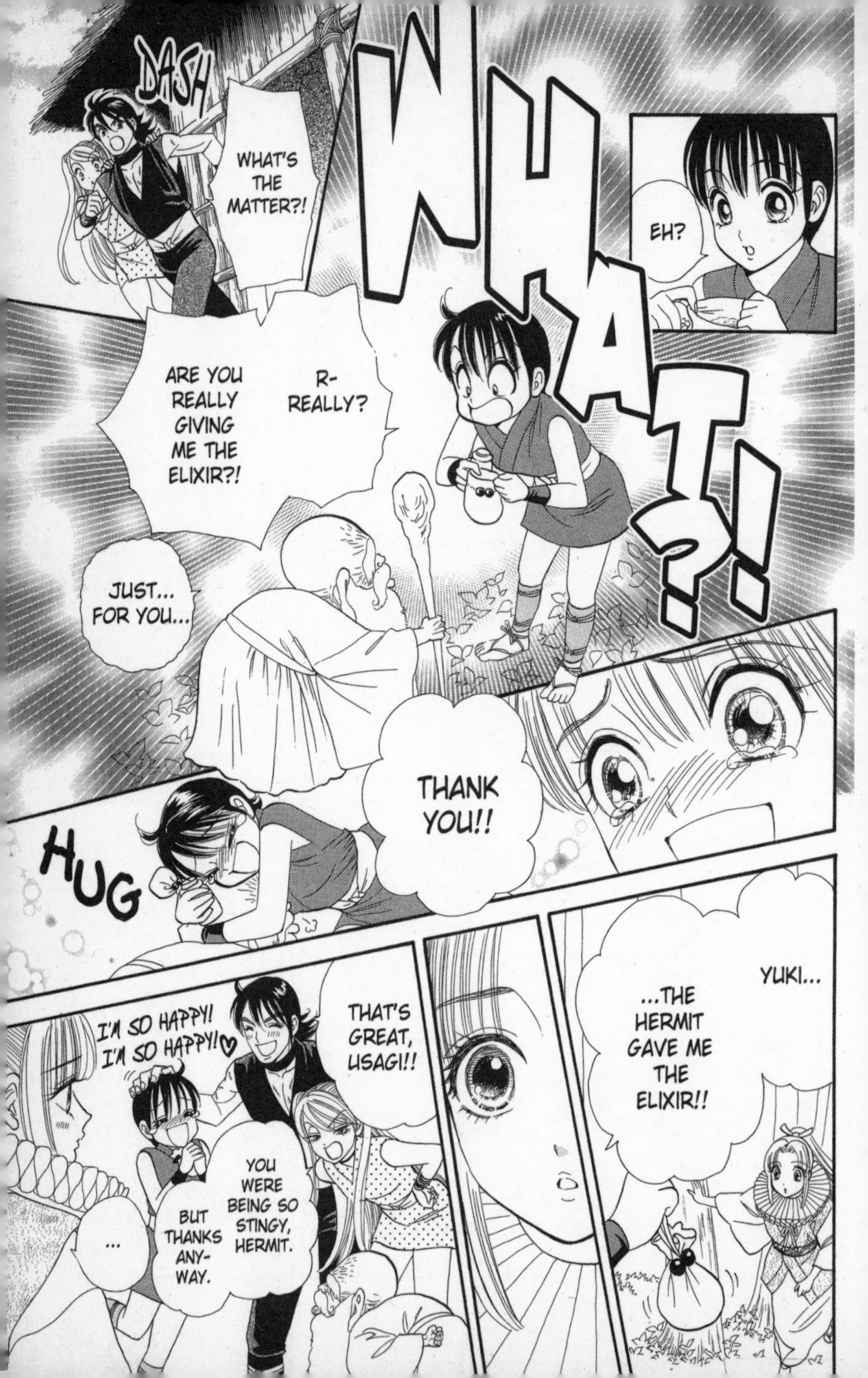

EH?
WHAT?!
DASH
WHAT'S THE MATTER?!
R-REALLY?
ARE YOU REALLY GIVING ME THE ELIXIR?!
JUST... FOR YOU...
THANK YOU!!
HUG
YUKI...
...THE HERMIT GAVE ME THE ELIXIR!!
THAT'S GREAT, USAGI!!
I'M SO HAPPY! I'M SO HAPPY!♡
YOU WERE BEING SO STINGY, HERMIT.
BUT THANKS ANY-WAY.
...

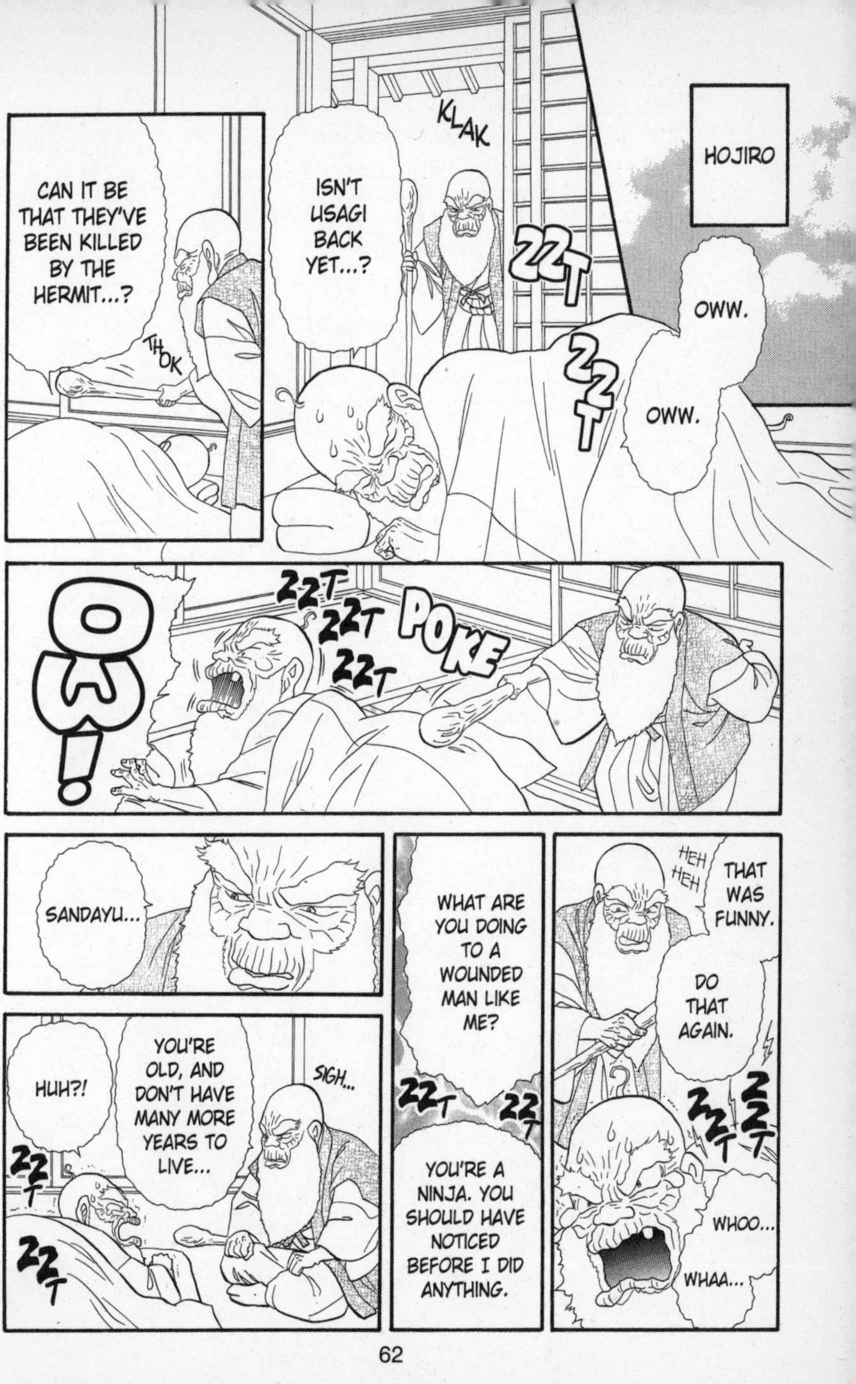

HOJIRO
KLAK
ISN'T USAGI BACK YET...?
ZZT
OWW.
ZZT
OWW.
CAN IT BE THAT THEY'VE BEEN KILLED BY THE HERMIT...?
THOK
POKE
ZZT
ZZT
ZZT
OW!
THAT WAS FUNNY.
HEH HEH
DO THAT AGAIN.
ZZT
ZZT
WHOO...
WHAA...
WHAT ARE YOU DOING TO A WOUNDED MAN LIKE ME?
ZZT
ZZT
YOU'RE A NINJA. YOU SHOULD HAVE NOTICED BEFORE I DID ANYTHING.
SANDAYU...
SIGH...
YOU'RE OLD, AND DON'T HAVE MANY MORE YEARS TO LIVE...
HUH?!
ZZT
ZZT

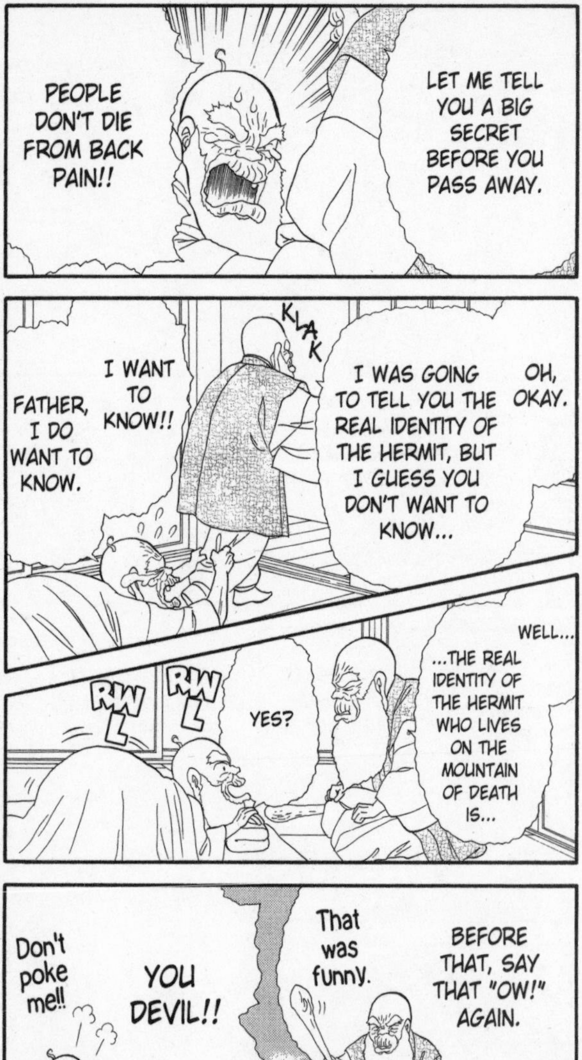
LET ME TELL YOU A BIG SECRET BEFORE YOU PASS AWAY.
PEOPLE DON'T DIE FROM BACK PAIN!!
OH, OKAY.
I WAS GOING TO TELL YOU THE REAL IDENTITY OF THE HERMIT, BUT I GUESS YOU DON'T WANT TO KNOW...
KLAK
I WANT TO KNOW!!
FATHER, I DO WANT TO KNOW.
WELL...
...THE REAL IDENTITY OF THE HERMIT WHO LIVES ON THE MOUNTAIN OF DEATH IS...
YES?
RWL
RWL
BEFORE THAT, SAY THAT "OW!" AGAIN.
That was funny.
YOU DEVIL!!
Don't poke me!!

Stories About My Research Trip #1

Iga is in Mie prefecture, and Kouka is right next to it in Shiga Prefecture.

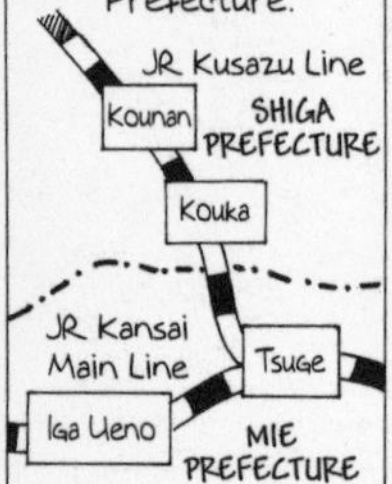
JR Kusazu Line
Kounan
SHIGA PREFECTURE
Kouka
JR Kansai Main Line
Tsuge
Iga Ueno
MIE PREFECTURE

I never knew that Iga and Kouka were so close to each other until I started creating this series.

The last time I went to Iga from my parents house in Nara, I took the Kintetsu Line towards Sakurai Station, but this time, I took JR's local train down to Kouka.

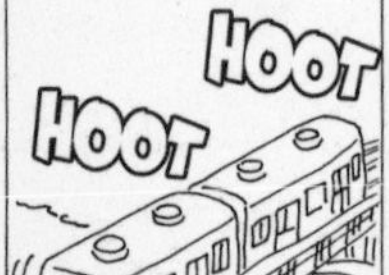
HOOT
HOOT

As I rode the train from Nara in the direction of Tsuge, I was able to see small valleys, and it felt like I was on a short excursion. ♪

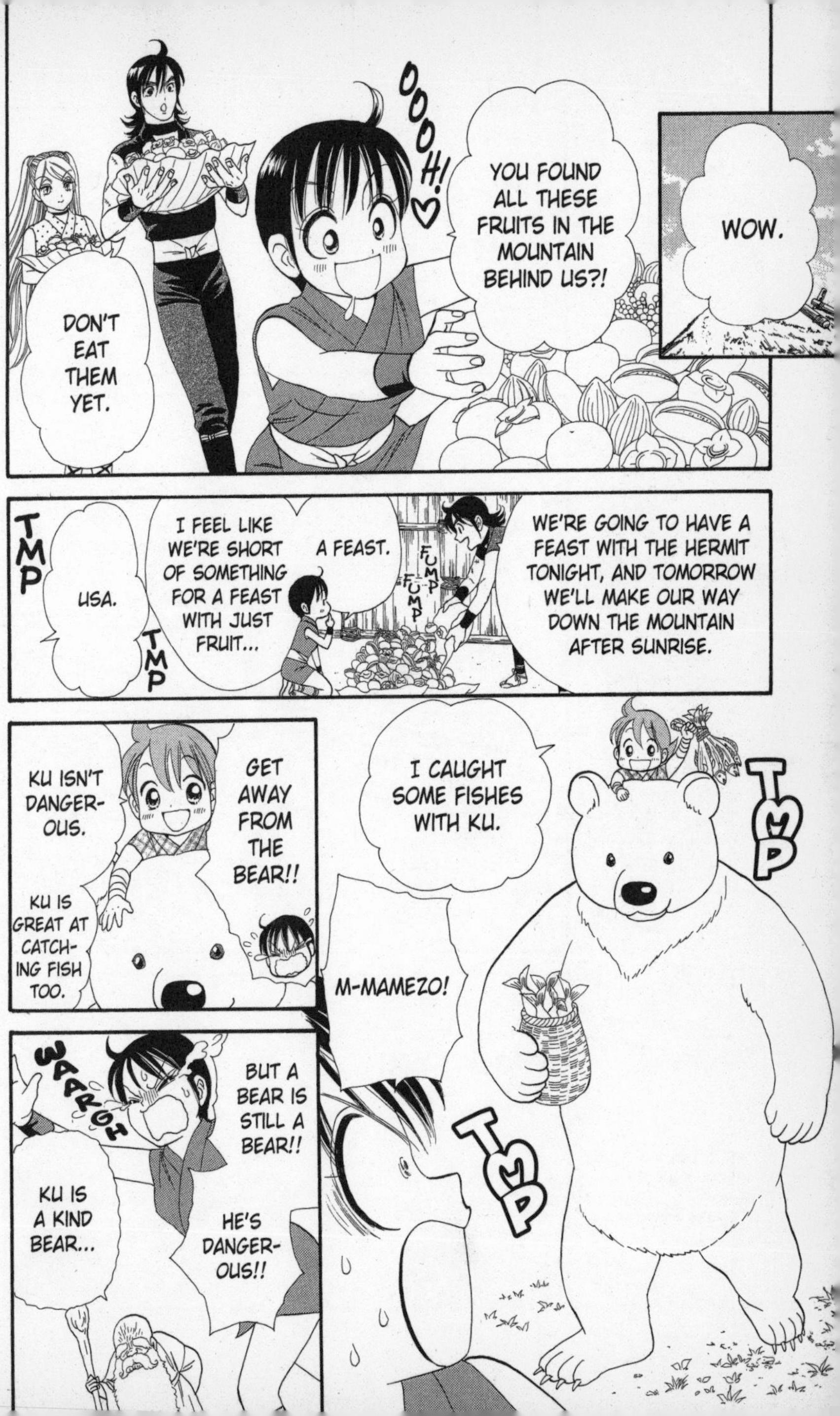
WOW.
OOOOH!♡
YOU FOUND ALL THESE FRUITS IN THE MOUNTAIN BEHIND US?!
DON'T EAT THEM YET.
WE'RE GOING TO HAVE A FEAST WITH THE HERMIT TONIGHT, AND TOMORROW WE'LL MAKE OUR WAY DOWN THE MOUNTAIN AFTER SUNRISE.
FUMP FUMP
A FEAST.
I FEEL LIKE WE'RE SHORT OF SOMETHING FOR A FEAST WITH JUST FRUIT...
TMP
USA.
TMP
TMP
I CAUGHT SOME FISHES WITH KU.
TMP
M-MAMEZO!
TMP
GET AWAY FROM THE BEAR!!
KU ISN'T DANGER-OUS.
KU IS GREAT AT CATCH-ING FISH TOO.
BUT A BEAR IS STILL A BEAR!!
WAARGH
HE'S DANGER-OUS!!
KU IS A KIND BEAR...

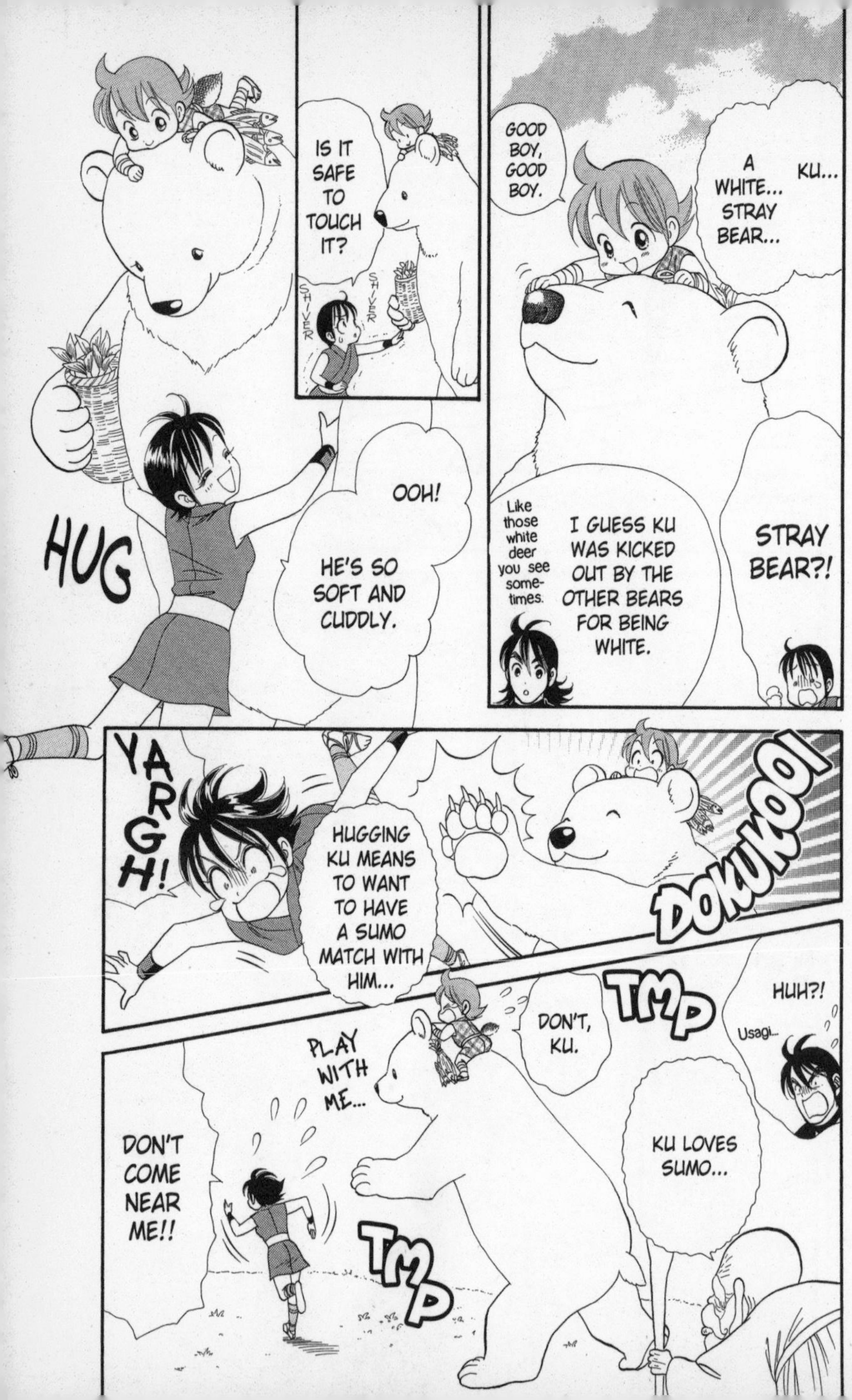
KU...
A WHITE... STRAY BEAR...
GOOD BOY, GOOD BOY.
STRAY BEAR?!
I GUESS KU WAS KICKED OUT BY THE OTHER BEARS FOR BEING WHITE.
Like those white deer you see some-times.
IS IT SAFE TO TOUCH IT?
SHIVER
SHIVER
OOH!
HE'S SO SOFT AND CUDDLY.
HUG
DOKUKOO!
HUGGING KU MEANS TO WANT TO HAVE A SUMO MATCH WITH HIM...
YARGH!
HUH?!
Usagi...
TMP
DON'T, KU.
PLAY WITH ME...
KU LOVES SUMO...
TMP
DON'T COME NEAR ME!!

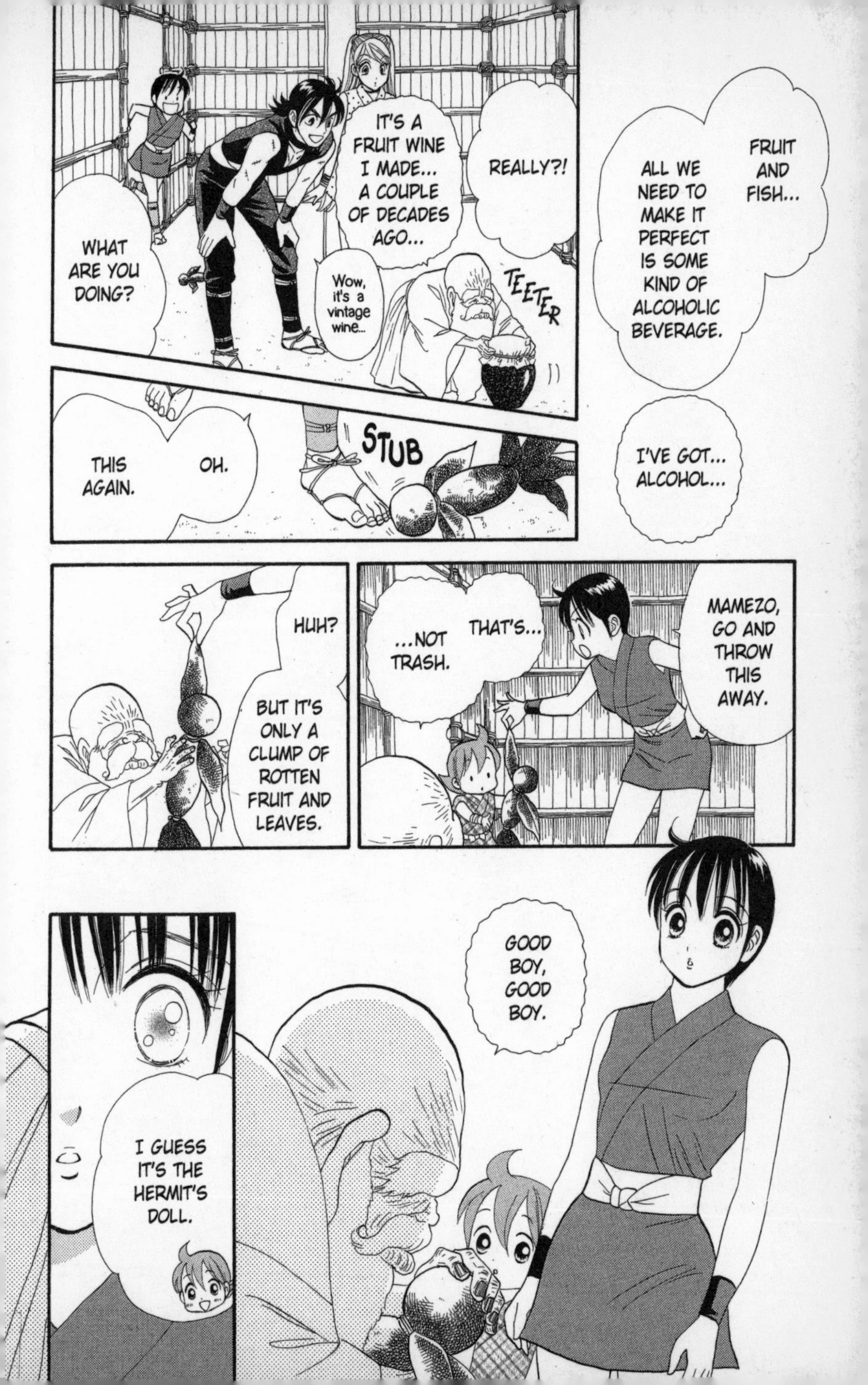
FRUIT AND FISH...
ALL WE NEED TO MAKE IT PERFECT IS SOME KIND OF ALCOHOLIC BEVERAGE.
I'VE GOT... ALCOHOL...
REALLY?!
IT'S A FRUIT WINE I MADE... A COUPLE OF DECADES AGO...
Wow, it's a vintage wine...
TEETER
WHAT ARE YOU DOING?
STUB
OH.
THIS AGAIN.
MAMEZO, GO AND THROW THIS AWAY.
THAT'S...
...NOT TRASH.
HUH?
BUT IT'S ONLY A CLUMP OF ROTTEN FRUIT AND LEAVES.
GOOD BOY, GOOD BOY.
I GUESS IT'S THE HERMIT'S DOLL.

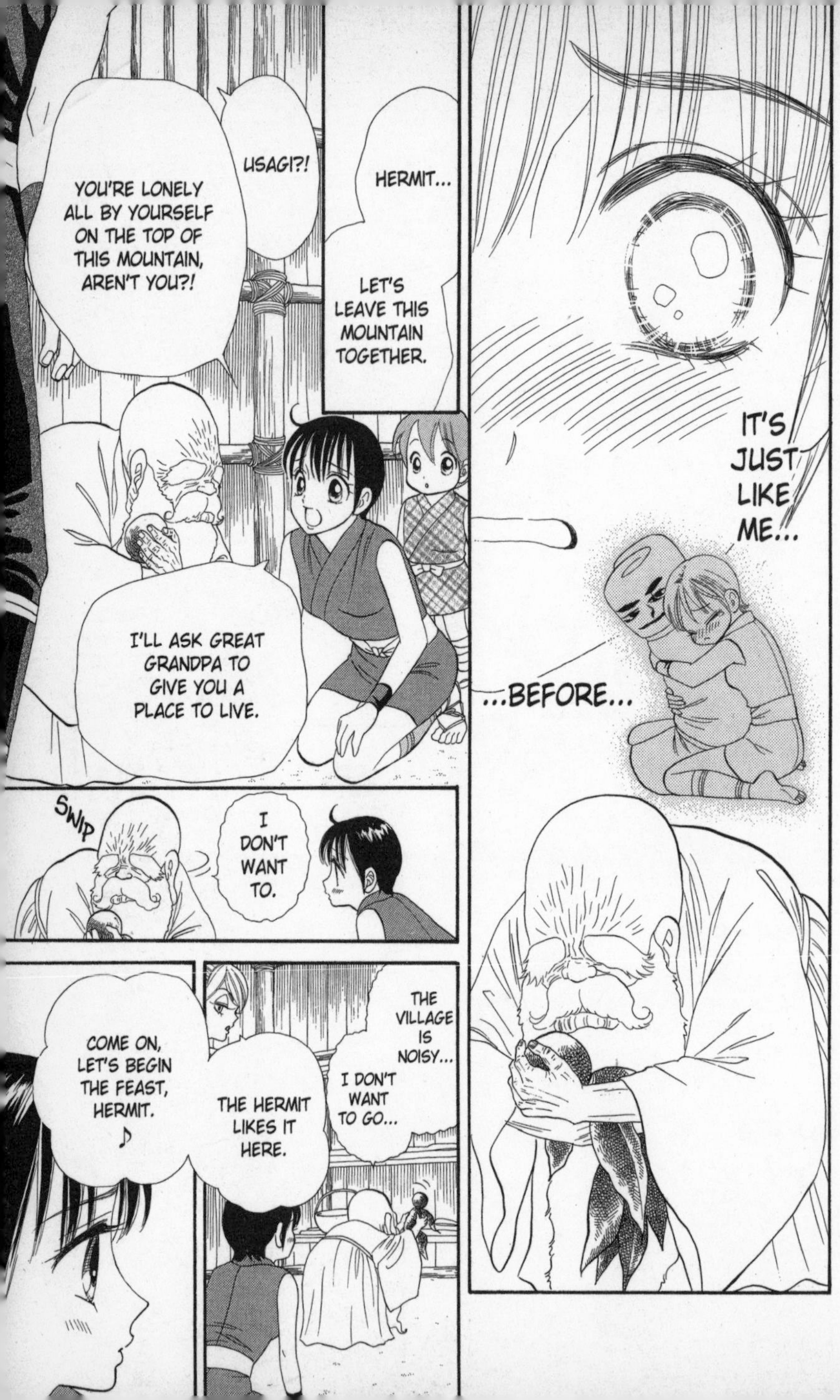
IT'S JUST LIKE ME...
...BEFORE...
HERMIT...
LET'S LEAVE THIS MOUNTAIN TOGETHER.
USAGI?!
YOU'RE LONELY ALL BY YOURSELF ON THE TOP OF THIS MOUNTAIN, AREN'T YOU?!
I'LL ASK GREAT GRANDPA TO GIVE YOU A PLACE TO LIVE.
I DON'T WANT TO.
SWIP
THE VILLAGE IS NOISY...
I DON'T WANT TO GO...
THE HERMIT LIKES IT HERE.
COME ON, LET'S BEGIN THE FEAST, HERMIT. ♪

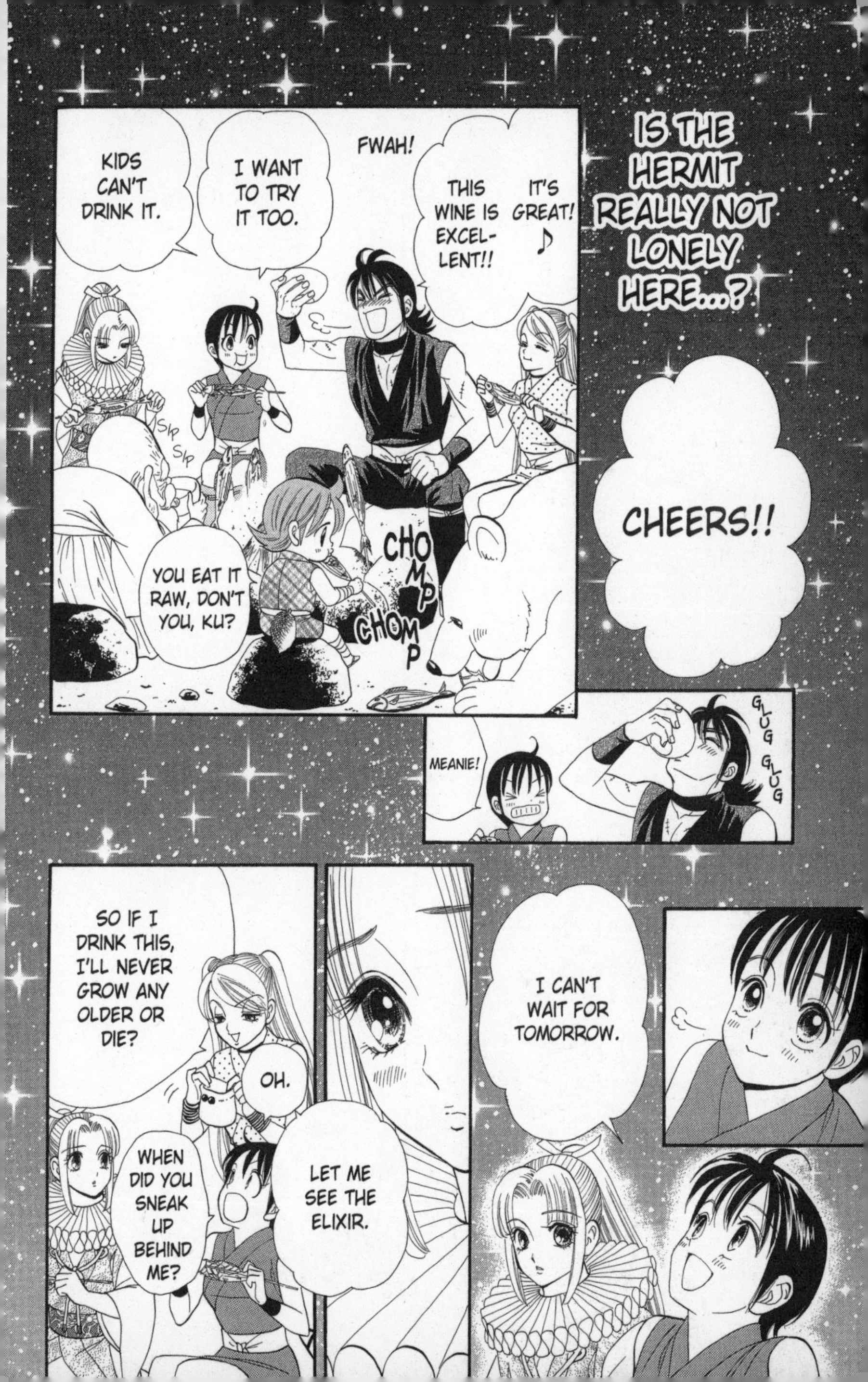
IS THE HERMIT REALLY NOT LONELY HERE...?
CHEERS!!
IT'S GREAT! ♪
THIS WINE IS EXCEL-LENT!!
FWAH!
I WANT TO TRY IT TOO.
KIDS CAN'T DRINK IT.
SIP SIP
CHOMP CHOMP
YOU EAT IT RAW, DON'T YOU, KU?
GLUG GLUG
MEANIE!
I CAN'T WAIT FOR TOMORROW.
LET ME SEE THE ELIXIR.
SO IF I DRINK THIS, I'LL NEVER GROW ANY OLDER OR DIE?
OH.
WHEN DID YOU SNEAK UP BEHIND ME?

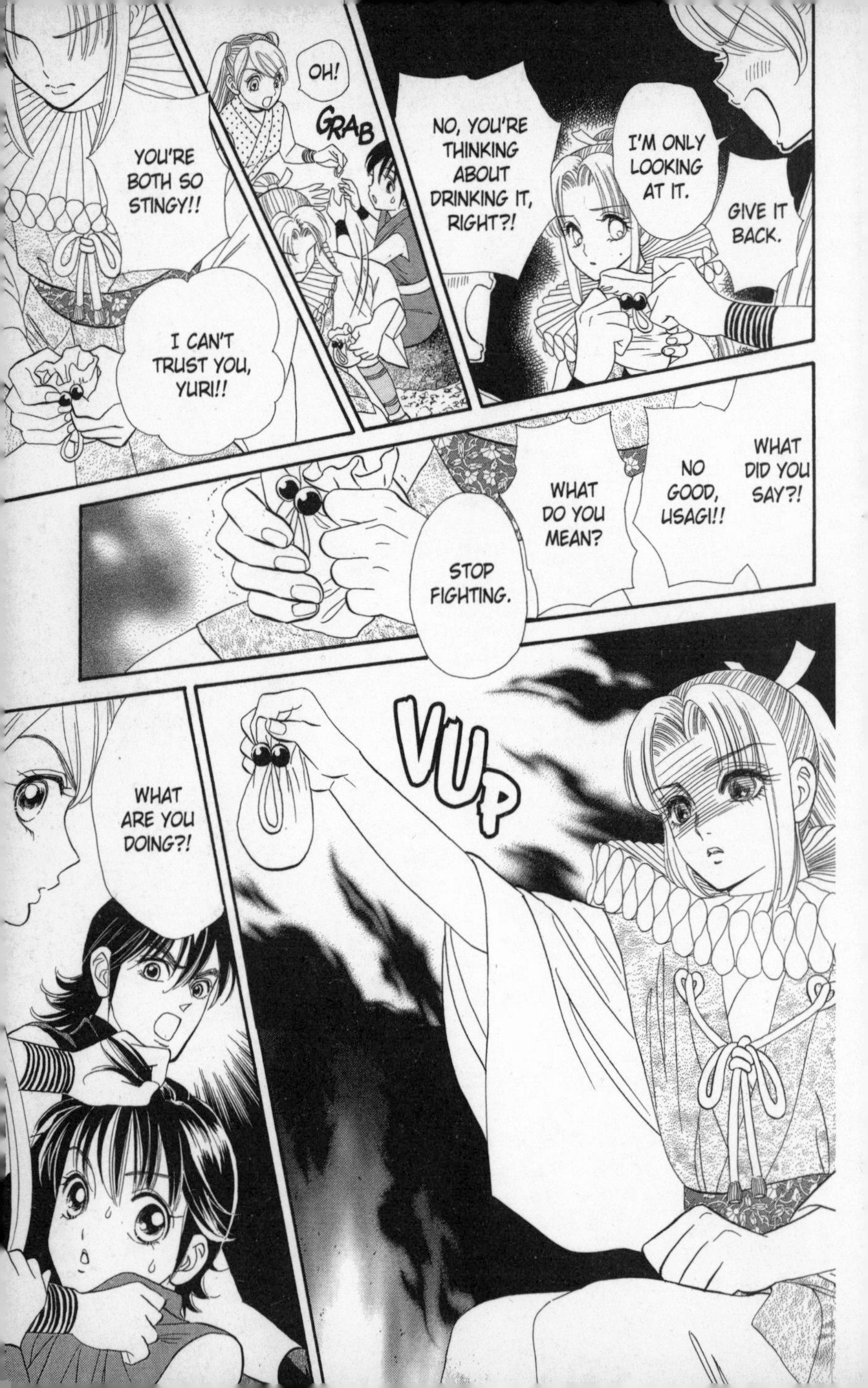
GIVE IT BACK.
I'M ONLY LOOKING AT IT.
NO, YOU'RE THINKING ABOUT DRINKING IT, RIGHT?!
OH!
GRAB
YOU'RE BOTH SO STINGY!!
I CAN'T TRUST YOU, YURI!!
WHAT DID YOU SAY?!
NO GOOD, USAGI!!
WHAT DO YOU MEAN?
STOP FIGHTING.
VUP
WHAT ARE YOU DOING?!

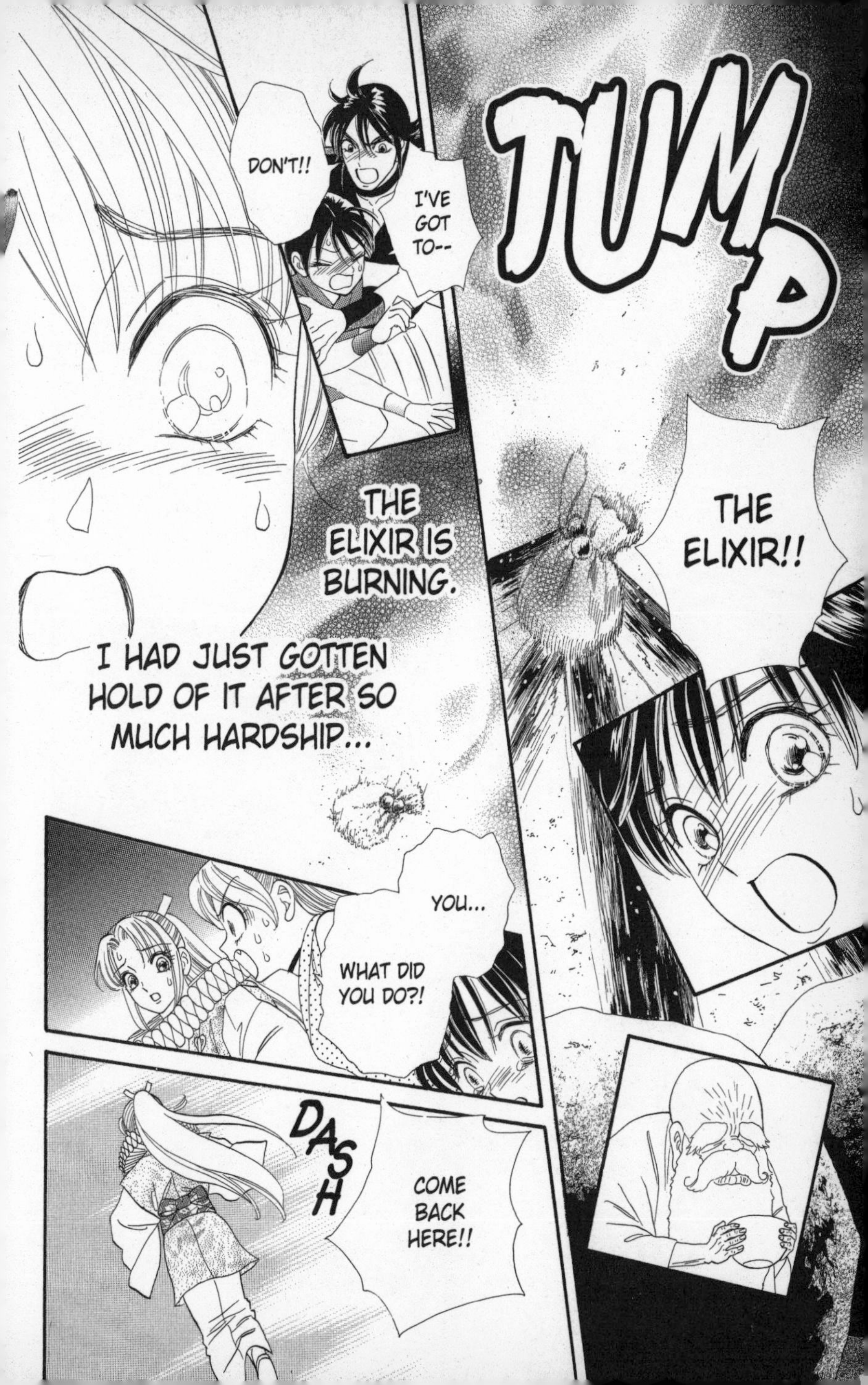
TUMP
THE ELIXIR!!
DON'T!!
I'VE GOT TO--
THE ELIXIR IS BURNING.
I HAD JUST GOTTEN HOLD OF IT AFTER SO MUCH HARDSHIP...
YOU...
WHAT DID YOU DO?!
DASH
COME BACK HERE!!

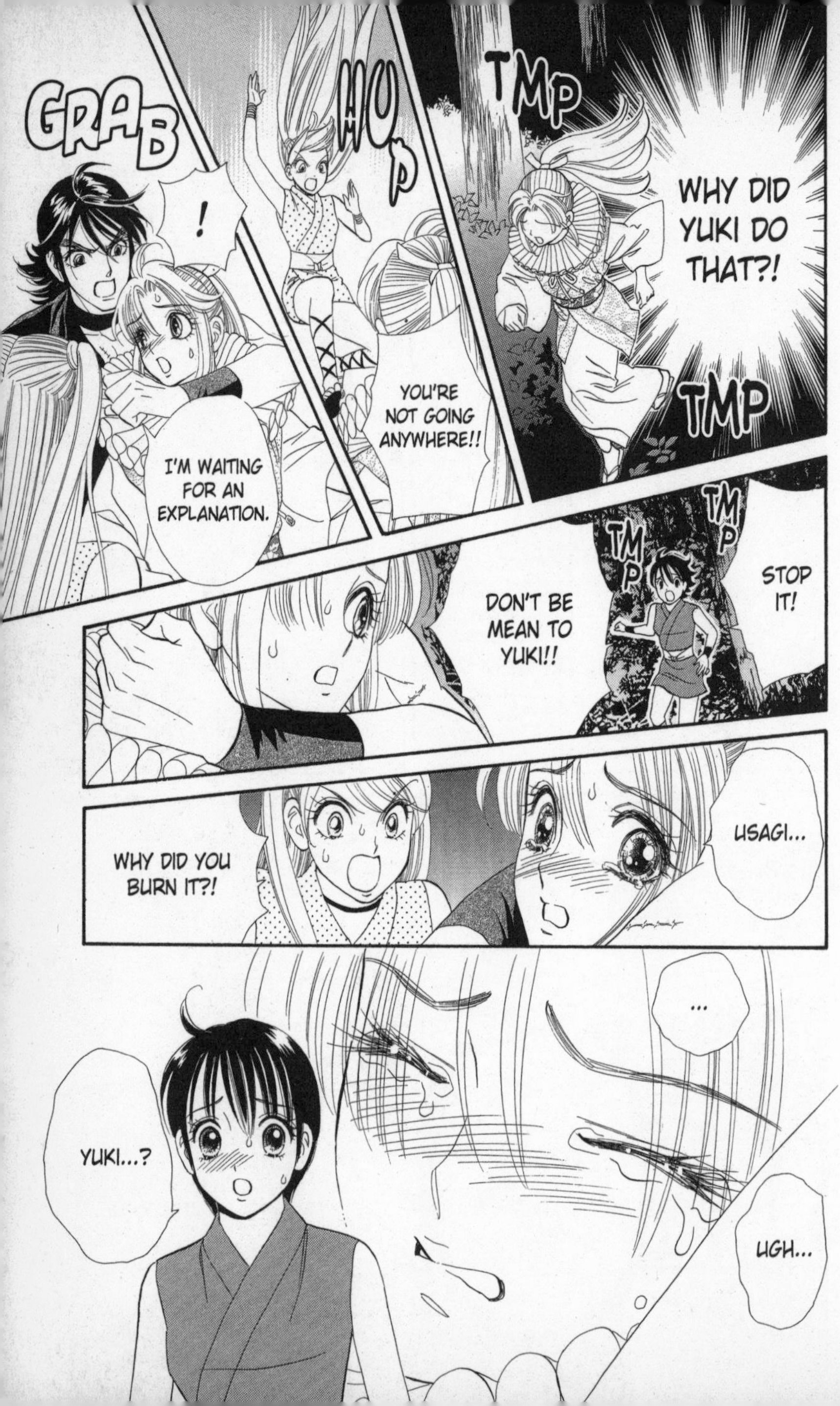
TMP
WHY DID YUKI DO THAT?!
TMP
HUP
YOU'RE NOT GOING ANYWHERE!!
GRAB
!
I'M WAITING FOR AN EXPLANATION.
TMP
TMP
STOP IT!
DON'T BE MEAN TO YUKI!!
USAGI...
WHY DID YOU BURN IT?!
...
UGH...
YUKI...?

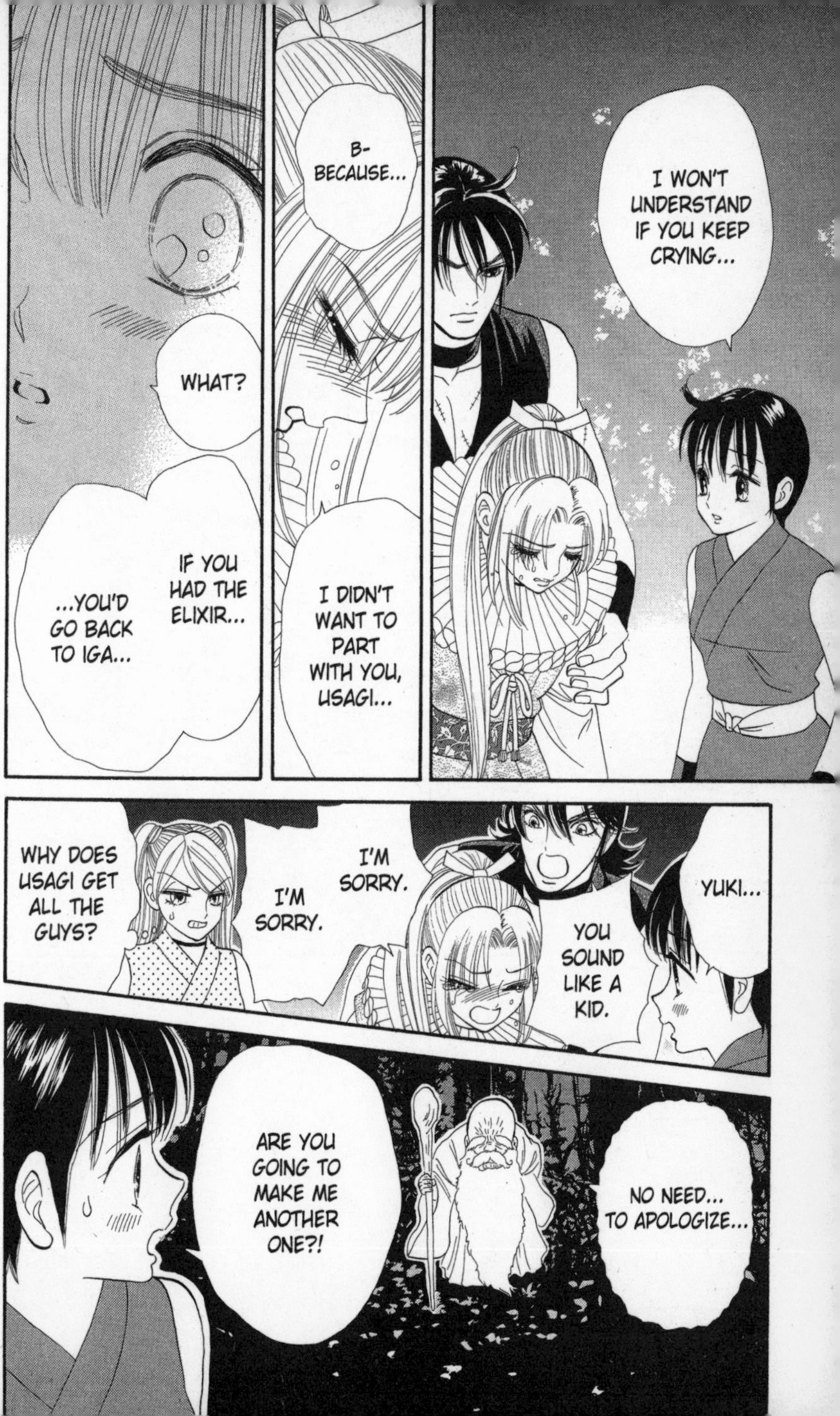
I WON'T UNDERSTAND IF YOU KEEP CRYING...
B- BECAUSE...
I DIDN'T WANT TO PART WITH YOU, USAGI...
WHAT?
IF YOU HAD THE ELIXIR...
...YOU'D GO BACK TO IGA...
YUKI...
YOU SOUND LIKE A KID.
I'M SORRY.
I'M SORRY.
WHY DOES USAGI GET ALL THE GUYS?
NO NEED... TO APOLOGIZE...
ARE YOU GOING TO MAKE ME ANOTHER ONE?!

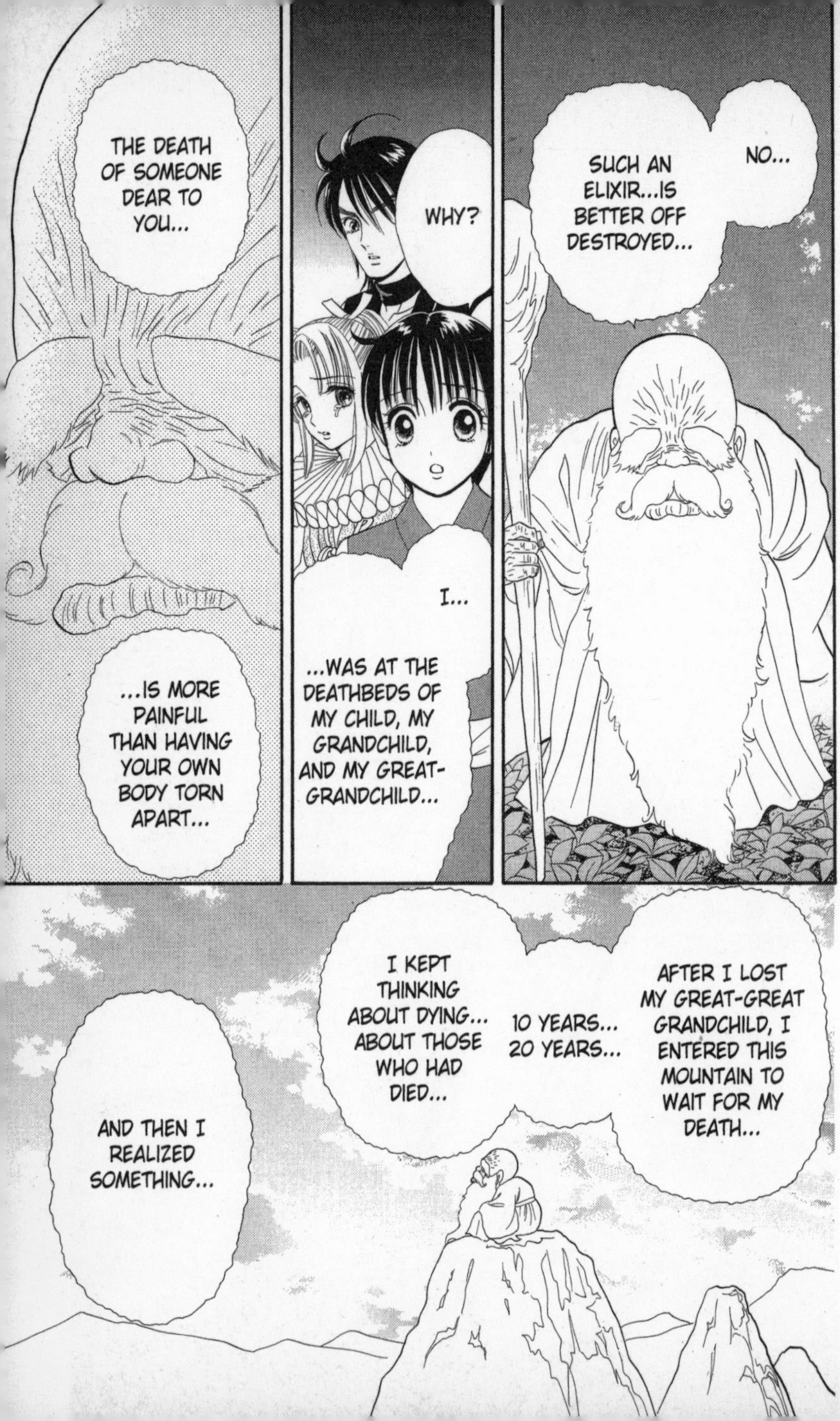
NO...
SUCH AN ELIXIR...IS BETTER OFF DESTROYED...
WHY?
I...
...WAS AT THE DEATHBEDS OF MY CHILD, MY GRANDCHILD, AND MY GREAT-GRANDCHILD...
THE DEATH OF SOMEONE DEAR TO YOU...
...IS MORE PAINFUL THAN HAVING YOUR OWN BODY TORN APART...
AFTER I LOST MY GREAT-GREAT GRANDCHILD, I ENTERED THIS MOUNTAIN TO WAIT FOR MY DEATH...
10 YEARS... 20 YEARS...
I KEPT THINKING ABOUT DYING... ABOUT THOSE WHO HAD DIED...
AND THEN I REALIZED SOMETHING...

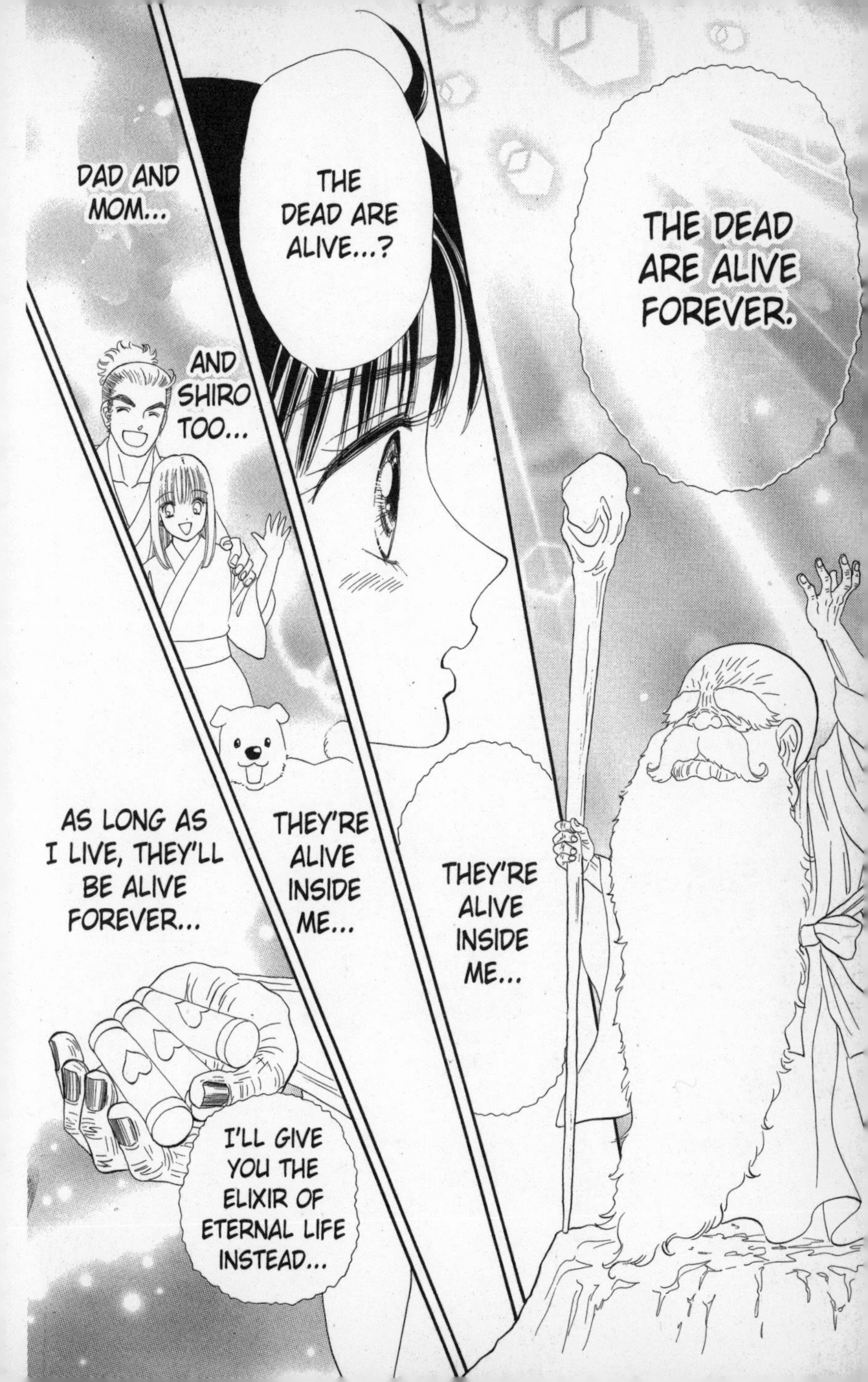
THE DEAD ARE ALIVE FOREVER.
THE DEAD ARE ALIVE...?
DAD AND MOM...
AND SHIRO TOO...
THEY'RE ALIVE INSIDE ME...
THEY'RE ALIVE INSIDE ME...
AS LONG AS I LIVE, THEY'LL BE ALIVE FOREVER...
I'LL GIVE YOU THE ELIXIR OF ETERNAL LIFE INSTEAD...

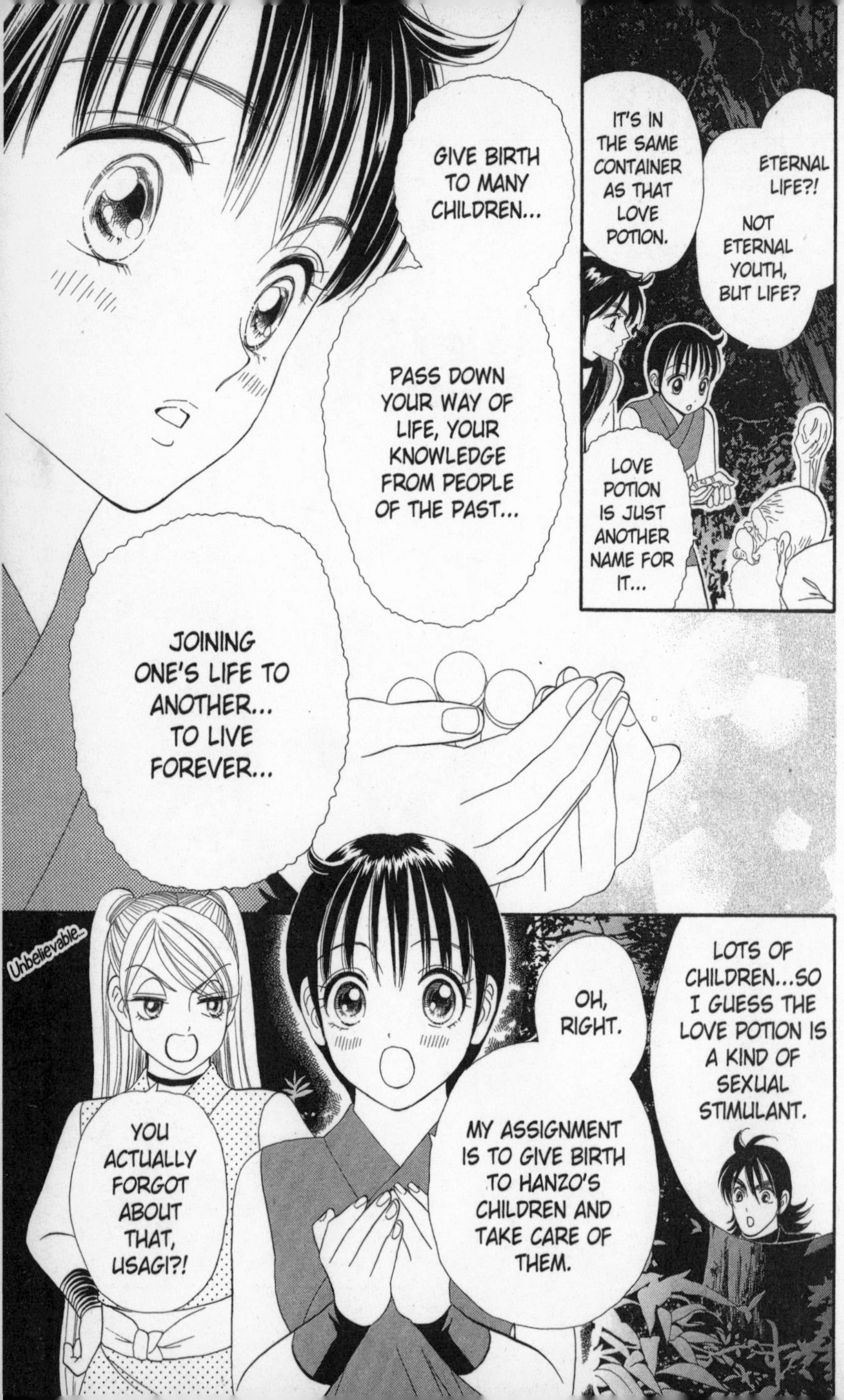
ETERNAL LIFE?!
NOT ETERNAL YOUTH, BUT LIFE?
IT'S IN THE SAME CONTAINER AS THAT LOVE POTION.
LOVE POTION IS JUST ANOTHER NAME FOR IT...
GIVE BIRTH TO MANY CHILDREN...
PASS DOWN YOUR WAY OF LIFE, YOUR KNOWLEDGE FROM PEOPLE OF THE PAST...
JOINING ONE'S LIFE TO ANOTHER... TO LIVE FOREVER...
LOTS OF CHILDREN...SO I GUESS THE LOVE POTION IS A KIND OF SEXUAL STIMULANT.
OH, RIGHT.
MY ASSIGNMENT IS TO GIVE BIRTH TO HANZO'S CHILDREN AND TAKE CARE OF THEM.
YOU ACTUALLY FORGOT ABOUT THAT, USAGI?!
Unbelievable...

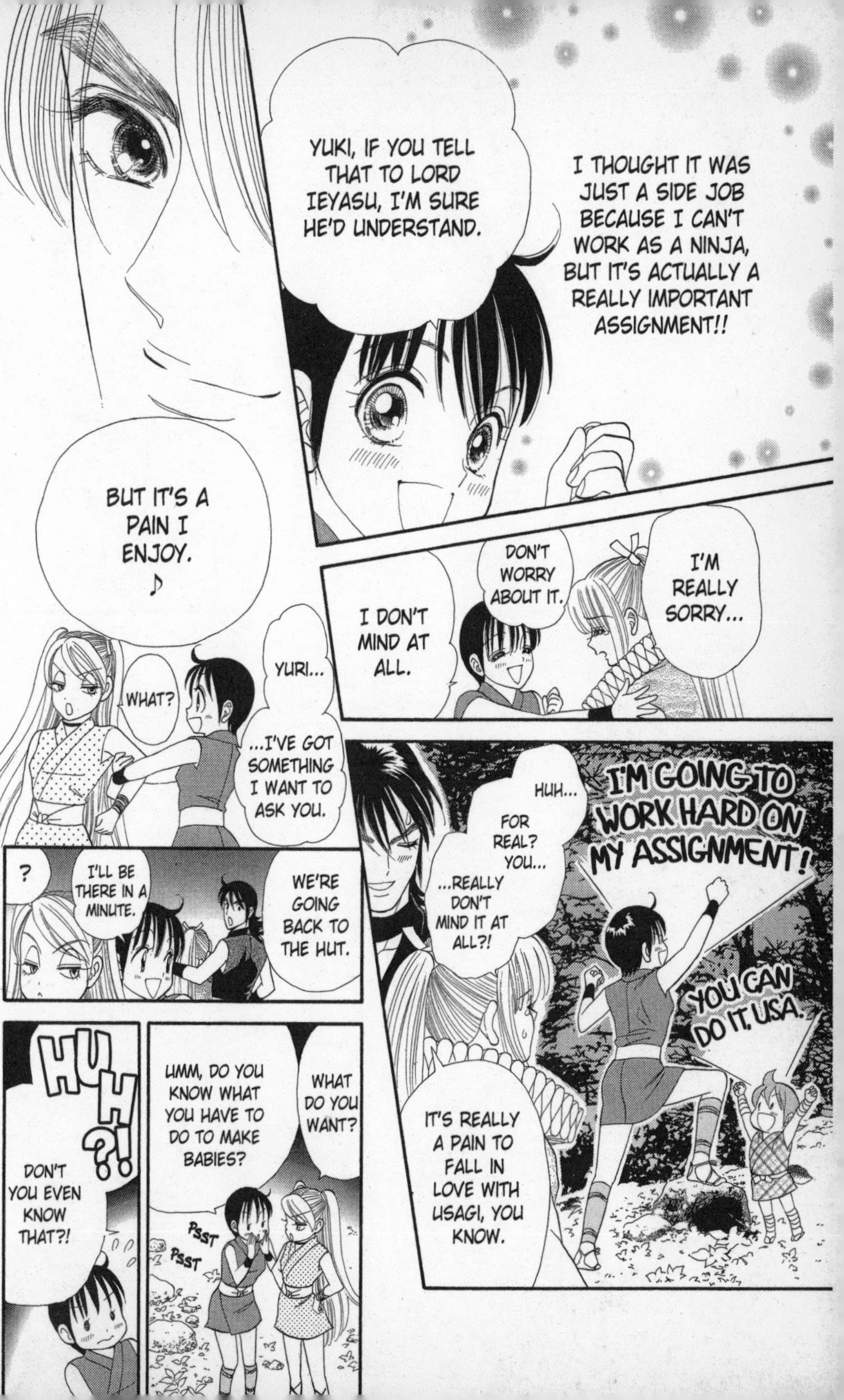

I THOUGHT IT WAS JUST A SIDE JOB BECAUSE I CAN'T WORK AS A NINJA, BUT IT'S ACTUALLY A REALLY IMPORTANT ASSIGNMENT!!
YUKI, IF YOU TELL THAT TO LORD IEYASU, I'M SURE HE'D UNDERSTAND.
BUT IT'S A PAIN I ENJOY. ♪
I'M REALLY SORRY...
DON'T WORRY ABOUT IT.
I DON'T MIND AT ALL.
YURI...
WHAT?
...I'VE GOT SOMETHING I WANT TO ASK YOU.
I'M GOING TO WORK HARD ON MY ASSIGNMENT!
YOU CAN DO IT, USA.
HUH...
FOR REAL? YOU...
...REALLY DON'T MIND IT AT ALL?!
IT'S REALLY A PAIN TO FALL IN LOVE WITH USAGI, YOU KNOW.
WE'RE GOING BACK TO THE HUT.
I'LL BE THERE IN A MINUTE.
?
WHAT DO YOU WANT?
UMM, DO YOU KNOW WHAT YOU HAVE TO DO TO MAKE BABIES?
PSST
PSST
HUH?!
DON'T YOU EVEN KNOW THAT?!

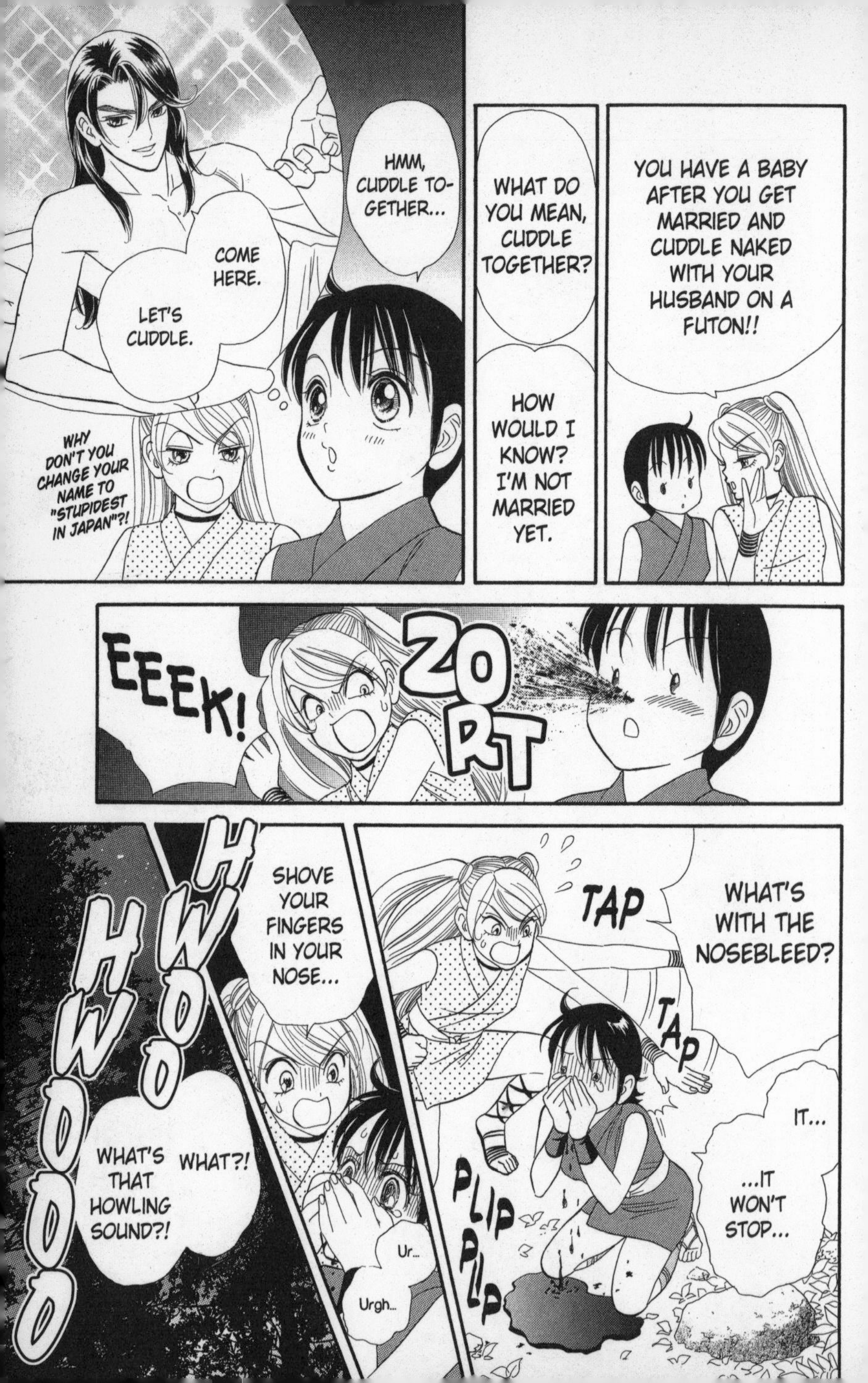
YOU HAVE A BABY AFTER YOU GET MARRIED AND CUDDLE NAKED WITH YOUR HUSBAND ON A FUTON!!
WHAT DO YOU MEAN, CUDDLE TOGETHER?
HOW WOULD I KNOW? I'M NOT MARRIED YET.
HMM, CUDDLE TO-GETHER...
COME HERE.
LET'S CUDDLE.
WHY DON'T YOU CHANGE YOUR NAME TO "STUPIDEST IN JAPAN"?!
ZORT
EEEK!
TAP
WHAT'S WITH THE NOSEBLEED?
TAP
IT...
...IT WON'T STOP...
PLIP PLIP PLIP
SHOVE YOUR FINGERS IN YOUR NOSE...
WHAT?!
Ur...
Urgh...
HWOOOO
HWWOOOOOO
WHAT'S THAT HOWLING SOUND?!

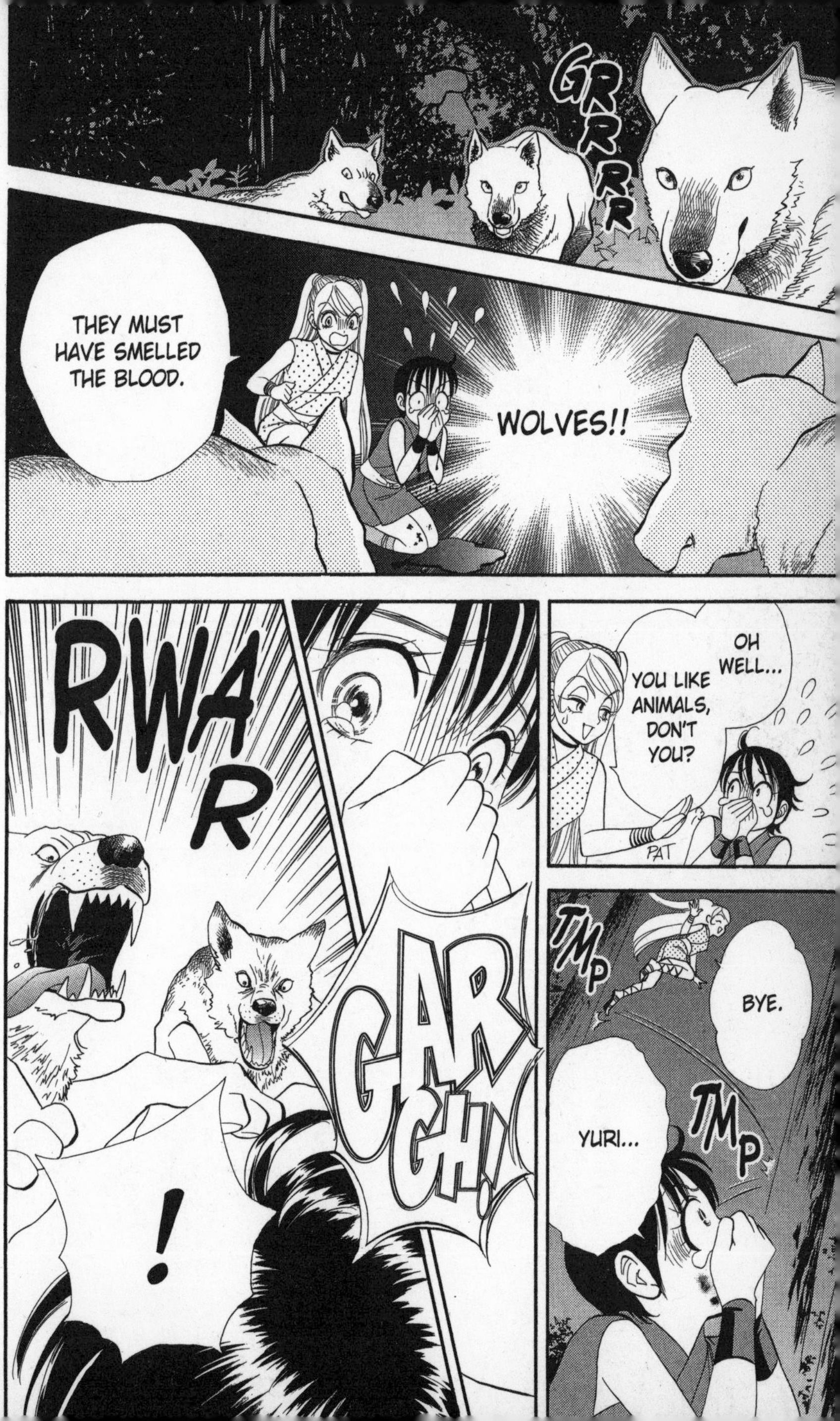
GRRRR
WOLVES!!
THEY MUST HAVE SMELLED THE BLOOD.
OH WELL...
YOU LIKE ANIMALS, DON'T YOU?
PAT
TMP
BYE.
TMP
YURI...
GARGH!
RWAR
!

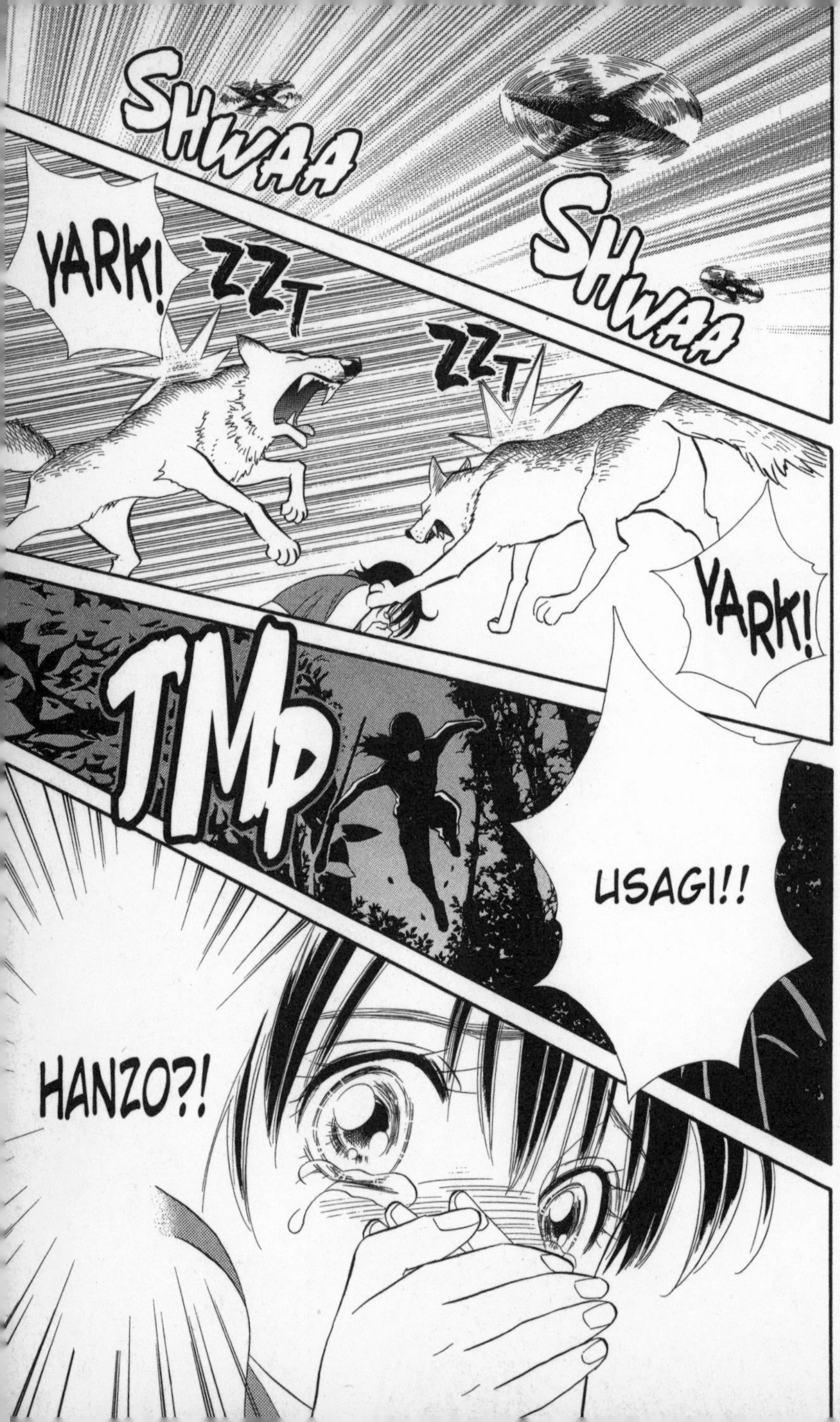
SHWAA
SHWAA
ZZT
YARK!
ZZT
YARK!
TMP
USAGI!!
HANZO?!

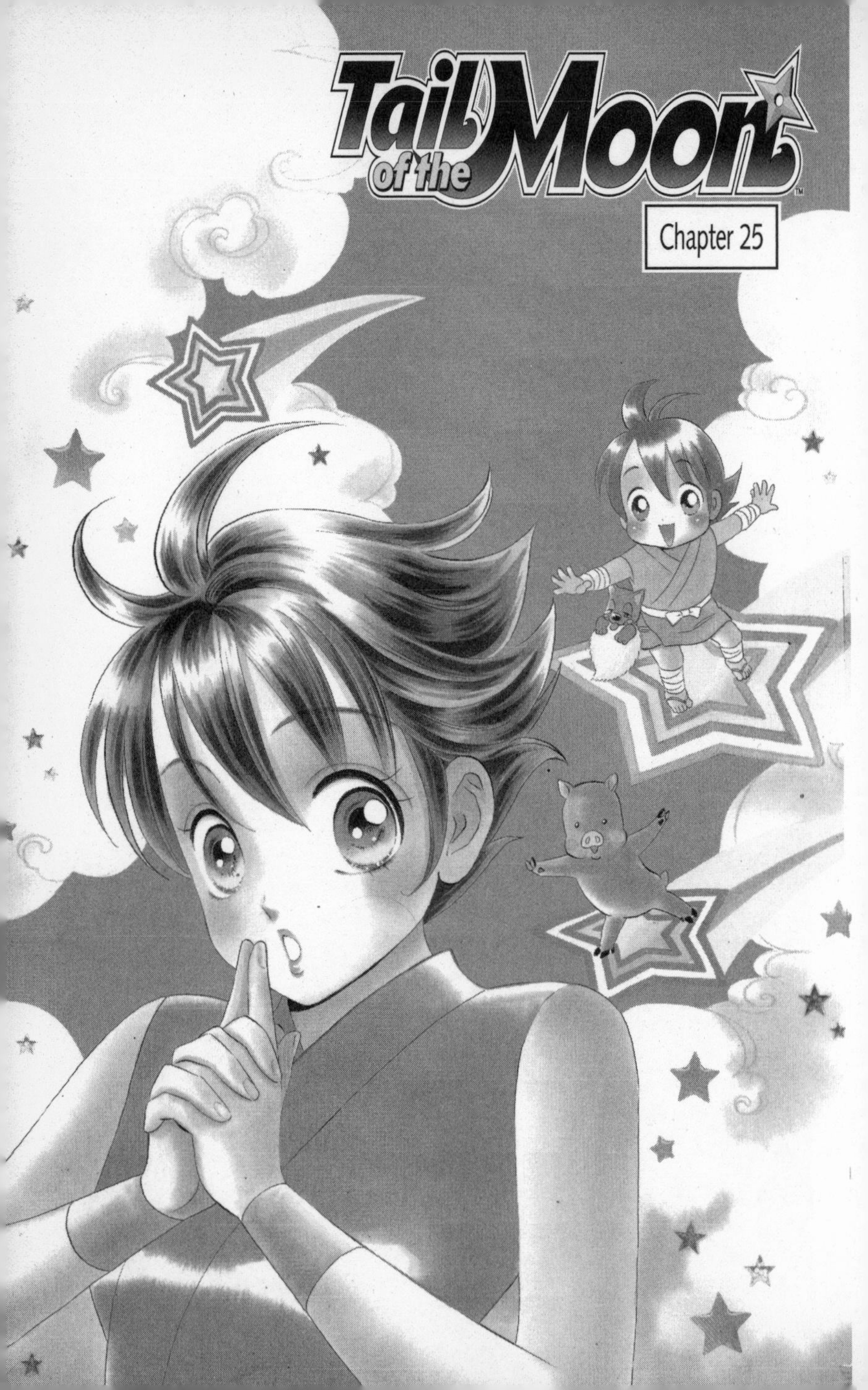
Tail of the Moon™
Chapter 25

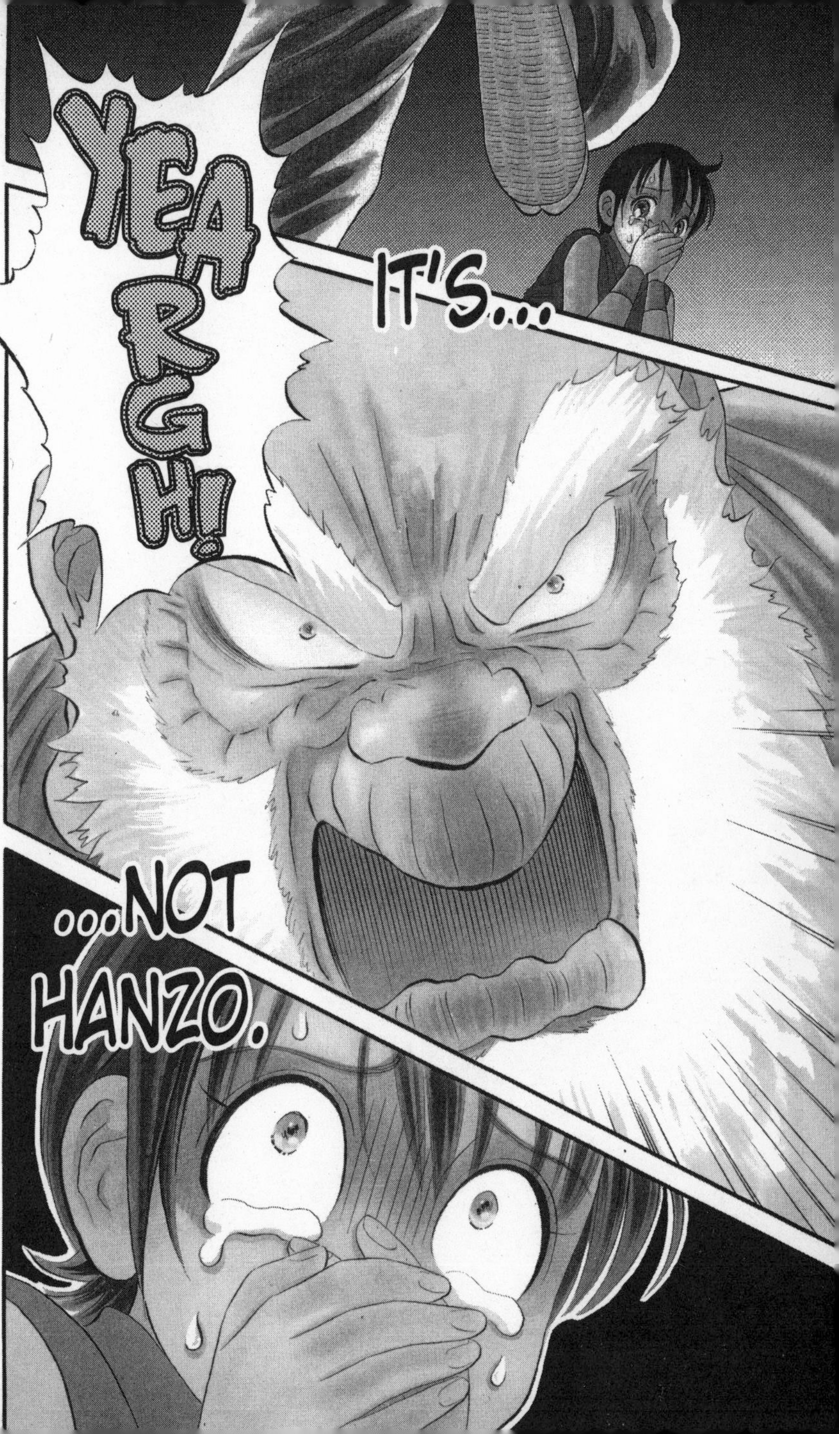
YEARGH!
IT'S...
...NOT HANZO.

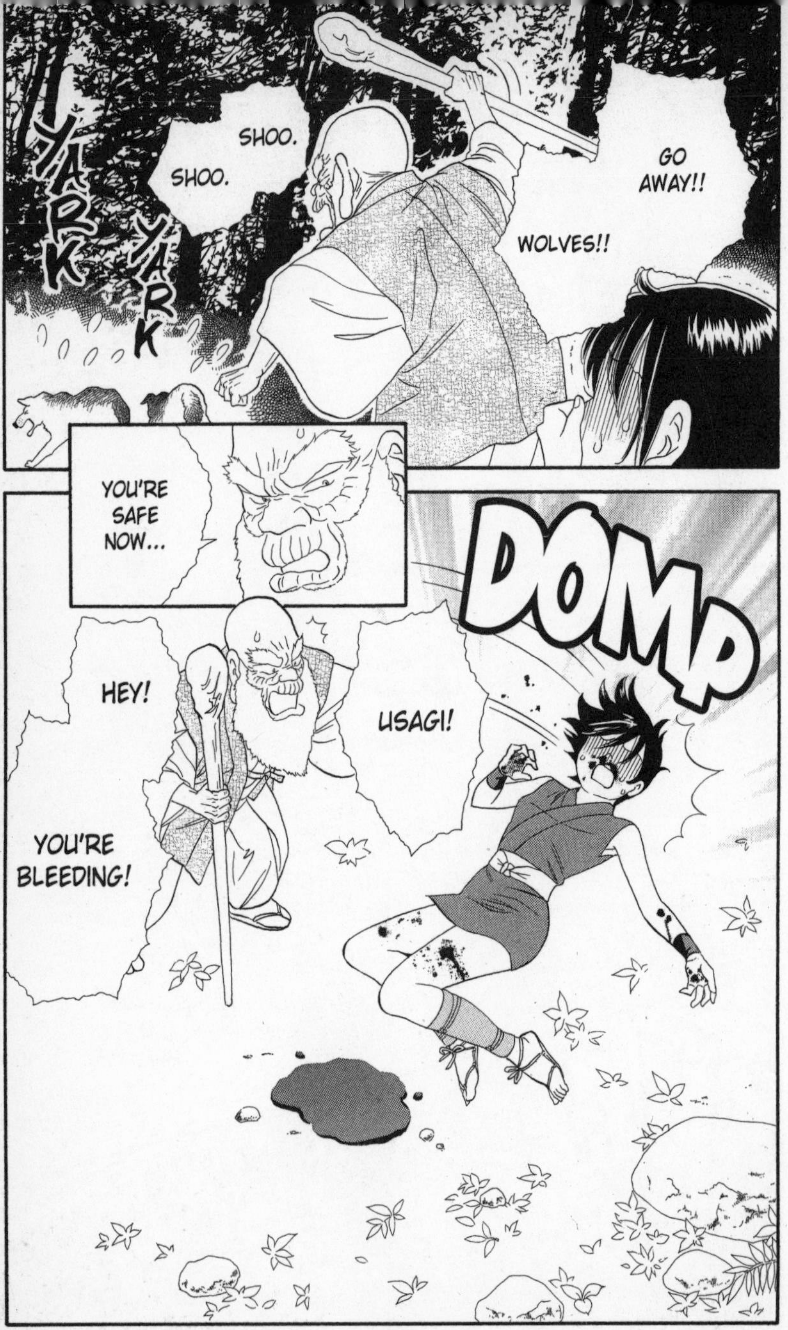
GO AWAY!!
WOLVES!!
SHOO.
SHOO.
YARK
YARK
YOU'RE SAFE NOW...
DOMP
USAGI!
HEY!
YOU'RE BLEEDING!

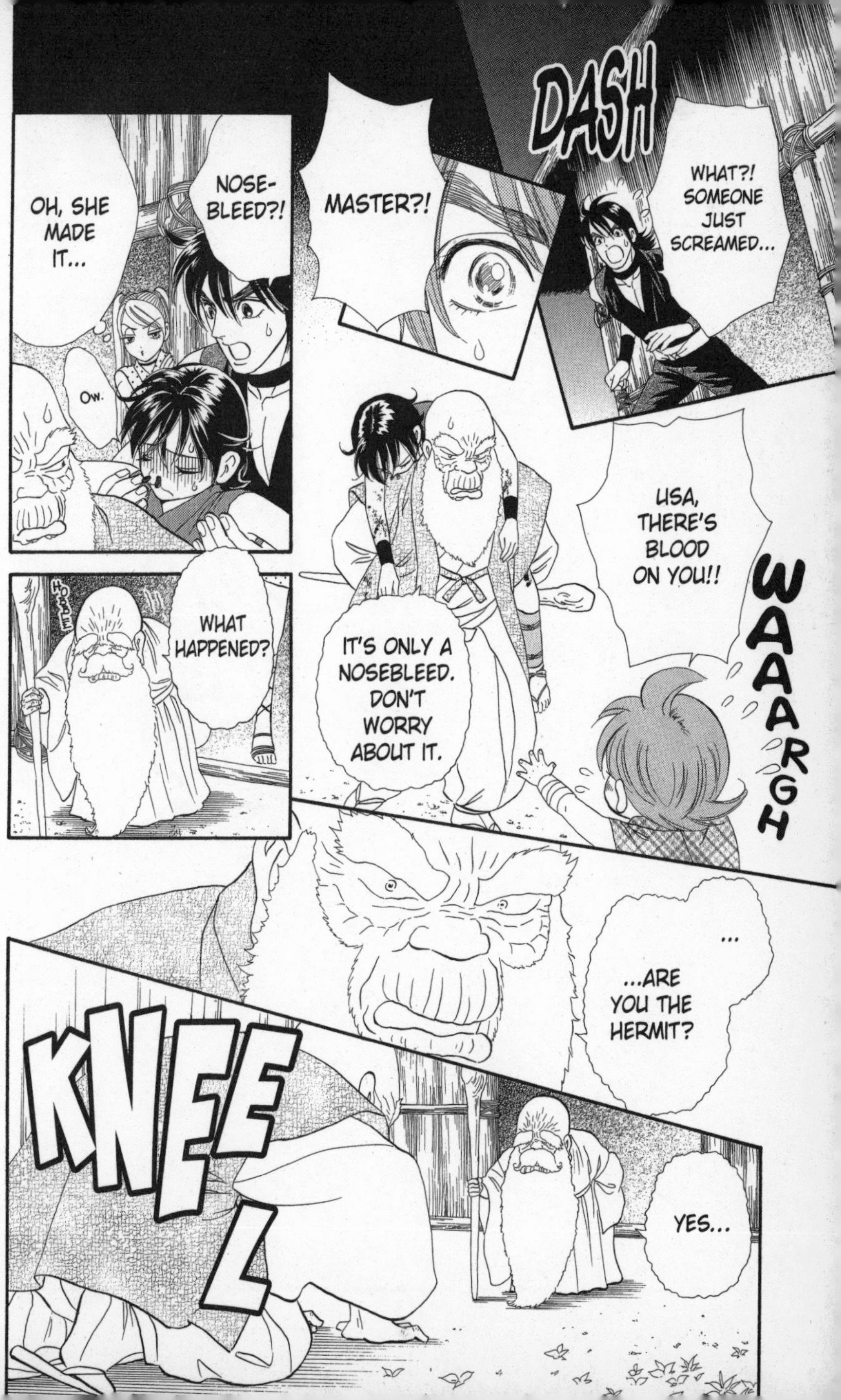
DASH
WHAT?! SOMEONE JUST SCREAMED...
MASTER?!
NOSE-BLEED?!
OH, SHE MADE IT...
OW.
USA, THERE'S BLOOD ON YOU!!
WAAAARGH
IT'S ONLY A NOSEBLEED. DON'T WORRY ABOUT IT.
HOBBLE
WHAT HAPPENED?
...
...ARE YOU THE HERMIT?
KNEEL
YES...

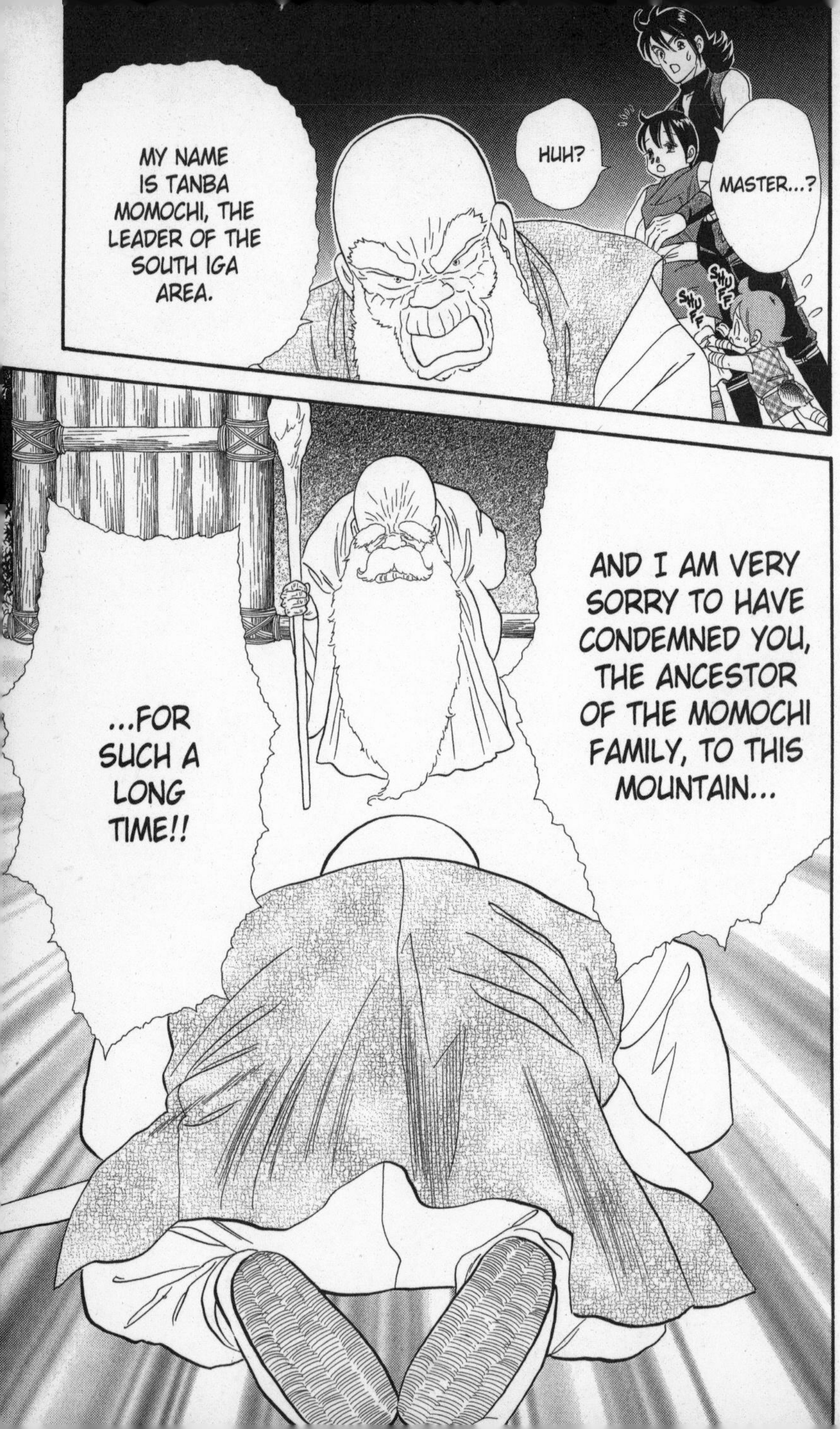
MASTER...?
SHUFF
SHUFF
HUH?
MY NAME IS TANBA MOMOCHI, THE LEADER OF THE SOUTH IGA AREA.
AND I AM VERY SORRY TO HAVE CONDEMNED YOU, THE ANCESTOR OF THE MOMOCHI FAMILY, TO THIS MOUNTAIN...
...FOR SUCH A LONG TIME!!

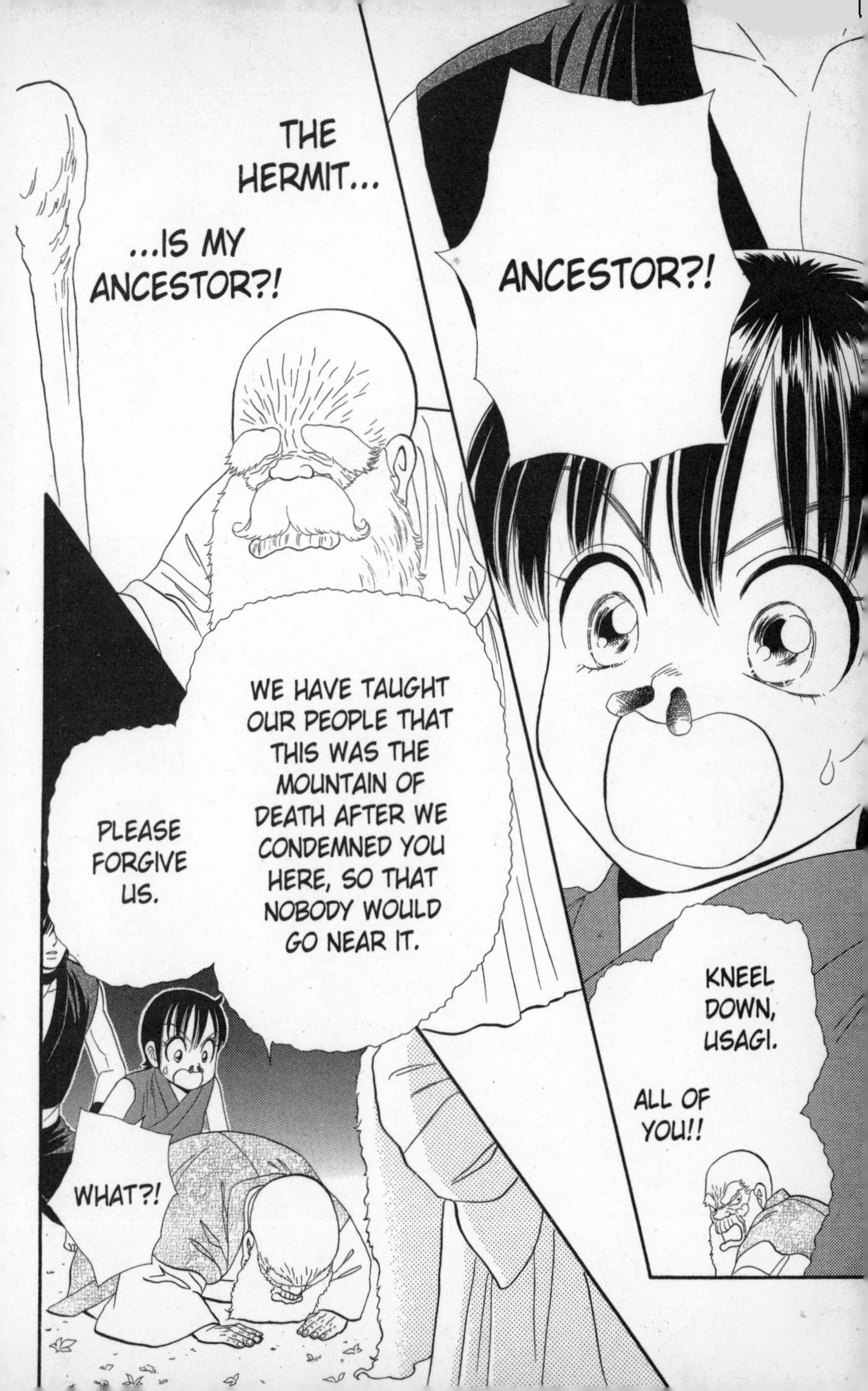
ANCESTOR?!
KNEEL DOWN, USAGI.
ALL OF YOU!!
THE HERMIT...
...IS MY ANCESTOR?!
WE HAVE TAUGHT OUR PEOPLE THAT THIS WAS THE MOUNTAIN OF DEATH AFTER WE CONDEMNED YOU HERE, SO THAT NOBODY WOULD GO NEAR IT.
PLEASE FORGIVE US.
WHAT?!

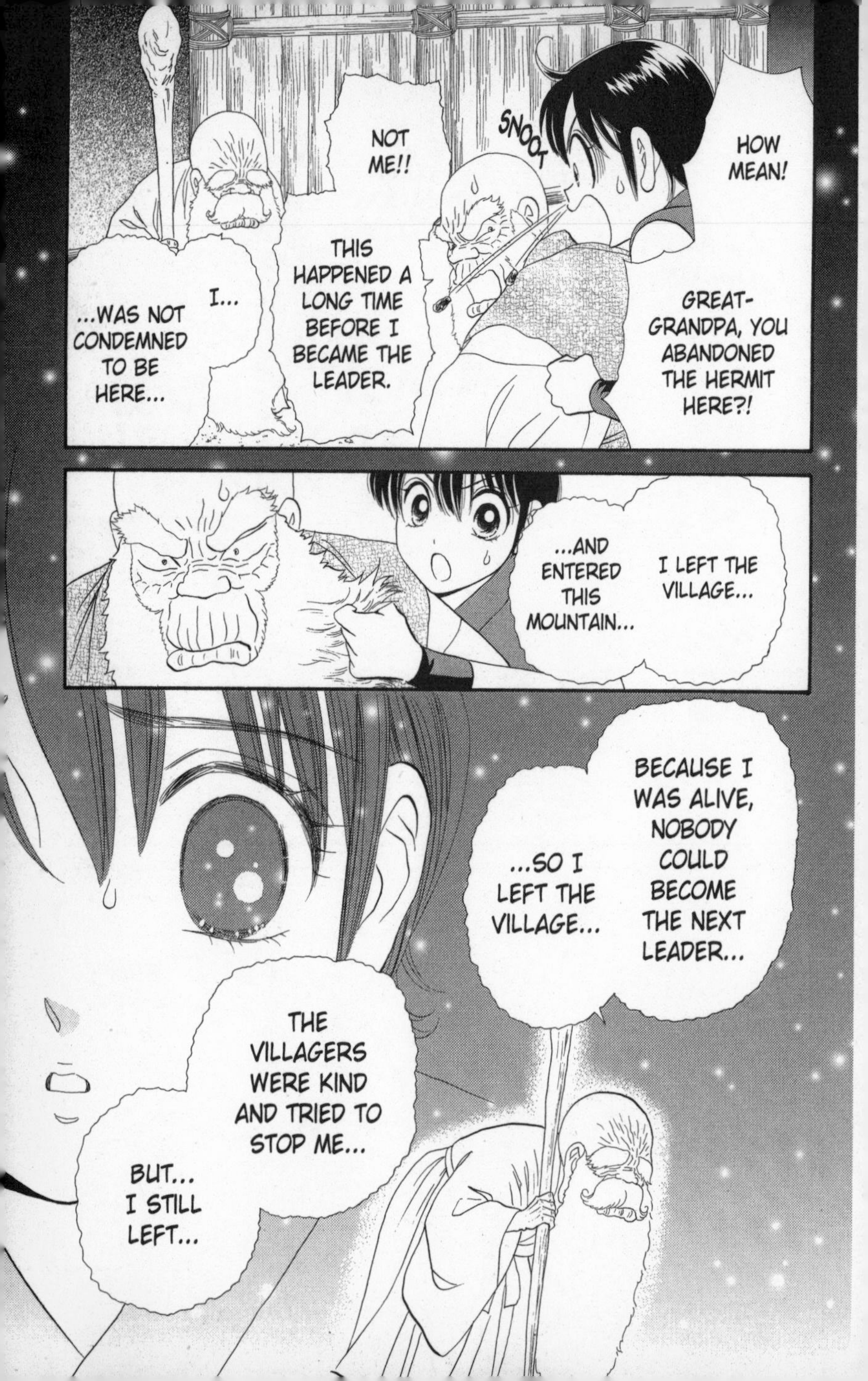
HOW MEAN!
SNOOT
GREAT-GRANDPA, YOU ABANDONED THE HERMIT HERE?!
NOT ME!!
THIS HAPPENED A LONG TIME BEFORE I BECAME THE LEADER.
I...
...WAS NOT CONDEMNED TO BE HERE...
I LEFT THE VILLAGE...
...AND ENTERED THIS MOUNTAIN...
BECAUSE I WAS ALIVE, NOBODY COULD BECOME THE NEXT LEADER...
...SO I LEFT THE VILLAGE...
THE VILLAGERS WERE KIND AND TRIED TO STOP ME...
BUT... I STILL LEFT...

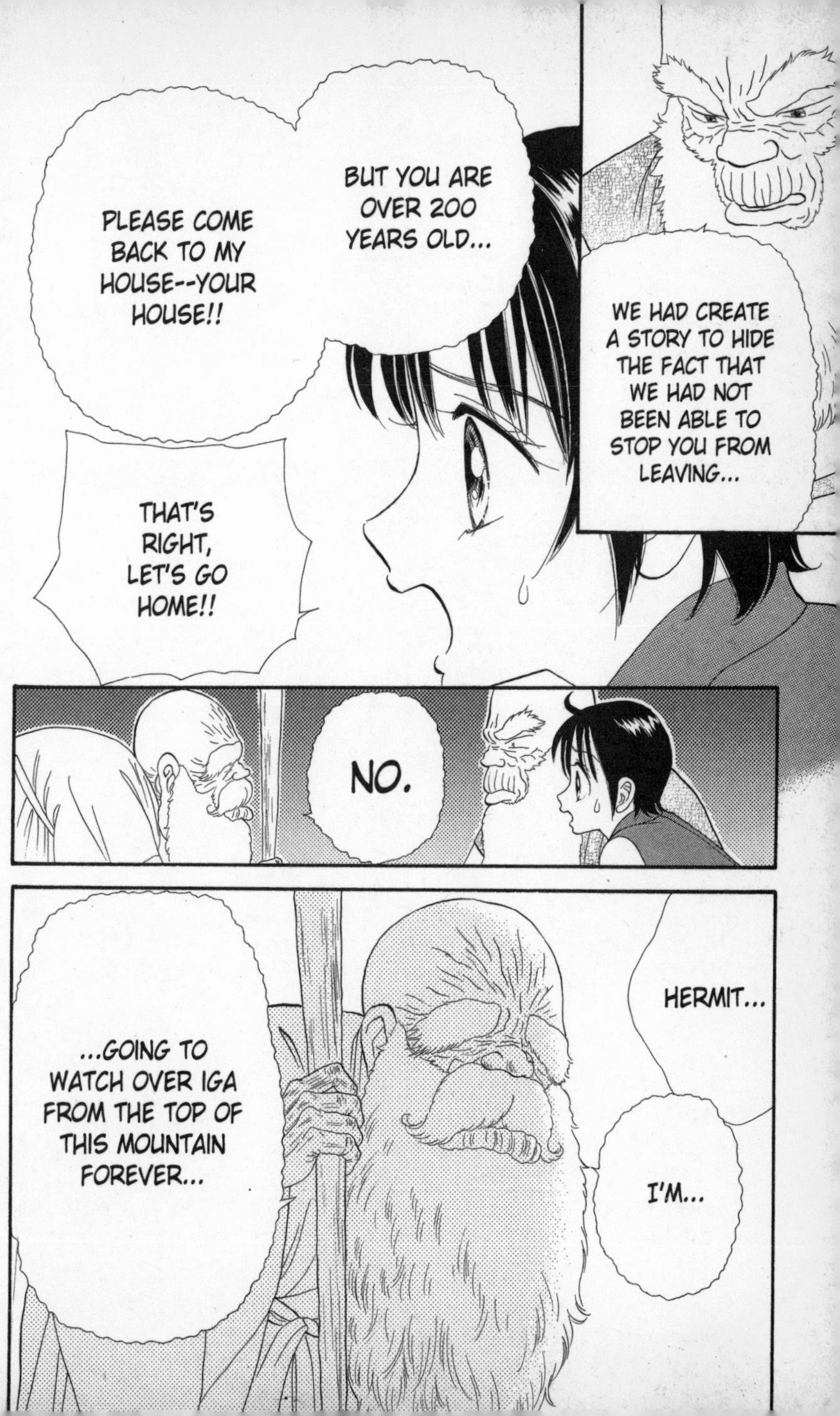
WE HAD CREATE A STORY TO HIDE THE FACT THAT WE HAD NOT BEEN ABLE TO STOP YOU FROM LEAVING...
BUT YOU ARE OVER 200 YEARS OLD...
PLEASE COME BACK TO MY HOUSE--YOUR HOUSE!!
THAT'S RIGHT, LET'S GO HOME!!
NO.
HERMIT...
I'M...
...GOING TO WATCH OVER IGA FROM THE TOP OF THIS MOUNTAIN FOREVER...

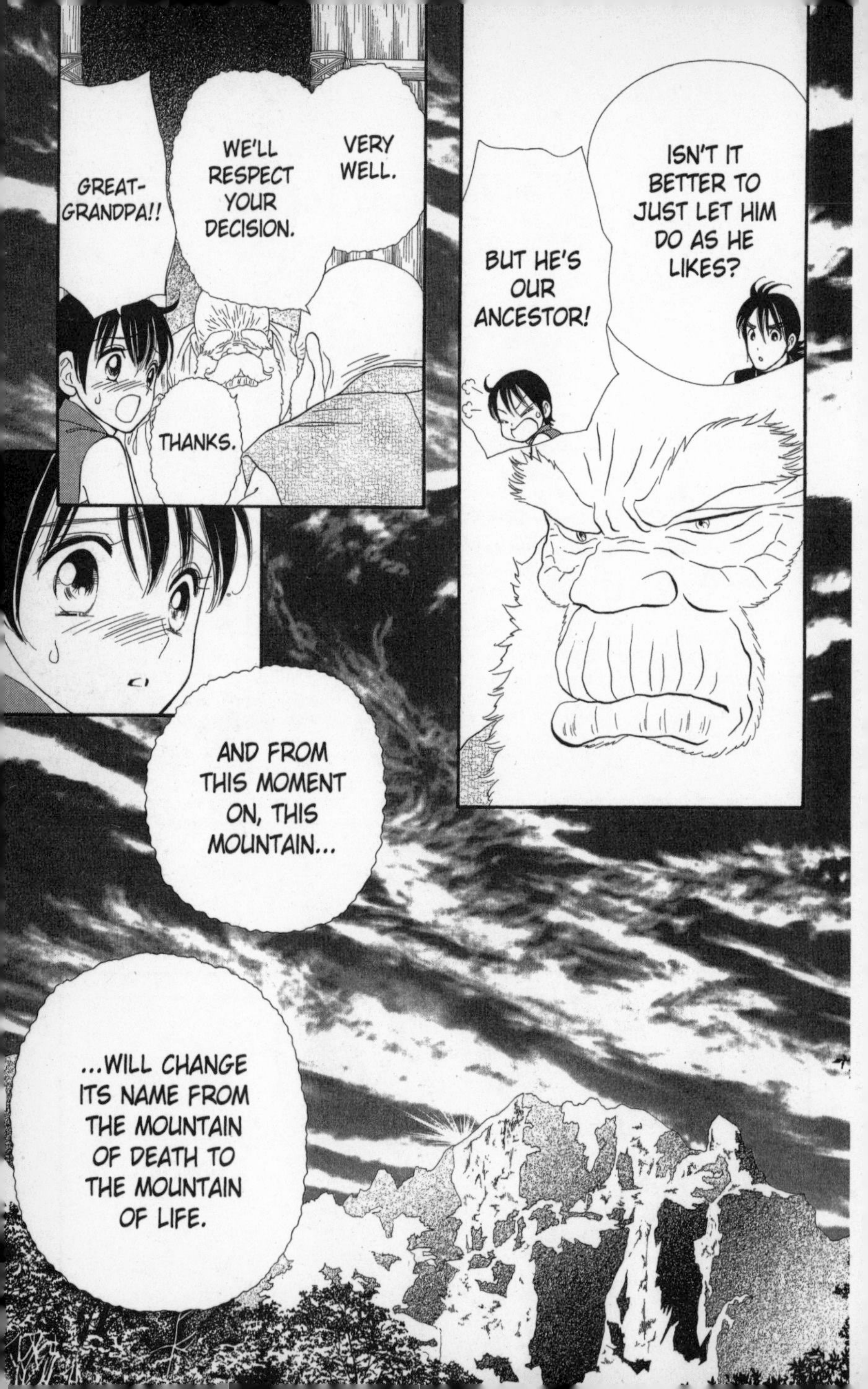
ISN'T IT BETTER TO JUST LET HIM DO AS HE LIKES?
BUT HE'S OUR ANCESTOR!
VERY WELL.
WE'LL RESPECT YOUR DECISION.
GREAT-GRANDPA!!
THANKS.
AND FROM THIS MOMENT ON, THIS MOUNTAIN...
...WILL CHANGE ITS NAME FROM THE MOUNTAIN OF DEATH TO THE MOUNTAIN OF LIFE.

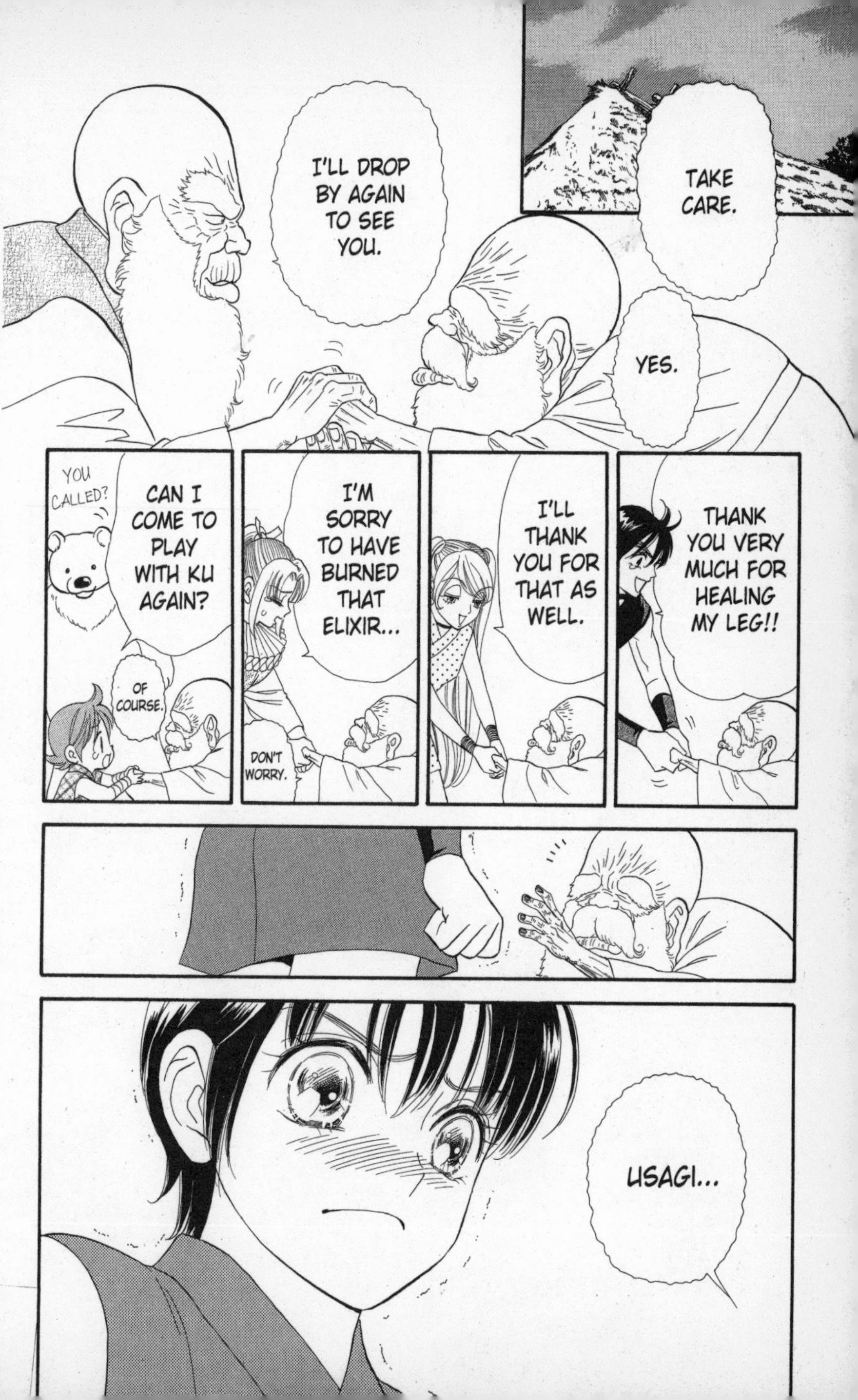
TAKE CARE.
I'LL DROP BY AGAIN TO SEE YOU.
YES.
THANK YOU VERY MUCH FOR HEALING MY LEG!!
I'LL THANK YOU FOR THAT AS WELL.
I'M SORRY TO HAVE BURNED THAT ELIXIR...
DON'T WORRY.
CAN I COME TO PLAY WITH KU AGAIN?
YOU CALLED?
OF COURSE.
USAGI...

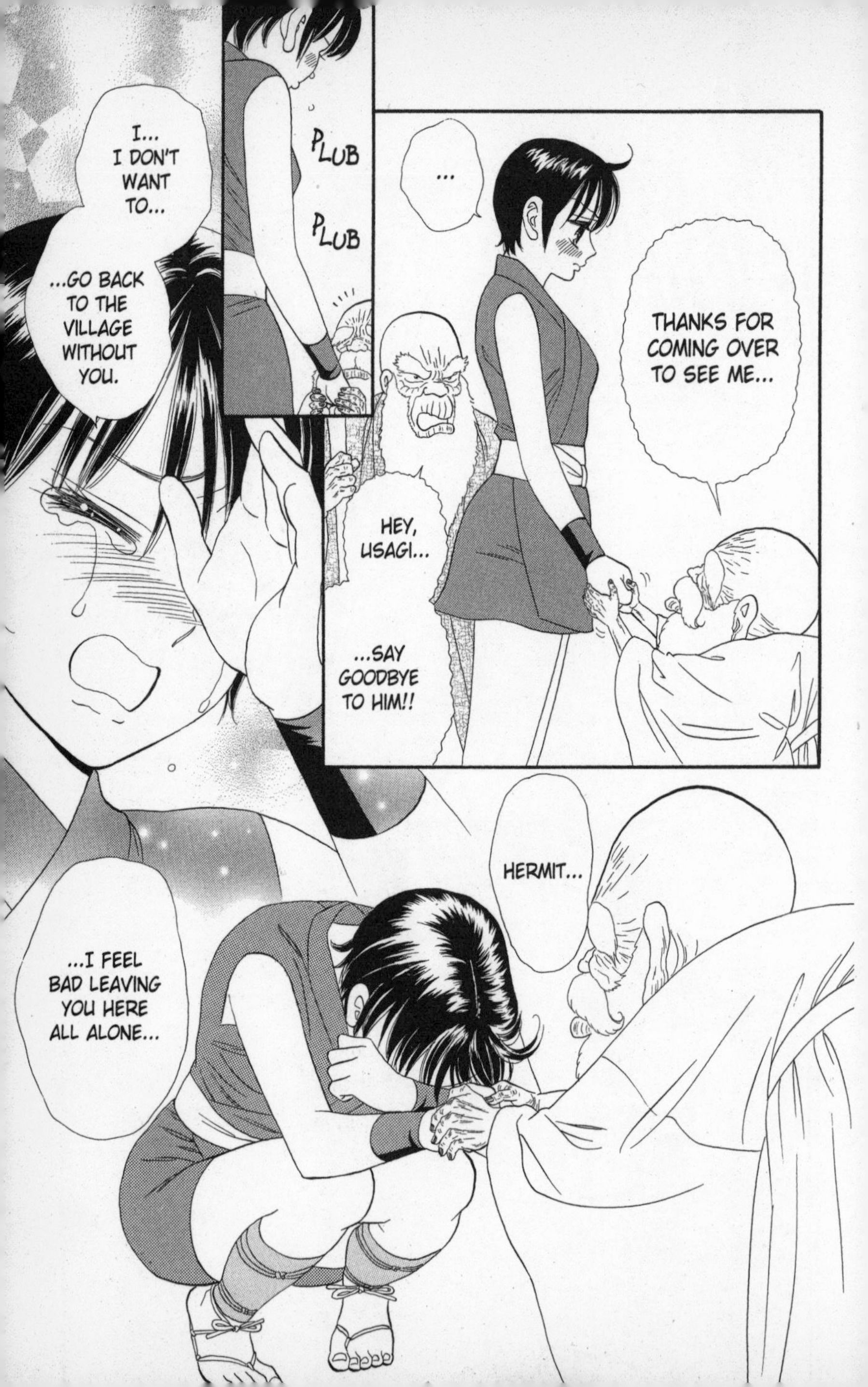
THANKS FOR COMING OVER TO SEE ME...
...
HEY, USAGI...
...SAY GOODBYE TO HIM!!
PLUB
PLUB
I... I DON'T WANT TO...
...GO BACK TO THE VILLAGE WITHOUT YOU.
HERMIT...
...I FEEL BAD LEAVING YOU HERE ALL ALONE...

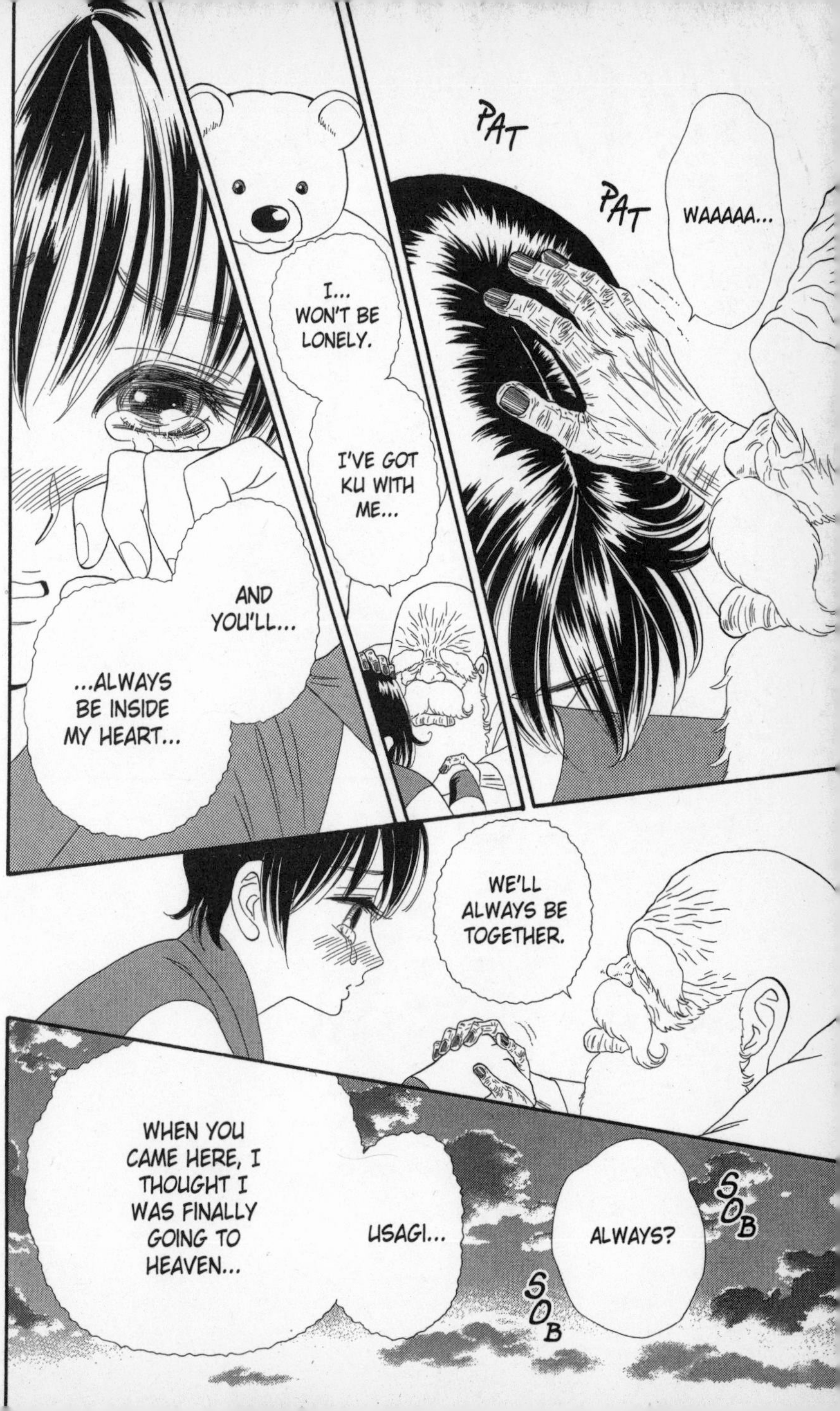
WAAAAA...
PAT
PAT
I... WON'T BE LONELY.
I'VE GOT KU WITH ME...
AND YOU'LL...
...ALWAYS BE INSIDE MY HEART...
WE'LL ALWAYS BE TOGETHER.
SOB
ALWAYS?
SOB
USAGI...
WHEN YOU CAME HERE, I THOUGHT I WAS FINALLY GOING TO HEAVEN...

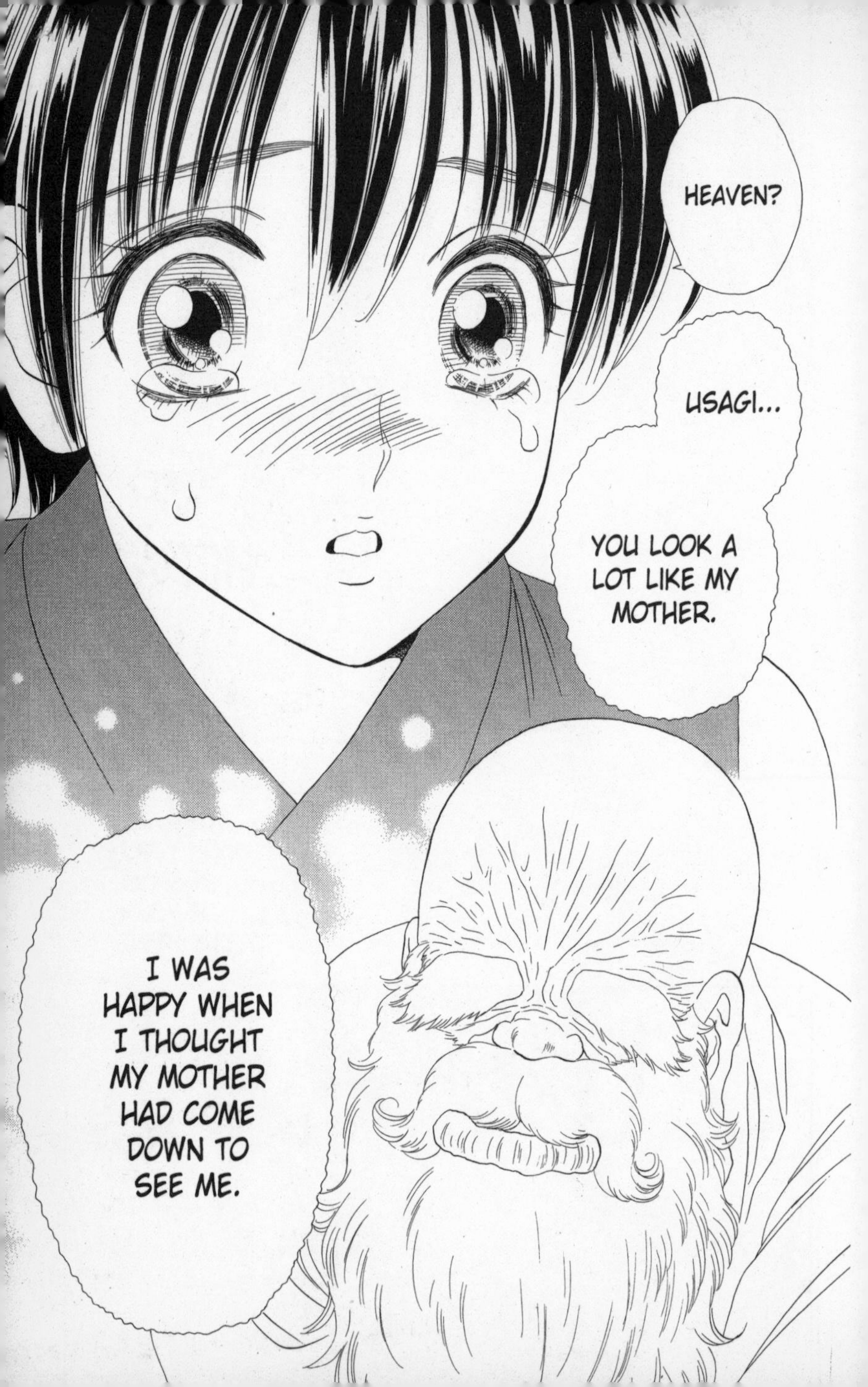
HEAVEN?
USAGI...
YOU LOOK A LOT LIKE MY MOTHER.
I WAS HAPPY WHEN I THOUGHT MY MOTHER HAD COME DOWN TO SEE ME.

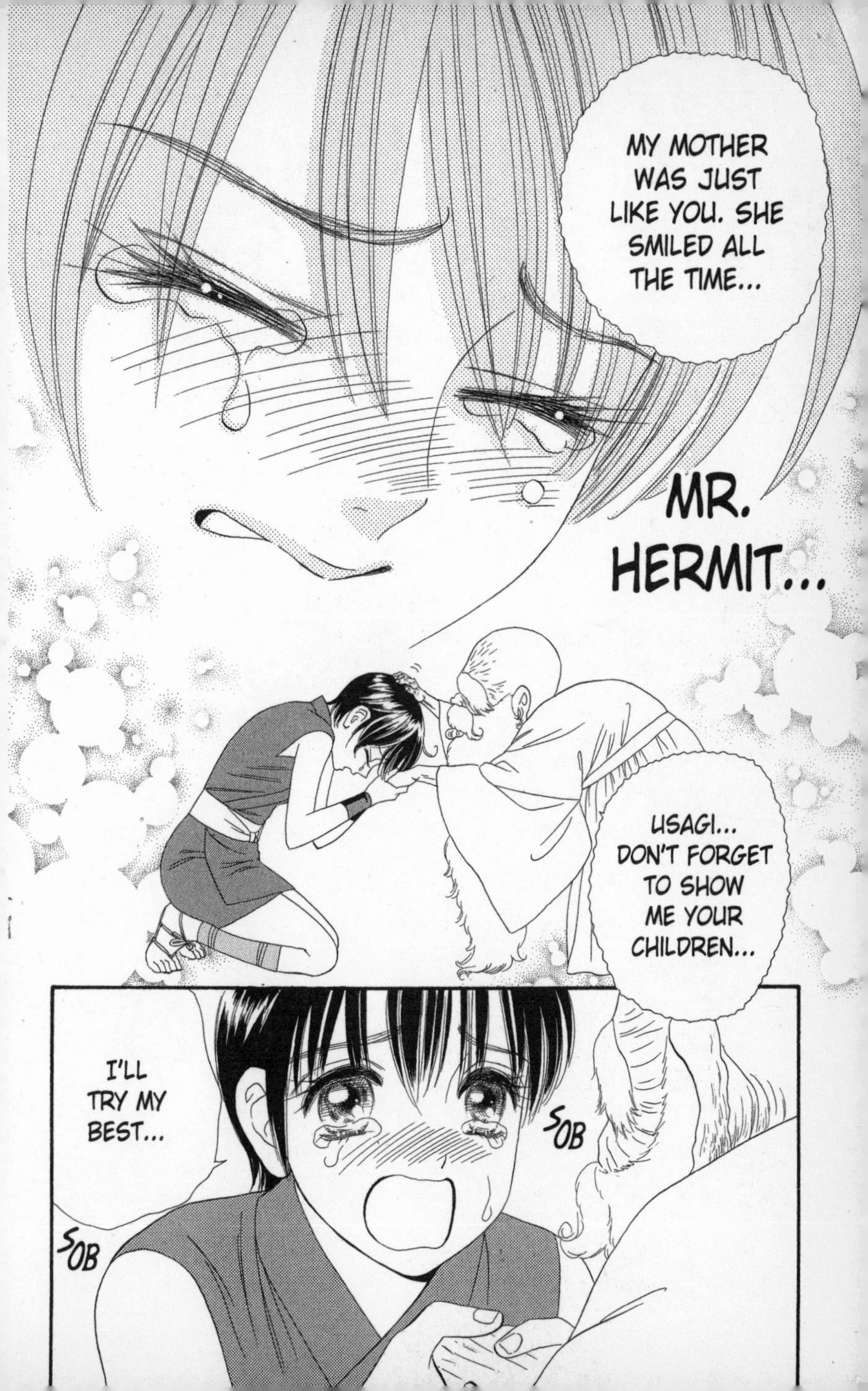
MY MOTHER WAS JUST LIKE YOU. SHE SMILED ALL THE TIME...
MR. HERMIT...
USAGI... DON'T FORGET TO SHOW ME YOUR CHILDREN...
SOB
I'LL TRY MY BEST...
SOB

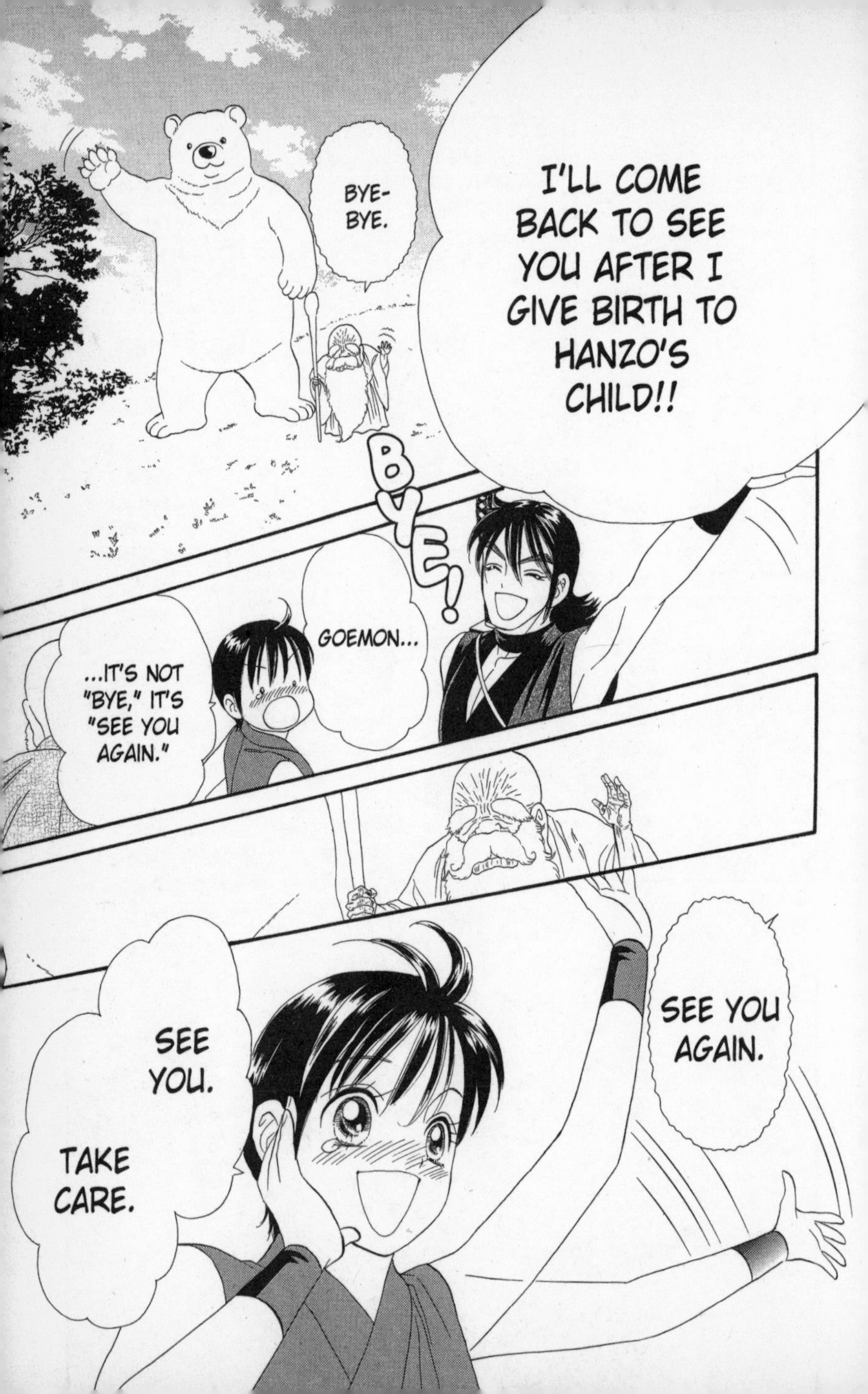
I'LL COME BACK TO SEE YOU AFTER I GIVE BIRTH TO HANZO'S CHILD!!
BYE-BYE.
BYE!
GOEMON...
...IT'S NOT "BYE," IT'S "SEE YOU AGAIN."
SEE YOU AGAIN.
SEE YOU.
TAKE CARE.

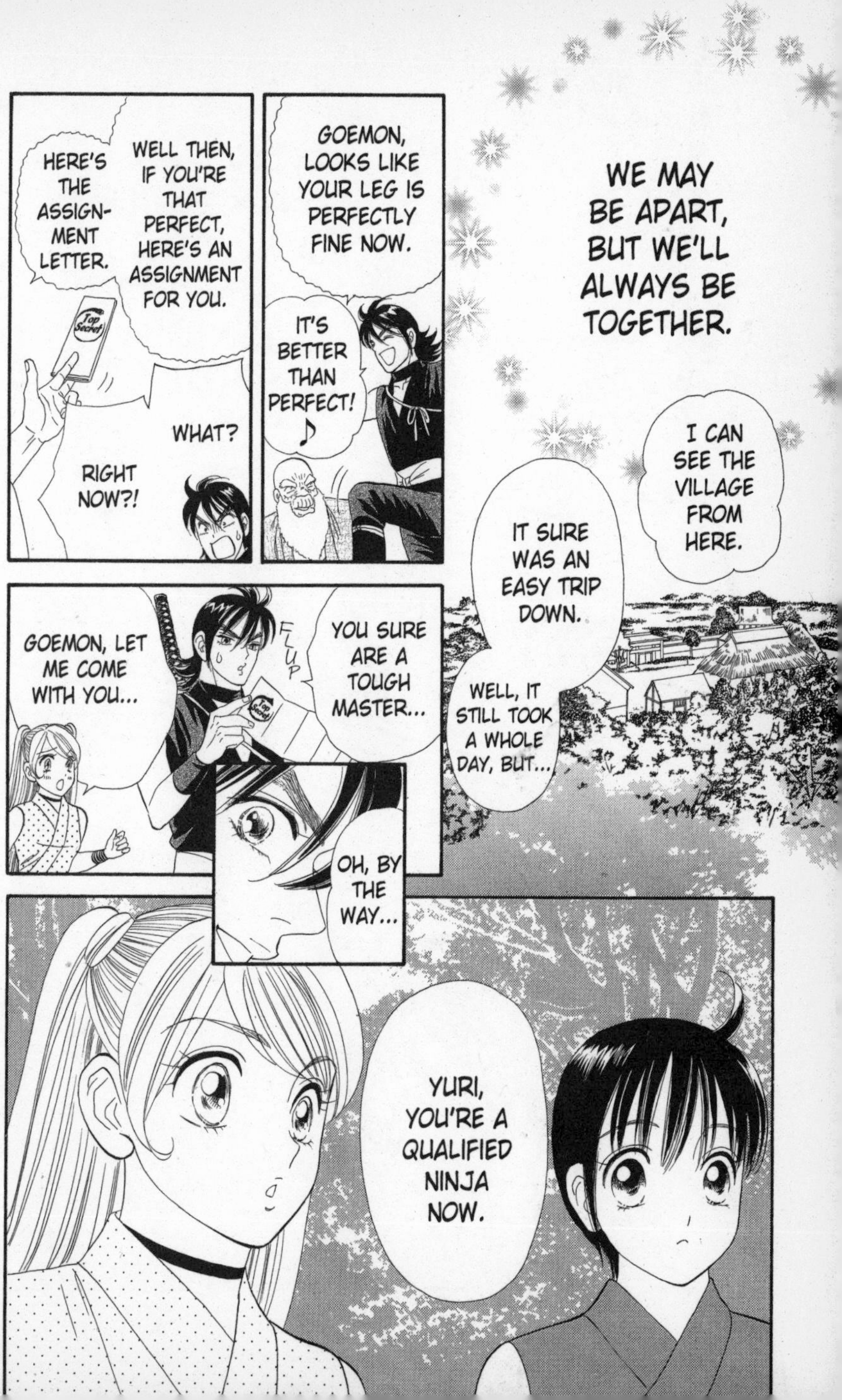
WE MAY BE APART, BUT WE'LL ALWAYS BE TOGETHER.
I CAN SEE THE VILLAGE FROM HERE.
IT SURE WAS AN EASY TRIP DOWN.
WELL, IT STILL TOOK A WHOLE DAY, BUT...
GOEMON, LOOKS LIKE YOUR LEG IS PERFECTLY FINE NOW.
IT'S BETTER THAN PERFECT! ♪
WELL THEN, IF YOU'RE THAT PERFECT, HERE'S AN ASSIGNMENT FOR YOU.
HERE'S THE ASSIGNMENT LETTER.
Top Secret
WHAT?
RIGHT NOW?!
YOU SURE ARE A TOUGH MASTER...
FLUP
Top Secret
GOEMON, LET ME COME WITH YOU...
OH, BY THE WAY...
YURI, YOU'RE A QUALIFIED NINJA NOW.

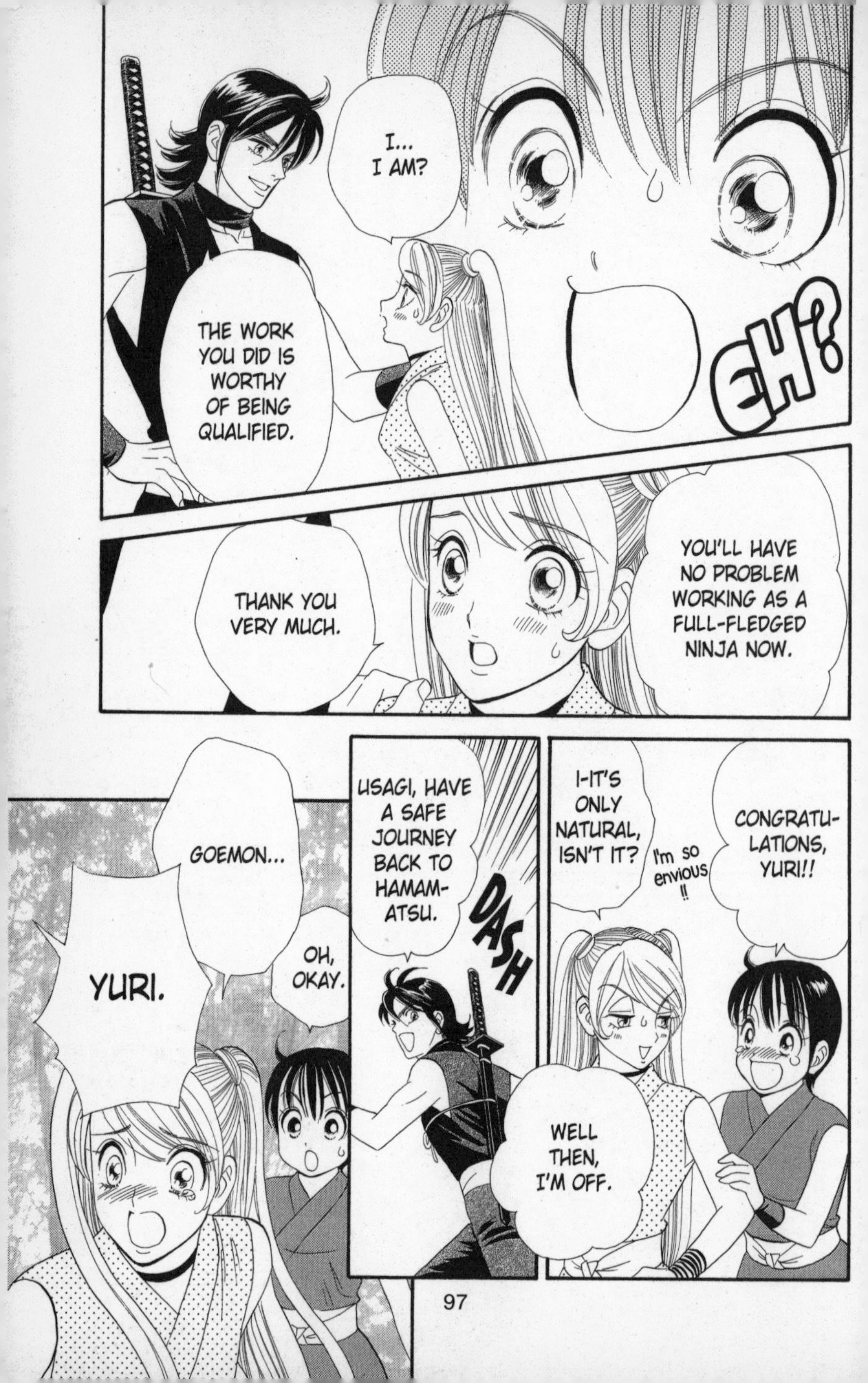
EH?
I... I AM?
THE WORK YOU DID IS WORTHY OF BEING QUALIFIED.
YOU'LL HAVE NO PROBLEM WORKING AS A FULL-FLEDGED NINJA NOW.
THANK YOU VERY MUCH.
CONGRATU-LATIONS, YURI!!
I-IT'S ONLY NATURAL, ISN'T IT?
I'm so envious !!
WELL THEN, I'M OFF.
USAGI, HAVE A SAFE JOURNEY BACK TO HAMAM-ATSU.
DASH
GOEMON...
OH, OKAY.
YURI.

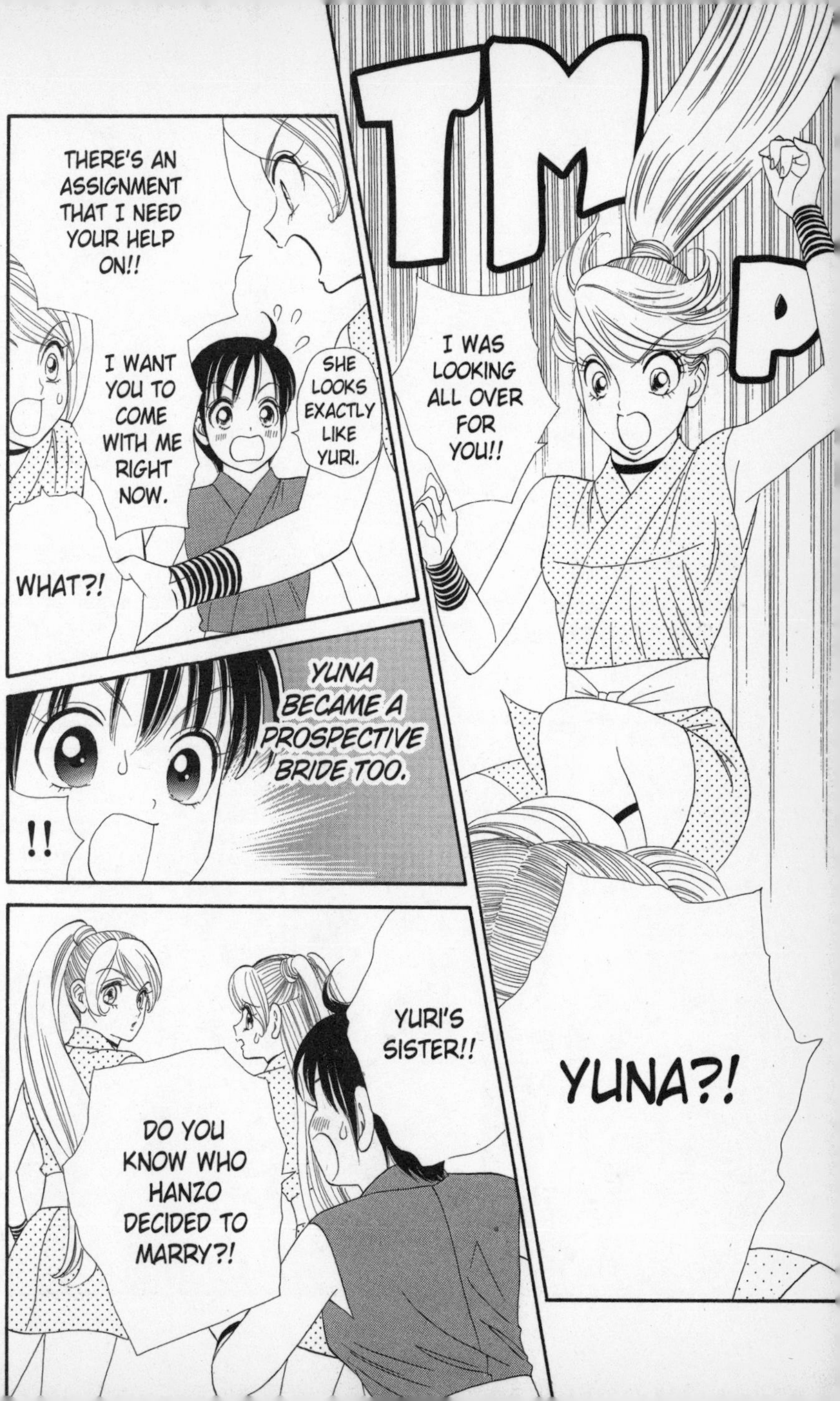
TMP
I WAS LOOKING ALL OVER FOR YOU!!
YUNA?!
THERE'S AN ASSIGNMENT THAT I NEED YOUR HELP ON!!
I WANT YOU TO COME WITH ME RIGHT NOW.
SHE LOOKS EXACTLY LIKE YURI.
WHAT?!
YUNA BECAME A PROSPECTIVE BRIDE TOO.
!!
YURI'S SISTER!!
DO YOU KNOW WHO HANZO DECIDED TO MARRY?!

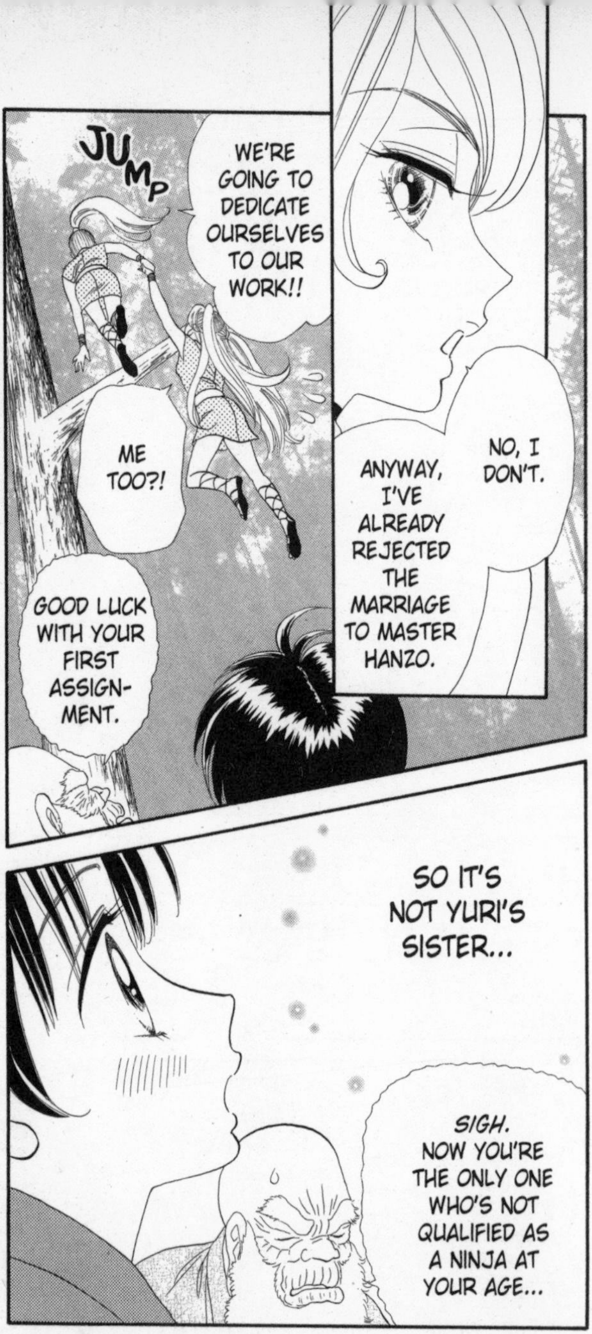
NO, I DON'T.
ANYWAY, I'VE ALREADY REJECTED THE MARRIAGE TO MASTER HANZO.
JUMP
WE'RE GOING TO DEDICATE OURSELVES TO OUR WORK!!
ME TOO?!
GOOD LUCK WITH YOUR FIRST ASSIGNMENT.
SO IT'S NOT YURI'S SISTER...
SIGH. NOW YOU'RE THE ONLY ONE WHO'S NOT QUALIFIED AS A NINJA AT YOUR AGE...

Stories About My Research Trip #2

The aim of this trip was to visit the Kouga-ryu Ninjutsu House. It is located 2 minutes away from Kounan station!!

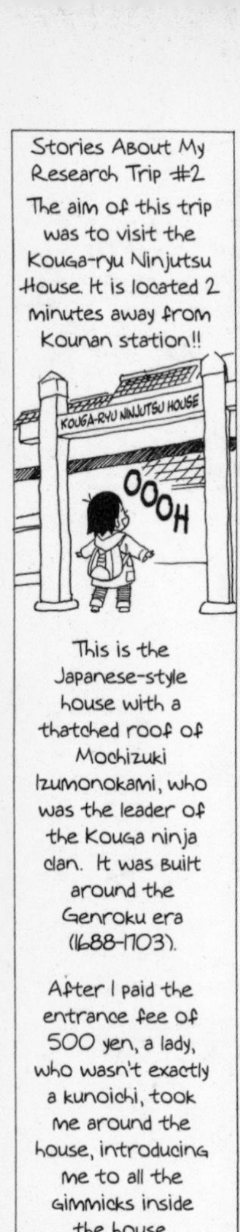
KOUGA-RYU NINJUTSU HOUSE
OOOH

This is the Japanese-style house with a thatched roof of Mochizuki Izumonokami, who was the leader of the Kouga ninja clan. It was built around the Genroku era (1688-1703).

After I paid the entrance fee of 500 yen, a lady, who wasn't exactly a kunoichi, took me around the house, introducing me to all the gimmicks inside the house.

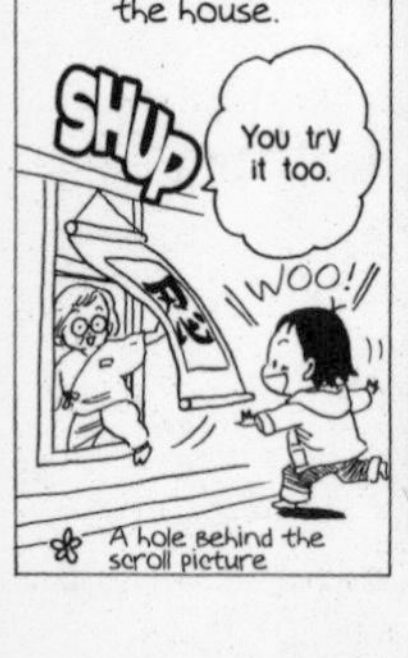
SHUP
You try it too.
WOO!

A hole behind the scroll picture

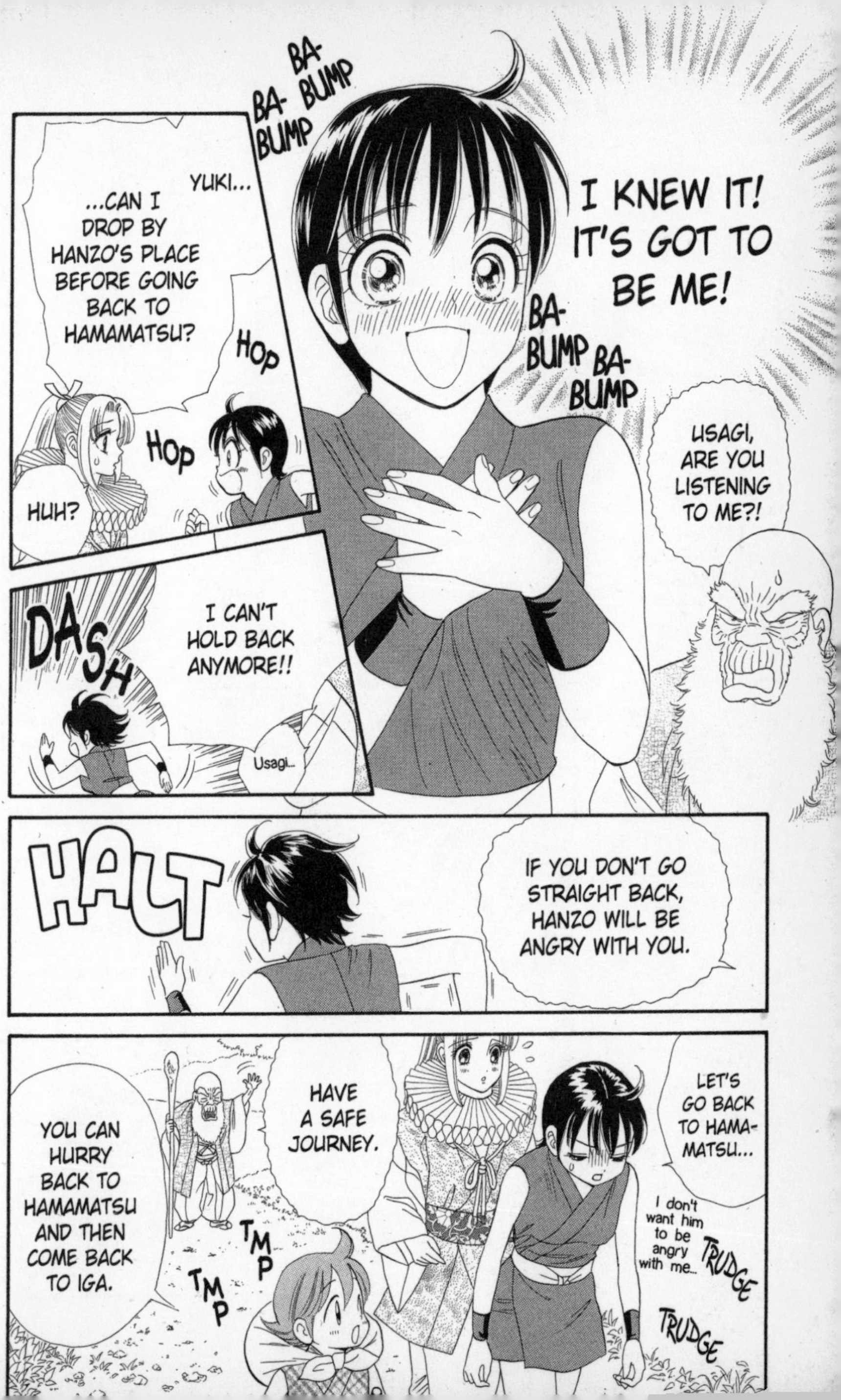
BA-BUMP
BA-BUMP
I KNEW IT! IT'S GOT TO BE ME!
BA-BUMP
BA-BUMP
USAGI, ARE YOU LISTENING TO ME?!
YUKI...
...CAN I DROP BY HANZO'S PLACE BEFORE GOING BACK TO HAMAMATSU?
HOP
HOP
HUH?
I CAN'T HOLD BACK ANYMORE!!
DASH
Usagi...
IF YOU DON'T GO STRAIGHT BACK, HANZO WILL BE ANGRY WITH YOU.
HALT
LET'S GO BACK TO HAMA-MATSU...
I don't want him to be angry with me...
TRUDGE
TRUDGE
HAVE A SAFE JOURNEY.
YOU CAN HURRY BACK TO HAMAMATSU AND THEN COME BACK TO IGA.
TMP
TMP

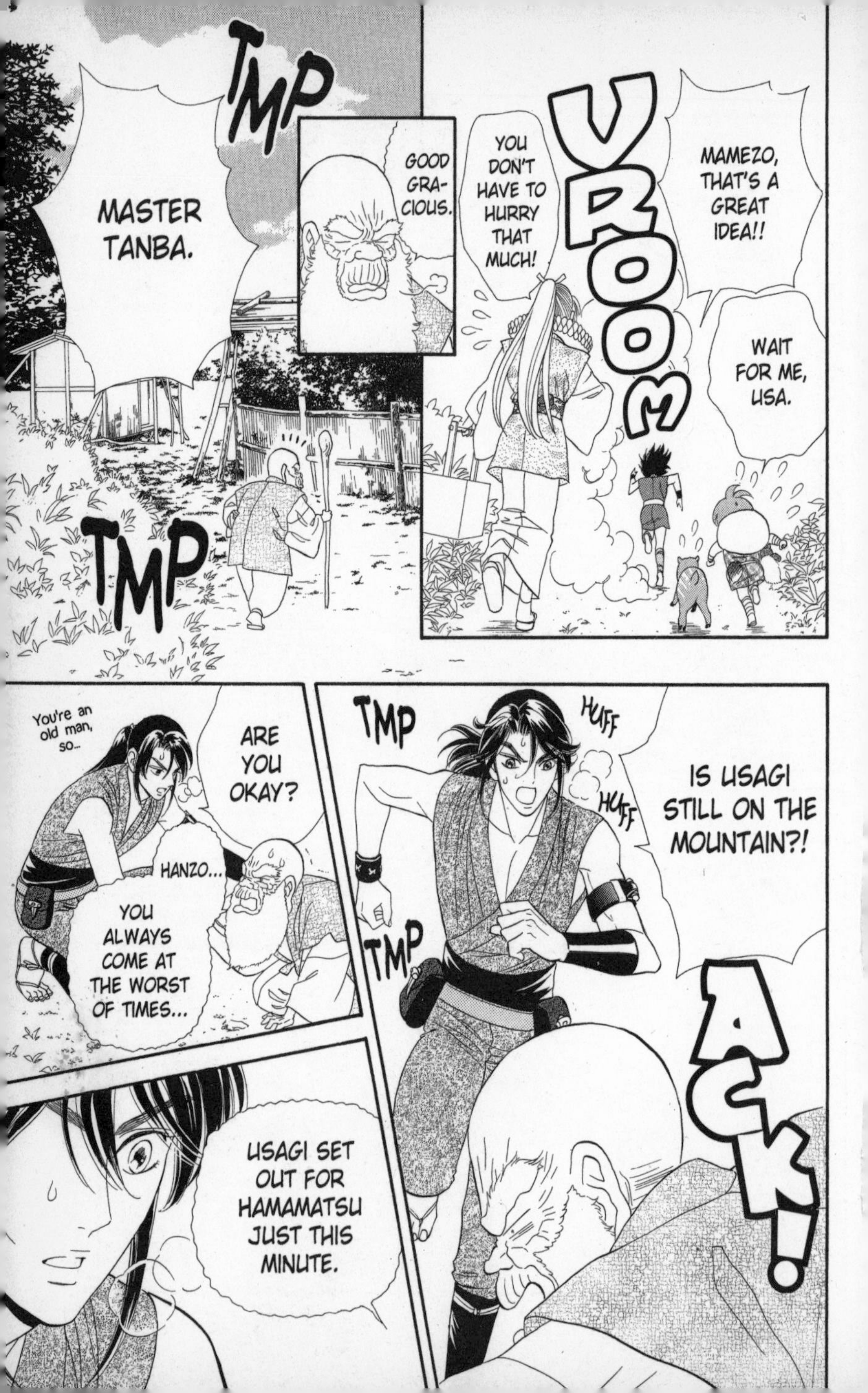

MAMEZO, THAT'S A GREAT IDEA!!
VROOOM
YOU DON'T HAVE TO HURRY THAT MUCH!
WAIT FOR ME, USA.
TMP
GOOD GRA-CIOUS.
MASTER TANBA.
TMP
TMP
HUFF
HUFF
IS USAGI STILL ON THE MOUNTAIN?!
TMP
ACK!
ARE YOU OKAY?
You're an old man, so...
HANZO...
YOU ALWAYS COME AT THE WORST OF TIMES...
USAGI SET OUT FOR HAMAMATSU JUST THIS MINUTE.

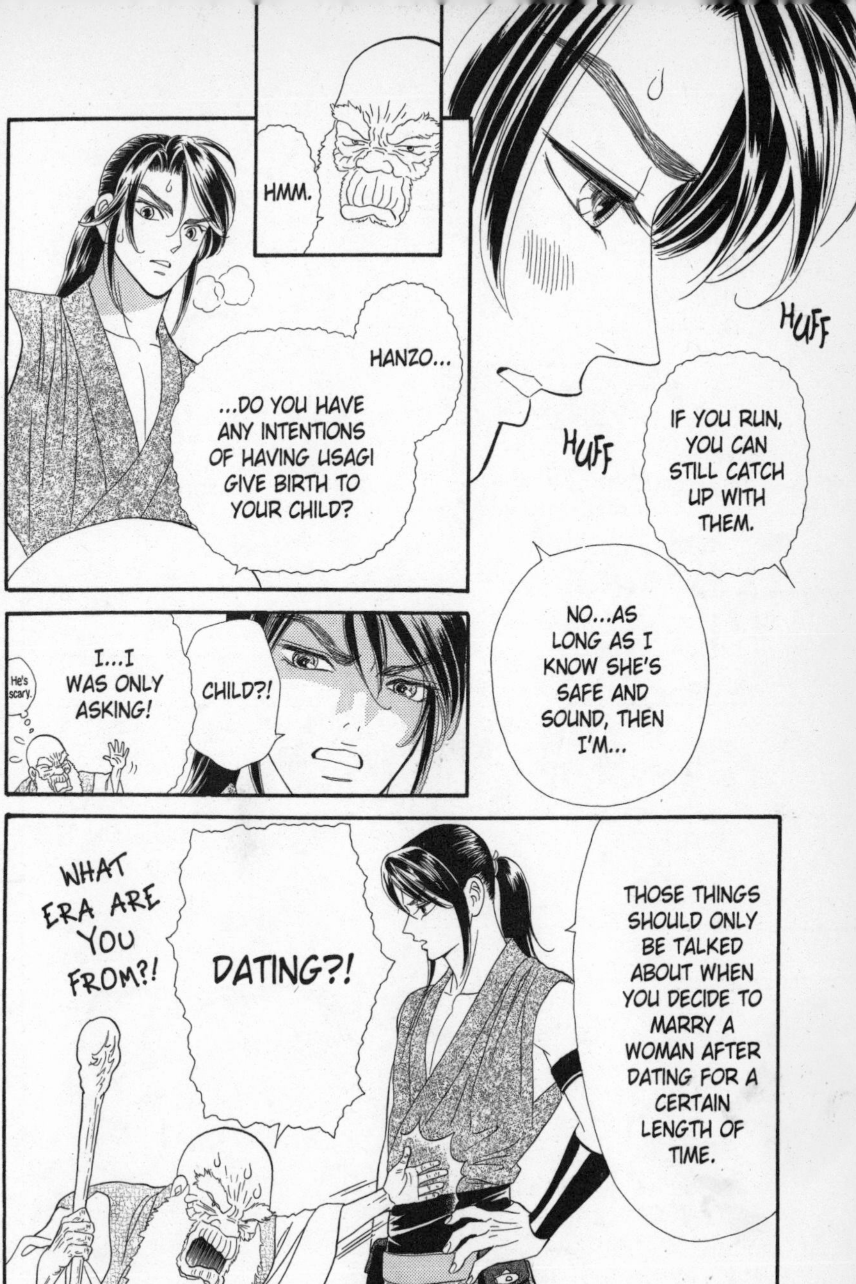
HUFF
HUFF
IF YOU RUN, YOU CAN STILL CATCH UP WITH THEM.
NO...AS LONG AS I KNOW SHE'S SAFE AND SOUND, THEN I'M...
HMM.
HANZO...
...DO YOU HAVE ANY INTENTIONS OF HAVING USAGI GIVE BIRTH TO YOUR CHILD?
CHILD?!
I...I WAS ONLY ASKING!
He's scary.
THOSE THINGS SHOULD ONLY BE TALKED ABOUT WHEN YOU DECIDE TO MARRY A WOMAN AFTER DATING FOR A CERTAIN LENGTH OF TIME.
DATING?!
WHAT ERA ARE YOU FROM?!

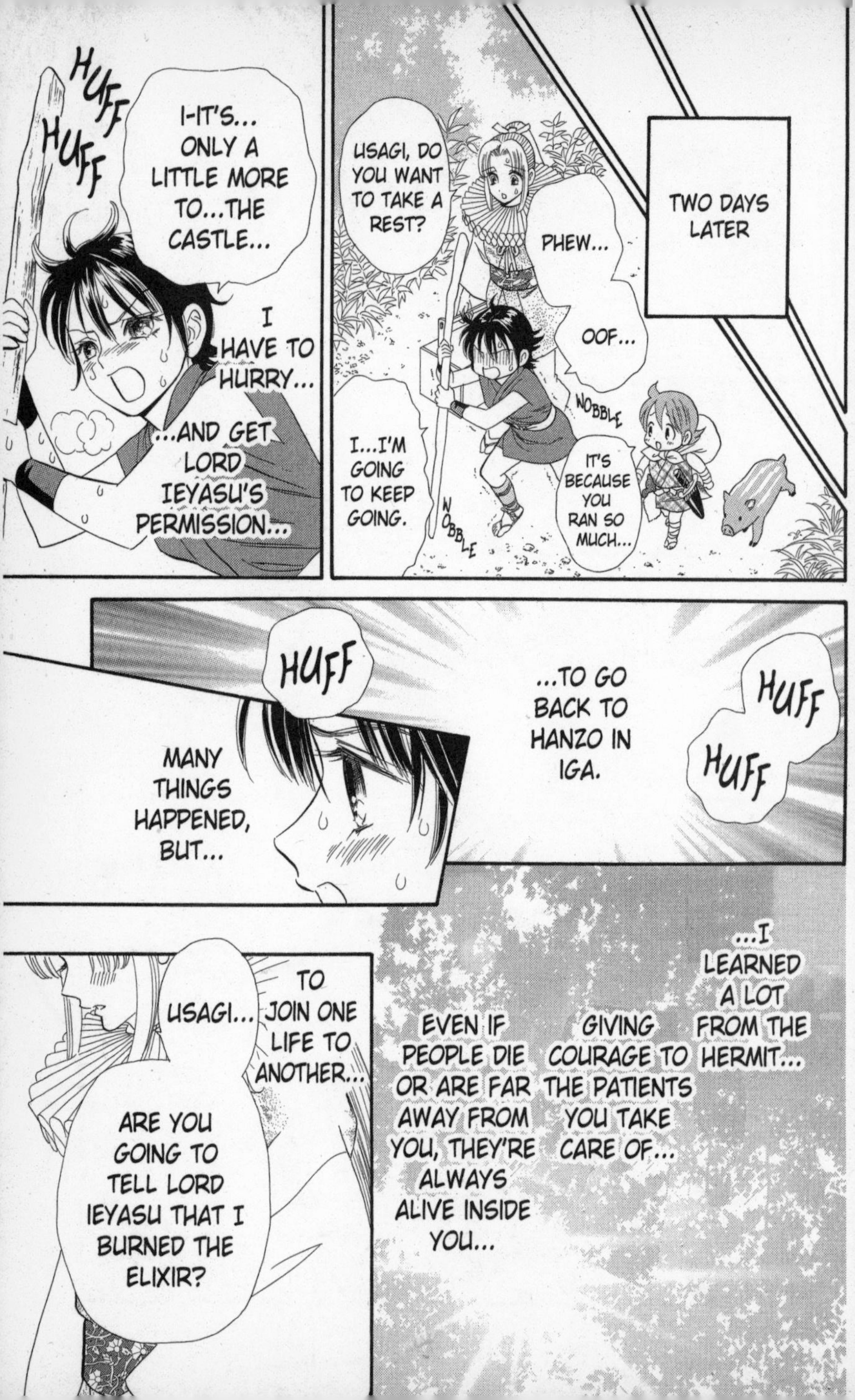
TWO DAYS LATER
PHEW...
OOF...
USAGI, DO YOU WANT TO TAKE A REST?
WOBBLE
IT'S BECAUSE YOU RAN SO MUCH...
I...I'M GOING TO KEEP GOING.
WOBBLE
HUFF HUFF
I-IT'S... ONLY A LITTLE MORE TO...THE CASTLE...
I HAVE TO HURRY...
...AND GET LORD IEYASU'S PERMISSION...
HUFF HUFF
...TO GO BACK TO HANZO IN IGA.
HUFF
MANY THINGS HAPPENED, BUT...
...I LEARNED A LOT FROM THE HERMIT...
GIVING COURAGE TO THE PATIENTS YOU TAKE CARE OF...
EVEN IF PEOPLE DIE OR ARE FAR AWAY FROM YOU, THEY'RE ALWAYS ALIVE INSIDE YOU...
TO JOIN ONE LIFE TO ANOTHER...
USAGI...
ARE YOU GOING TO TELL LORD IEYASU THAT I BURNED THE ELIXIR?

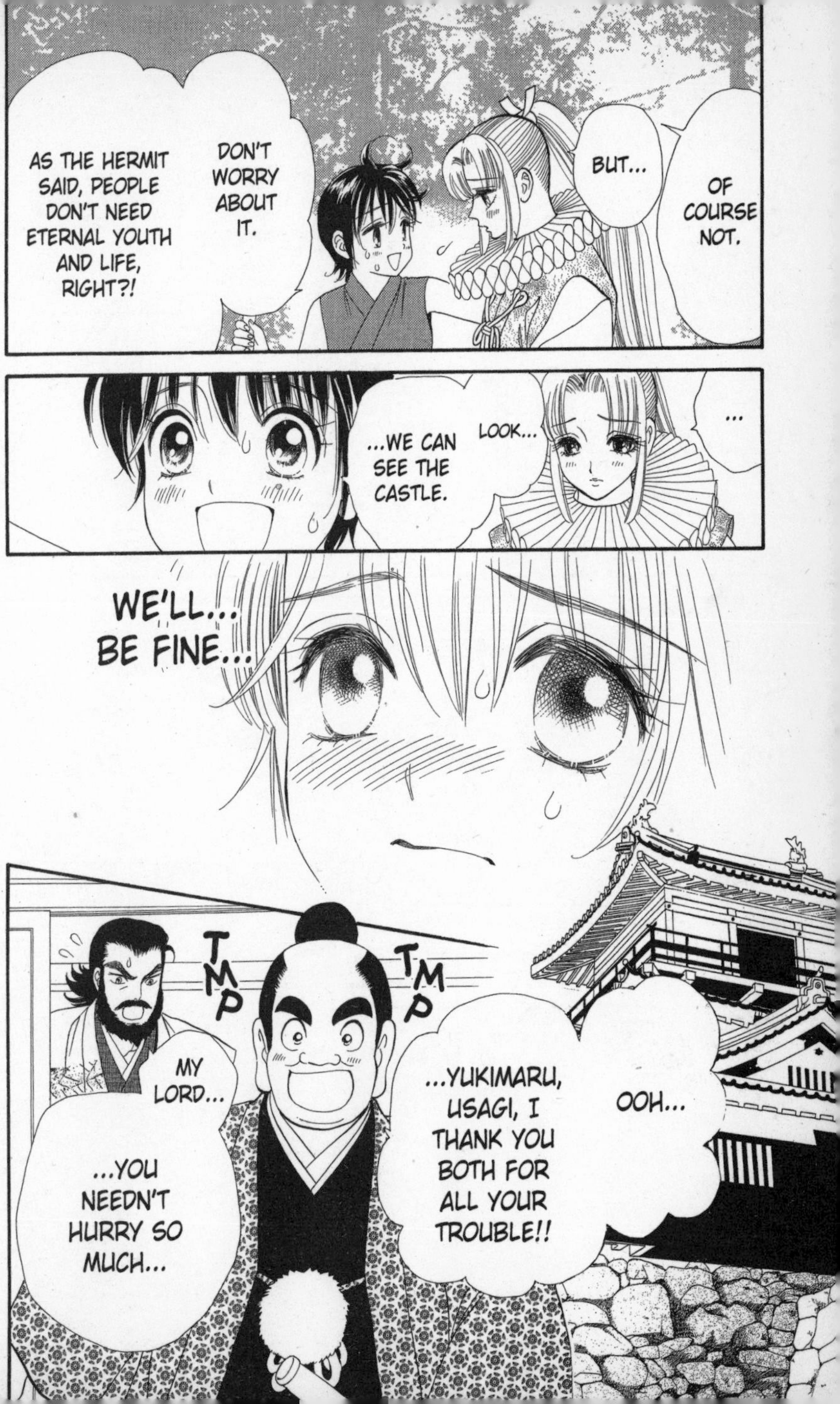
OF COURSE NOT.
BUT...
DON'T WORRY ABOUT IT.
AS THE HERMIT SAID, PEOPLE DON'T NEED ETERNAL YOUTH AND LIFE, RIGHT?!
...
LOOK...
...WE CAN SEE THE CASTLE.
WE'LL... BE FINE...
TMP
OOH...
...YUKIMARU, USAGI, I THANK YOU BOTH FOR ALL YOUR TROUBLE!!
TMP
MY LORD...
...YOU NEEDN'T HURRY SO MUCH...

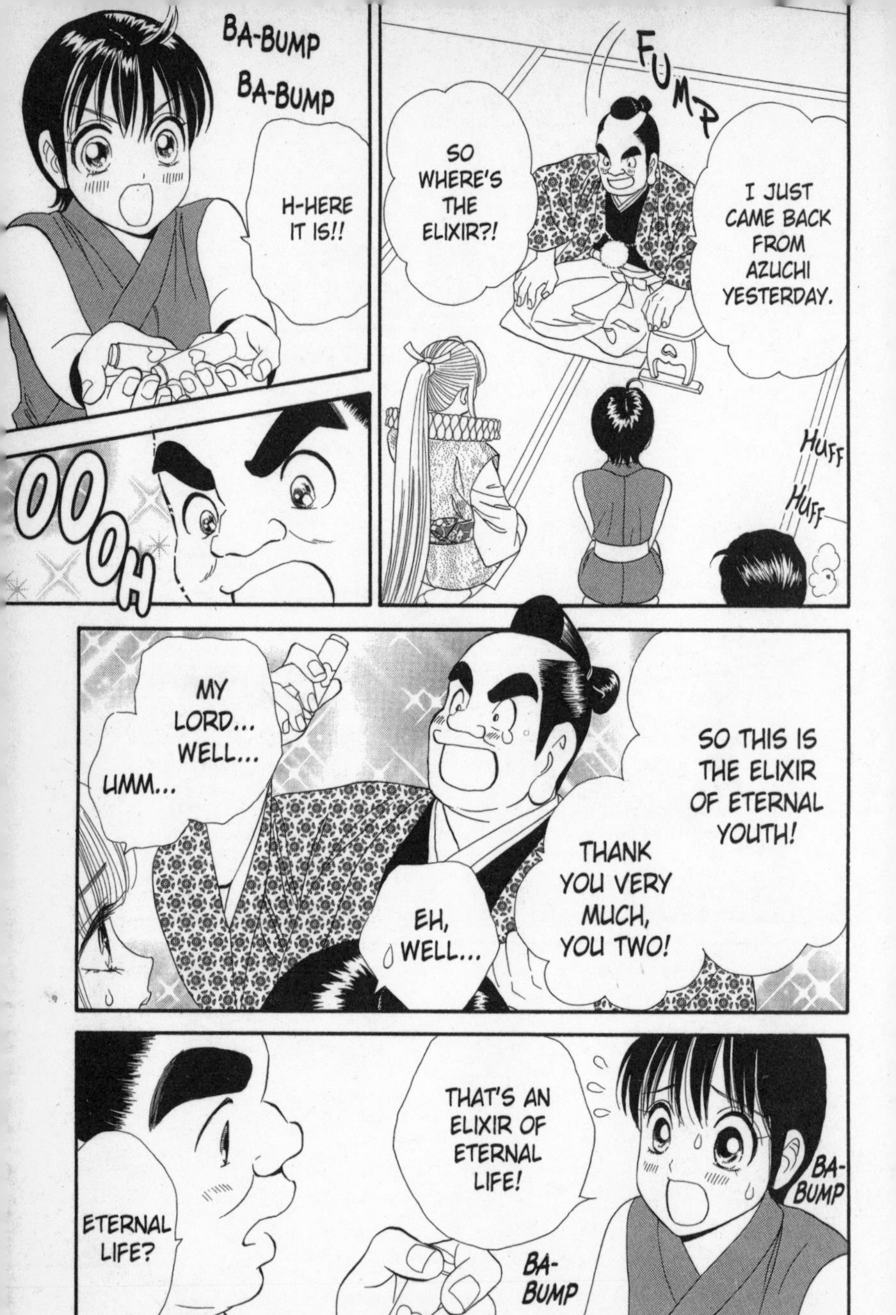
FUMP
I JUST CAME BACK FROM AZUCHI YESTERDAY.
SO WHERE'S THE ELIXIR?!
HUFF
HUFF
BA-BUMP
BA-BUMP
H-HERE IT IS!!
OOOOH
SO THIS IS THE ELIXIR OF ETERNAL YOUTH!
THANK YOU VERY MUCH, YOU TWO!
EH, WELL...
MY LORD... WELL...
UMM...
BA-BUMP
THAT'S AN ELIXIR OF ETERNAL LIFE!
BA-BUMP
ETERNAL LIFE?

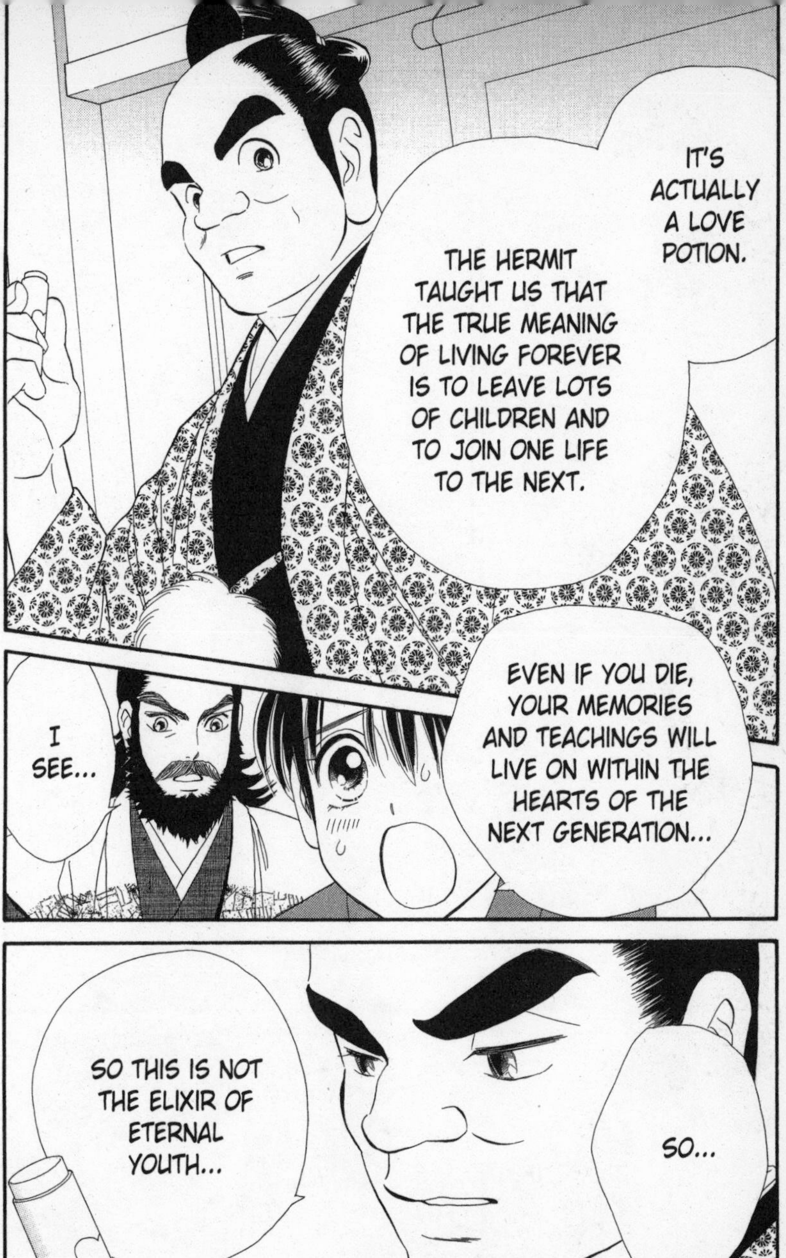
IT'S ACTUALLY A LOVE POTION.
THE HERMIT TAUGHT US THAT THE TRUE MEANING OF LIVING FOREVER IS TO LEAVE LOTS OF CHILDREN AND TO JOIN ONE LIFE TO THE NEXT.
EVEN IF YOU DIE, YOUR MEMORIES AND TEACHINGS WILL LIVE ON WITHIN THE HEARTS OF THE NEXT GENERATION...
I SEE...
SO...
SO THIS IS NOT THE ELIXIR OF ETERNAL YOUTH...

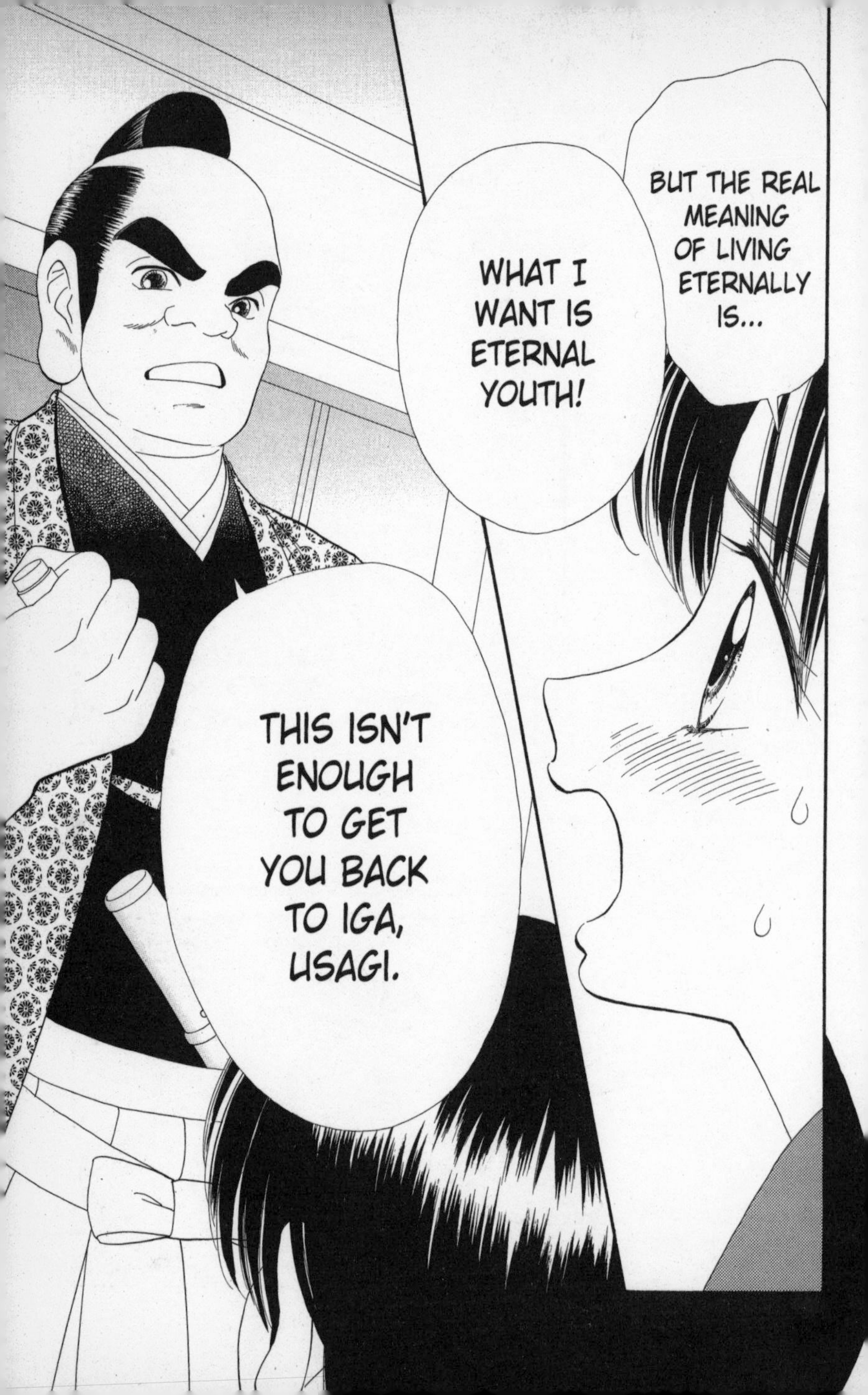
BUT THE REAL MEANING OF LIVING ETERNALLY IS...
WHAT I WANT IS ETERNAL YOUTH!
THIS ISN'T ENOUGH TO GET YOU BACK TO IGA, USAGI.

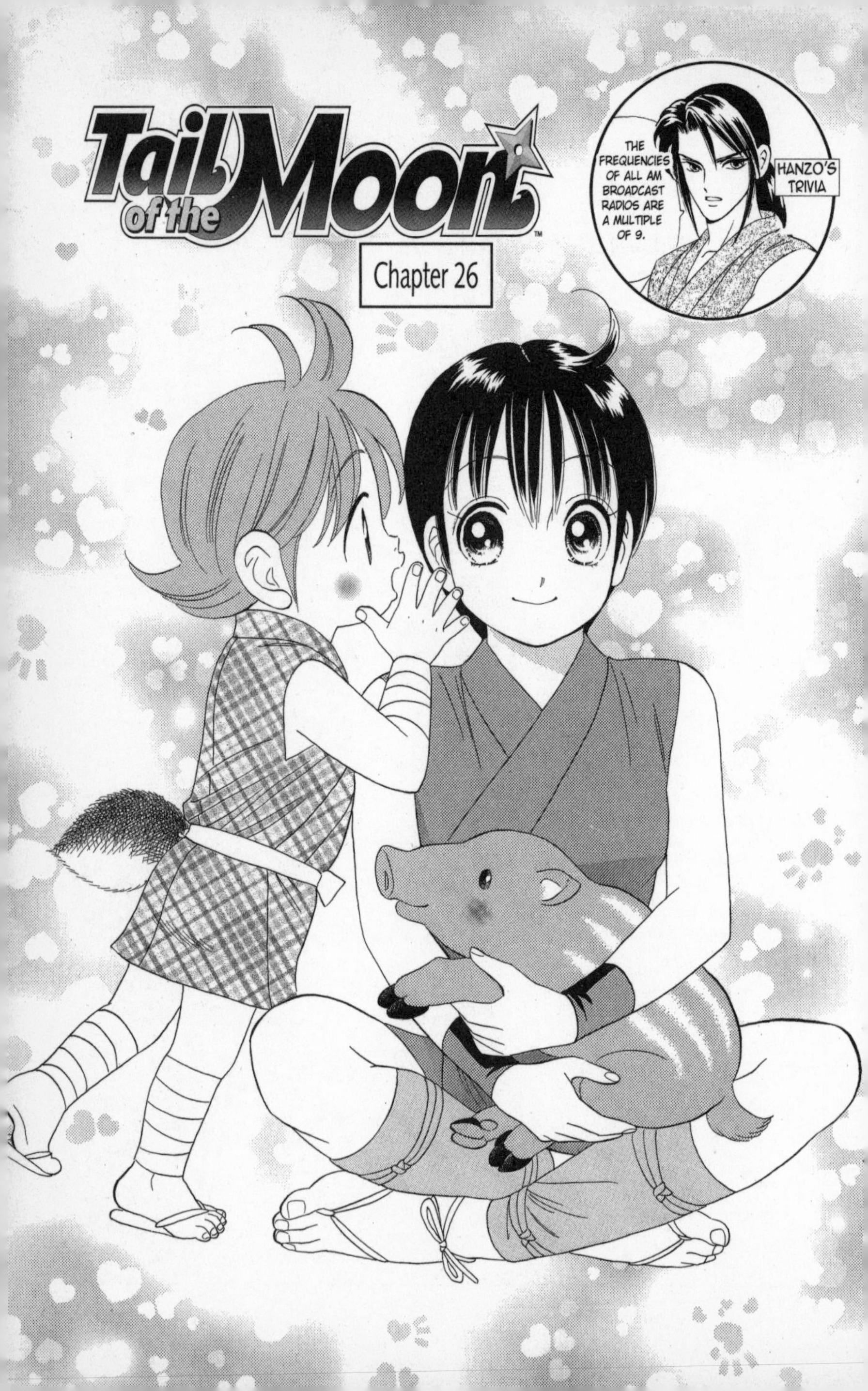
Tail of the Moon™
Chapter 26
THE FREQUENCIES OF ALL AM BROADCAST RADIOS ARE A MULTIPLE OF 9.
HANZO'S TRIVIA

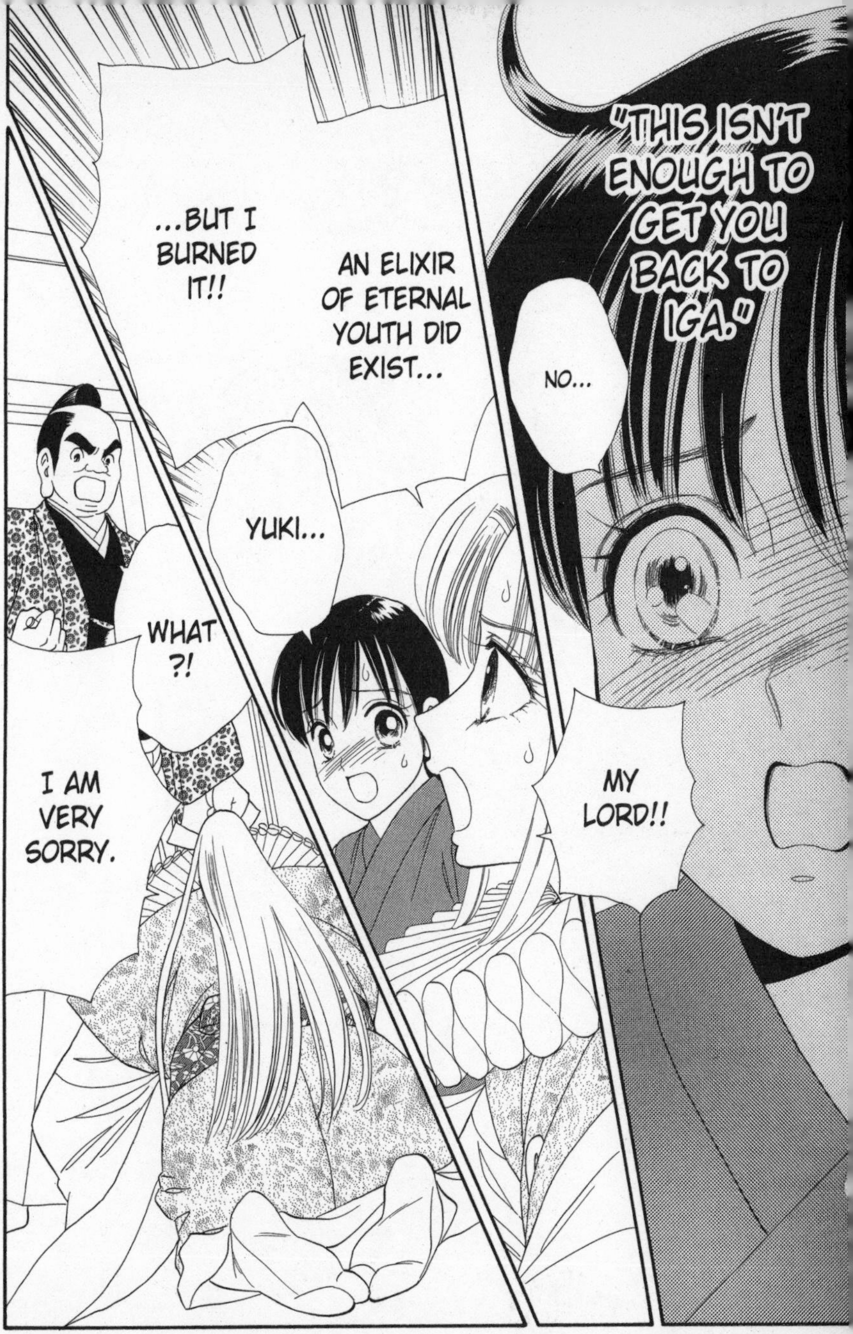
"THIS ISN'T ENOUGH TO GET YOU BACK TO IGA."
NO...
MY LORD!!
AN ELIXIR OF ETERNAL YOUTH DID EXIST...
YUKI...
...BUT I BURNED IT!!
WHAT?!
I AM VERY SORRY.

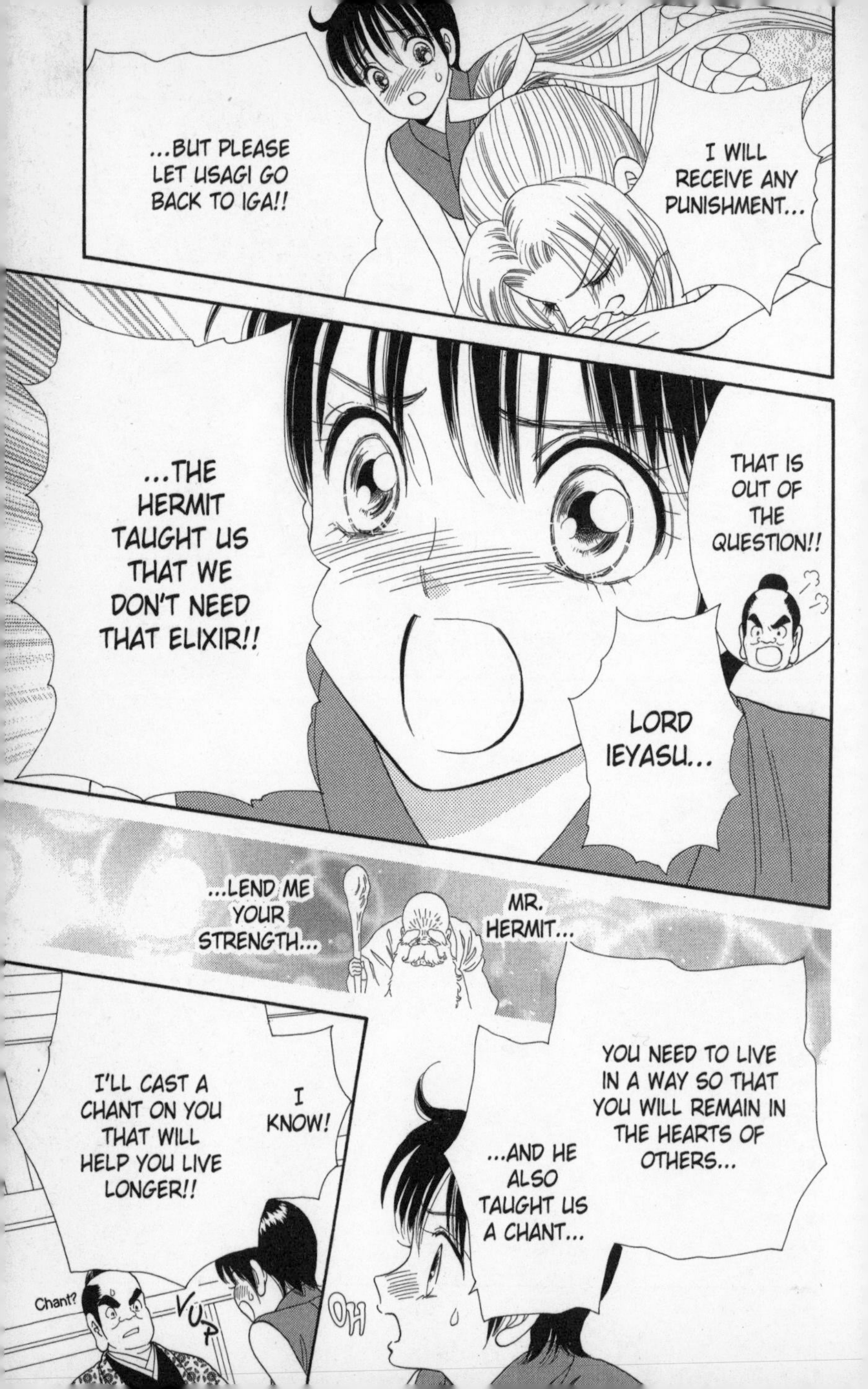
I WILL RECEIVE ANY PUNISHMENT...
...BUT PLEASE LET USAGI GO BACK TO IGA!!
THAT IS OUT OF THE QUESTION!!
LORD IEYASU...
...THE HERMIT TAUGHT US THAT WE DON'T NEED THAT ELIXIR!!
MR. HERMIT...
...LEND ME YOUR STRENGTH...
YOU NEED TO LIVE IN A WAY SO THAT YOU WILL REMAIN IN THE HEARTS OF OTHERS...
...AND HE ALSO TAUGHT US A CHANT...
OH
I KNOW!
I'LL CAST A CHANT ON YOU THAT WILL HELP YOU LIVE LONGER!!
VUP
Chant?

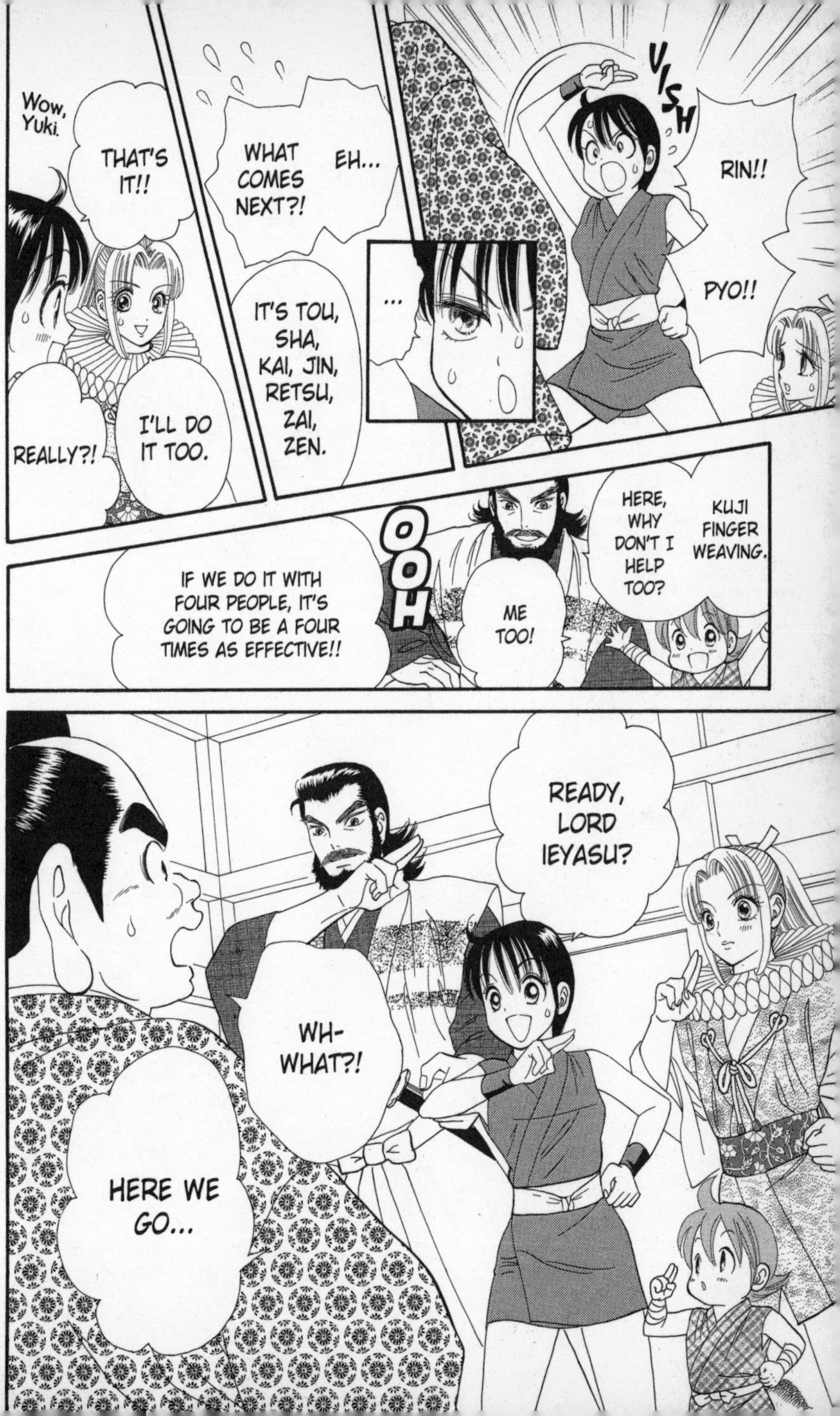
VISH
RIN!!
PYO!!
...
EH...
WHAT COMES NEXT?!
IT'S TOU, SHA, KAI, JIN, RETSU, ZAI, ZEN.
THAT'S IT!!
Wow, Yuki.
I'LL DO IT TOO.
REALLY?!
KUJI FINGER WEAVING.
HERE, WHY DON'T I HELP TOO?
OOH
ME TOO!
IF WE DO IT WITH FOUR PEOPLE, IT'S GOING TO BE A FOUR TIMES AS EFFECTIVE!!
READY, LORD IEYASU?
WH-WHAT?!
HERE WE GO...

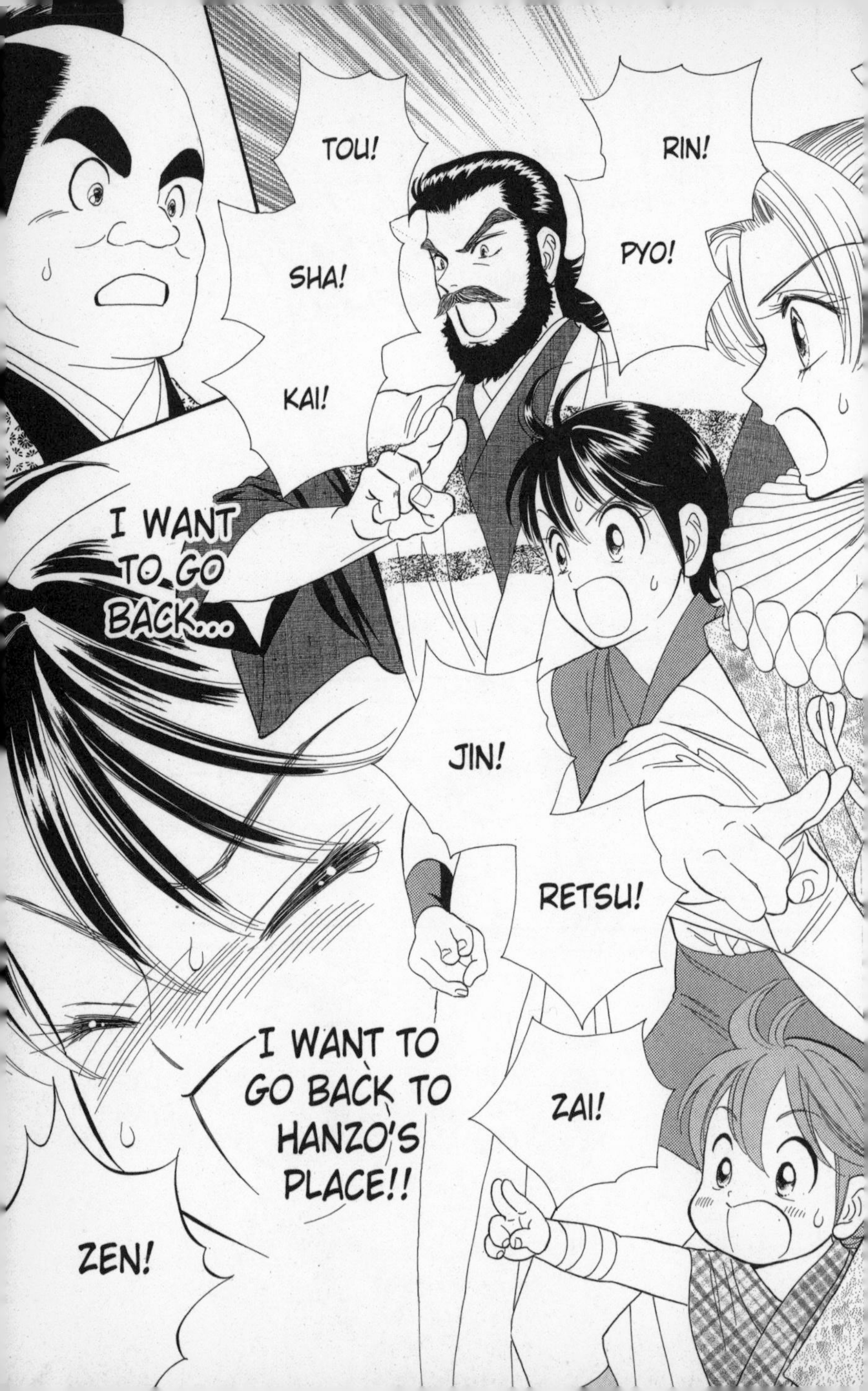
RIN!
PYO!
TOU!
SHA!
KAI!
I WANT TO GO BACK...
JIN!
RETSU!
ZAI!
I WANT TO GO BACK TO HANZO'S PLACE!!
ZEN!

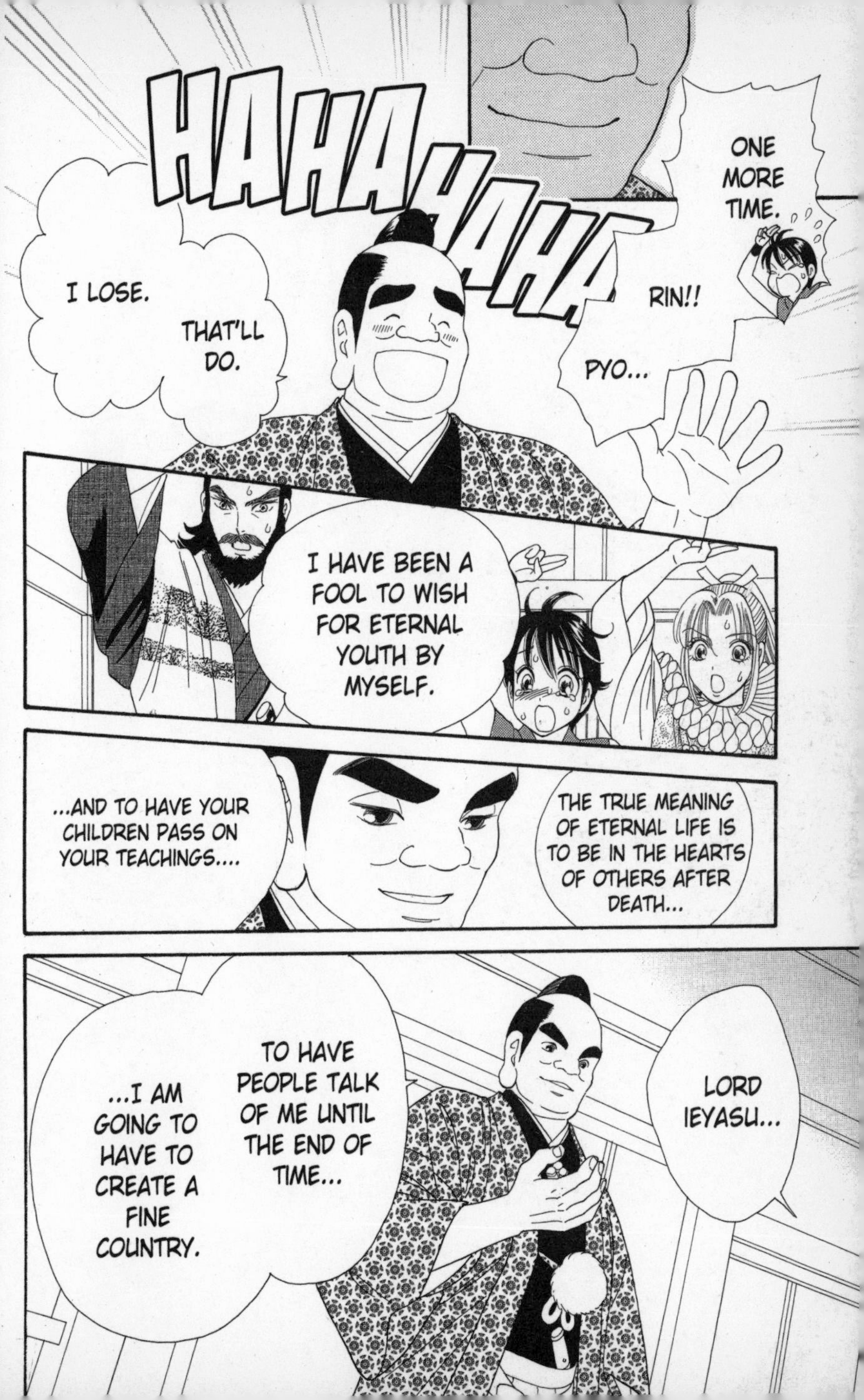
ONE MORE TIME.
HAHAHAHAHA
RIN!!
PYO...
I LOSE.
THAT'LL DO.
I HAVE BEEN A FOOL TO WISH FOR ETERNAL YOUTH BY MYSELF.
THE TRUE MEANING OF ETERNAL LIFE IS TO BE IN THE HEARTS OF OTHERS AFTER DEATH...
...AND TO HAVE YOUR CHILDREN PASS ON YOUR TEACHINGS....
LORD IEYASU...
TO HAVE PEOPLE TALK OF ME UNTIL THE END OF TIME...
...I AM GOING TO HAVE TO CREATE A FINE COUNTRY.

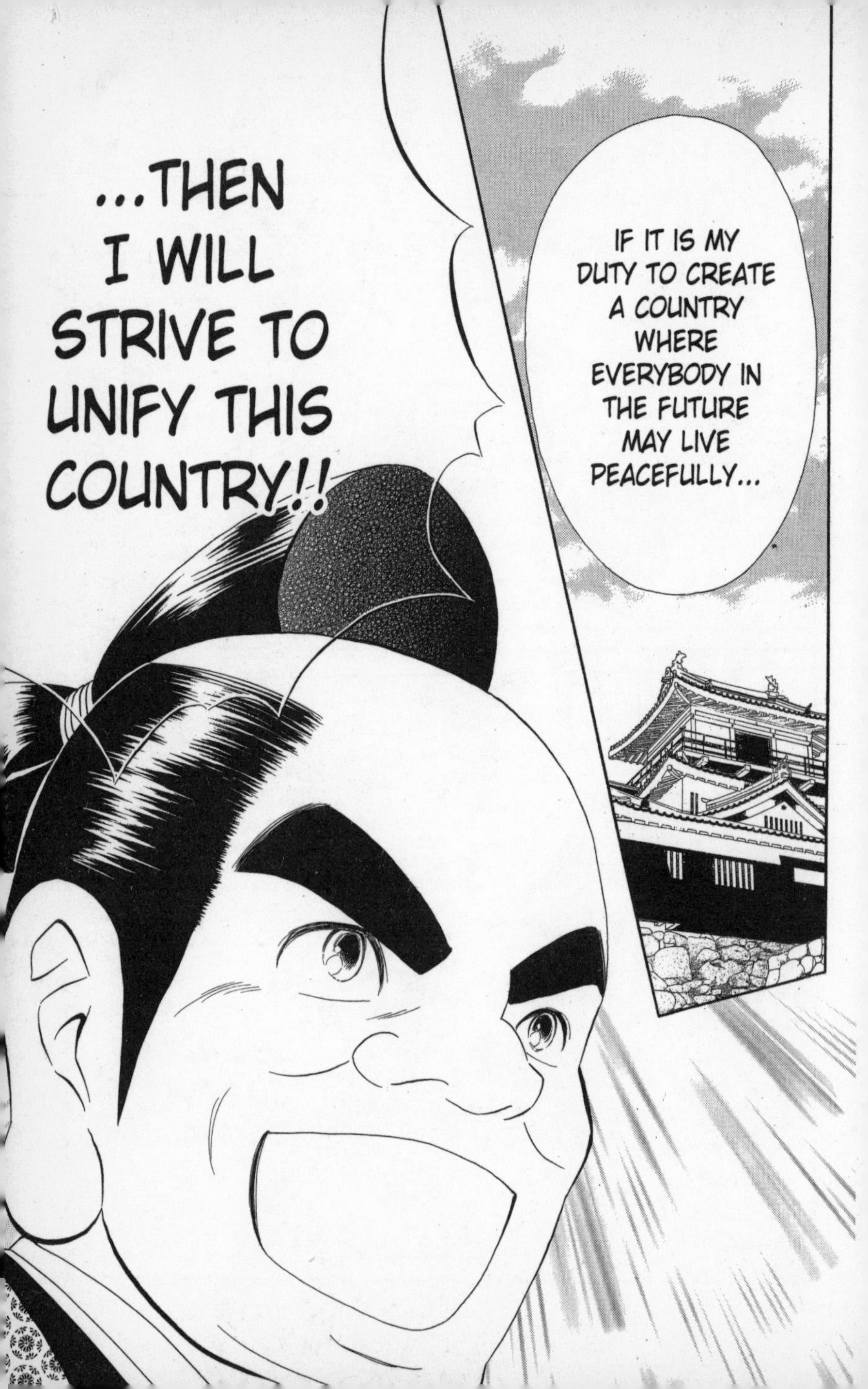
IF IT IS MY DUTY TO CREATE A COUNTRY WHERE EVERYBODY IN THE FUTURE MAY LIVE PEACEFULLY...
...THEN I WILL STRIVE TO UNIFY THIS COUNTRY!!

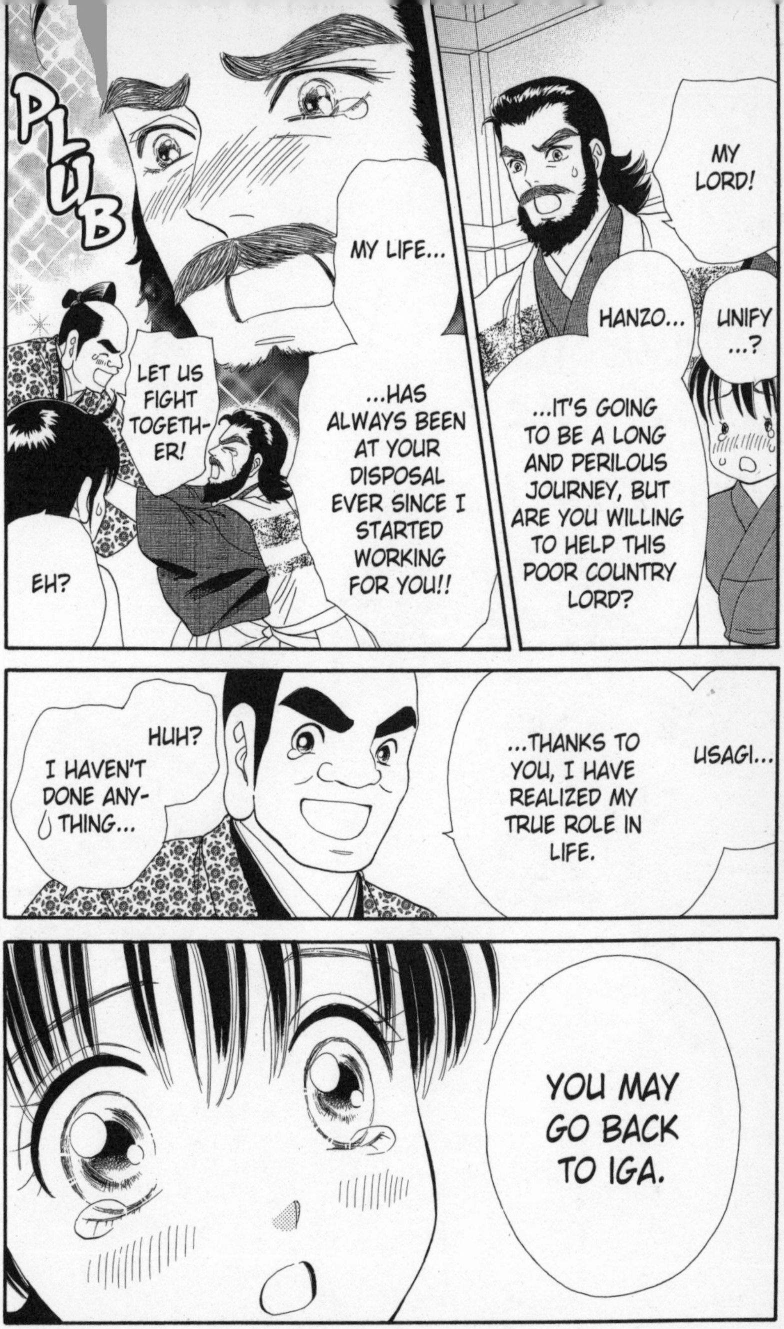
MY LORD!
UNIFY ...?
HANZO...
...IT'S GOING TO BE A LONG AND PERILOUS JOURNEY, BUT ARE YOU WILLING TO HELP THIS POOR COUNTRY LORD?
MY LIFE...
...HAS ALWAYS BEEN AT YOUR DISPOSAL EVER SINCE I STARTED WORKING FOR YOU!!
PLUB
LET US FIGHT TOGETH-ER!
EH?
USAGI...
...THANKS TO YOU, I HAVE REALIZED MY TRUE ROLE IN LIFE.
HUH?
I HAVEN'T DONE ANY-THING...
YOU MAY GO BACK TO IGA.

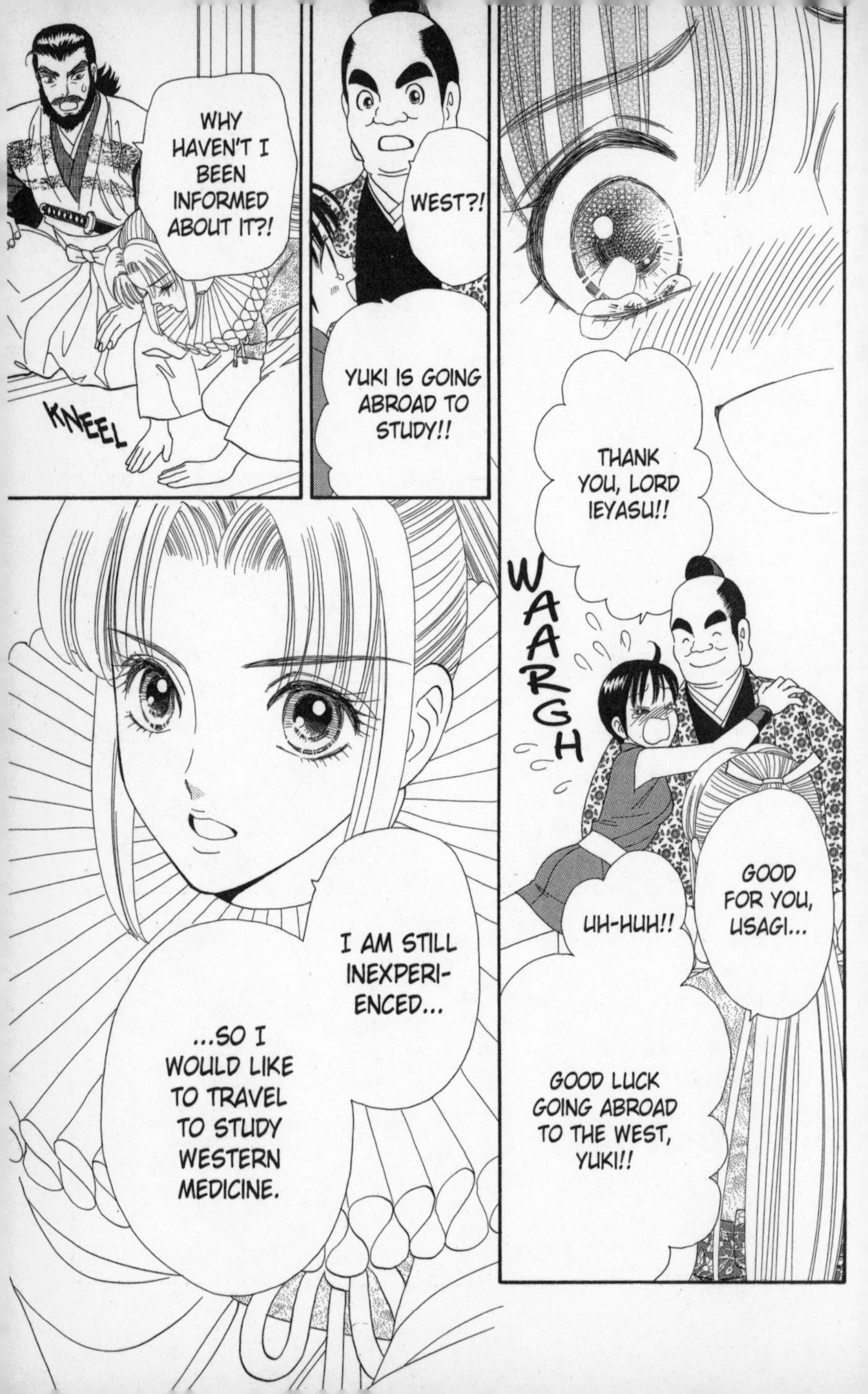
THANK YOU, LORD IEYASU!!
WAARGH
GOOD FOR YOU, USAGI...
UH-HUH!!
GOOD LUCK GOING ABROAD TO THE WEST, YUKI!!
WEST?!
YUKI IS GOING ABROAD TO STUDY!!
WHY HAVEN'T I BEEN INFORMED ABOUT IT?!
KNEEL
I AM STILL INEXPERIENCED...
...SO I WOULD LIKE TO TRAVEL TO STUDY WESTERN MEDICINE.

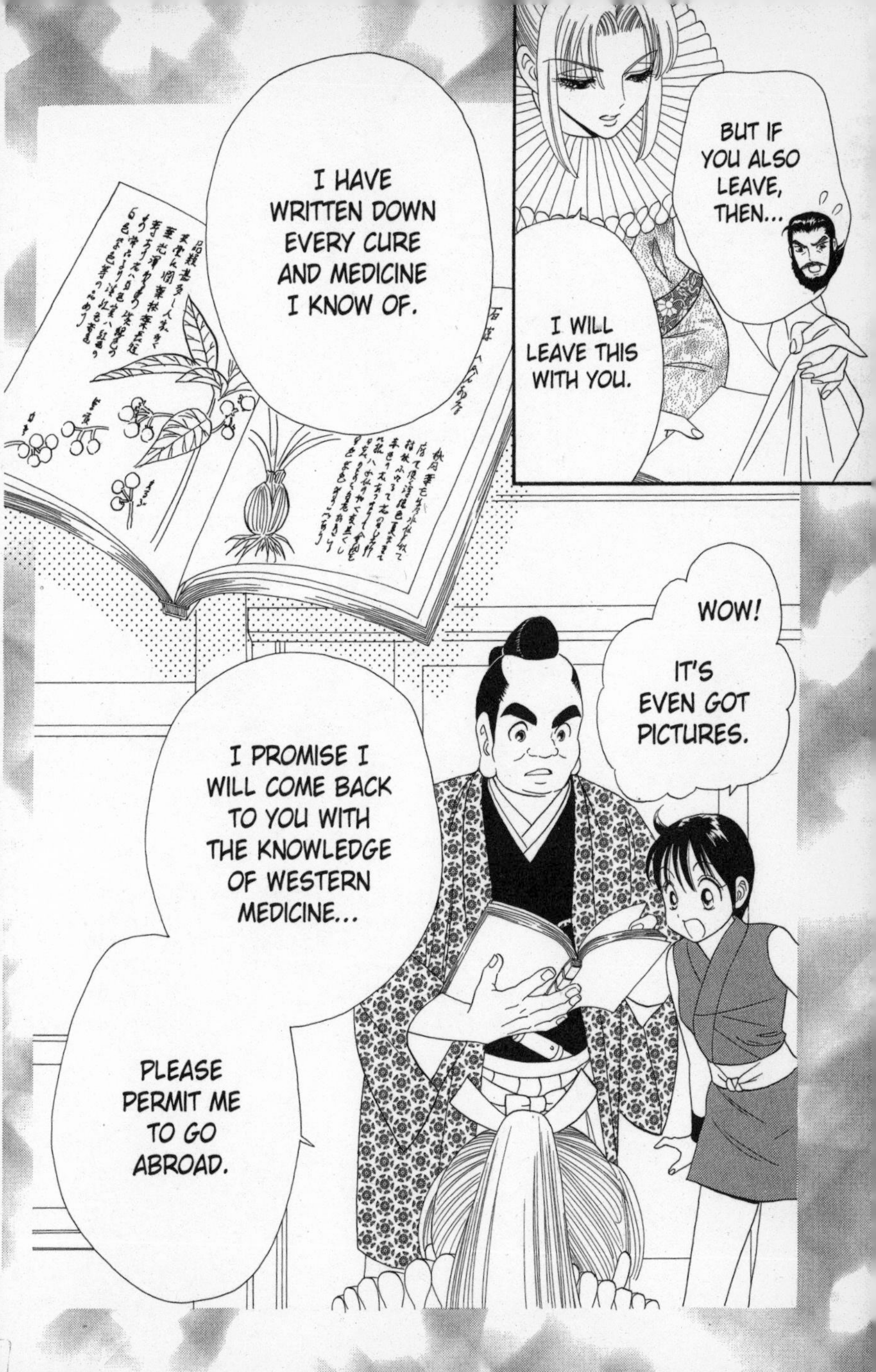
BUT IF YOU ALSO LEAVE, THEN...
I WILL LEAVE THIS WITH YOU.
I HAVE WRITTEN DOWN EVERY CURE AND MEDICINE I KNOW OF.
WOW!
IT'S EVEN GOT PICTURES.
I PROMISE I WILL COME BACK TO YOU WITH THE KNOWLEDGE OF WESTERN MEDICINE...
PLEASE PERMIT ME TO GO ABROAD.

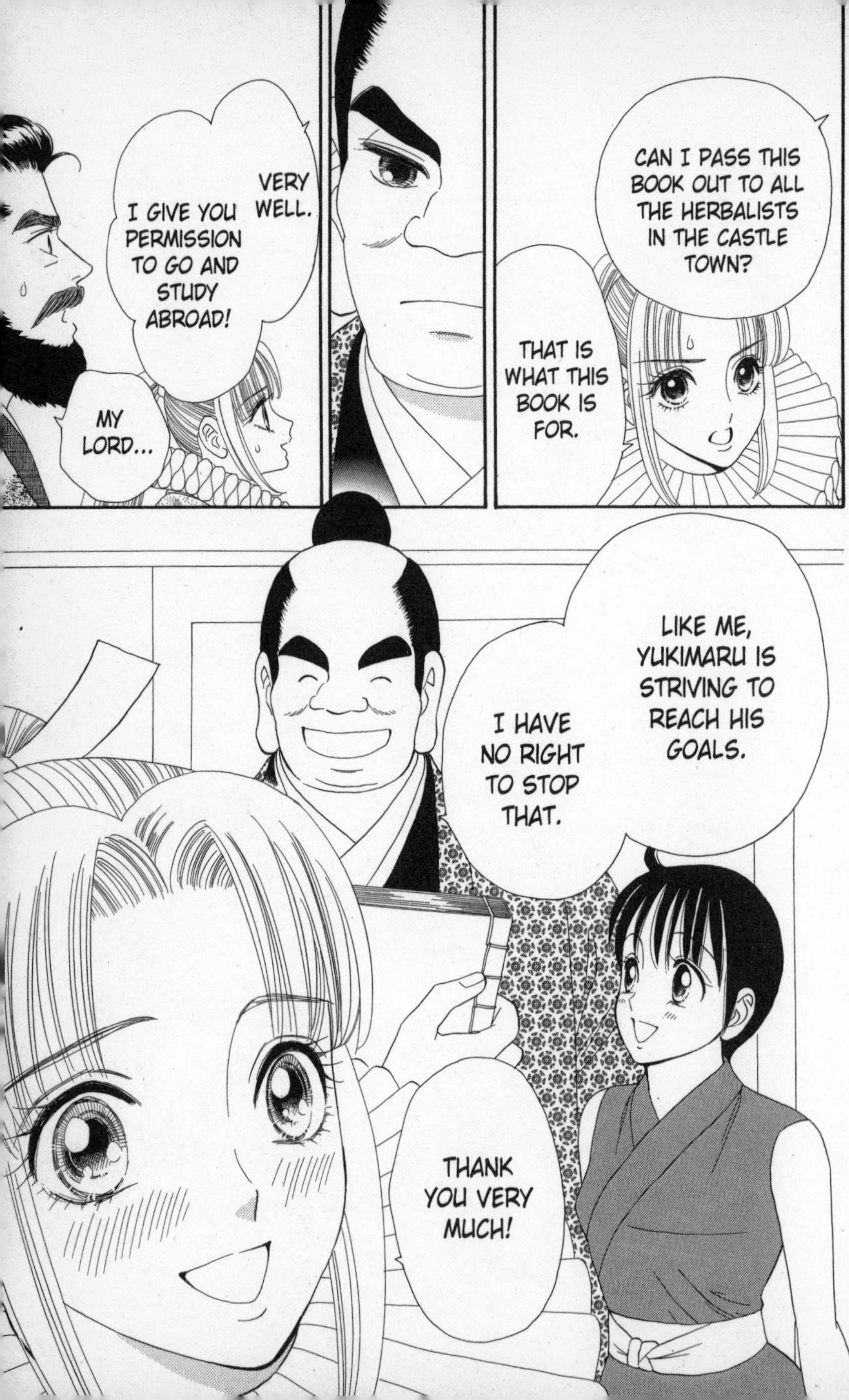
CAN I PASS THIS BOOK OUT TO ALL THE HERBALISTS IN THE CASTLE TOWN?
THAT IS WHAT THIS BOOK IS FOR.
VERY WELL.
I GIVE YOU PERMISSION TO GO AND STUDY ABROAD!
MY LORD...
LIKE ME, YUKIMARU IS STRIVING TO REACH HIS GOALS.
I HAVE NO RIGHT TO STOP THAT.
THANK YOU VERY MUCH!

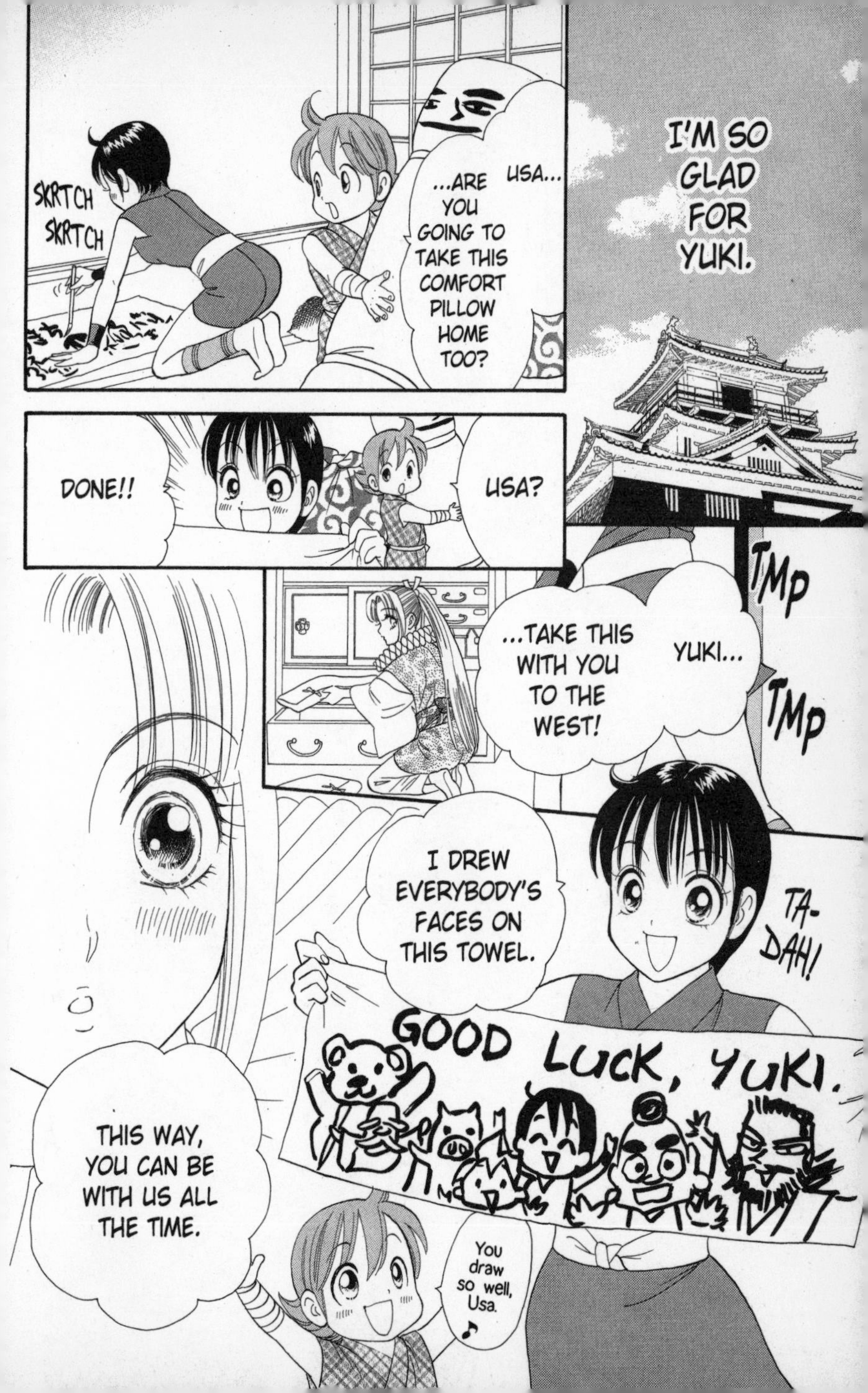
I'M SO GLAD FOR YUKI.
USA...
...ARE YOU GOING TO TAKE THIS COMFORT PILLOW HOME TOO?
SKRTCH SKRTCH
USA?
DONE!!
TMP TMP
YUKI...
...TAKE THIS WITH YOU TO THE WEST!
TA-DAH!
I DREW EVERYBODY'S FACES ON THIS TOWEL.
GOOD LUCK, YUKI.
THIS WAY, YOU CAN BE WITH US ALL THE TIME.
You draw so well, Usa. ♪

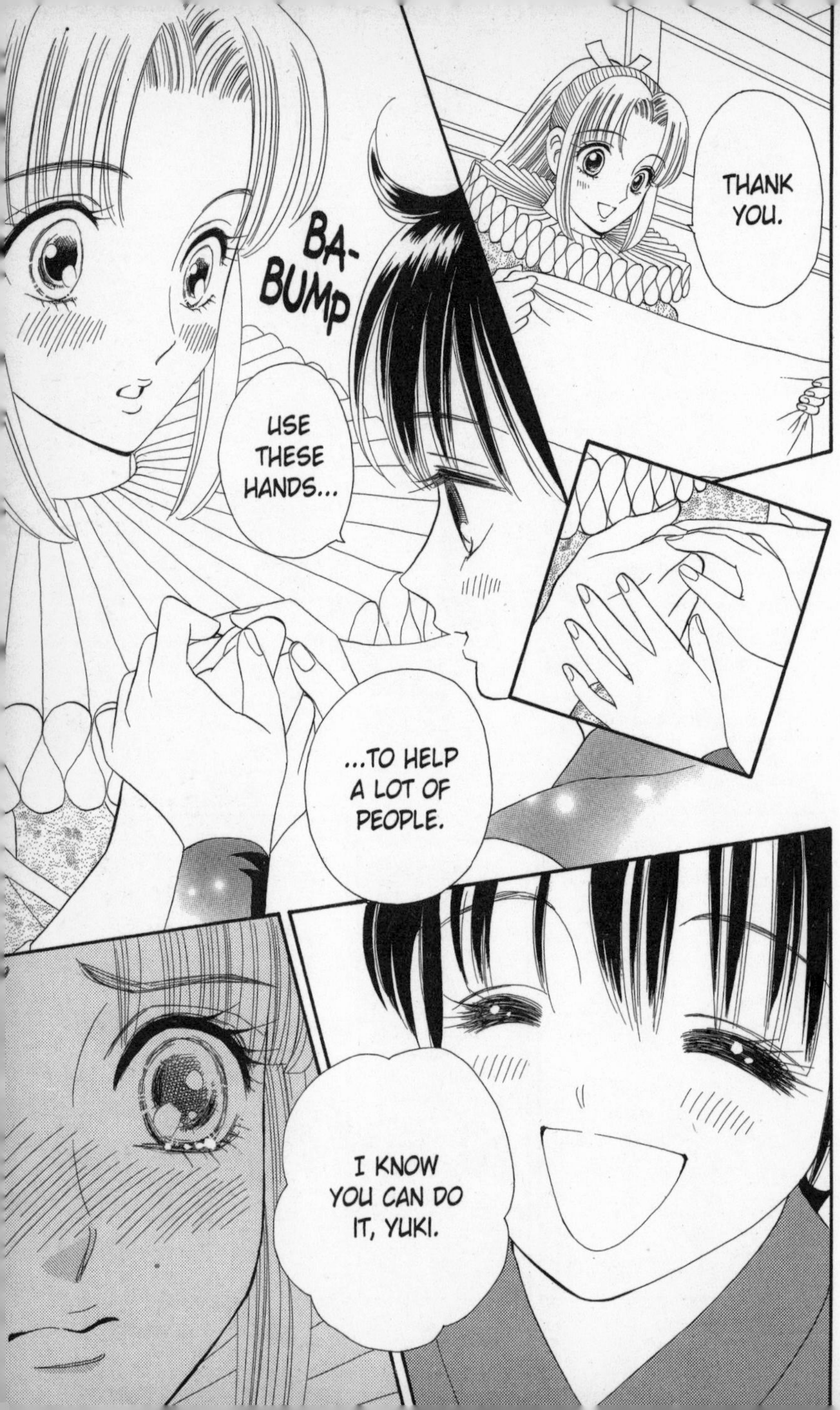
THANK YOU.
BA-BUMP
USE THESE HANDS...
...TO HELP A LOT OF PEOPLE.
I KNOW YOU CAN DO IT, YUKI.

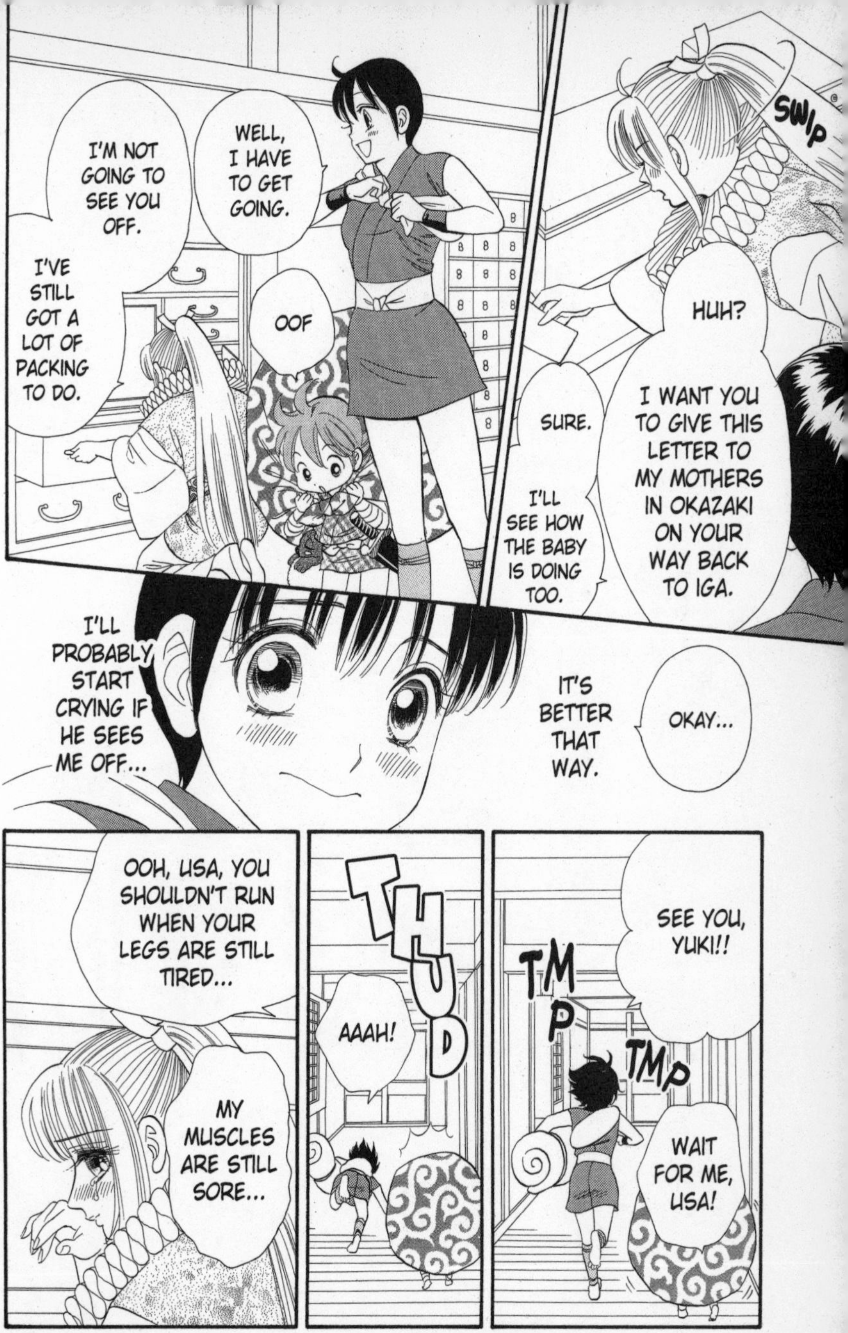
SWIP
HUH?
I WANT YOU TO GIVE THIS LETTER TO MY MOTHERS IN OKAZAKI ON YOUR WAY BACK TO IGA.
SURE.
I'LL SEE HOW THE BABY IS DOING TOO.
WELL, I HAVE TO GET GOING.
I'M NOT GOING TO SEE YOU OFF.
I'VE STILL GOT A LOT OF PACKING TO DO.
OOF
OKAY...
IT'S BETTER THAT WAY.
I'LL PROBABLY START CRYING IF HE SEES ME OFF...
SEE YOU, YUKI!!
TMP
TMP
WAIT FOR ME, USA!
THUD
AAAH!
OOH, USA, YOU SHOULDN'T RUN WHEN YOUR LEGS ARE STILL TIRED...
MY MUSCLES ARE STILL SORE...

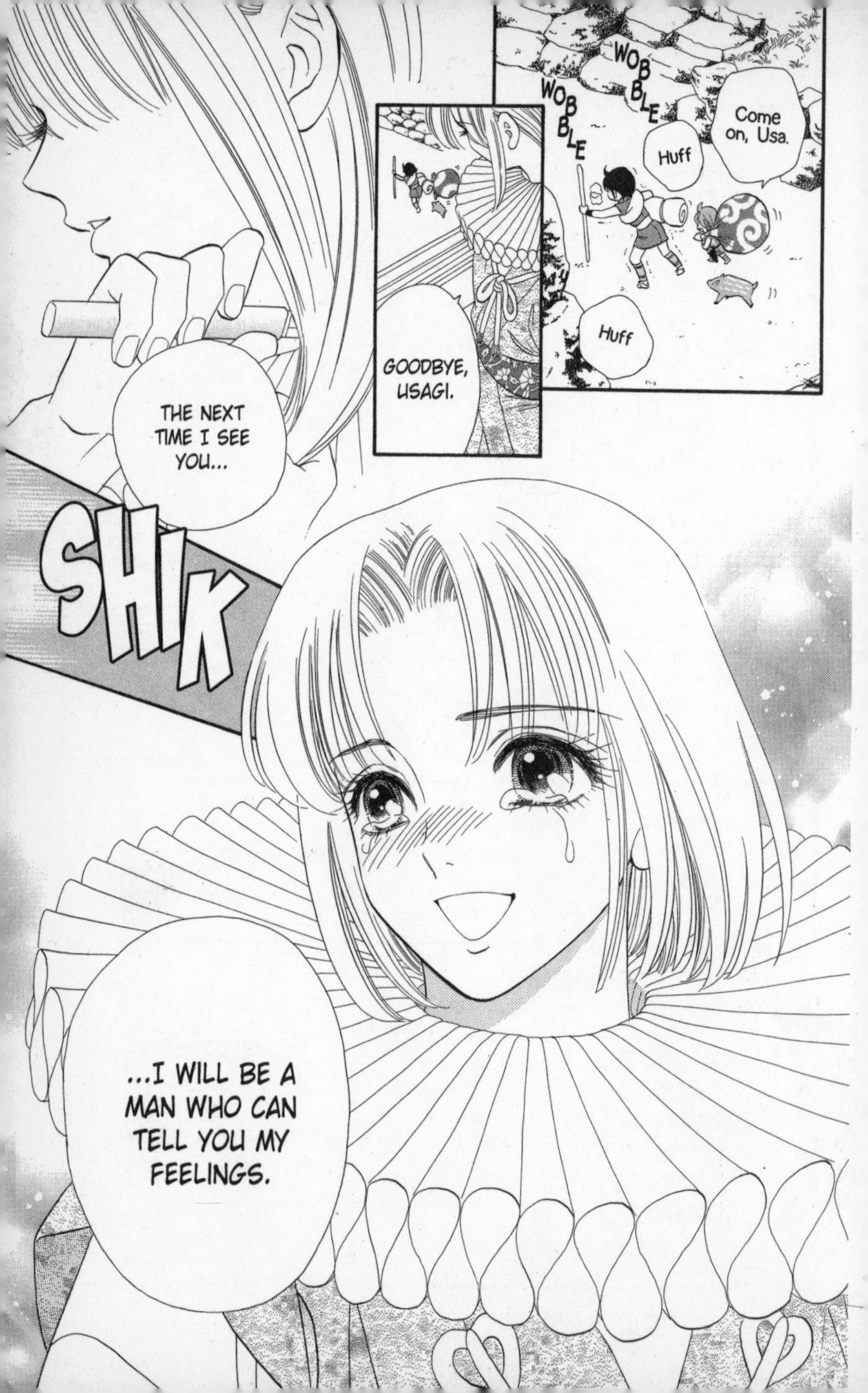
Come on, Usa.
WOBBLE
WOBBLE
Huff
Huff
GOODBYE, USAGI.
THE NEXT TIME I SEE YOU...
SHIK
...I WILL BE A MAN WHO CAN TELL YOU MY FEELINGS.

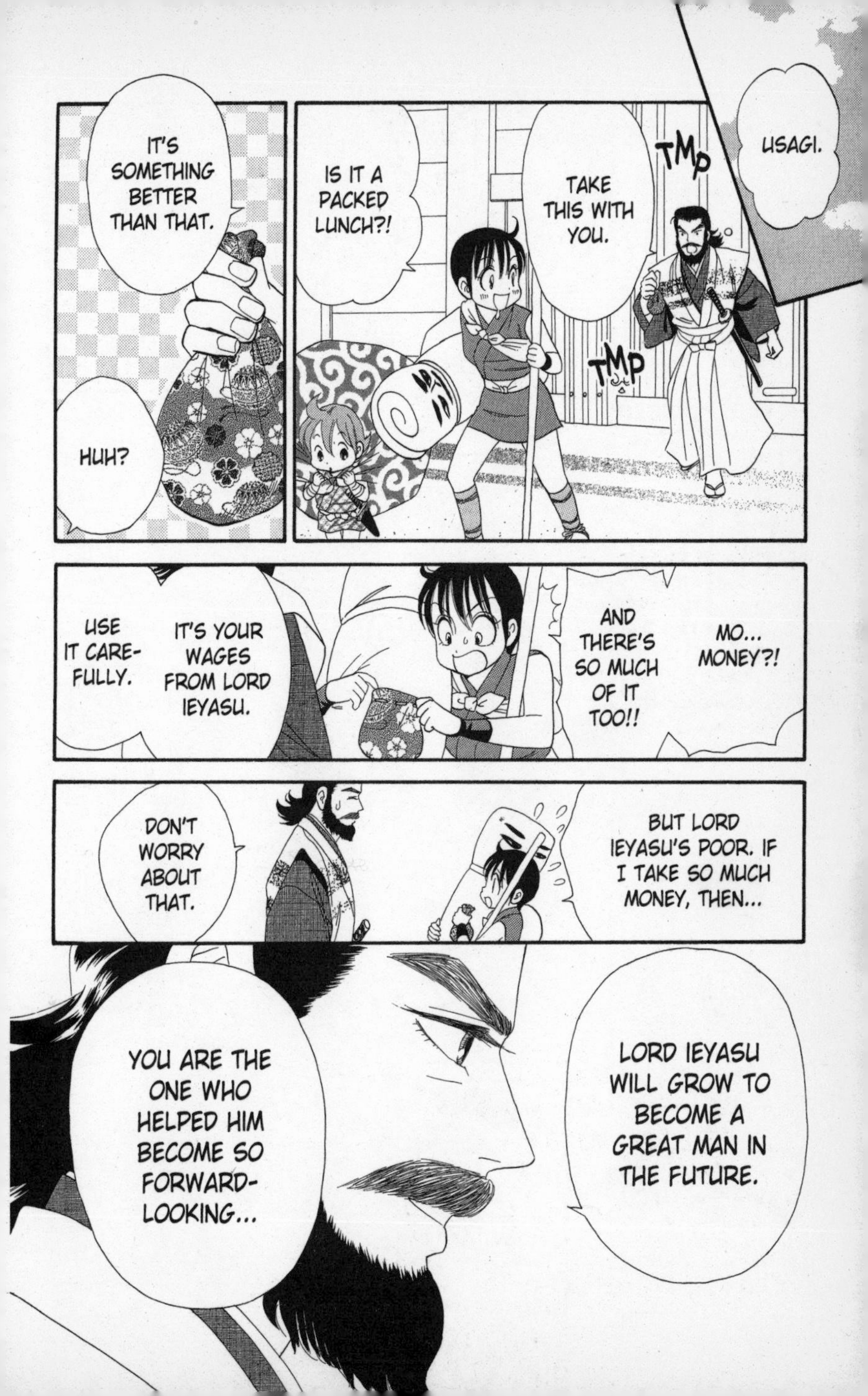
USAGI.
TMP
TAKE THIS WITH YOU.
TMP
IS IT A PACKED LUNCH?!
IT'S SOMETHING BETTER THAN THAT.
HUH?
MO... MONEY?!
AND THERE'S SO MUCH OF IT TOO!!
IT'S YOUR WAGES FROM LORD IEYASU.
USE IT CAREFULLY.
BUT LORD IEYASU'S POOR. IF I TAKE SO MUCH MONEY, THEN...
DON'T WORRY ABOUT THAT.
LORD IEYASU WILL GROW TO BECOME A GREAT MAN IN THE FUTURE.
YOU ARE THE ONE WHO HELPED HIM BECOME SO FORWARD-LOOKING...

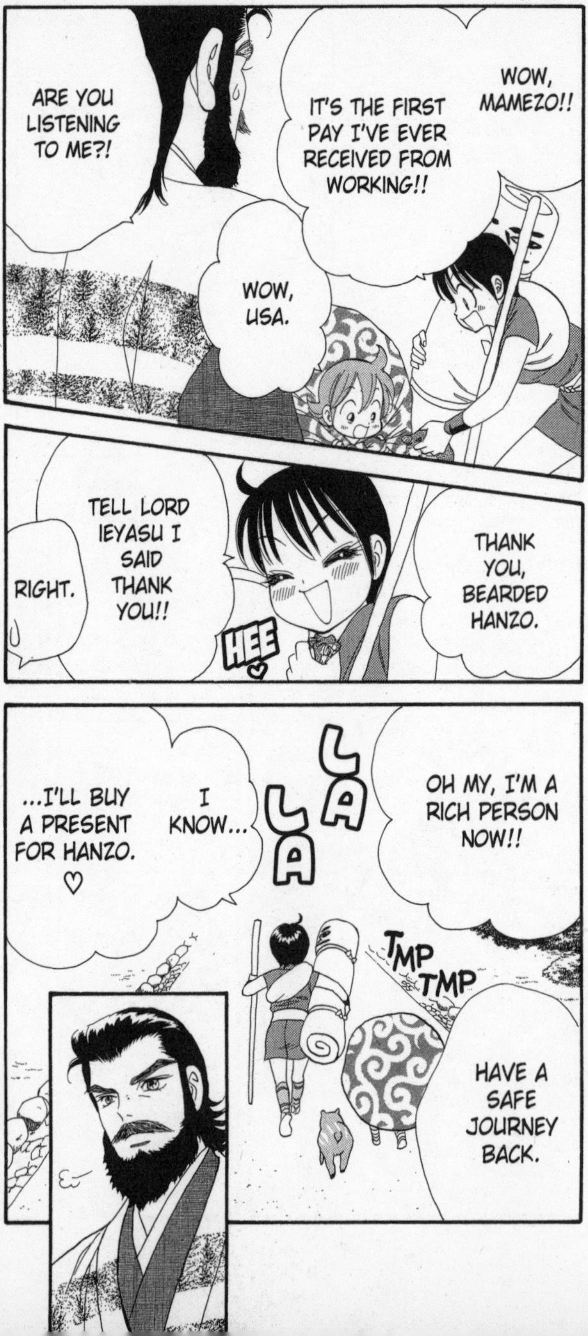
WOW, MAMEZO!!
IT'S THE FIRST PAY I'VE EVER RECEIVED FROM WORKING!!
WOW, USA.
ARE YOU LISTENING TO ME?!
THANK YOU, BEARDED HANZO.
HEE ♡
TELL LORD IEYASU I SAID THANK YOU!!
RIGHT.
OH MY, I'M A RICH PERSON NOW!!
LA LA
I KNOW...
...I'LL BUY A PRESENT FOR HANZO. ♡
TMP TMP
HAVE A SAFE JOURNEY BACK.

Stories About My Research Trip #3

The Kouga-ryu Ninjutsu House was filled with secret revolving doors, pitfalls, and secret passages. Just imagining that this was all part of daily life was a blast back to the Warring States Era!

Even more, the lady had me climb up to the suspended ceiling, revolve around the revolving door, and climb up a hidden ladder. I felt like I was fully immersed in the ninja experience!♪

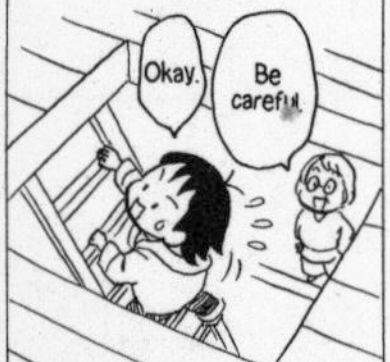
Okay.
Be careful.

The floor of the corridor came up to reveal a hidden well!!

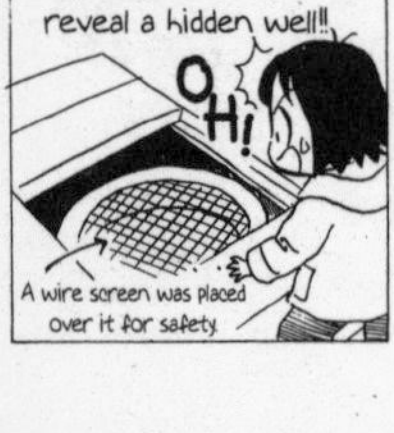
OH!
A wire screen was placed over it for safety.

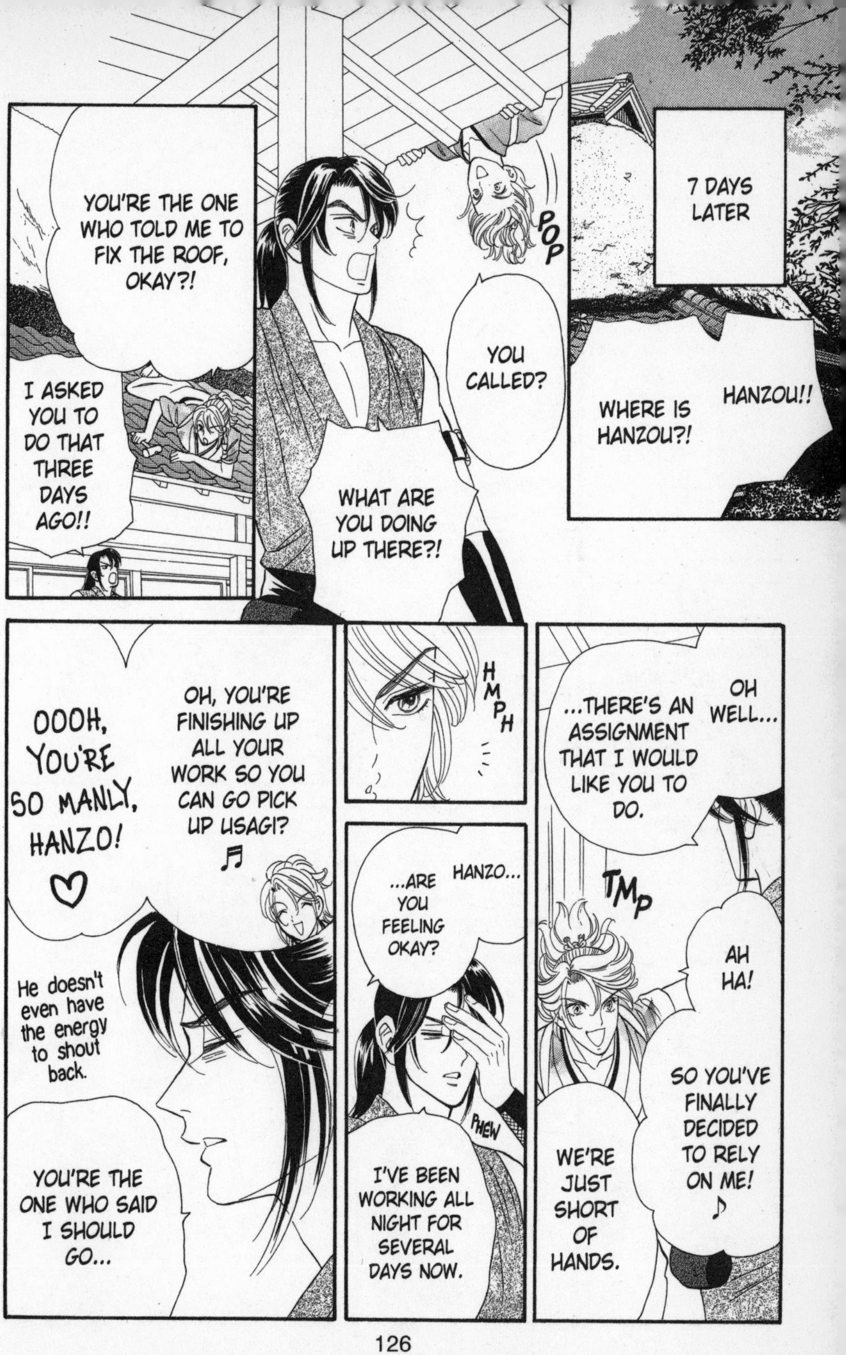
7 DAYS LATER
HANZOU!!
WHERE IS HANZOU?!
POP
YOU CALLED?
WHAT ARE YOU DOING UP THERE?!
YOU'RE THE ONE WHO TOLD ME TO FIX THE ROOF, OKAY?!
I ASKED YOU TO DO THAT THREE DAYS AGO!!
OH WELL...
...THERE'S AN ASSIGNMENT THAT I WOULD LIKE YOU TO DO.
TMP
AH HA!
SO YOU'VE FINALLY DECIDED TO RELY ON ME! ♪
WE'RE JUST SHORT OF HANDS.
HMPH
HANZO...
...ARE YOU FEELING OKAY?
PHEW
I'VE BEEN WORKING ALL NIGHT FOR SEVERAL DAYS NOW.
OH, YOU'RE FINISHING UP ALL YOUR WORK SO YOU CAN GO PICK UP USAGI? ♬
OOOH, YOU'RE SO MANLY, HANZO! ♡
He doesn't even have the energy to shout back.
YOU'RE THE ONE WHO SAID I SHOULD GO...

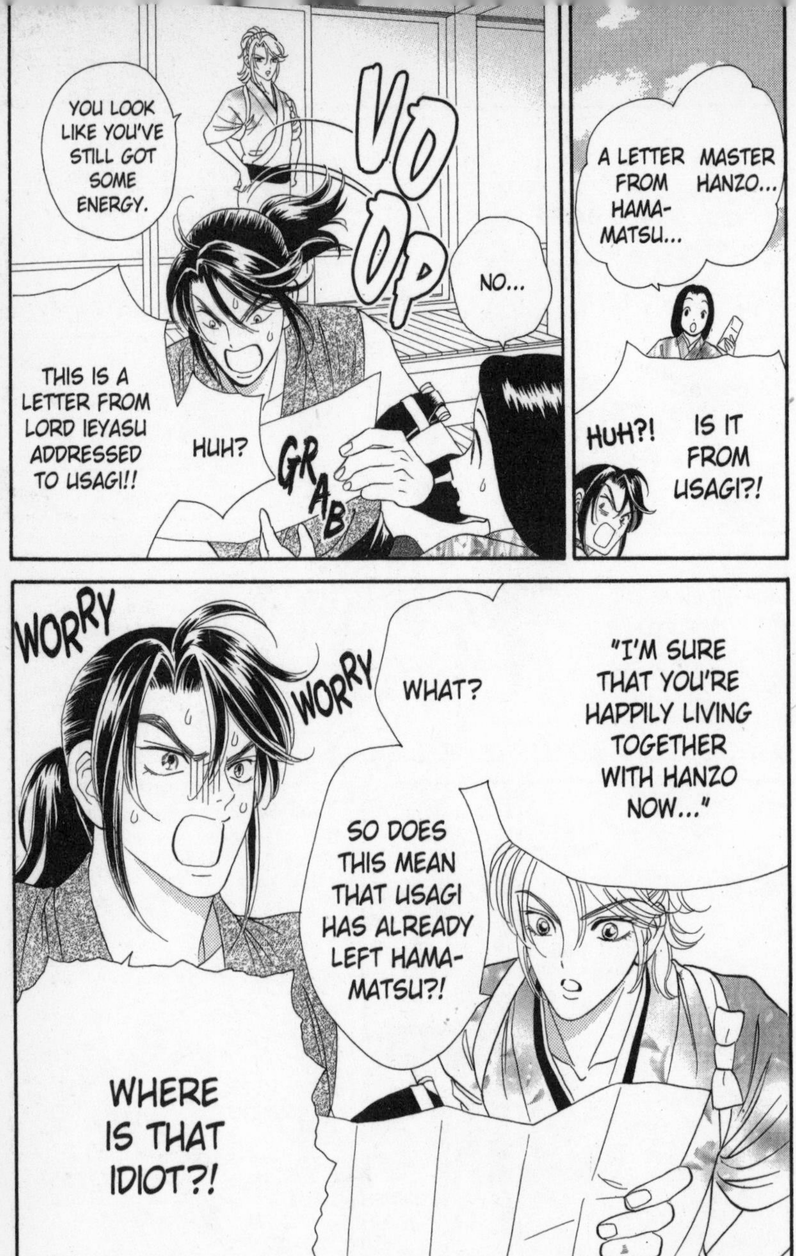
MASTER HANZO...
A LETTER FROM HAMA-MATSU...
IS IT FROM USAGI?!
HUH?!
NO...
VOOP
YOU LOOK LIKE YOU'VE STILL GOT SOME ENERGY.
HUH?
GRAB
THIS IS A LETTER FROM LORD IEYASU ADDRESSED TO USAGI!!
"I'M SURE THAT YOU'RE HAPPILY LIVING TOGETHER WITH HANZO NOW..."
WHAT?
WORRY
WORRY
SO DOES THIS MEAN THAT USAGI HAS ALREADY LEFT HAMA-MATSU?!
WHERE IS THAT IDIOT?!

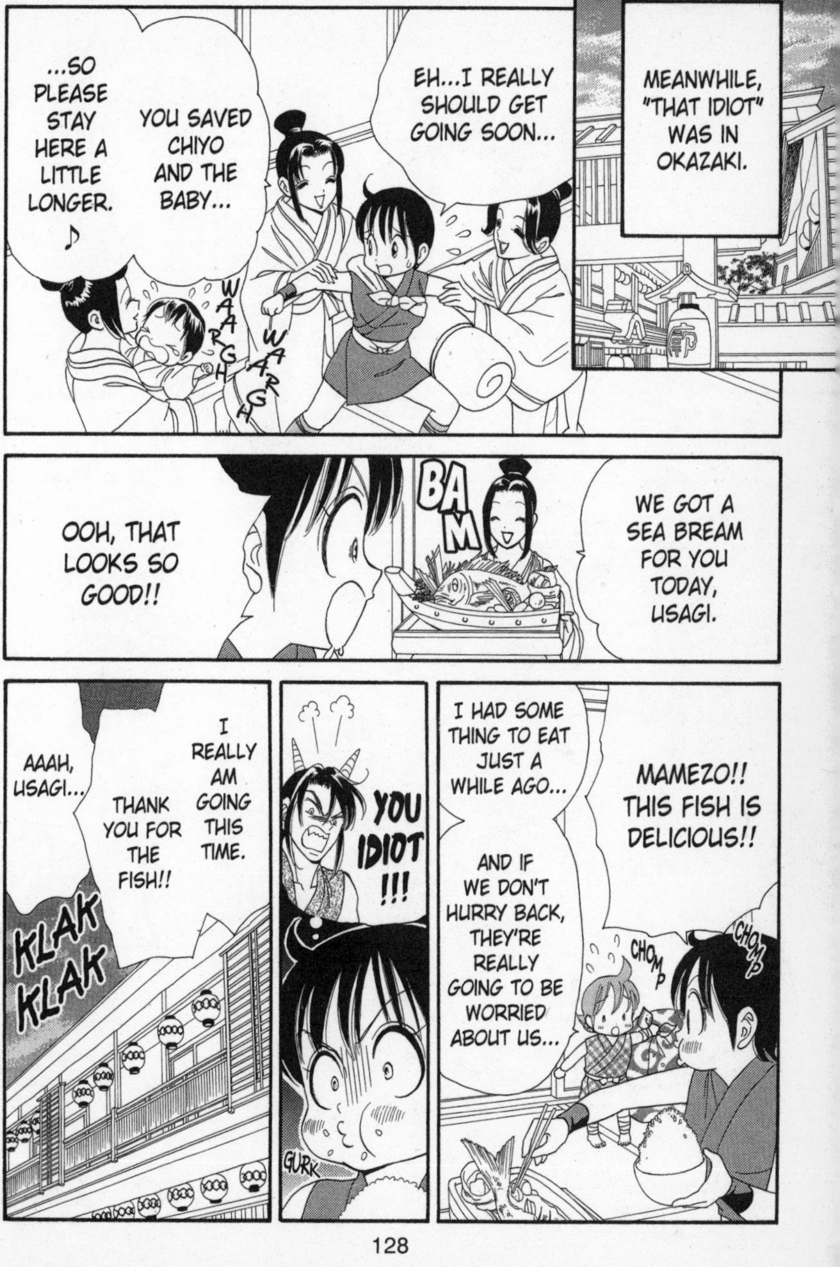
MEANWHILE, "THAT IDIOT" WAS IN OKAZAKI.
EH...I REALLY SHOULD GET GOING SOON...
YOU SAVED CHIYO AND THE BABY...
...SO PLEASE STAY HERE A LITTLE LONGER. ♪
WAARGH
WAARGH
WE GOT A SEA BREAM FOR YOU TODAY, USAGI.
BAM
OOH, THAT LOOKS SO GOOD!!
MAMEZO!! THIS FISH IS DELICIOUS!!
CHOMP
CHOMP
I HAD SOME THING TO EAT JUST A WHILE AGO...
AND IF WE DON'T HURRY BACK, THEY'RE REALLY GOING TO BE WORRIED ABOUT US...
YOU IDIOT!!!
GURK
I REALLY AM GOING THIS TIME.
THANK YOU FOR THE FISH!!
AAAH, USAGI...
KLAK KLAK

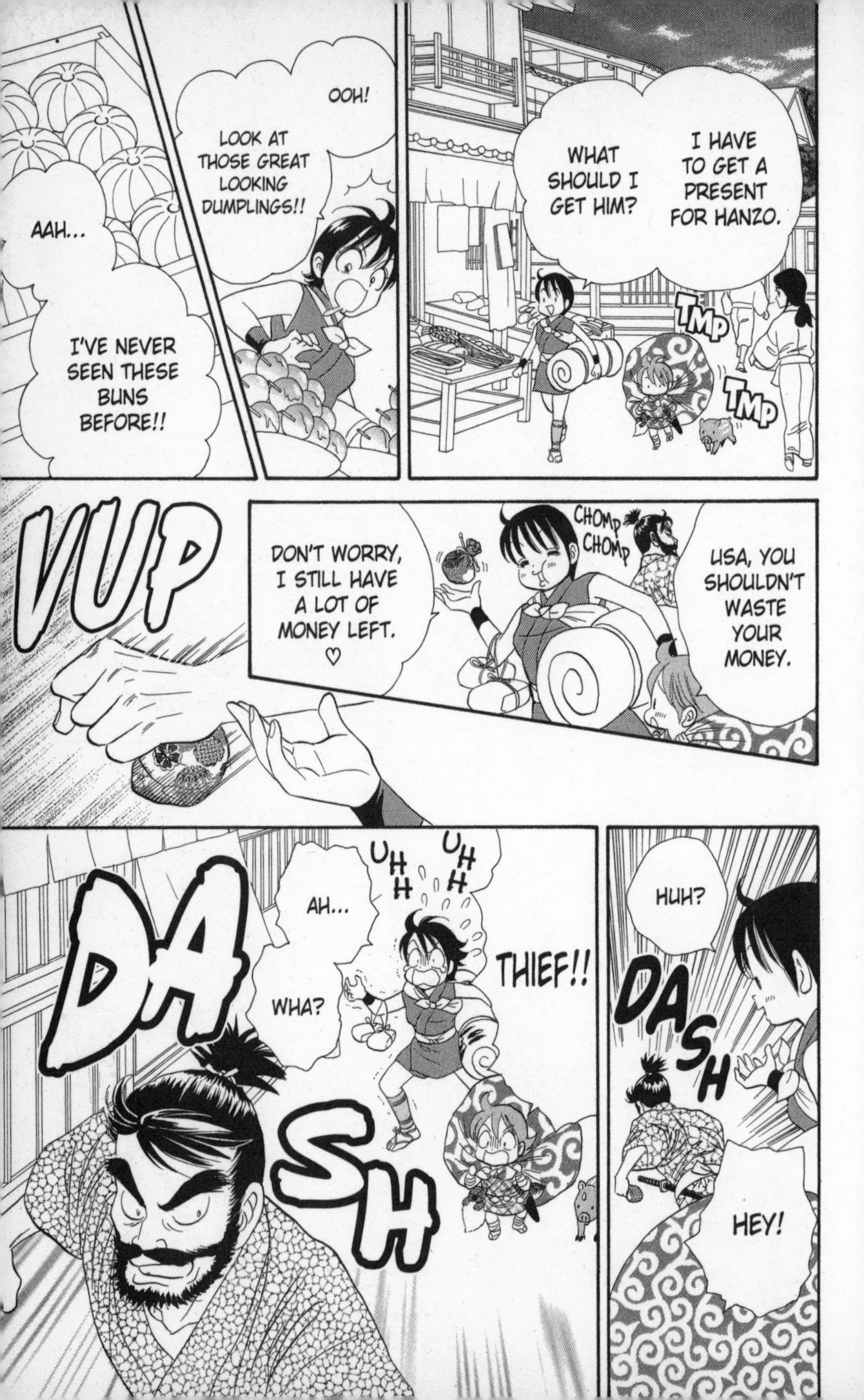
I HAVE TO GET A PRESENT FOR HANZO.
WHAT SHOULD I GET HIM?
TMP
TMP
OOH!
LOOK AT THOSE GREAT LOOKING DUMPLINGS!!
AAH...
I'VE NEVER SEEN THESE BUNS BEFORE!!
CHOMP CHOMP
USA, YOU SHOULDN'T WASTE YOUR MONEY.
DON'T WORRY, I STILL HAVE A LOT OF MONEY LEFT. ♡
VUP
HUH?
DASH
HEY!
UHH UHH
THIEF!!
AH...
WHA?
DASH

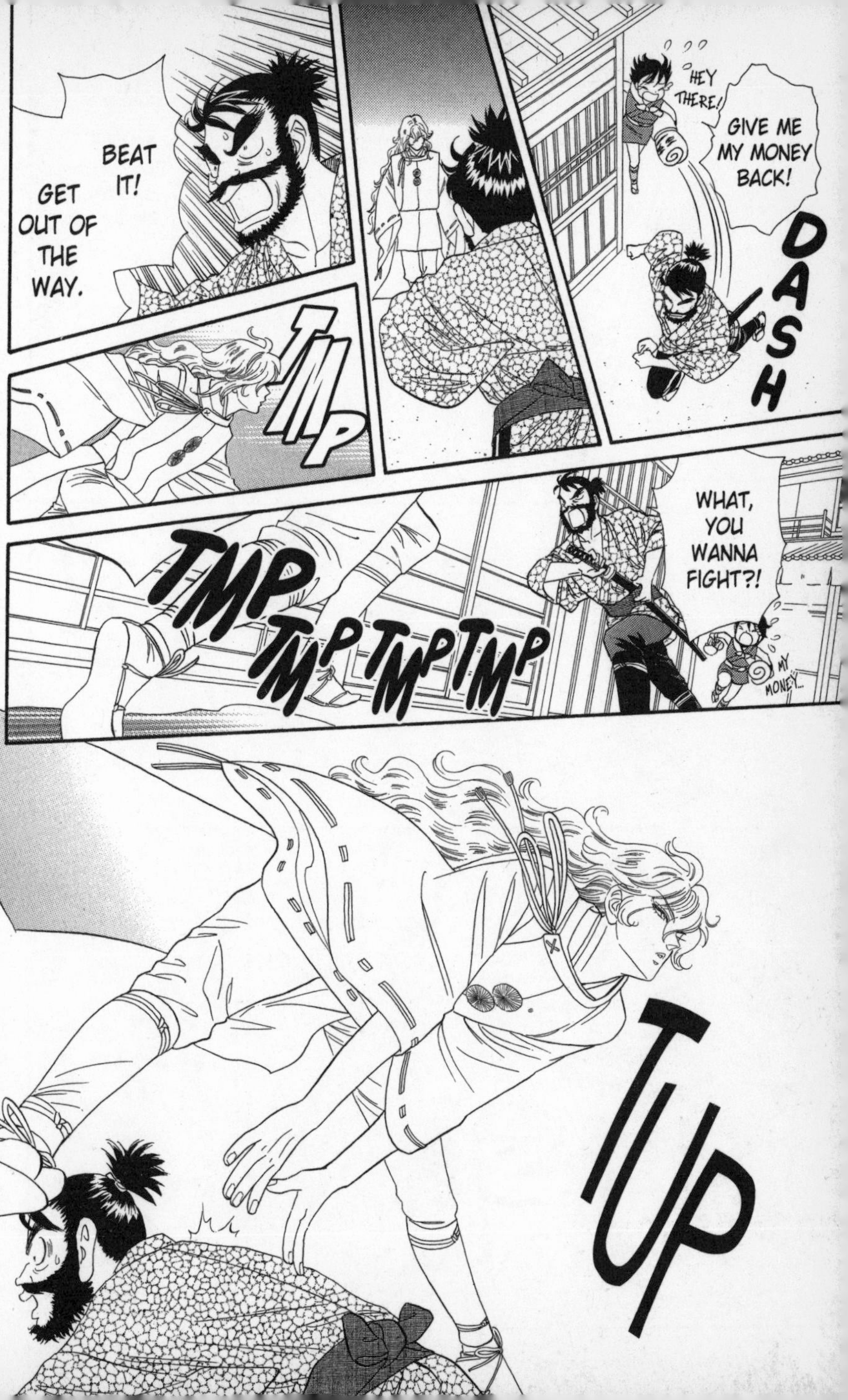
HEY THERE!
GIVE ME MY MONEY BACK!
DASH
BEAT IT!
GET OUT OF THE WAY.
TMP
WHAT, YOU WANNA FIGHT?!
MY MONEY...
TMP TMP TMP TMP
TUP

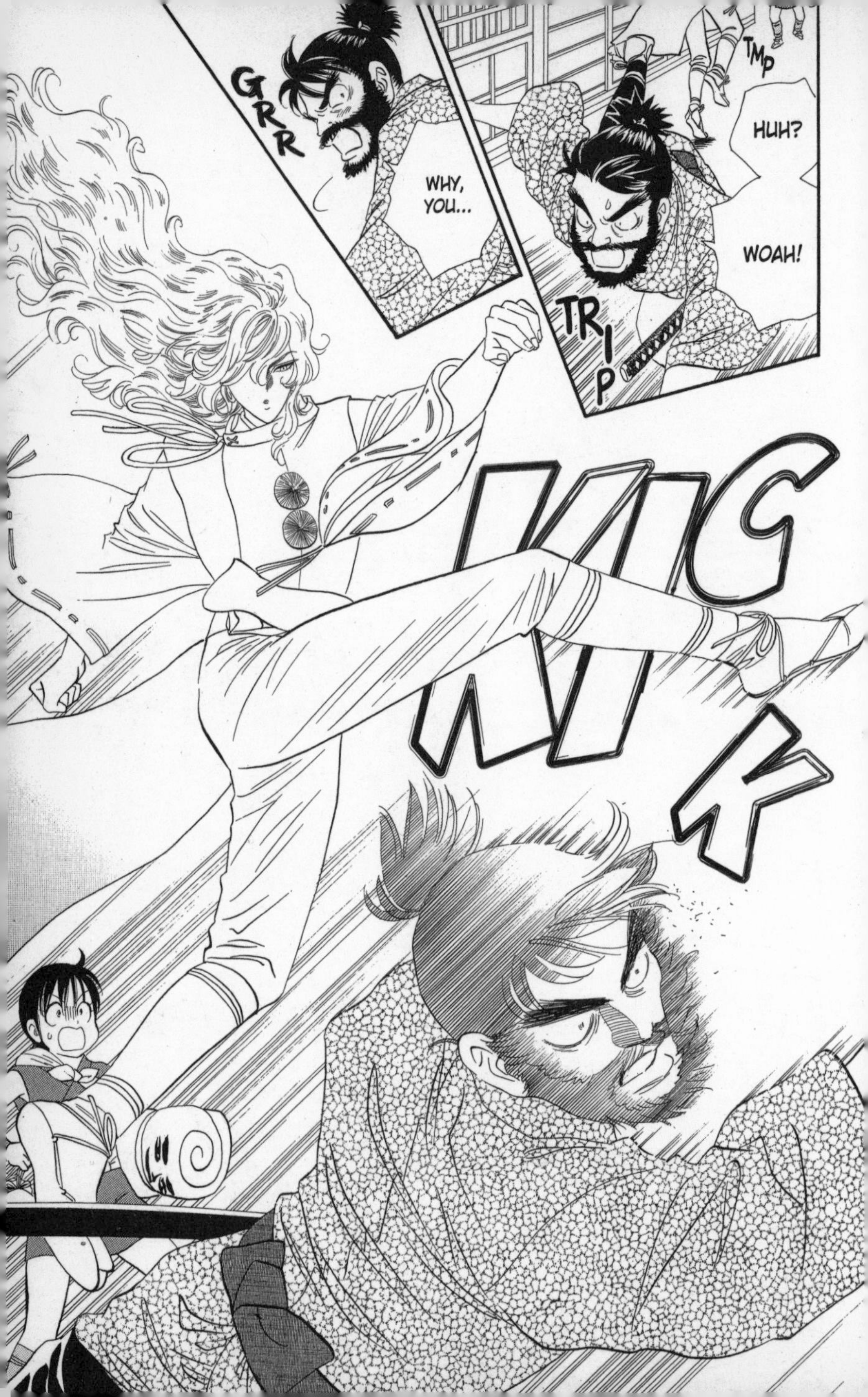
TMP
HUH?
WOAH!
TRIP
GRR
WHY, YOU...
KICK

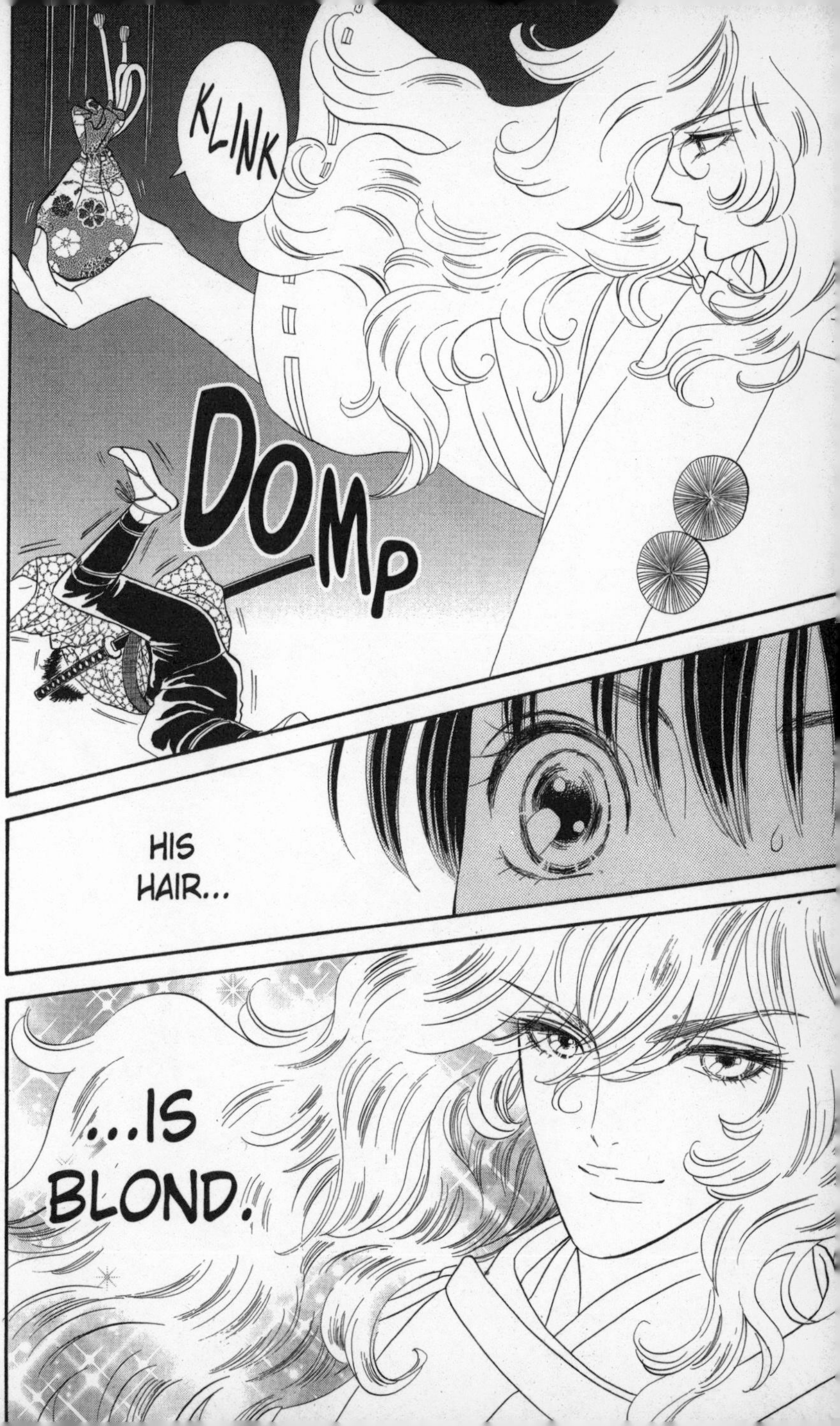
KLINK
DOMP
HIS HAIR...
...IS BLOND.

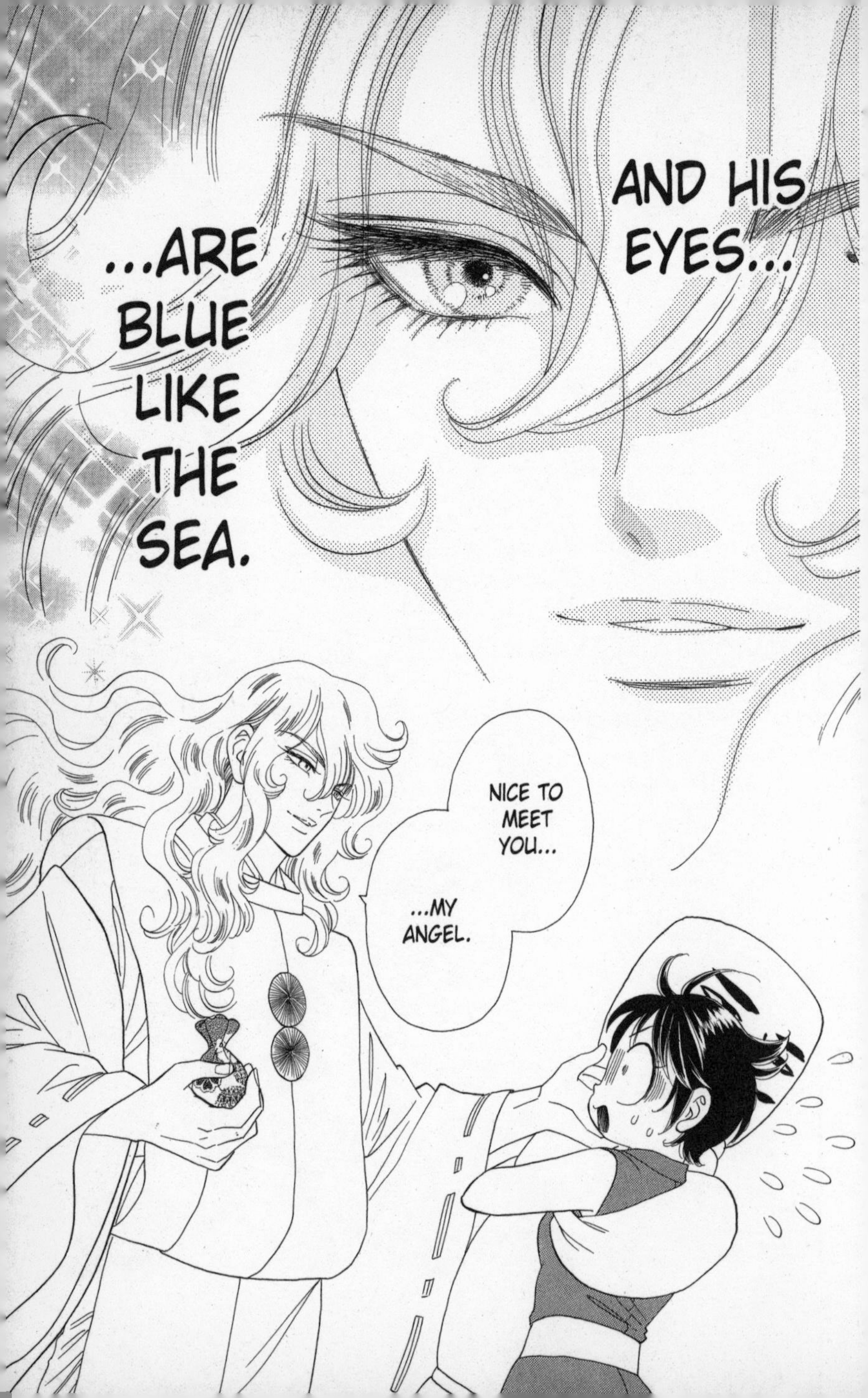
AND HIS EYES...
...ARE BLUE LIKE THE SEA.
NICE TO MEET YOU...
...MY ANGEL.

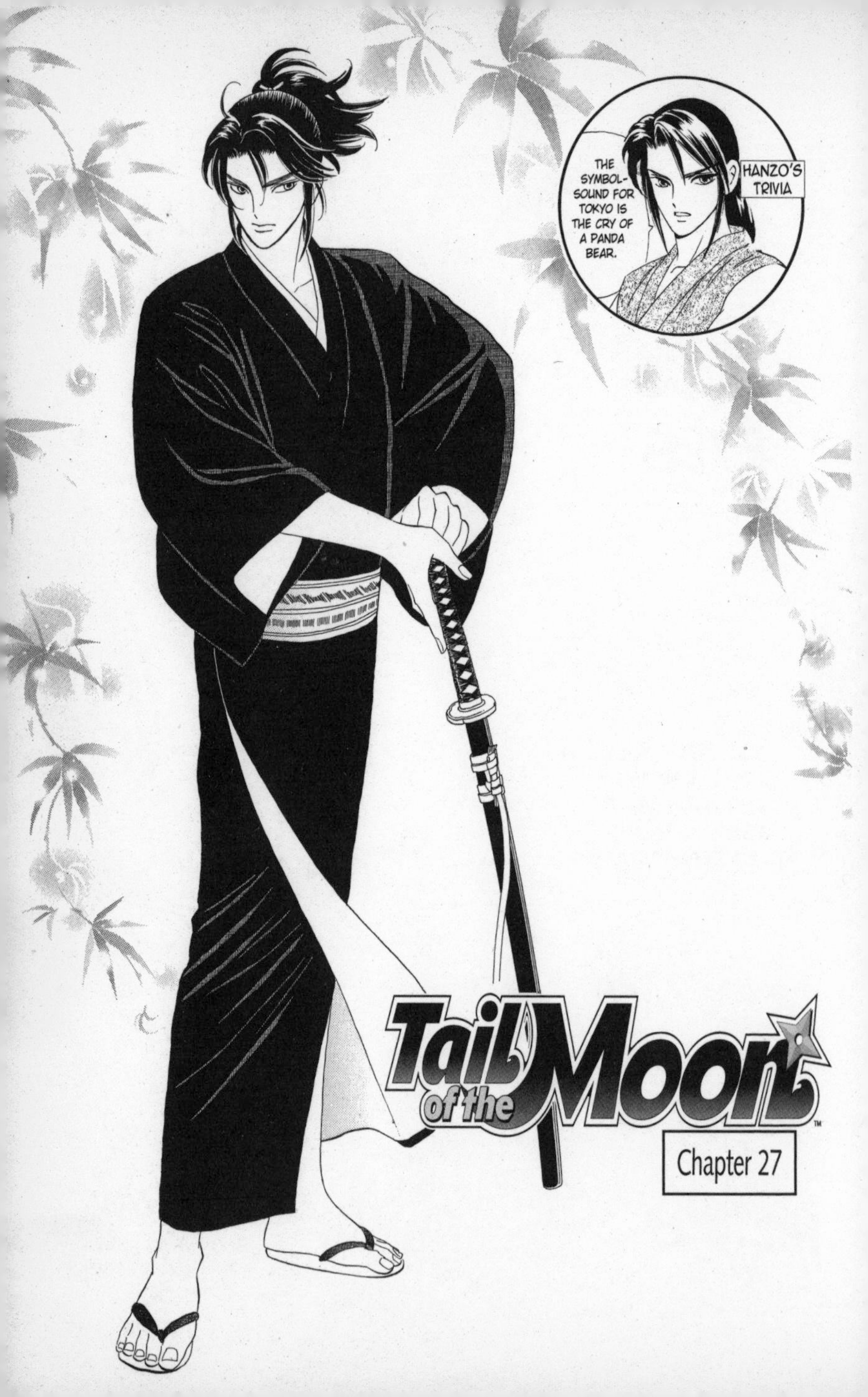
HANZO'S TRIVIA
THE SYMBOL-SOUND FOR TOKYO IS THE CRY OF A PANDA BEAR.
Tail of the Moon™
Chapter 27

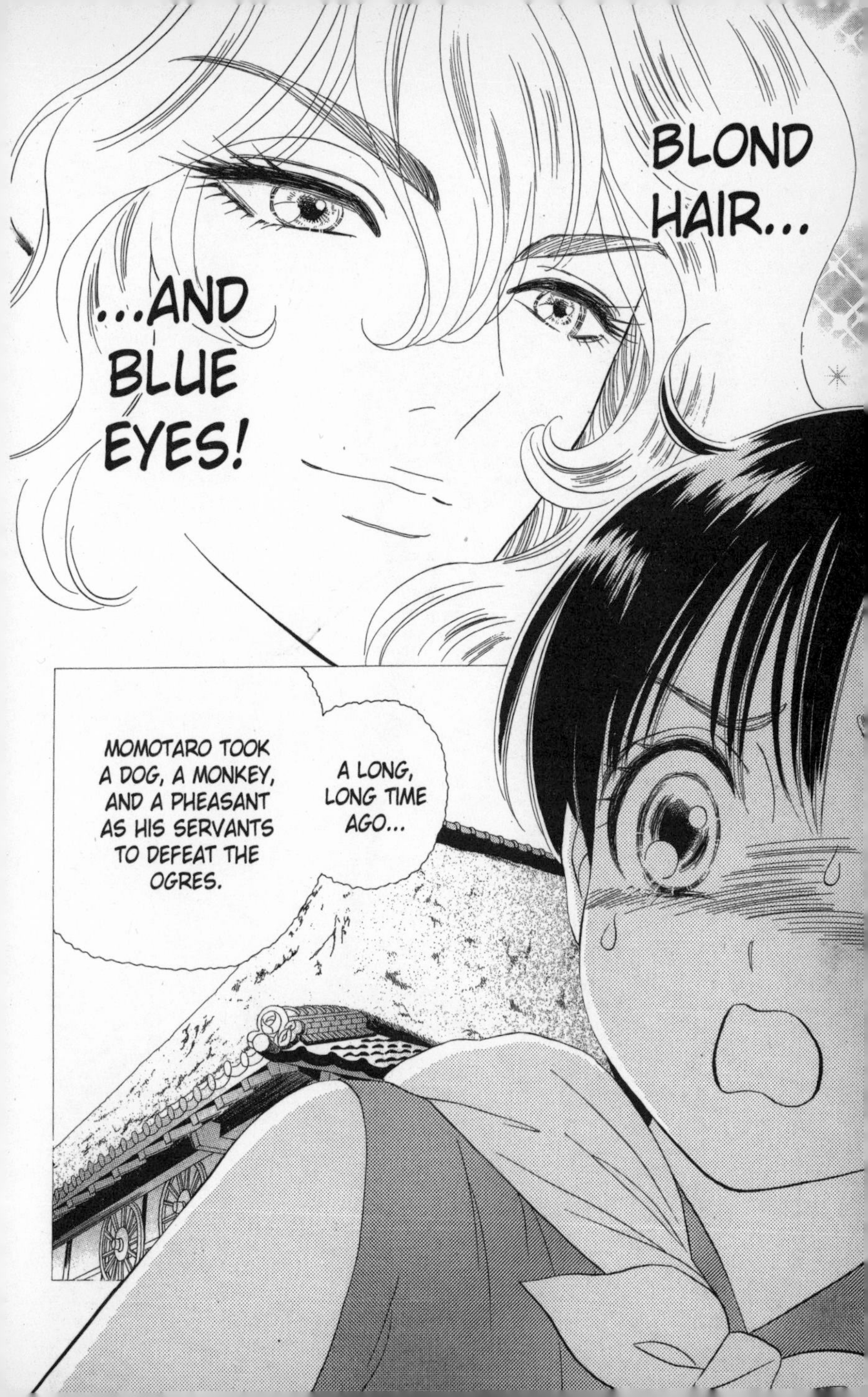
BLOND HAIR...
...AND BLUE EYES!
A LONG, LONG TIME AGO...
MOMOTARO TOOK A DOG, A MONKEY, AND A PHEASANT AS HIS SERVANTS TO DEFEAT THE OGRES.

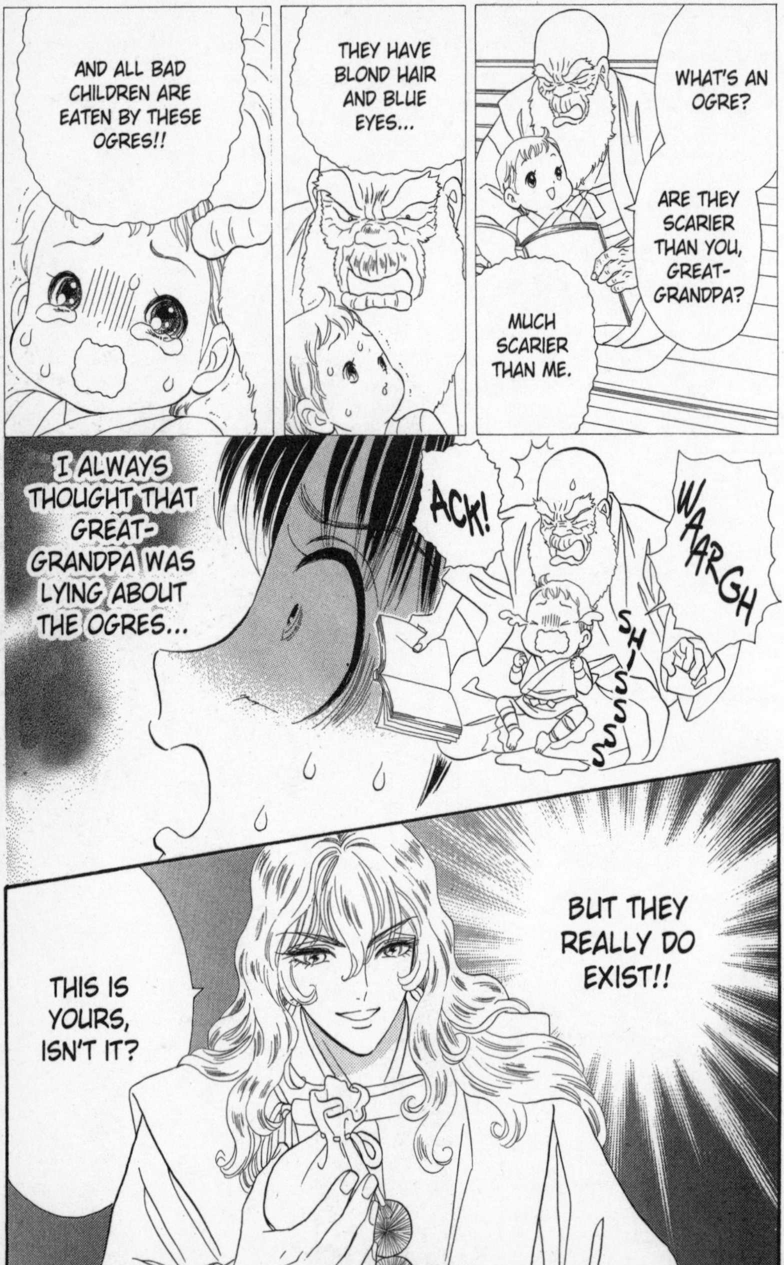
WHAT'S AN OGRE?
ARE THEY SCARIER THAN YOU, GREAT-GRANDPA?
MUCH SCARIER THAN ME.
THEY HAVE BLOND HAIR AND BLUE EYES...
AND ALL BAD CHILDREN ARE EATEN BY THESE OGRES!!
WAARGH
ACK!
SHISSSSS
I ALWAYS THOUGHT THAT GREAT-GRANDPA WAS LYING ABOUT THE OGRES...
BUT THEY REALLY DO EXIST!!
THIS IS YOURS, ISN'T IT?

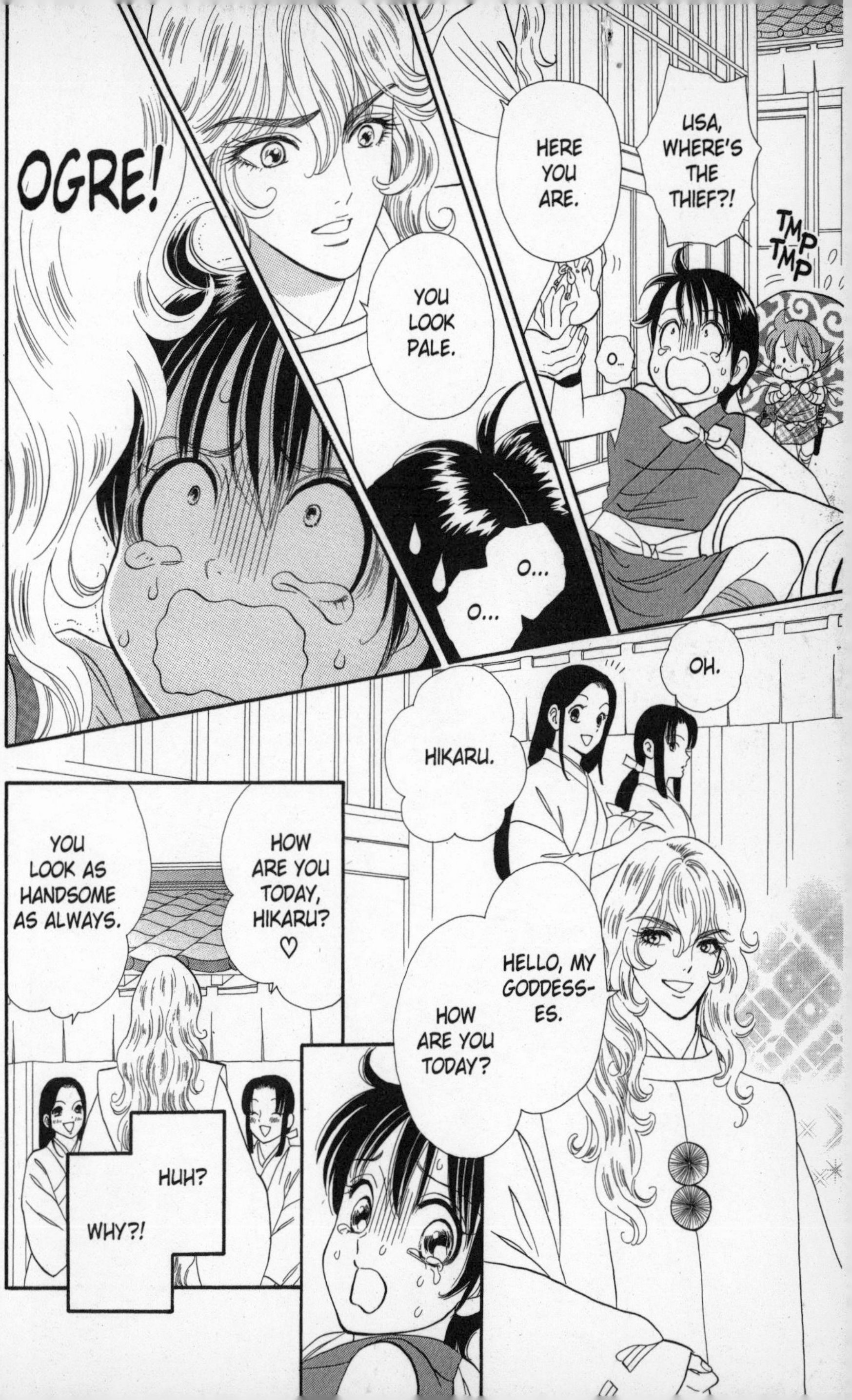

USA, WHERE'S THE THIEF?!
HERE YOU ARE.
TMP TMP
O...
YOU LOOK PALE.
O...
O...
OGRE!
OH.
HIKARU.
HELLO, MY GODDESS-ES.
HOW ARE YOU TODAY?
HOW ARE YOU TODAY, HIKARU? ♡
YOU LOOK AS HANDSOME AS ALWAYS.
HUH?
WHY?!

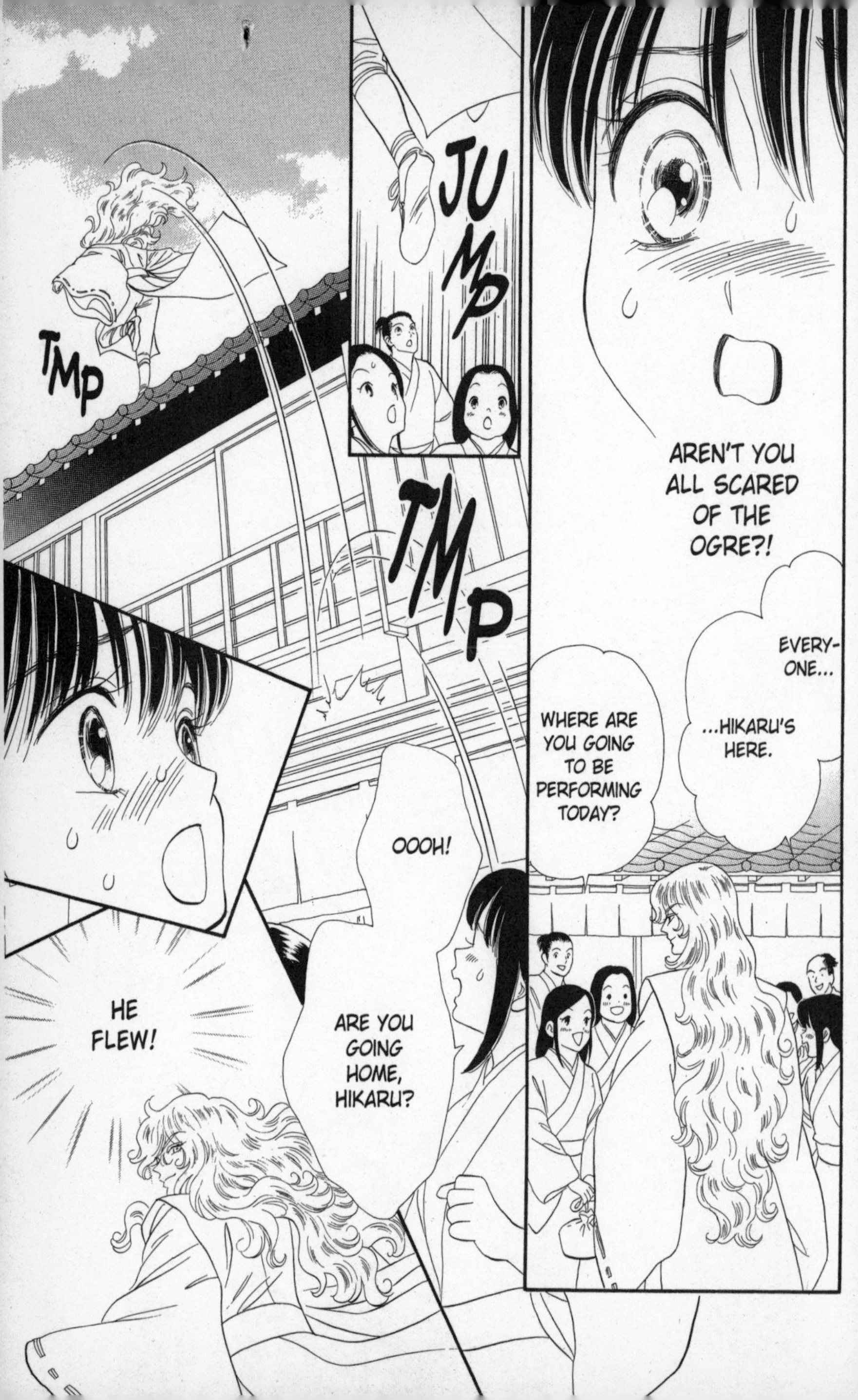
AREN'T YOU ALL SCARED OF THE OGRE?!
EVERY-ONE...
...HIKARU'S HERE.
WHERE ARE YOU GOING TO BE PERFORMING TODAY?
JUMP
TMp
TMP
OOOH!
ARE YOU GOING HOME, HIKARU?
HE FLEW!

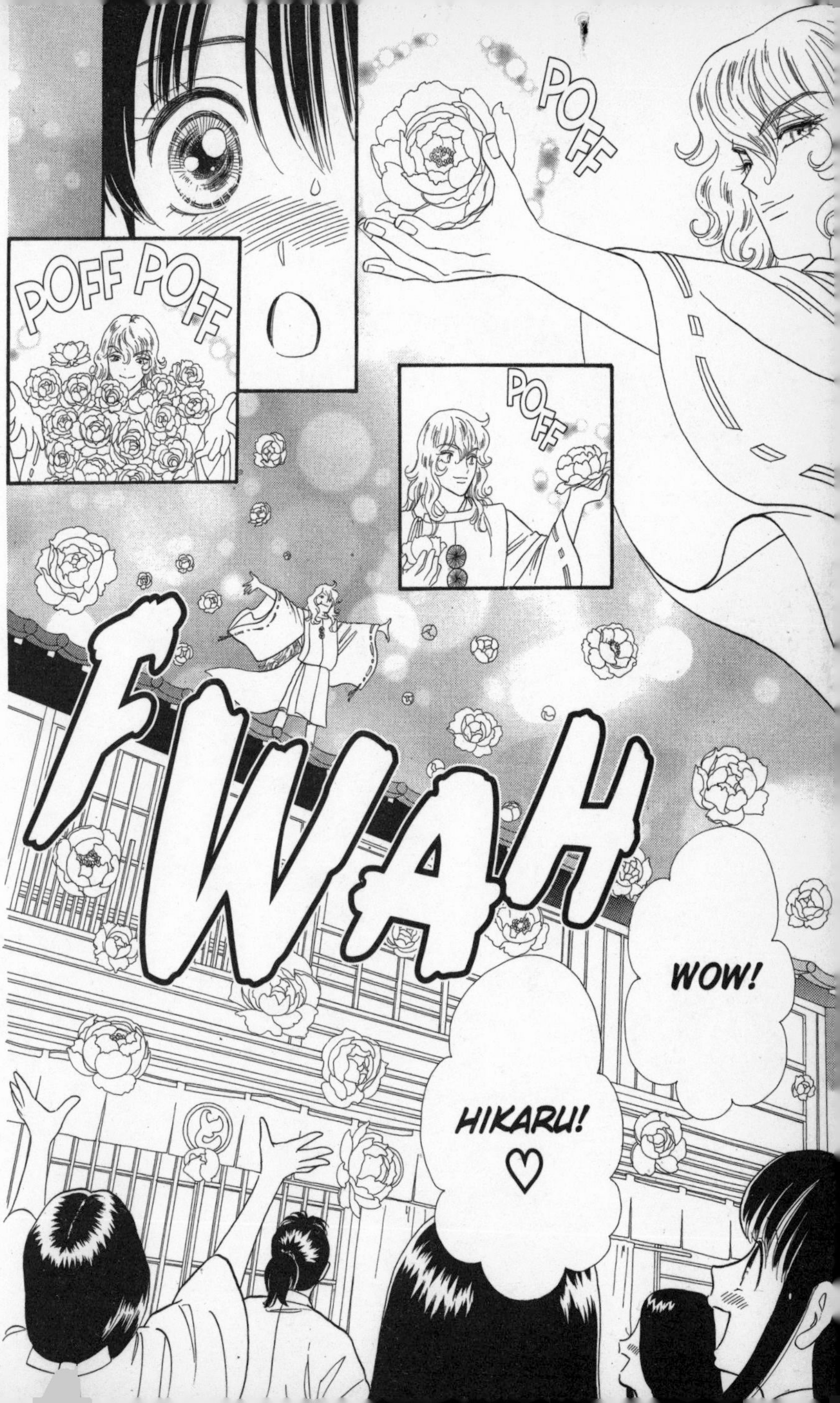
POFF
POFF POFF
POFF
IWAH
WOW!
HIKARU! ♡

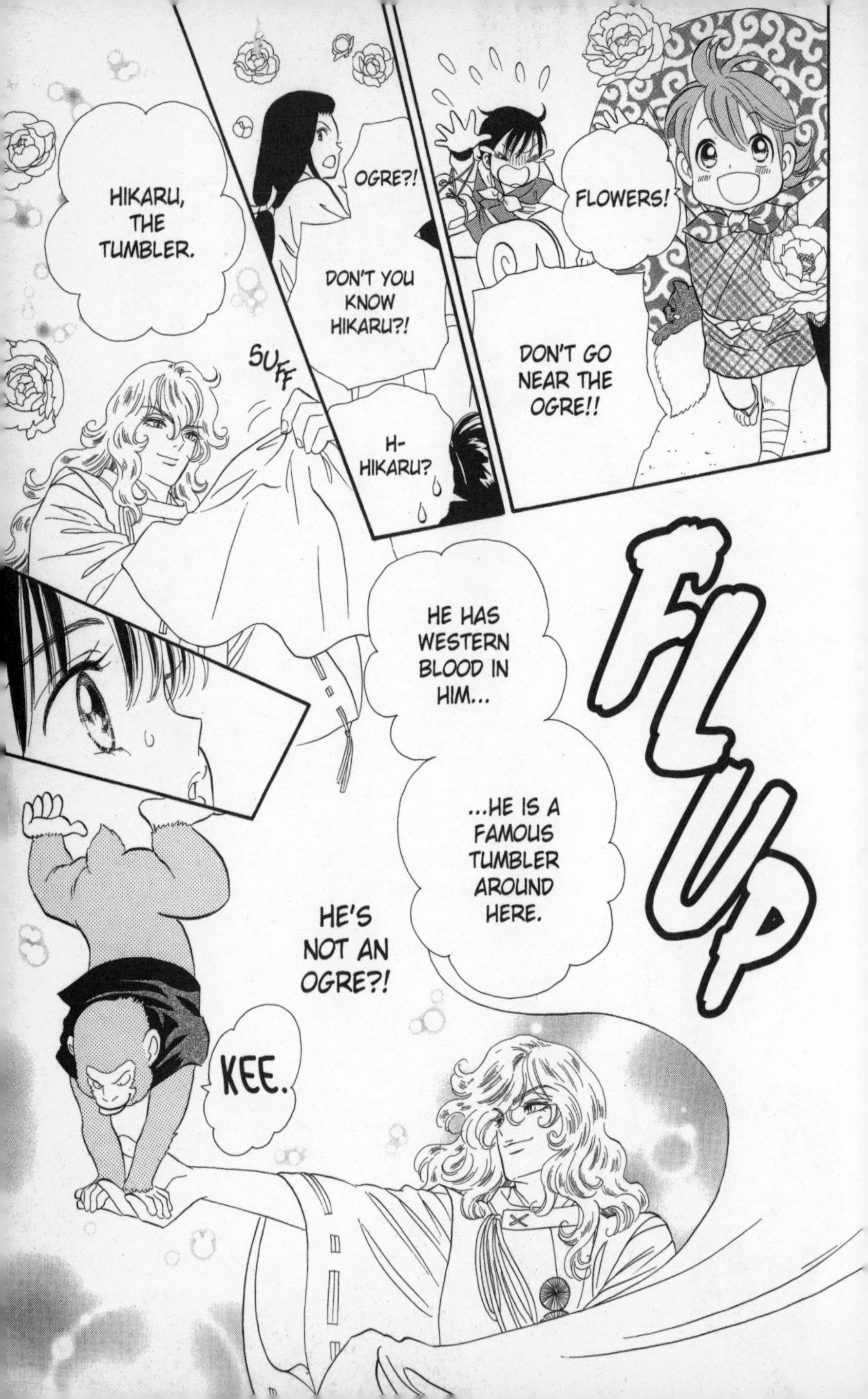
FLOWERS!
DON'T GO NEAR THE OGRE!!
OGRE?!
DON'T YOU KNOW HIKARU?!
H- HIKARU?
HIKARU, THE TUMBLER.
SUFF
FLUP
HE HAS WESTERN BLOOD IN HIM...
...HE IS A FAMOUS TUMBLER AROUND HERE.
HE'S NOT AN OGRE?!
KEE.

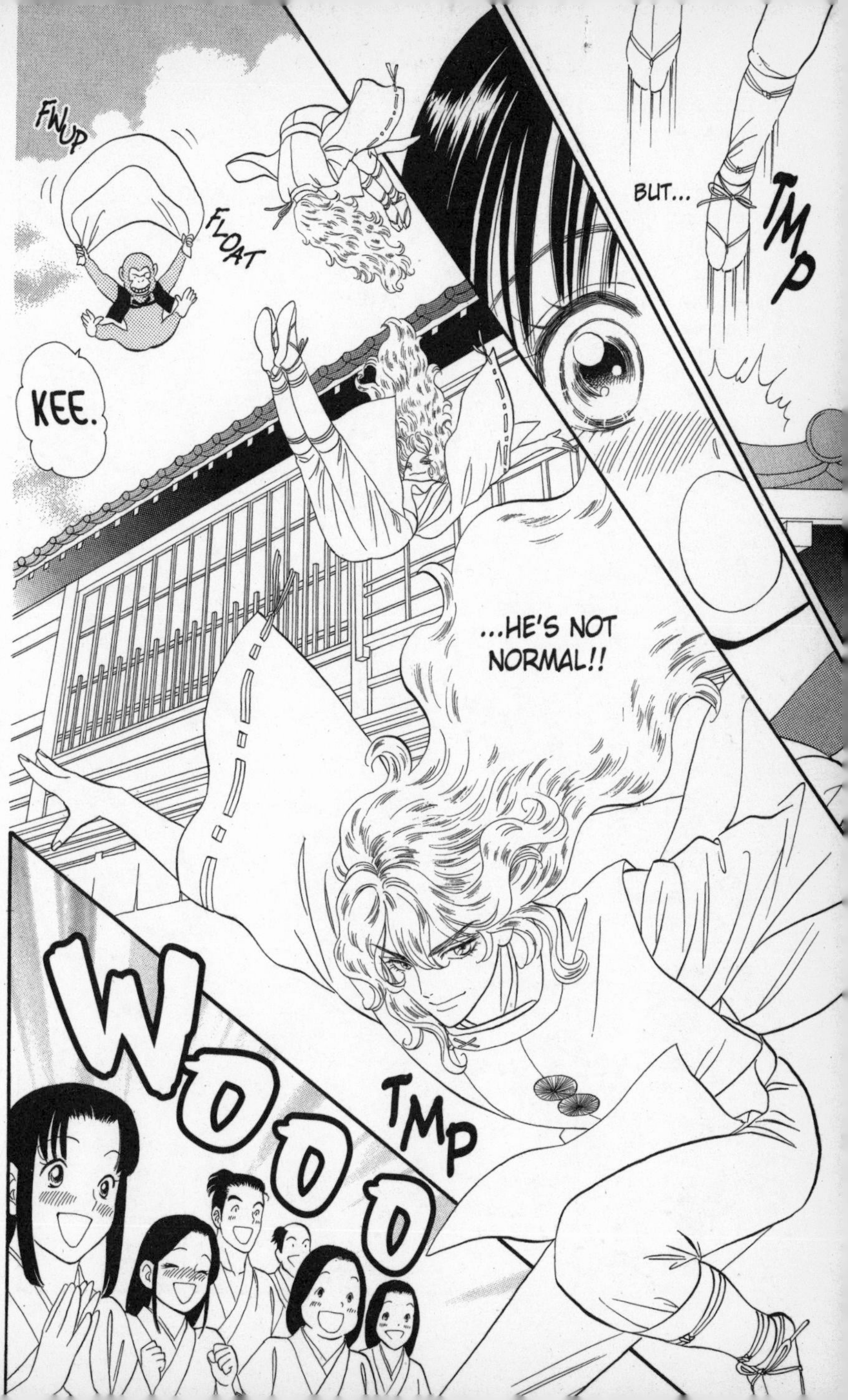

BUT...
TMP
...HE'S NOT NORMAL!!
FWUP
FLOAT
KEE.
TMP
WOOOO

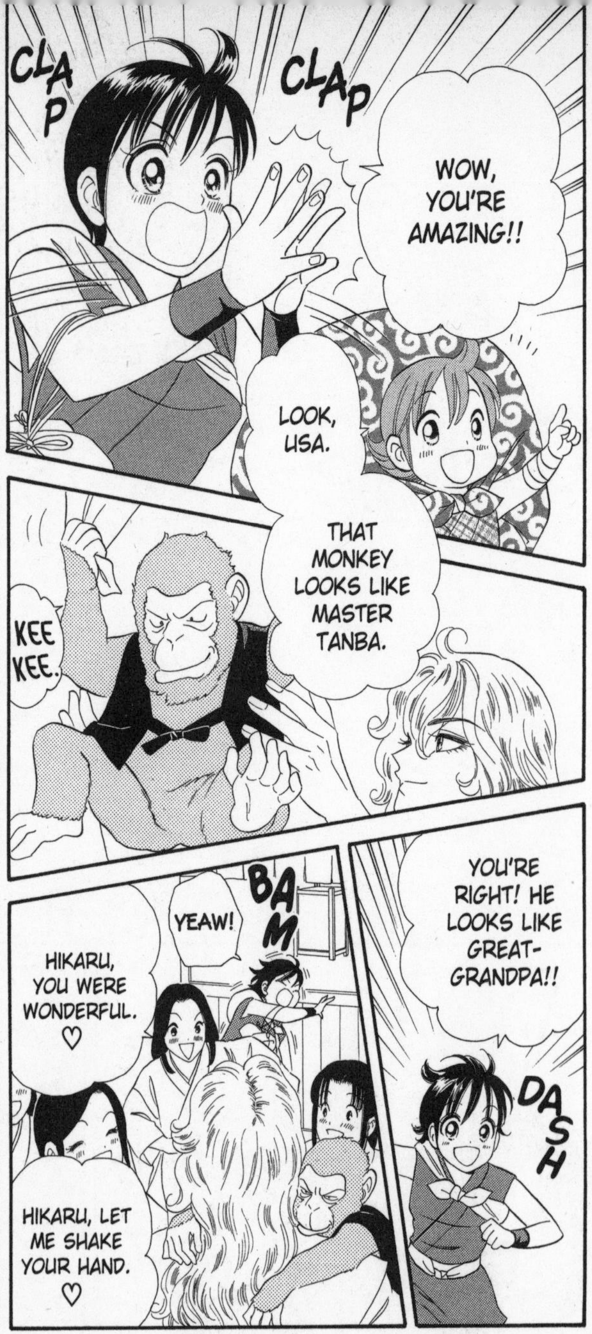
CLAP
CLAP
WOW, YOU'RE AMAZING!!
LOOK, USA.
THAT MONKEY LOOKS LIKE MASTER TANBA.
KEE KEE.
YOU'RE RIGHT! HE LOOKS LIKE GREAT-GRANDPA!!
DASH
BAM
YEAW!
HIKARU, YOU WERE WONDERFUL. ♡
HIKARU, LET ME SHAKE YOUR HAND. ♡

Stories About My Research Trip #5

I took my trip on a weekday morning, so I was the only one there. The guide did a one-on-one introduction session and told me all about the ninja stars and projectile weapons.

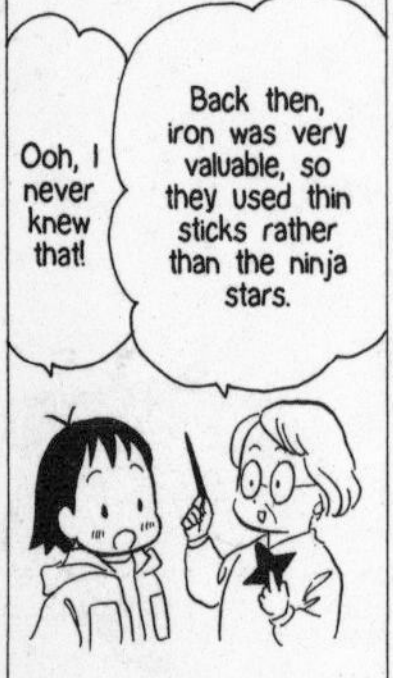
Back then, iron was very valuable, so they used thin sticks rather than the ninja stars.
Ooh, I never knew that!

I often see ninjas throwing ninja stars all the time in TV programs, animation, and manga, but I learned that was not the case.

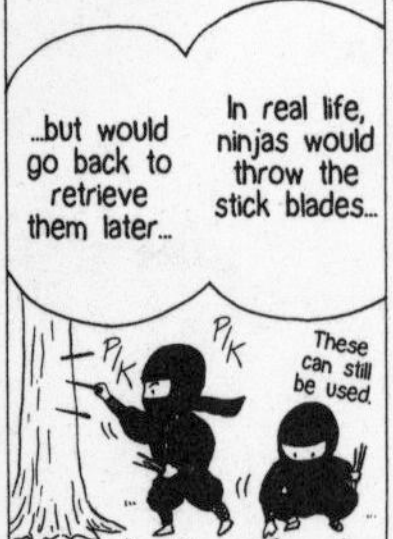
In real life, ninjas would throw the stick blades...
...but would go back to retrieve them later...
PIK
PIK
These can still be used.

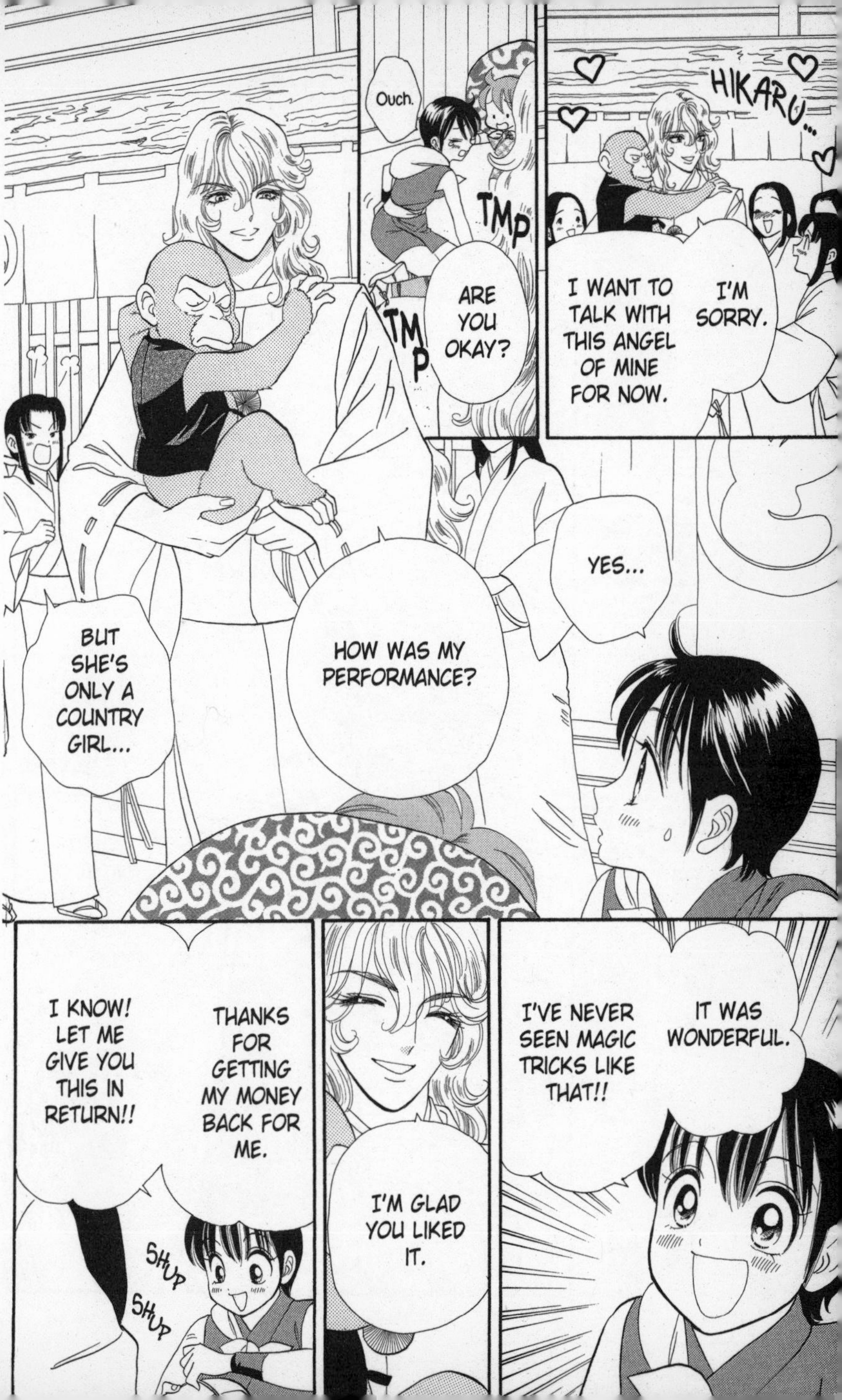
HIKARU...
I'M SORRY.
I WANT TO TALK WITH THIS ANGEL OF MINE FOR NOW.
Ouch.
TMP
ARE YOU OKAY?
TMP
YES...
HOW WAS MY PERFORMANCE?
BUT SHE'S ONLY A COUNTRY GIRL...
IT WAS WONDERFUL.
I'VE NEVER SEEN MAGIC TRICKS LIKE THAT!!
I'M GLAD YOU LIKED IT.
THANKS FOR GETTING MY MONEY BACK FOR ME.
I KNOW! LET ME GIVE YOU THIS IN RETURN!!
SHUP
SHUP

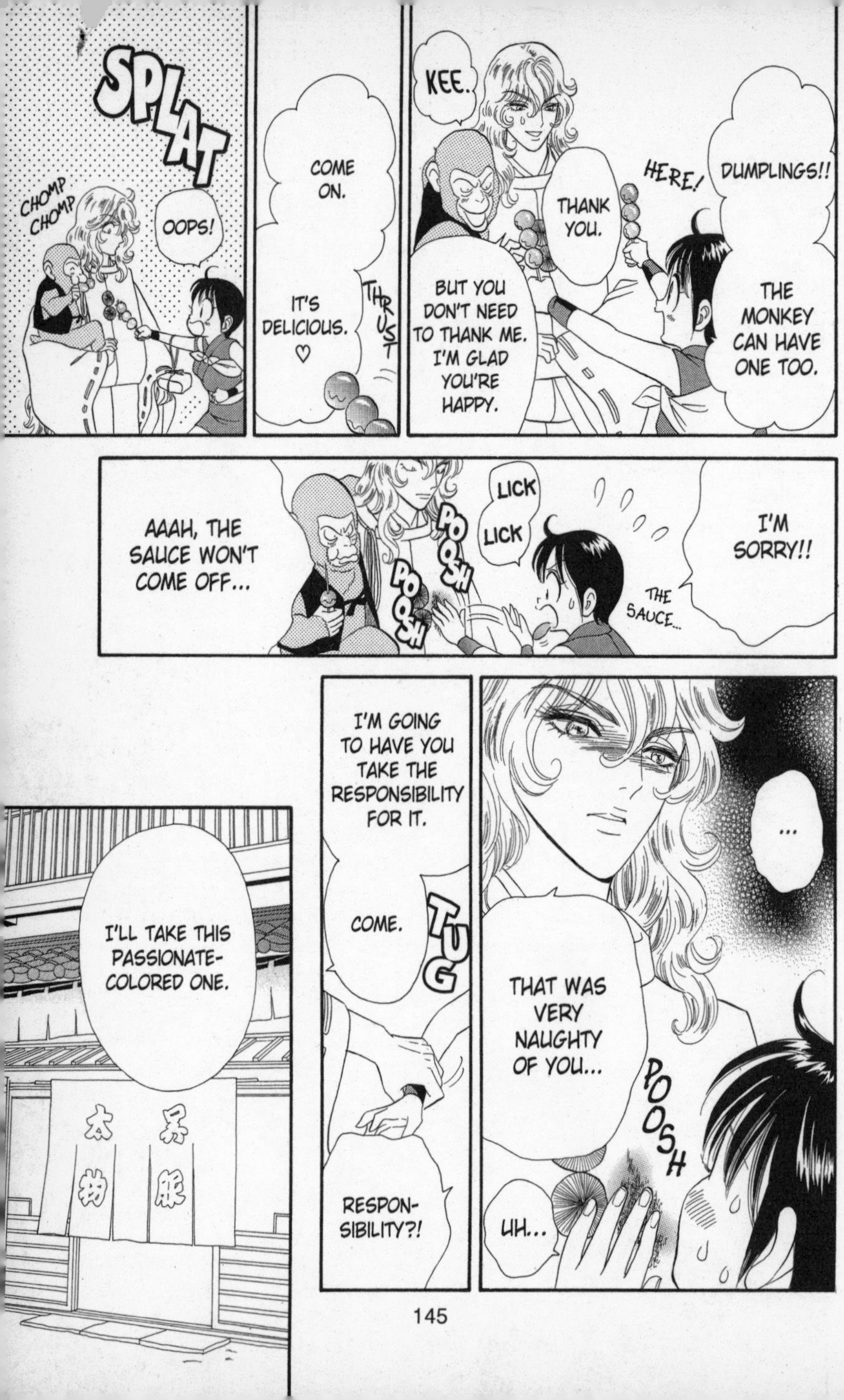
DUMPLINGS!!
HERE!
THE MONKEY CAN HAVE ONE TOO.
KEE..
THANK YOU.
BUT YOU DON'T NEED TO THANK ME. I'M GLAD YOU'RE HAPPY.
COME ON.
THRUST
IT'S DELICIOUS. ♡
SPLAT
OOPS!
CHOMP CHOMP
I'M SORRY!!
THE SAUCE...
LICK LICK
POOSH POOSH
AAAH, THE SAUCE WON'T COME OFF...
...
THAT WAS VERY NAUGHTY OF YOU...
POOSH
UH...
I'M GOING TO HAVE YOU TAKE THE RESPONSIBILITY FOR IT.
COME.
TUG
RESPON-SIBILITY?!
I'LL TAKE THIS PASSIONATE-COLORED ONE.
呉服
太物

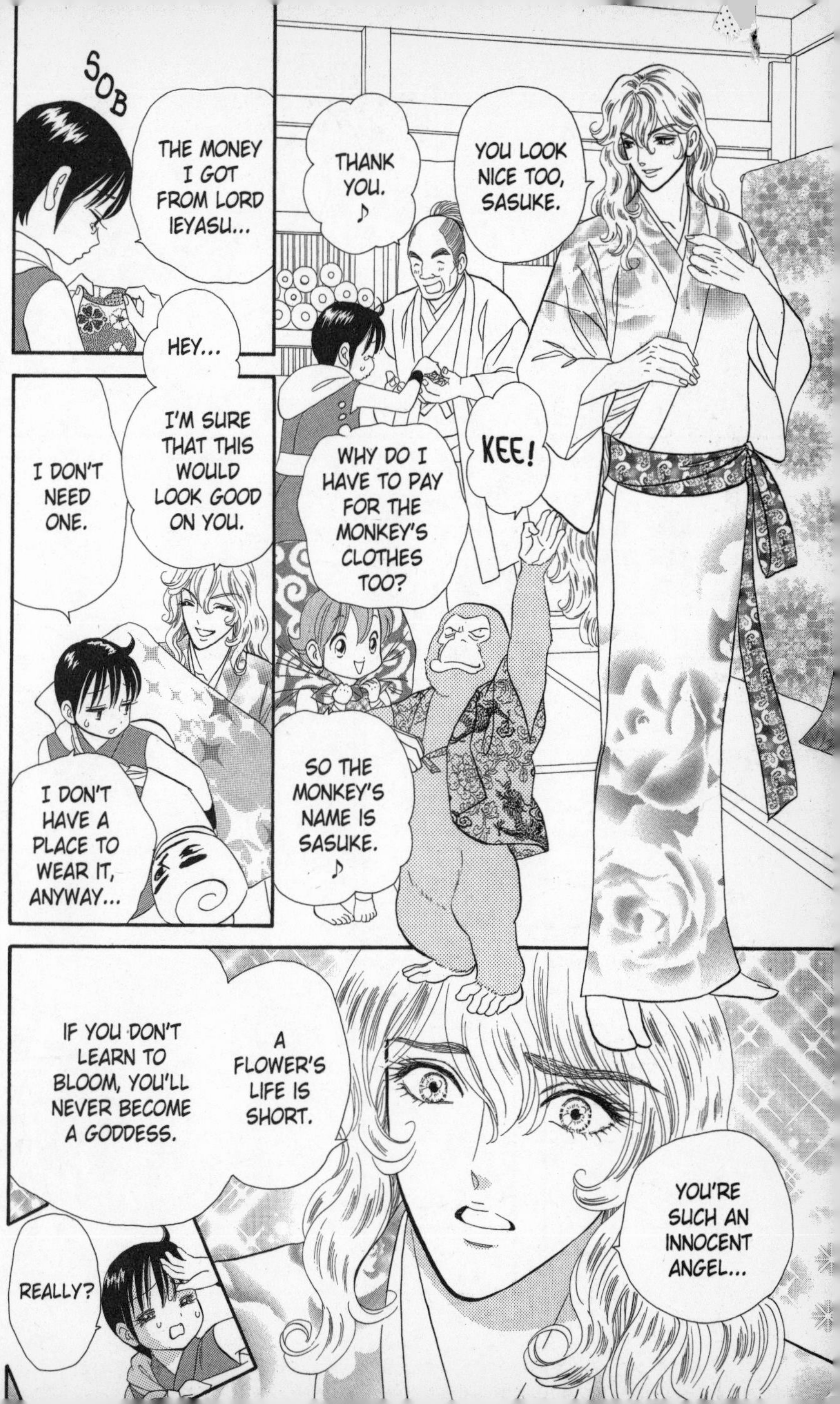
YOU LOOK NICE TOO, SASUKE.
THANK YOU. ♪
KEE!
WHY DO I HAVE TO PAY FOR THE MONKEY'S CLOTHES TOO?
SO THE MONKEY'S NAME IS SASUKE. ♪
SOB
THE MONEY I GOT FROM LORD IEYASU...
HEY...
I'M SURE THAT THIS WOULD LOOK GOOD ON YOU.
I DON'T NEED ONE.
I DON'T HAVE A PLACE TO WEAR IT, ANYWAY...
YOU'RE SUCH AN INNOCENT ANGEL...
A FLOWER'S LIFE IS SHORT.
IF YOU DON'T LEARN TO BLOOM, YOU'LL NEVER BECOME A GODDESS.
REALLY?

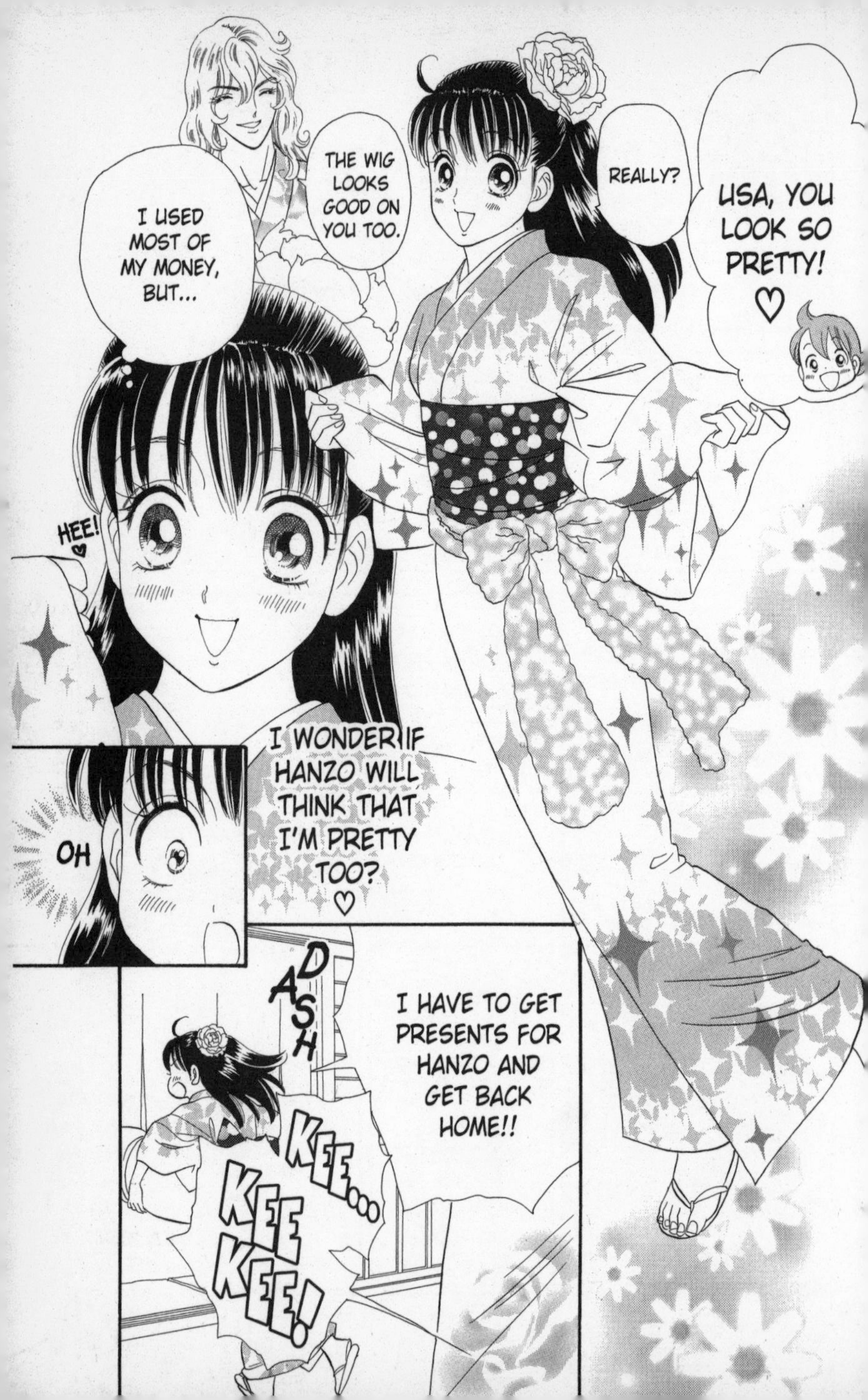
USA, YOU LOOK SO PRETTY! ♡
REALLY?
THE WIG LOOKS GOOD ON YOU TOO.
I USED MOST OF MY MONEY, BUT...
HEE! ♡
I WONDER IF HANZO WILL THINK THAT I'M PRETTY TOO? ♡
OH
I HAVE TO GET PRESENTS FOR HANZO AND GET BACK HOME!!
DASH
KEE...
KEE KEE!

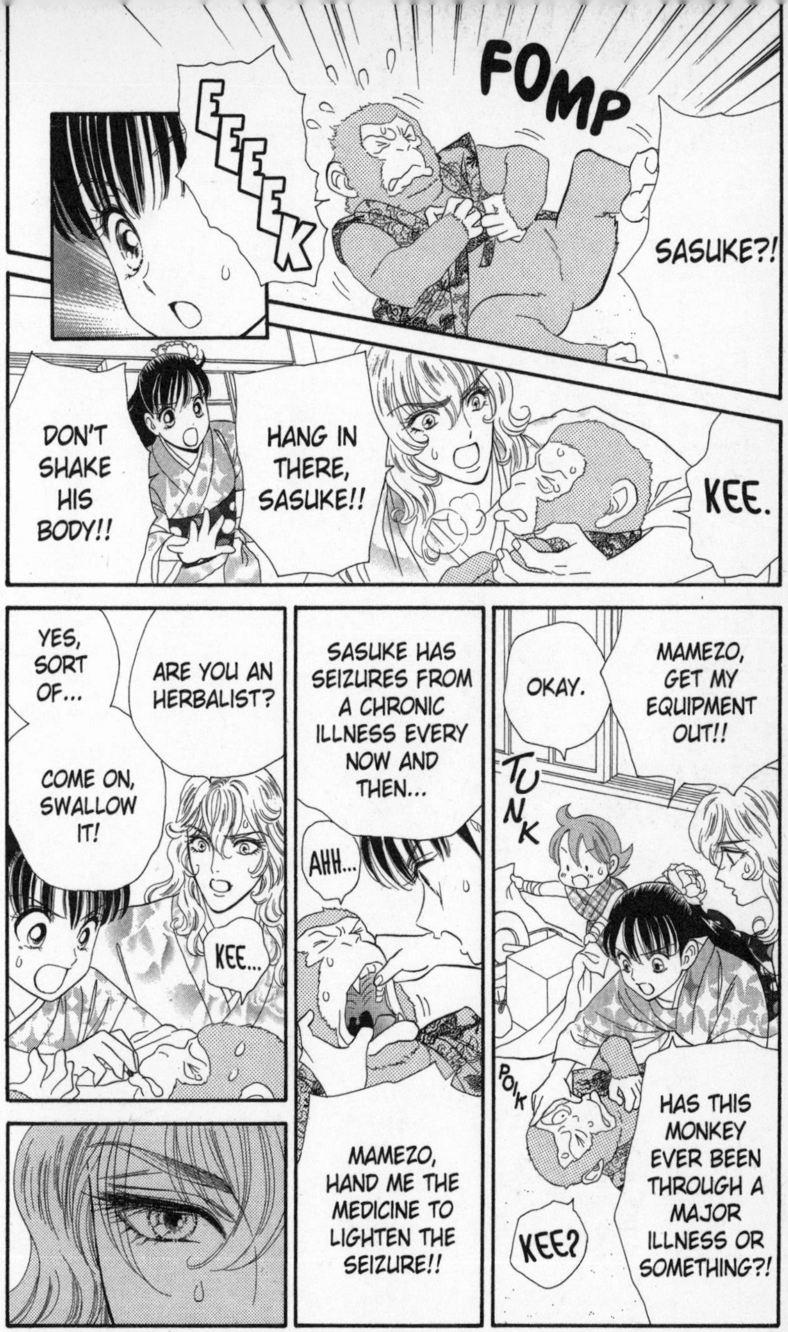
FOMP
SASUKE?!
EEEEK
KEE.
HANG IN THERE, SASUKE!!
DON'T SHAKE HIS BODY!!
MAMEZO, GET MY EQUIPMENT OUT!!
OKAY.
TUNK
HAS THIS MONKEY EVER BEEN THROUGH A MAJOR ILLNESS OR SOMETHING?!
POIK
KEE?
SASUKE HAS SEIZURES FROM A CHRONIC ILLNESS EVERY NOW AND THEN...
AHH...
MAMEZO, HAND ME THE MEDICINE TO LIGHTEN THE SEIZURE!!
ARE YOU AN HERBALIST?
YES, SORT OF...
COME ON, SWALLOW IT!
KEE...

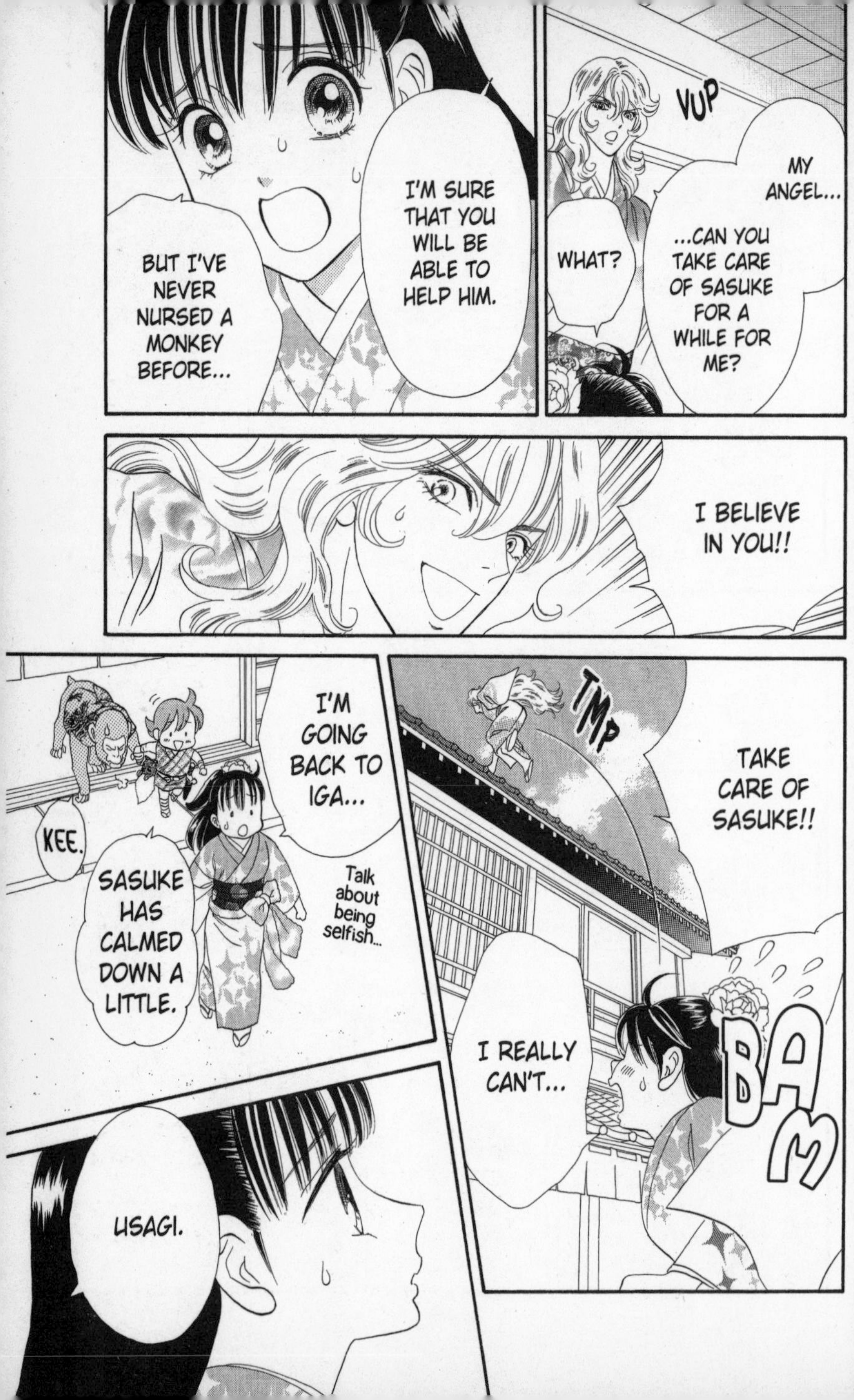
VUP
MY ANGEL...
...CAN YOU TAKE CARE OF SASUKE FOR A WHILE FOR ME?
WHAT?
I'M SURE THAT YOU WILL BE ABLE TO HELP HIM.
BUT I'VE NEVER NURSED A MONKEY BEFORE...
I BELIEVE IN YOU!!
TMP
TAKE CARE OF SASUKE!!
BAM
I REALLY CAN'T...
I'M GOING BACK TO IGA...
Talk about being selfish...
SASUKE HAS CALMED DOWN A LITTLE.
KEE.
USAGI.

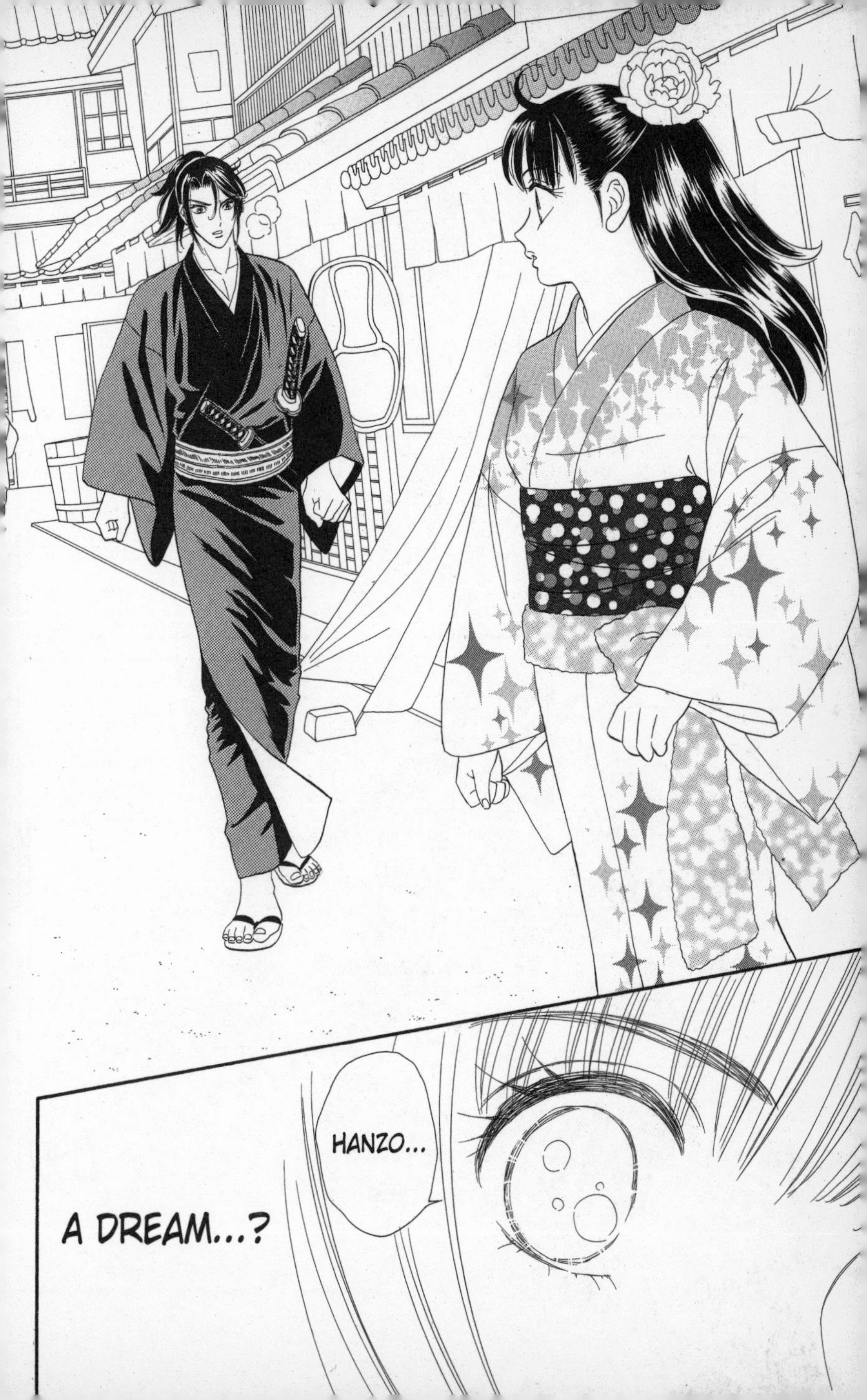
HANZO...
A DREAM...?

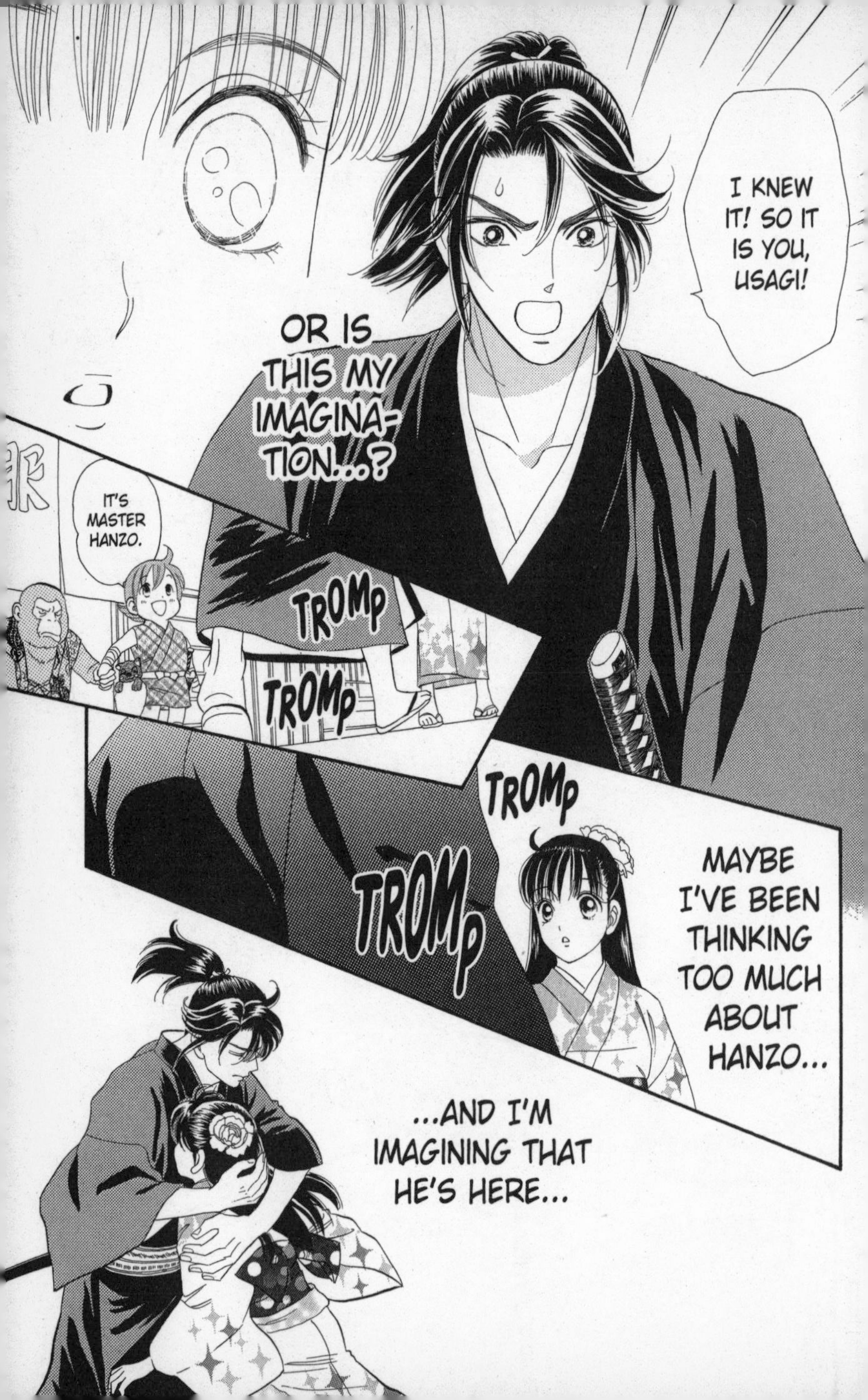
I KNEW IT! SO IT IS YOU, USAGI!
OR IS THIS MY IMAGINATION...?
IT'S MASTER HANZO.
TROMP
TROMP
TROMP
TROMP
MAYBE I'VE BEEN THINKING TOO MUCH ABOUT HANZO...
...AND I'M IMAGINING THAT HE'S HERE...

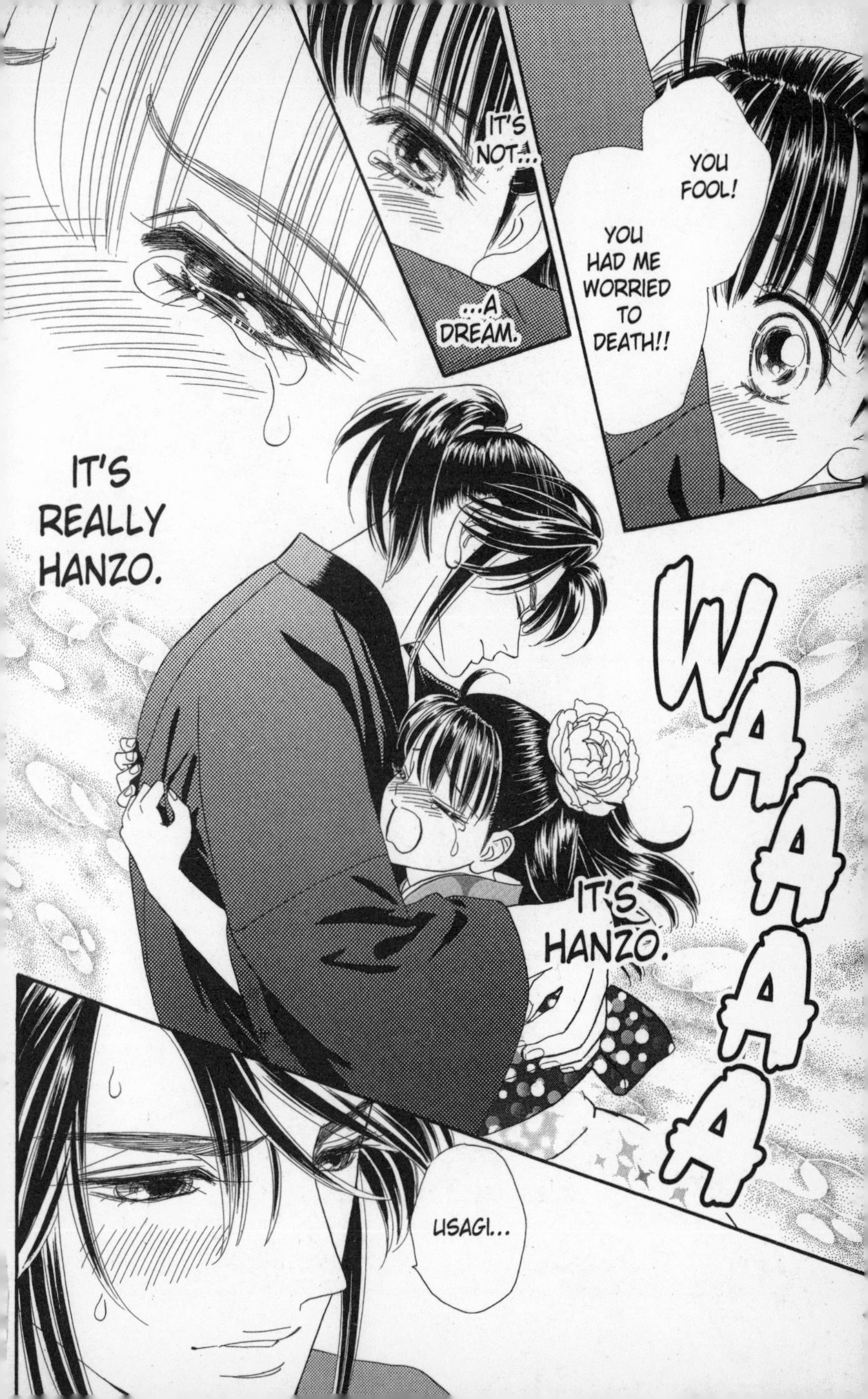
YOU FOOL!
YOU HAD ME WORRIED TO DEATH!!
IT'S NOT...
...A DREAM.
IT'S REALLY HANZO.
WAAAAA
IT'S HANZO.
USAGI...

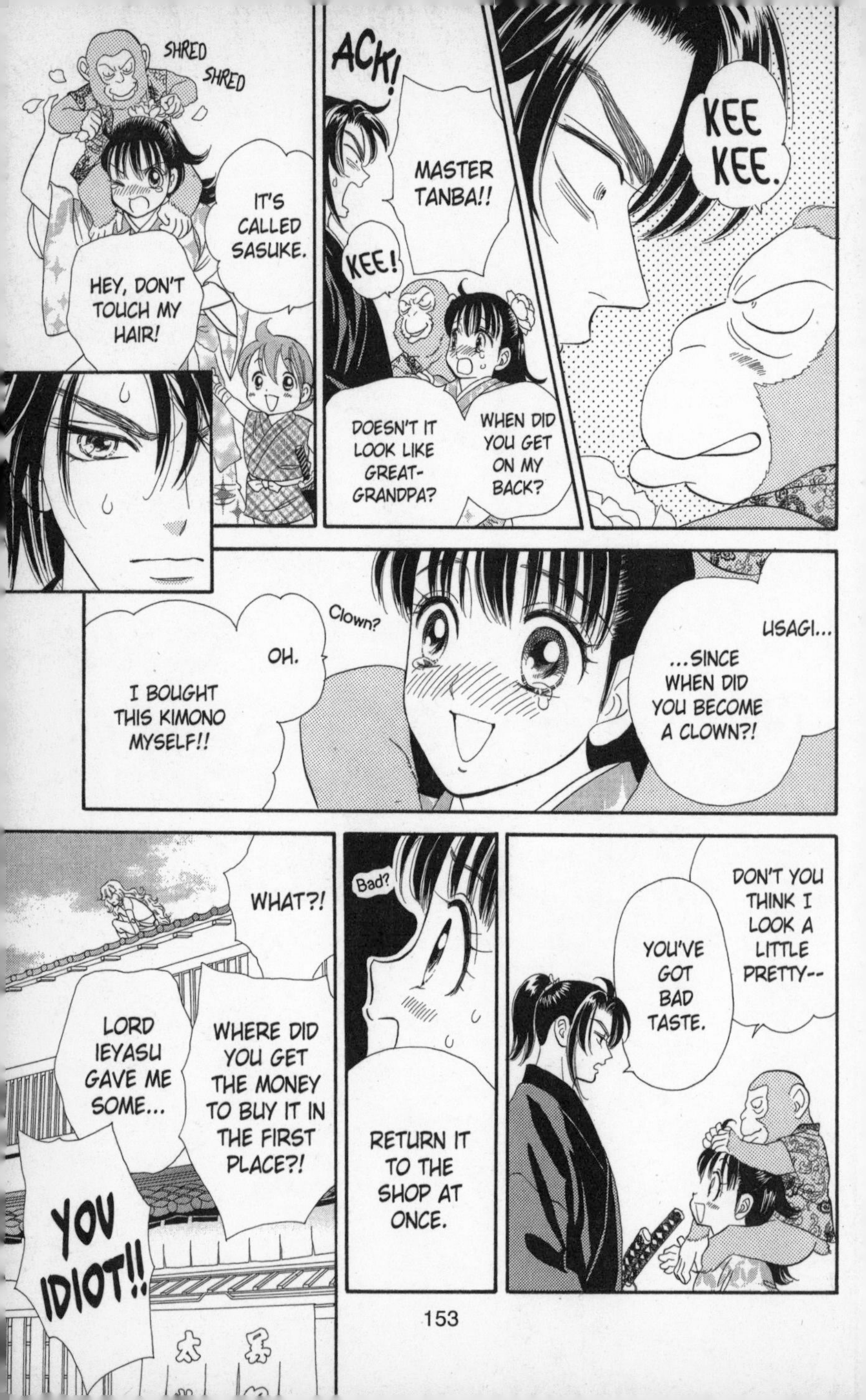
KEE KEE.
ACK!
MASTER TANBA!!
KEE!
WHEN DID YOU GET ON MY BACK?
DOESN'T IT LOOK LIKE GREAT-GRANDPA?
SHRED
SHRED
IT'S CALLED SASUKE.
HEY, DON'T TOUCH MY HAIR!
USAGI...
...SINCE WHEN DID YOU BECOME A CLOWN?!
Clown?
OH.
I BOUGHT THIS KIMONO MYSELF!!
DON'T YOU THINK I LOOK A LITTLE PRETTY--
YOU'VE GOT BAD TASTE.
Bad?
RETURN IT TO THE SHOP AT ONCE.
WHAT?!
WHERE DID YOU GET THE MONEY TO BUY IT IN THE FIRST PLACE?!
LORD IEYASU GAVE ME SOME...
YOU IDIOT!!

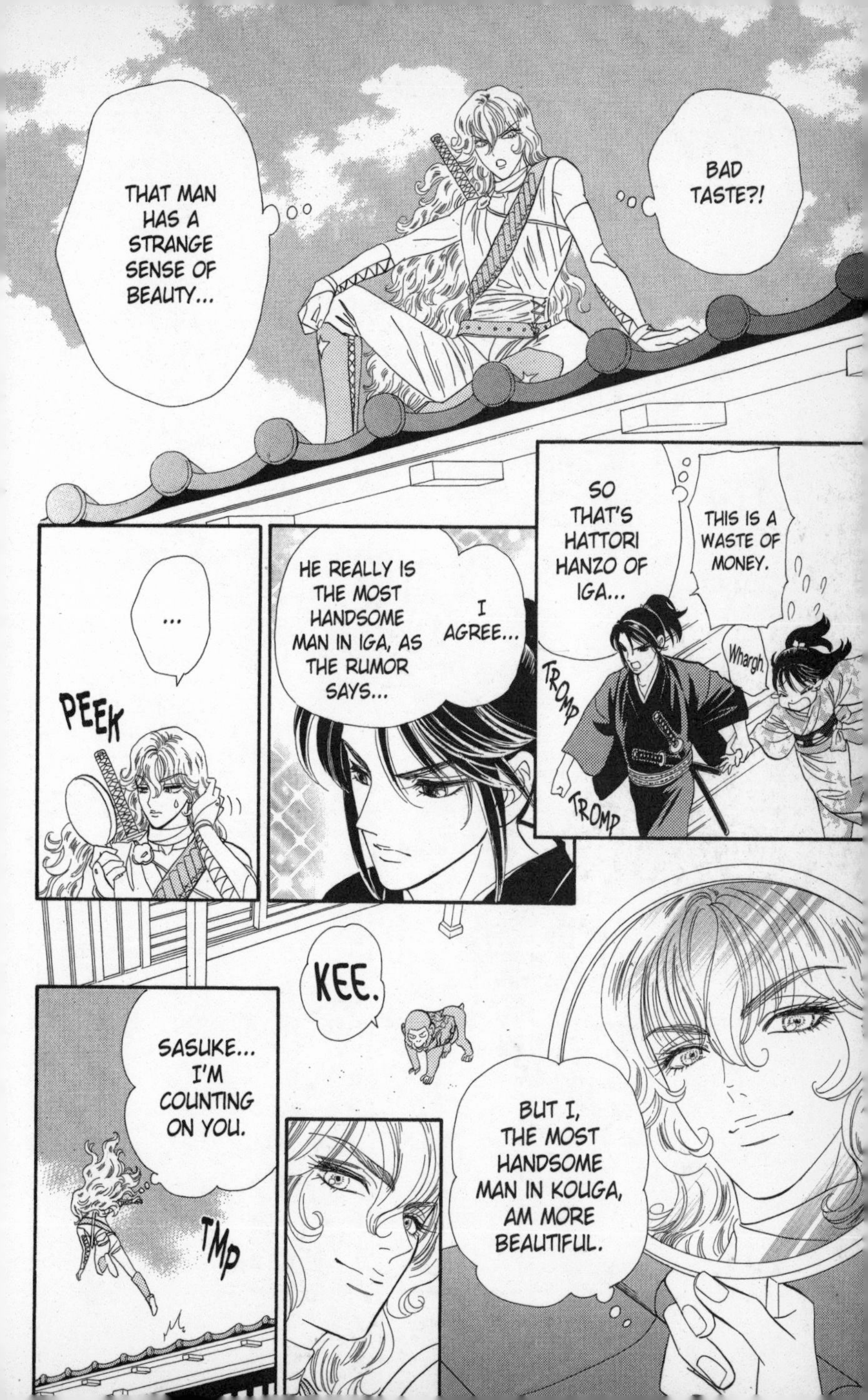
BAD TASTE?!
THAT MAN HAS A STRANGE SENSE OF BEAUTY...
THIS IS A WASTE OF MONEY.
SO THAT'S HATTORI HANZO OF IGA...
Whargh.
TROMP TROMP
HE REALLY IS THE MOST HANDSOME MAN IN IGA, AS THE RUMOR SAYS...
I AGREE...
...
PEEK
BUT I, THE MOST HANDSOME MAN IN KOUGA, AM MORE BEAUTIFUL.
KEE.
SASUKE... I'M COUNTING ON YOU.
TMP

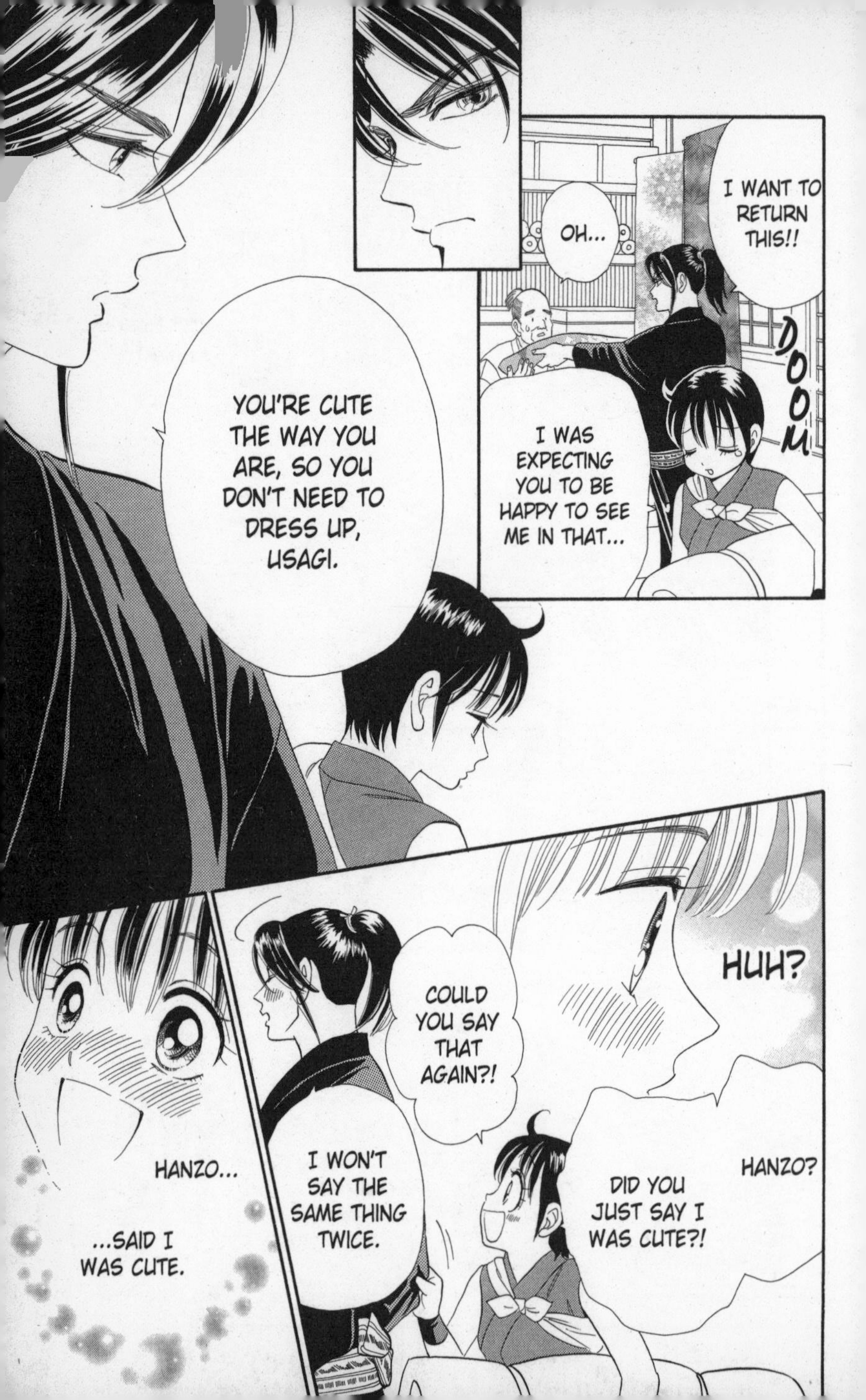
I WANT TO RETURN THIS!!
OH...
DOOOM
I WAS EXPECTING YOU TO BE HAPPY TO SEE ME IN THAT...
YOU'RE CUTE THE WAY YOU ARE, SO YOU DON'T NEED TO DRESS UP, USAGI.
HUH?
HANZO?
DID YOU JUST SAY I WAS CUTE?!
COULD YOU SAY THAT AGAIN?!
I WON'T SAY THE SAME THING TWICE.
HANZO...
...SAID I WAS CUTE.

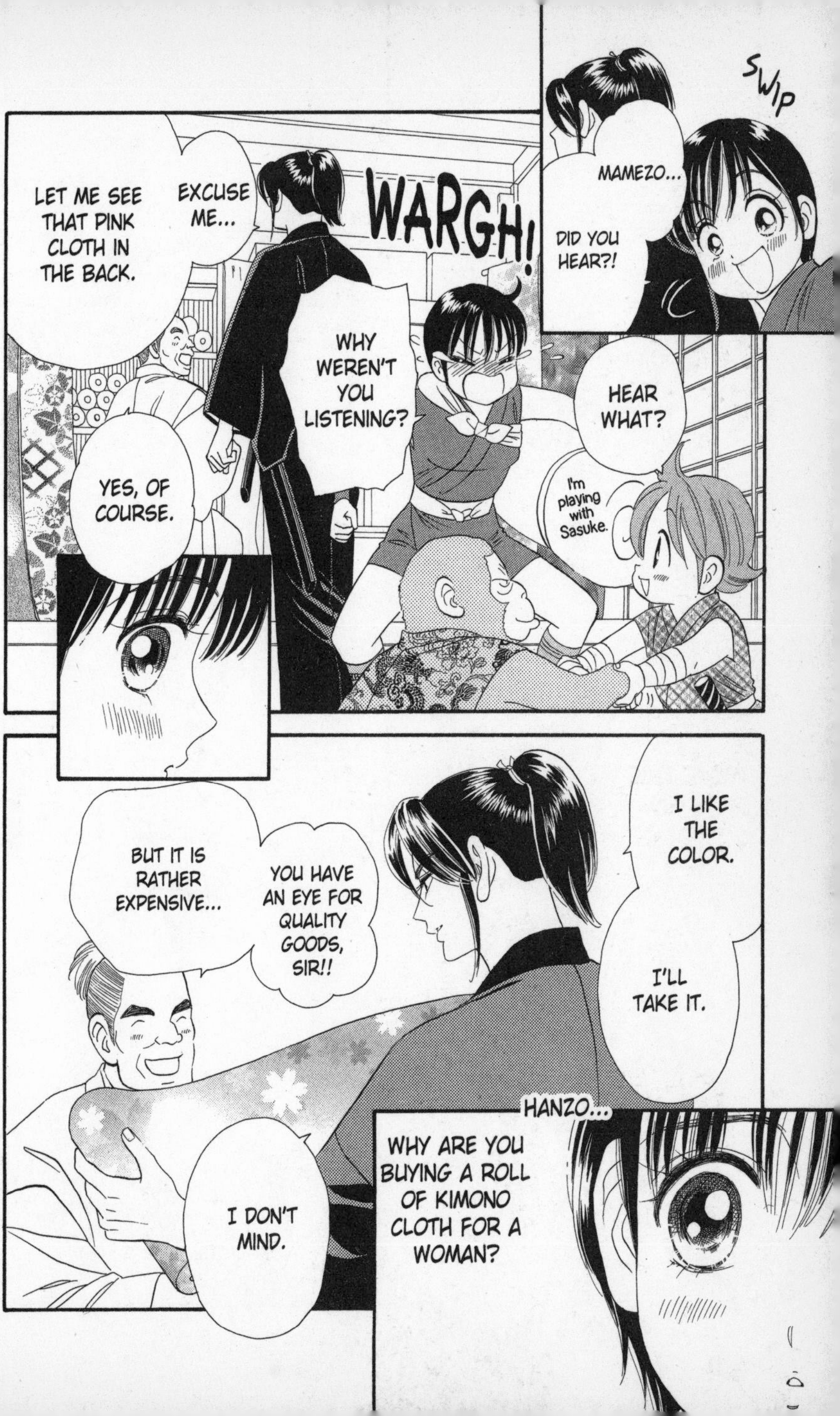
SWIP
MAMEZO...
DID YOU HEAR?!
HEAR WHAT?
I'm playing with Sasuke.
WHY WEREN'T YOU LISTENING?
WARGH!
EXCUSE ME...
LET ME SEE THAT PINK CLOTH IN THE BACK.
YES, OF COURSE.
I LIKE THE COLOR.
I'LL TAKE IT.
YOU HAVE AN EYE FOR QUALITY GOODS, SIR!!
BUT IT IS RATHER EXPENSIVE...
I DON'T MIND.
HANZO...
WHY ARE YOU BUYING A ROLL OF KIMONO CLOTH FOR A WOMAN?

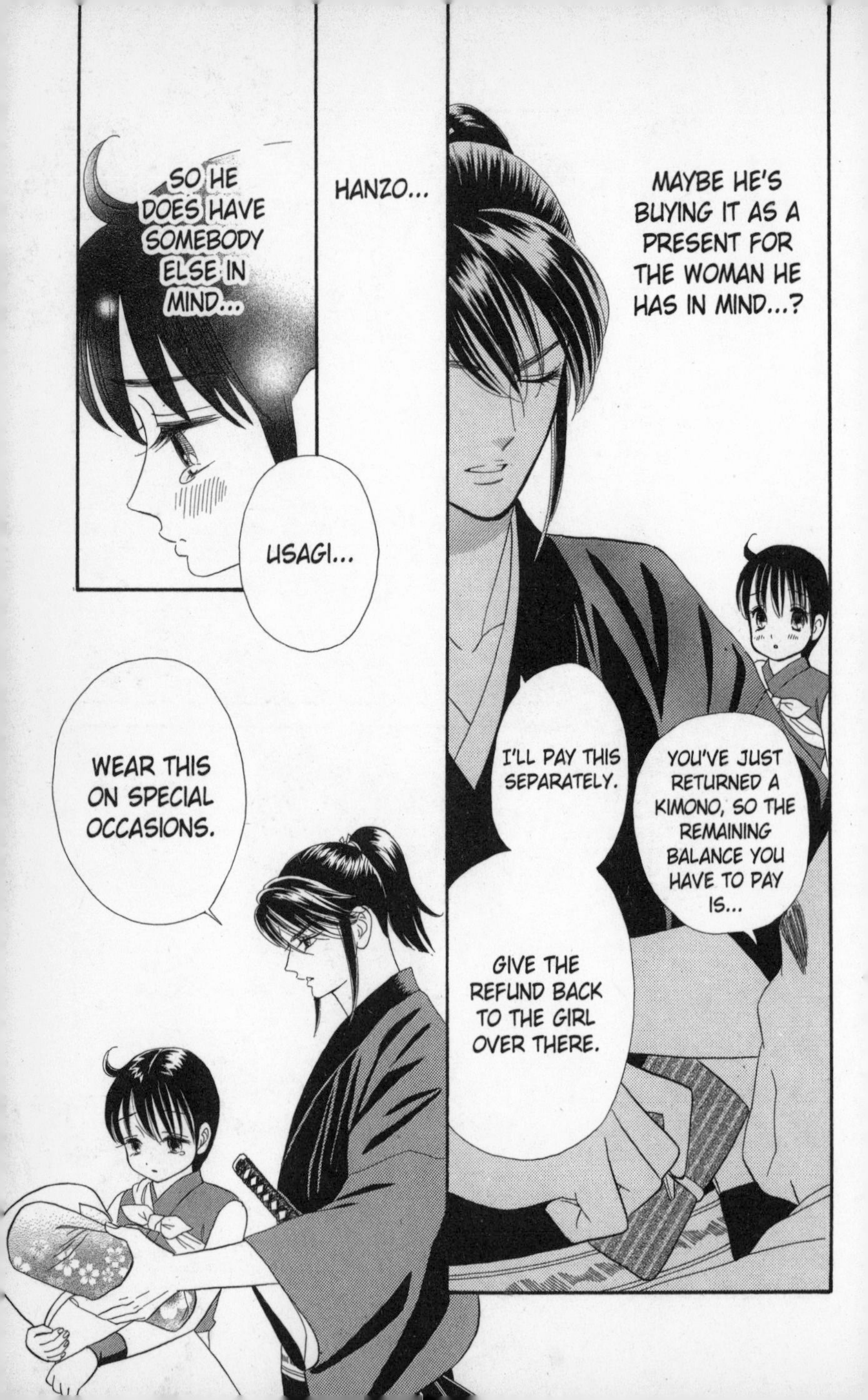
MAYBE HE'S BUYING IT AS A PRESENT FOR THE WOMAN HE HAS IN MIND...?
YOU'VE JUST RETURNED A KIMONO, SO THE REMAINING BALANCE YOU HAVE TO PAY IS...
I'LL PAY THIS SEPARATELY.
GIVE THE REFUND BACK TO THE GIRL OVER THERE.
HANZO...
SO HE DOES HAVE SOMEBODY ELSE IN MIND...
USAGI...
WEAR THIS ON SPECIAL OCCASIONS.

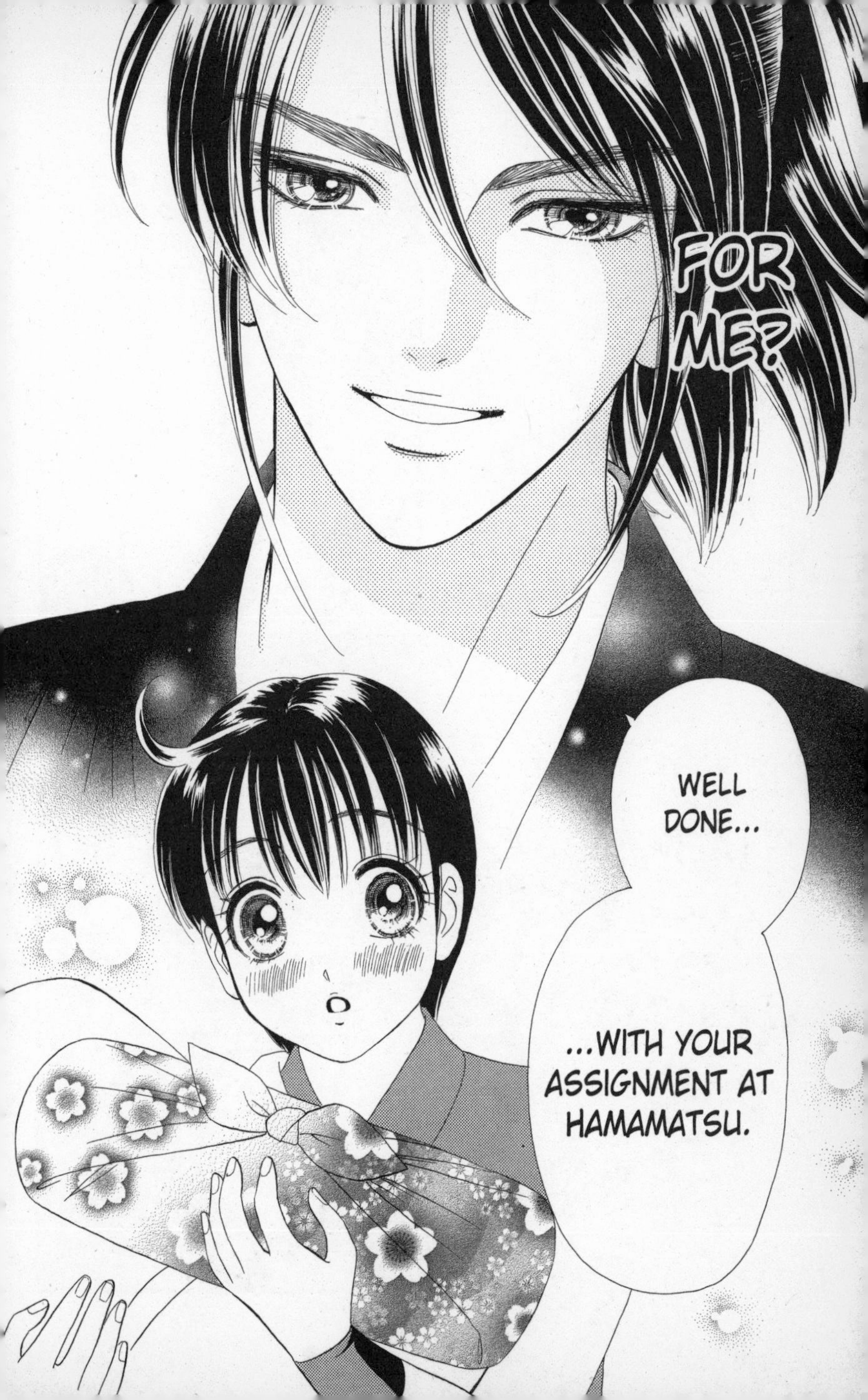
FOR ME?
WELL DONE...
...WITH YOUR ASSIGNMENT AT HAMAMATSU.

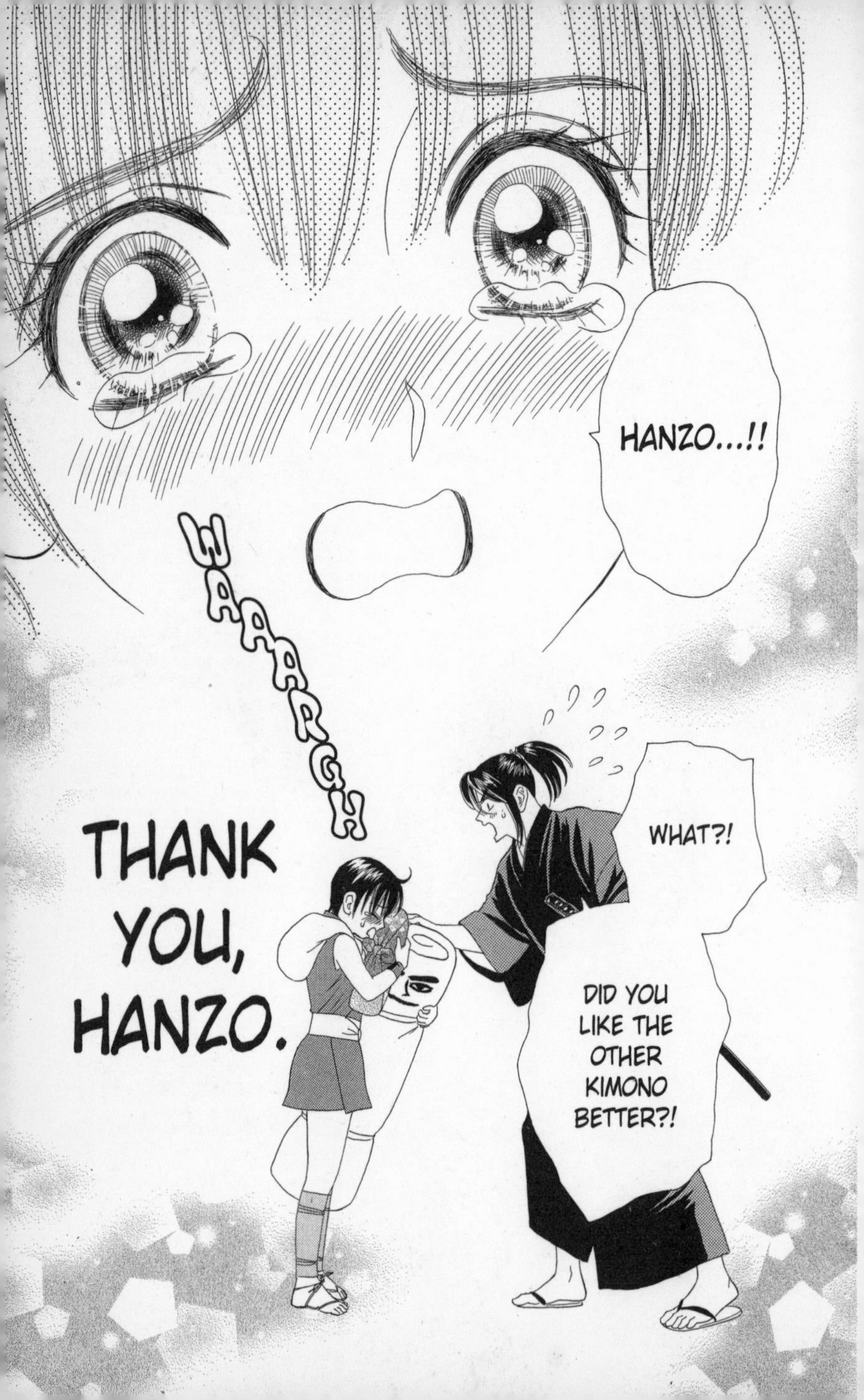

HANZO...!!
WAAARGH
WHAT?!
DID YOU LIKE THE OTHER KIMONO BETTER?!
THANK YOU, HANZO.

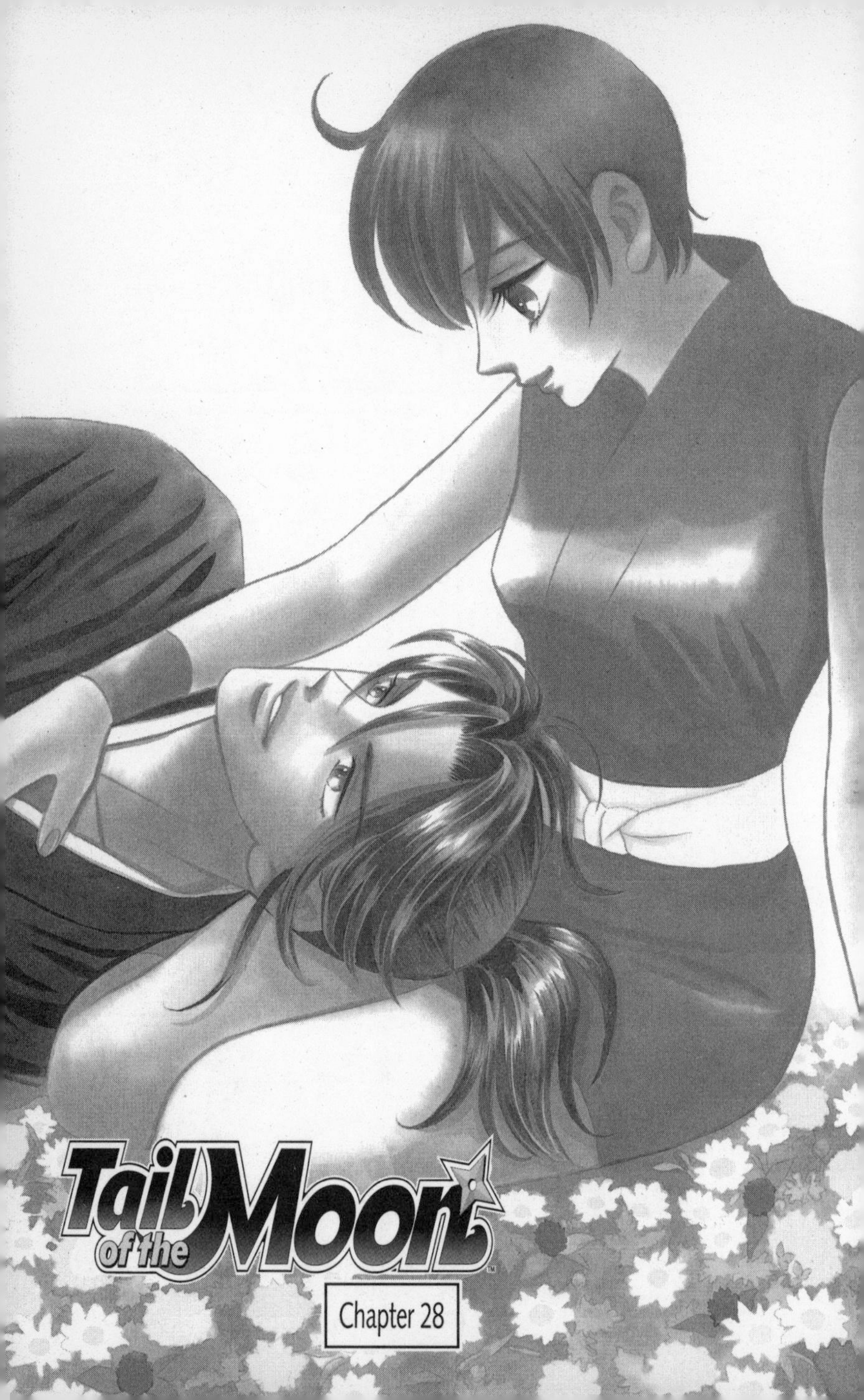
Tail of the Moon™
Chapter 28

USAGI'S SECRET ①

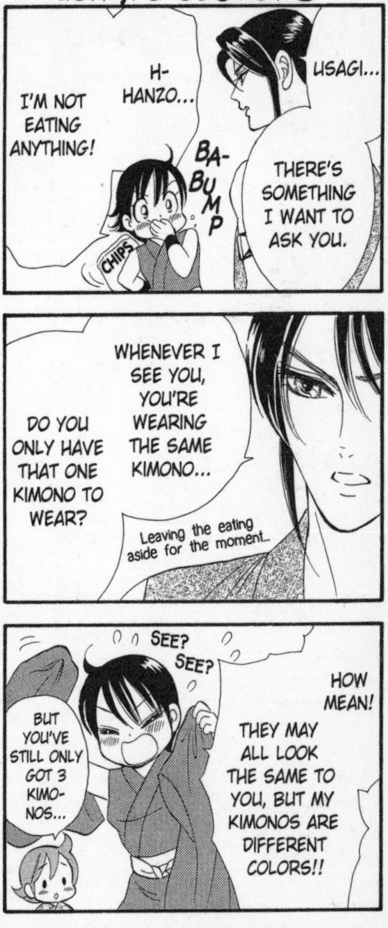
USAGI...
THERE'S SOMETHING I WANT TO ASK YOU.
H-HANZO...
BA-BUMP
I'M NOT EATING ANYTHING!
CHIPS
WHENEVER I SEE YOU, YOU'RE WEARING THE SAME KIMONO...
DO YOU ONLY HAVE THAT ONE KIMONO TO WEAR?
Leaving the eating aside for the moment...
HOW MEAN!
THEY MAY ALL LOOK THE SAME TO YOU, BUT MY KIMONOS ARE DIFFERENT COLORS!!
SEE? SEE?
BUT YOU'VE STILL ONLY GOT 3 KIMO-NOS...
I... I SEE...
Sorry.
I DIDN'T NOTICE SINCE THEY ALL LOOK THE SAME...
TO TELL YOU THE TRUTH, I HAVE MANY DIFFERENT ONES TOO...
I have lots of kimo-nos!

USAGI'S SECRET ②

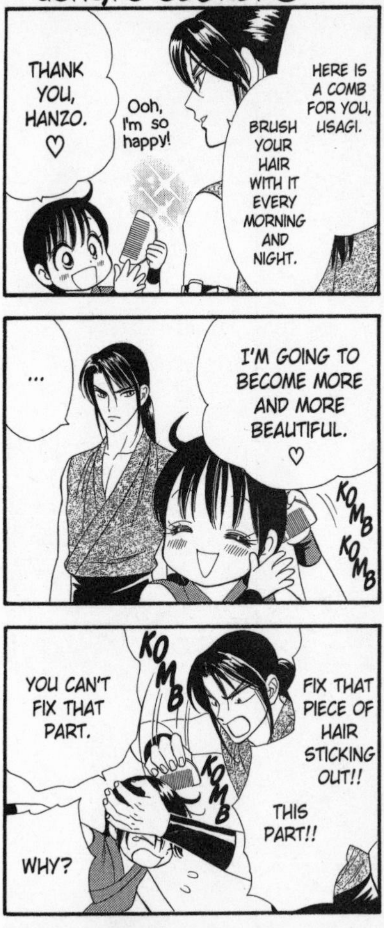
HERE IS A COMB FOR YOU, USAGI.
BRUSH YOUR HAIR WITH IT EVERY MORNING AND NIGHT.
Ooh, I'm so happy!
THANK YOU, HANZO. ♡
I'M GOING TO BECOME MORE AND MORE BEAUTIFUL. ♡
KOMB KOMB
...
FIX THAT PIECE OF HAIR STICKING OUT!!
KOMB
KOMB
THIS PART!!
YOU CAN'T FIX THAT PART.
WHY?
IT'S OKAY.
I DON'T MIND IT ANYMORE.
HUFF HUFF
BOIK
I MIND!!

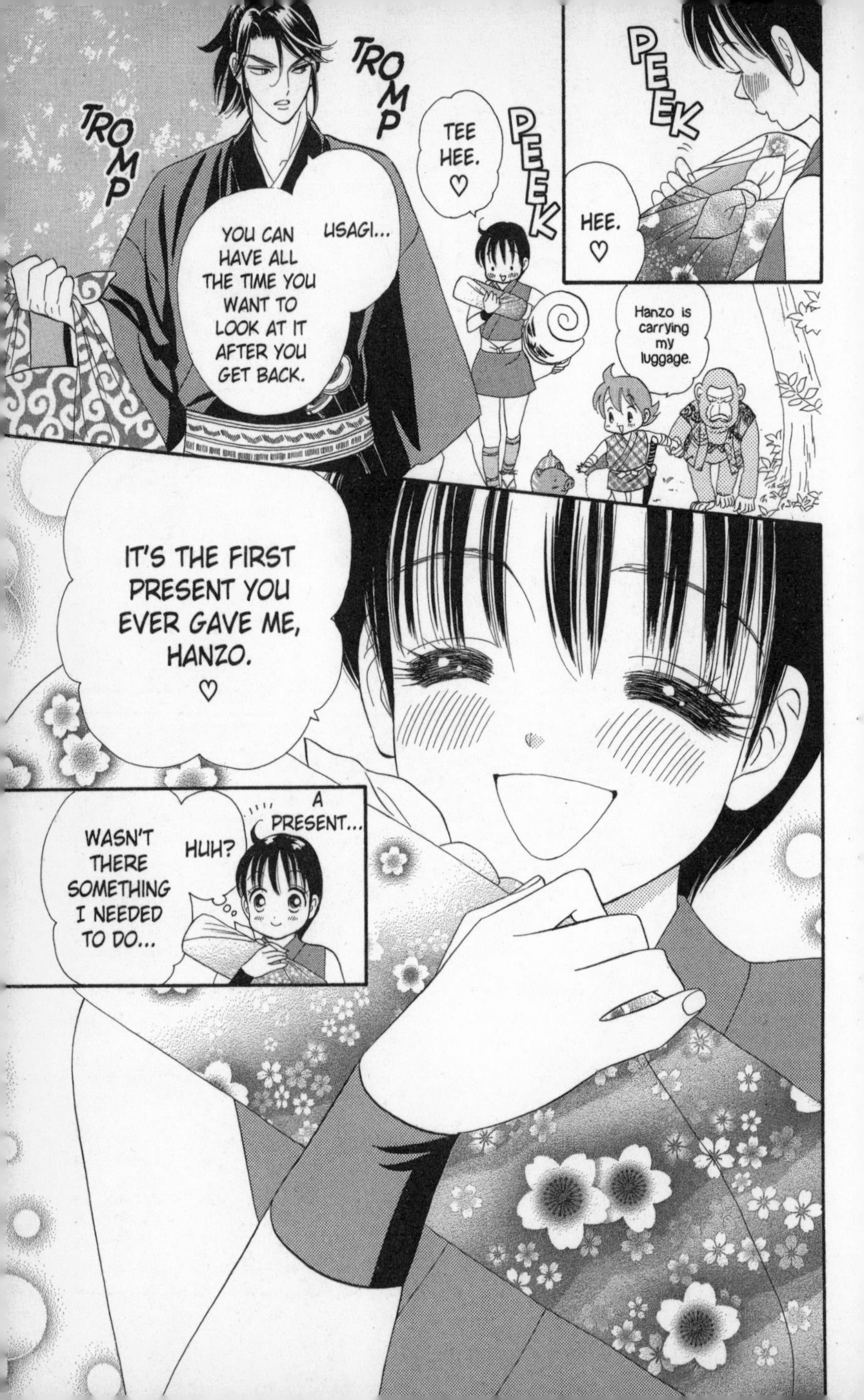
PEEK
HEE. ♡
PEEK
TEE HEE. ♡
Hanzo is carrying my luggage.
TROMP
TROMP
USAGI...
YOU CAN HAVE ALL THE TIME YOU WANT TO LOOK AT IT AFTER YOU GET BACK.
IT'S THE FIRST PRESENT YOU EVER GAVE ME, HANZO. ♡
A PRESENT...
HUH?
WASN'T THERE SOMETHING I NEEDED TO DO...

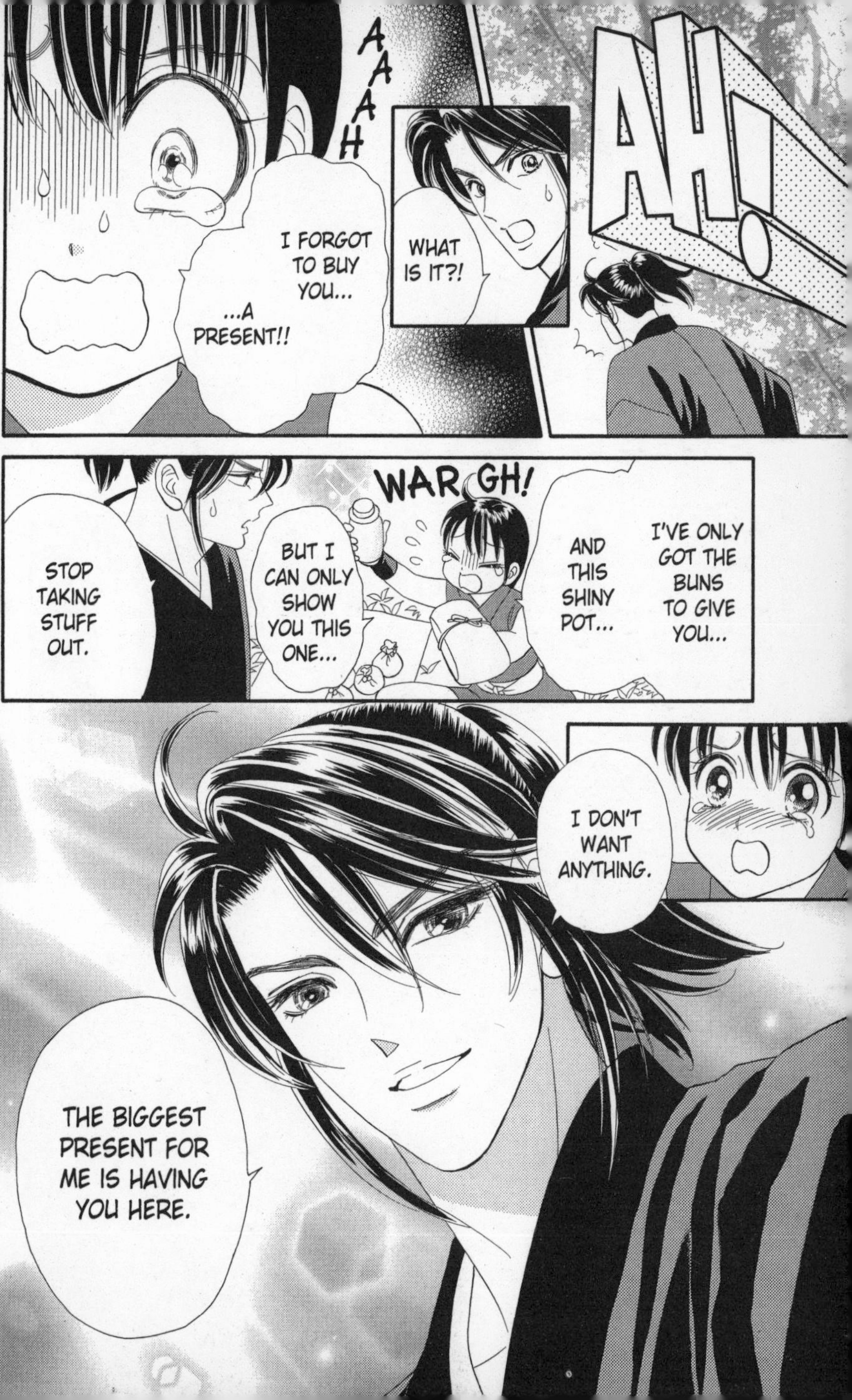
AH!
WHAT IS IT?!
AAAAH
I FORGOT TO BUY YOU...
...A PRESENT!!
I'VE ONLY GOT THE BUNS TO GIVE YOU...
AND THIS SHINY POT...
WARGH!
BUT I CAN ONLY SHOW YOU THIS ONE...
STOP TAKING STUFF OUT.
I DON'T WANT ANYTHING.
THE BIGGEST PRESENT FOR ME IS HAVING YOU HERE.

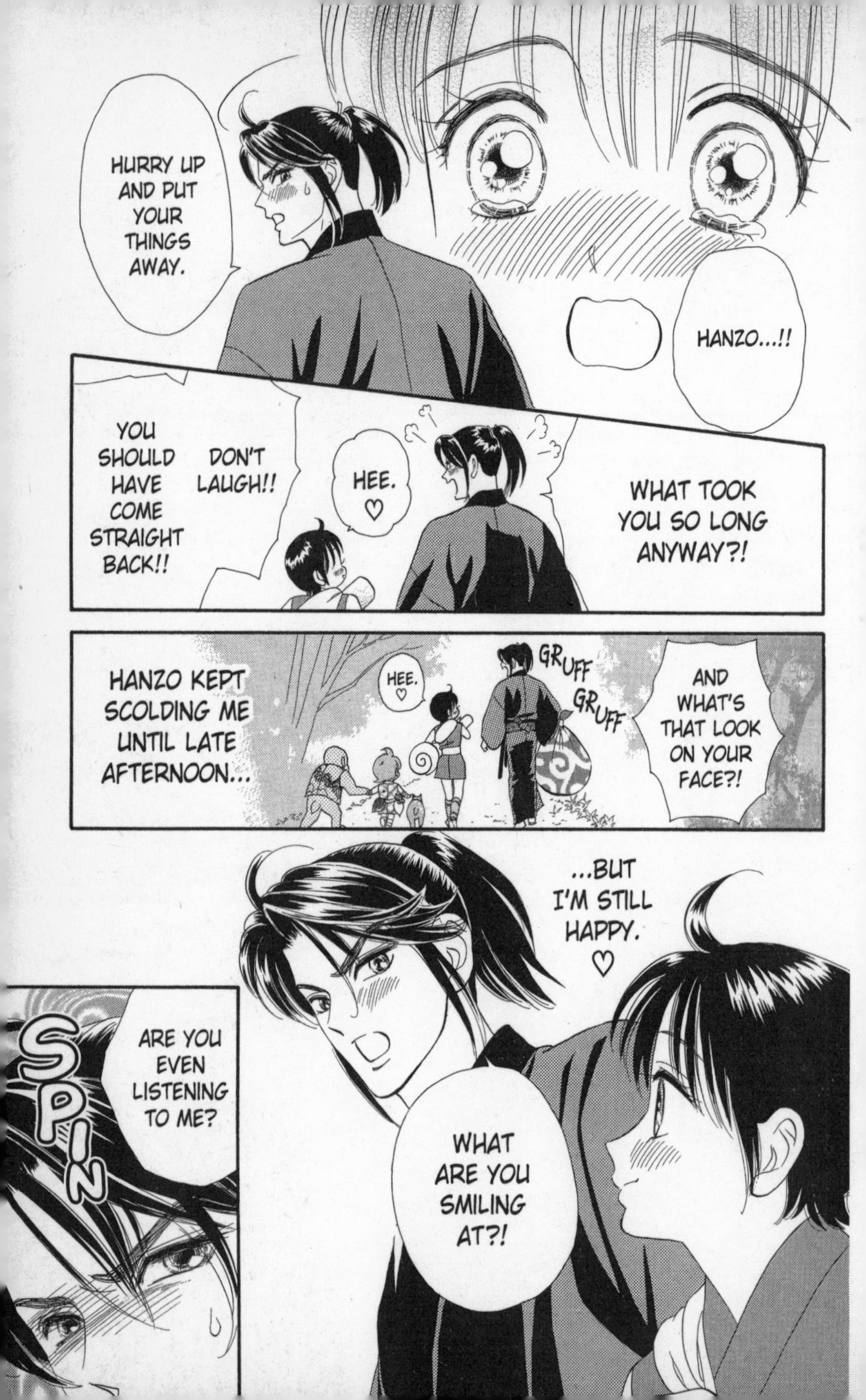
HANZO...!!
HURRY UP AND PUT YOUR THINGS AWAY.
WHAT TOOK YOU SO LONG ANYWAY?!
HEE. ♡
DON'T LAUGH!!
YOU SHOULD HAVE COME STRAIGHT BACK!!
AND WHAT'S THAT LOOK ON YOUR FACE?!
GRUFF GRUFF
HEE. ♡
HANZO KEPT SCOLDING ME UNTIL LATE AFTERNOON...
...BUT I'M STILL HAPPY. ♡
WHAT ARE YOU SMILING AT?!
SPIN
ARE YOU EVEN LISTENING TO ME?

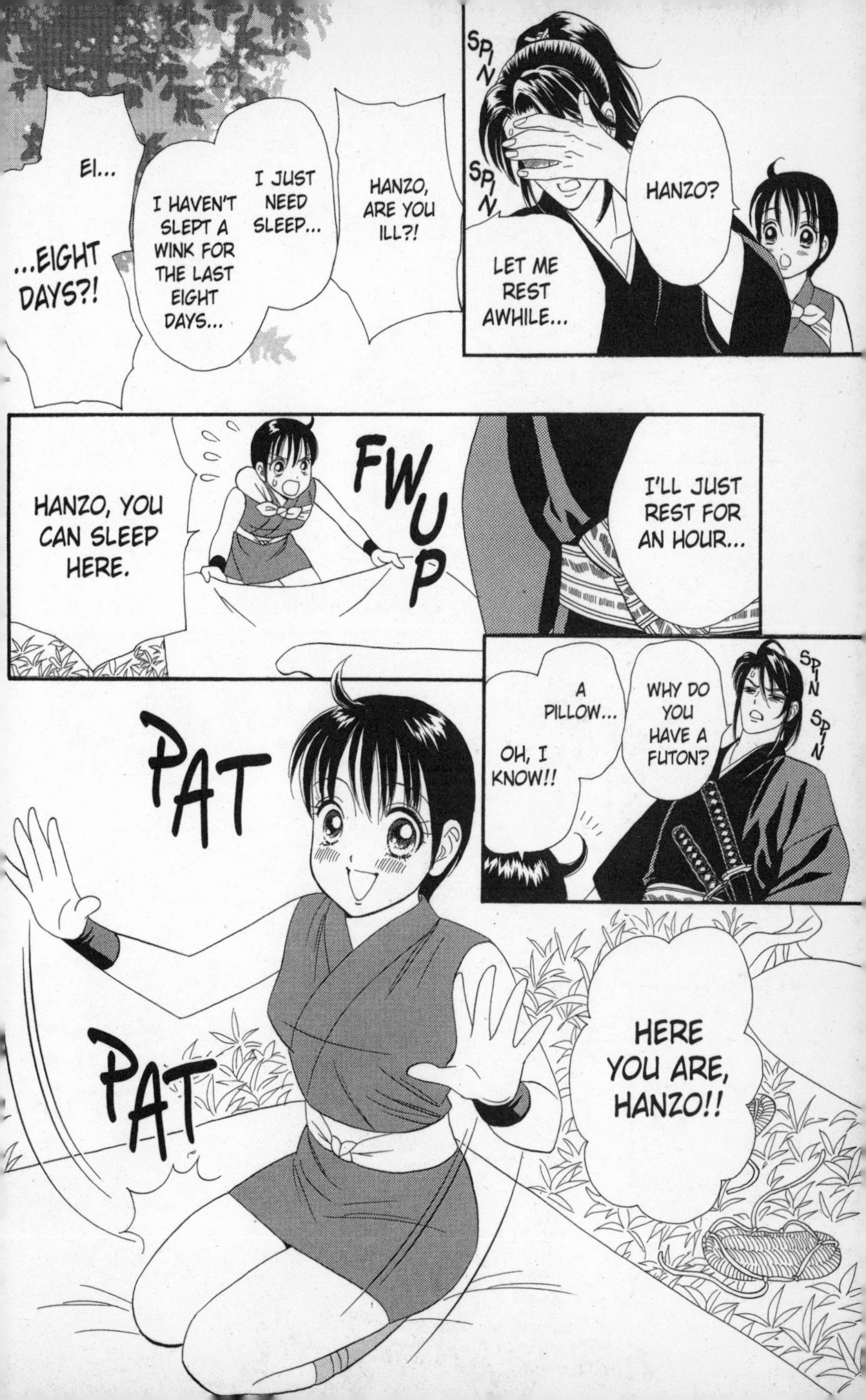
HANZO?
SPIN
SPIN
LET ME REST AWHILE...
HANZO, ARE YOU ILL?!
I JUST NEED SLEEP...
I HAVEN'T SLEPT A WINK FOR THE LAST EIGHT DAYS...
EI...
...EIGHT DAYS?!
I'LL JUST REST FOR AN HOUR...
FWUP
HANZO, YOU CAN SLEEP HERE.
SPIN
SPIN
WHY DO YOU HAVE A FUTON?
A PILLOW...
OH, I KNOW!!
HERE YOU ARE, HANZO!!
PAT
PAT

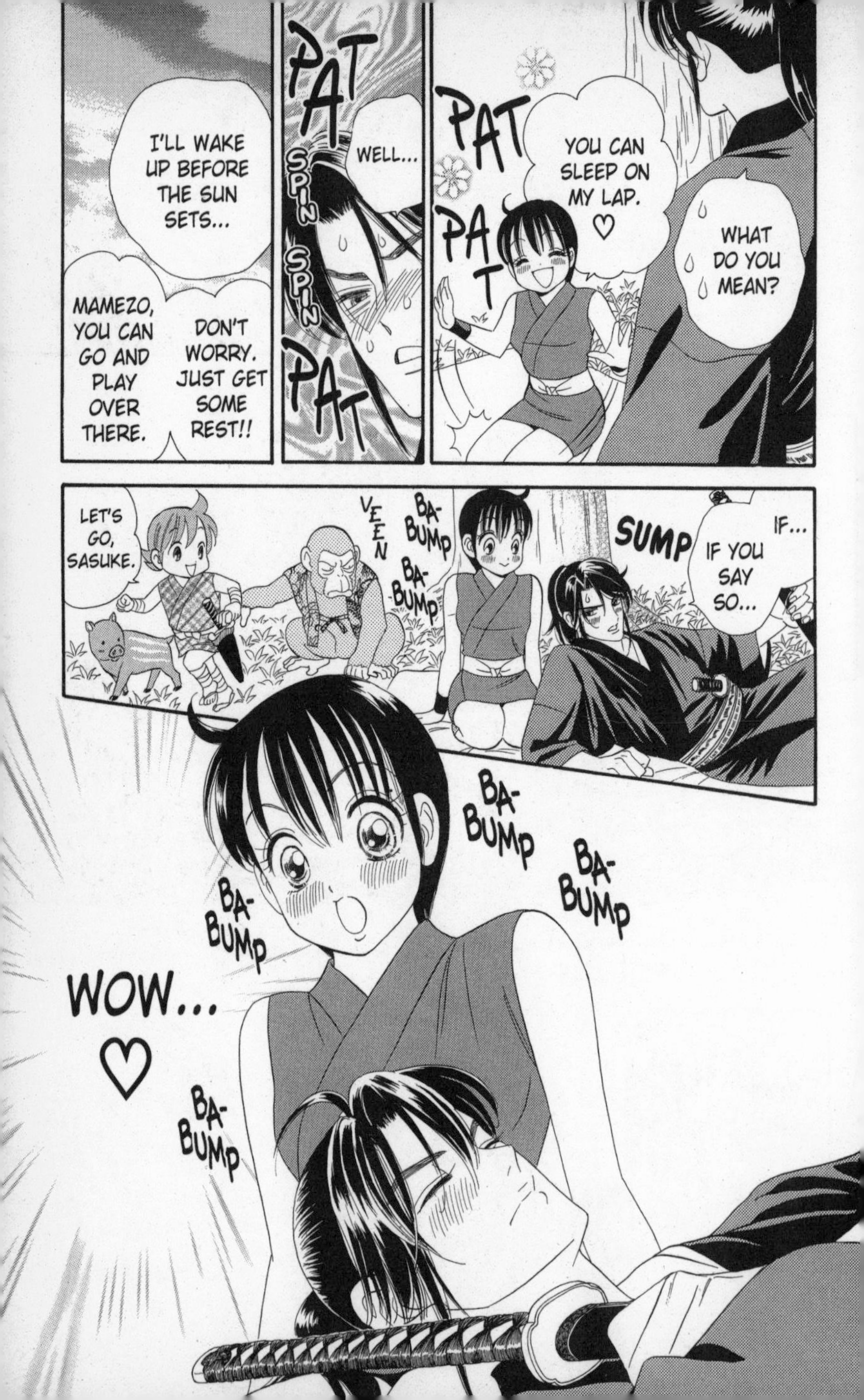
PAT
PAT
PAT
YOU CAN SLEEP ON MY LAP. ♡
WHAT DO YOU MEAN?
PAT
WELL...
SPIN SPIN
PAT
I'LL WAKE UP BEFORE THE SUN SETS...
DON'T WORRY. JUST GET SOME REST!!
MAMEZO, YOU CAN GO AND PLAY OVER THERE.
IF... IF YOU SAY SO...
SUMP
BA-BUMP
BA-BUMP
VEEN
LET'S GO, SASUKE.
BA-BUMP
BA-BUMP
BA-BUMP
WOW... ♡
BA-BUMP

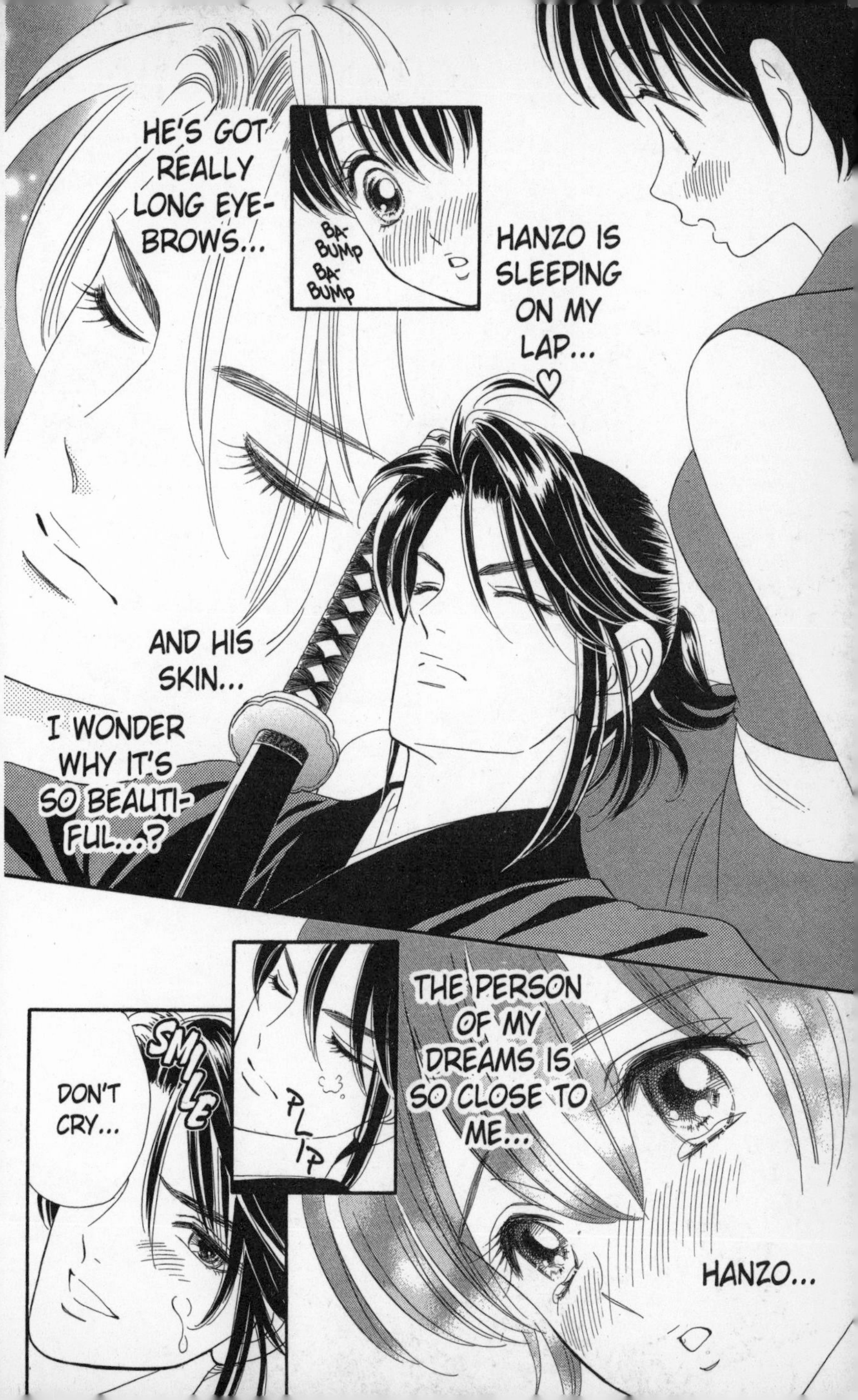
HANZO IS SLEEPING ON MY LAP... ♡
BA-BUMP BA-BUMP
HE'S GOT REALLY LONG EYE-BROWS...
AND HIS SKIN...
I WONDER WHY IT'S SO BEAUTI-FUL...?
THE PERSON OF MY DREAMS IS SO CLOSE TO ME...
HANZO...
PLIP
SMILE
DON'T CRY...

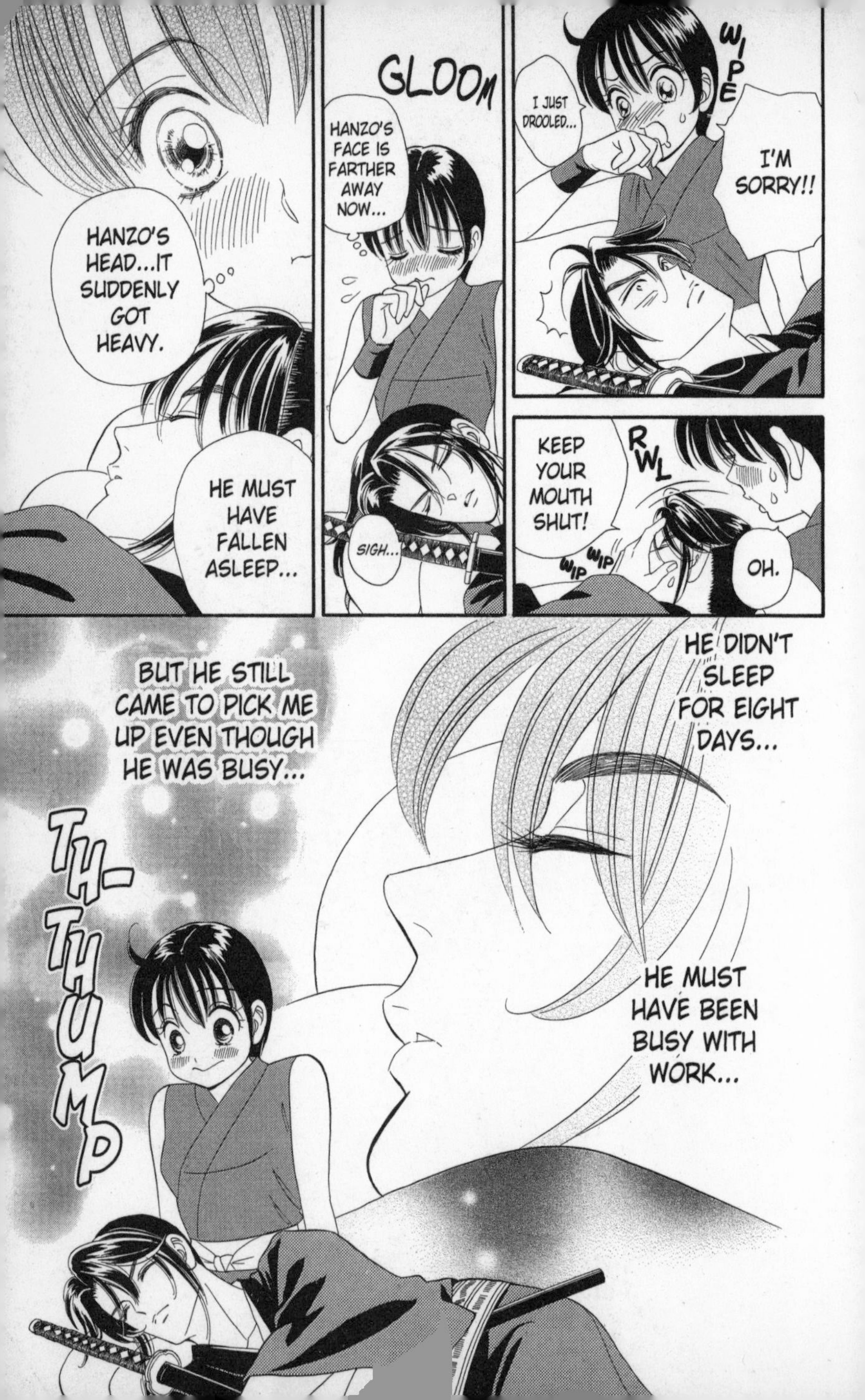
WIPE
I JUST DROOLED...
I'M SORRY!!
RWL
KEEP YOUR MOUTH SHUT!
OH.
WIP WIP
GLOOM
HANZO'S FACE IS FARTHER AWAY NOW...
SIGH...
HANZO'S HEAD...IT SUDDENLY GOT HEAVY.
HE MUST HAVE FALLEN ASLEEP...
HE DIDN'T SLEEP FOR EIGHT DAYS...
HE MUST HAVE BEEN BUSY WITH WORK...
BUT HE STILL CAME TO PICK ME UP EVEN THOUGH HE WAS BUSY...
TH-THUMP

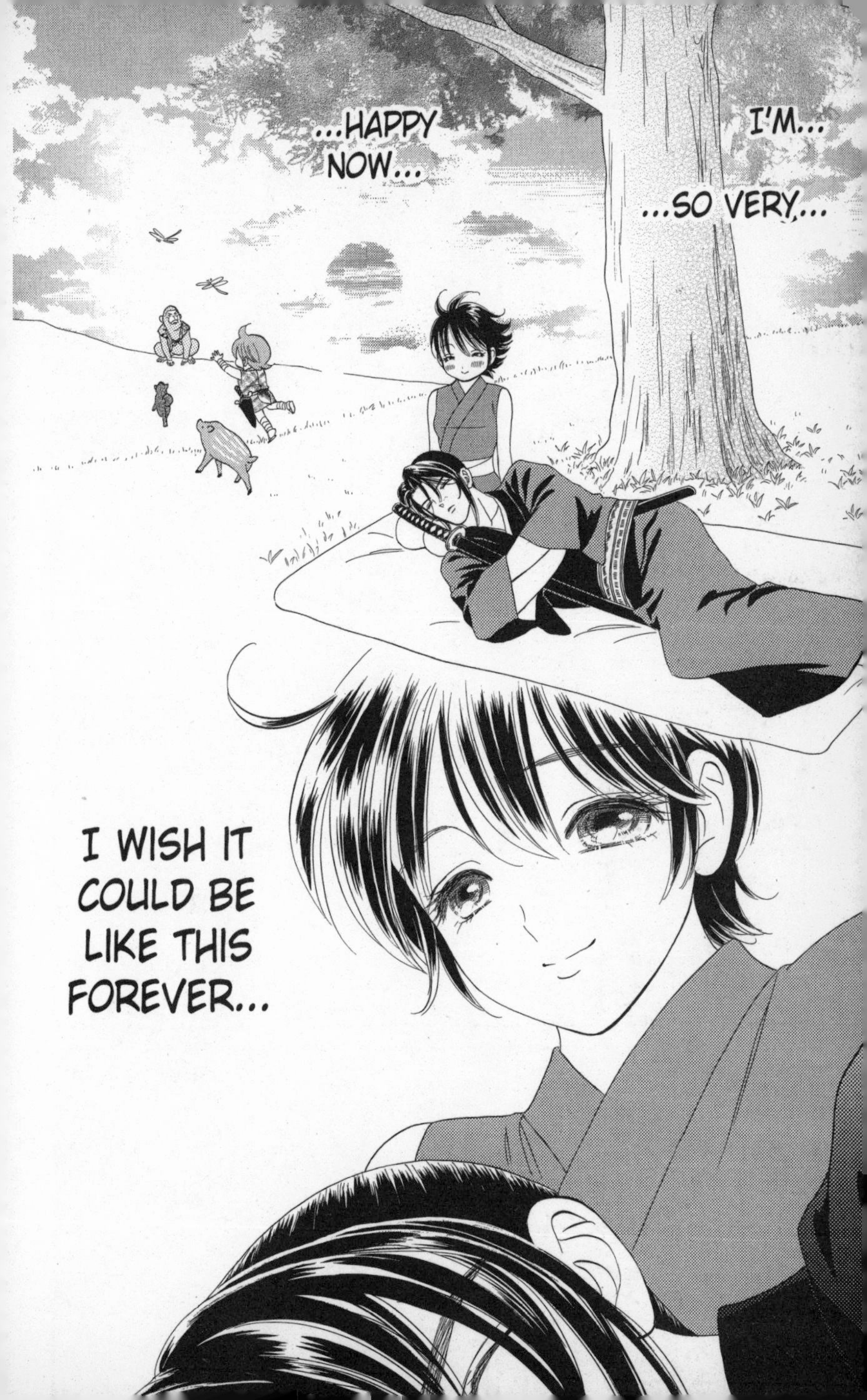
I'M...
...SO VERY...
...HAPPY NOW...
I WISH IT COULD BE LIKE THIS FOREVER...

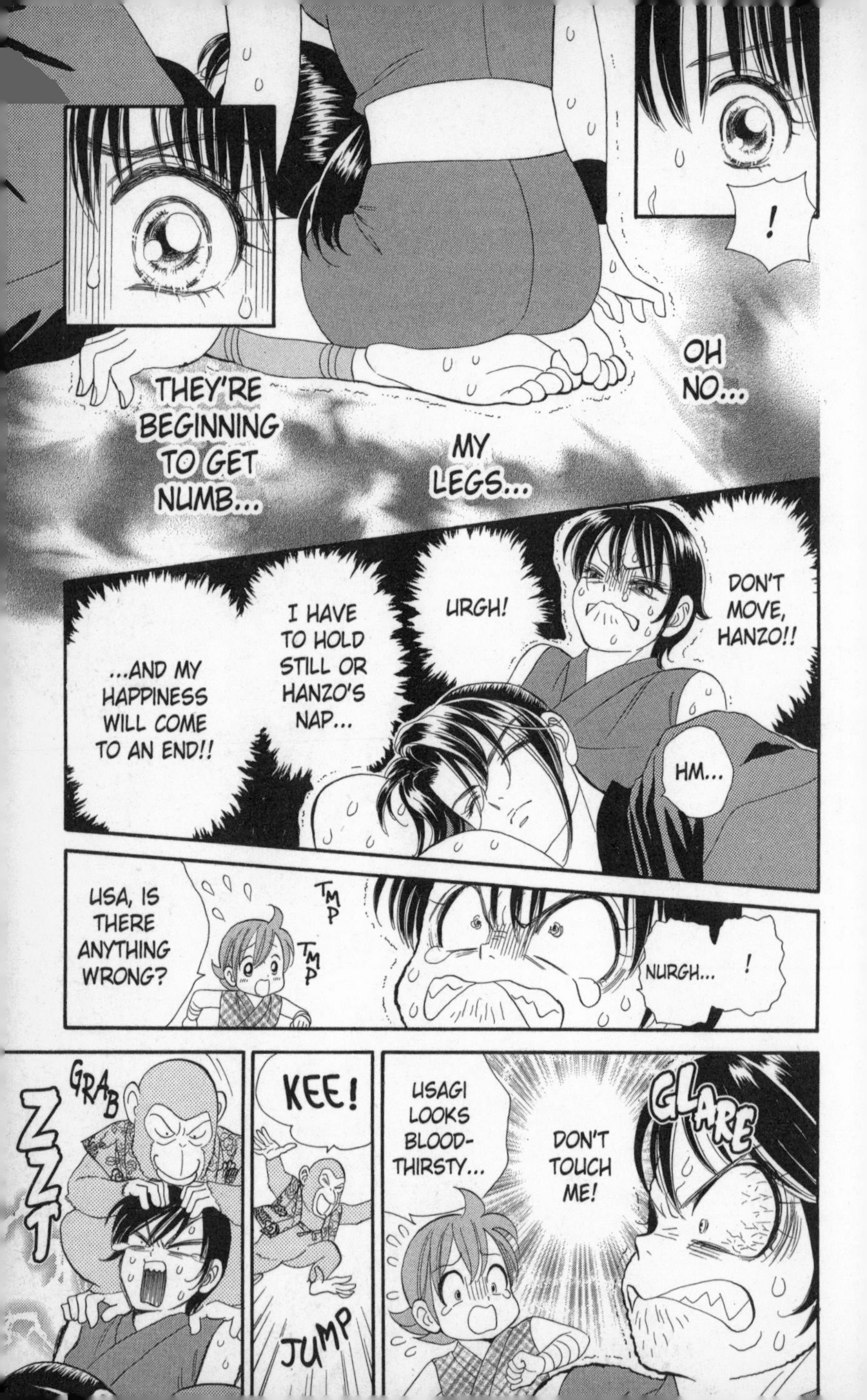
!
OH NO...
MY LEGS...
THEY'RE BEGINNING TO GET NUMB...
DON'T MOVE, HANZO!!
HM...
URGH!
I HAVE TO HOLD STILL OR HANZO'S NAP...
...AND MY HAPPINESS WILL COME TO AN END!!
NURGH... !
TMP
TMP
USA, IS THERE ANYTHING WRONG?
GLARE
DON'T TOUCH ME!
USAGI LOOKS BLOOD-THIRSTY...
KEE!
JUMP
GRAB
ZZZT

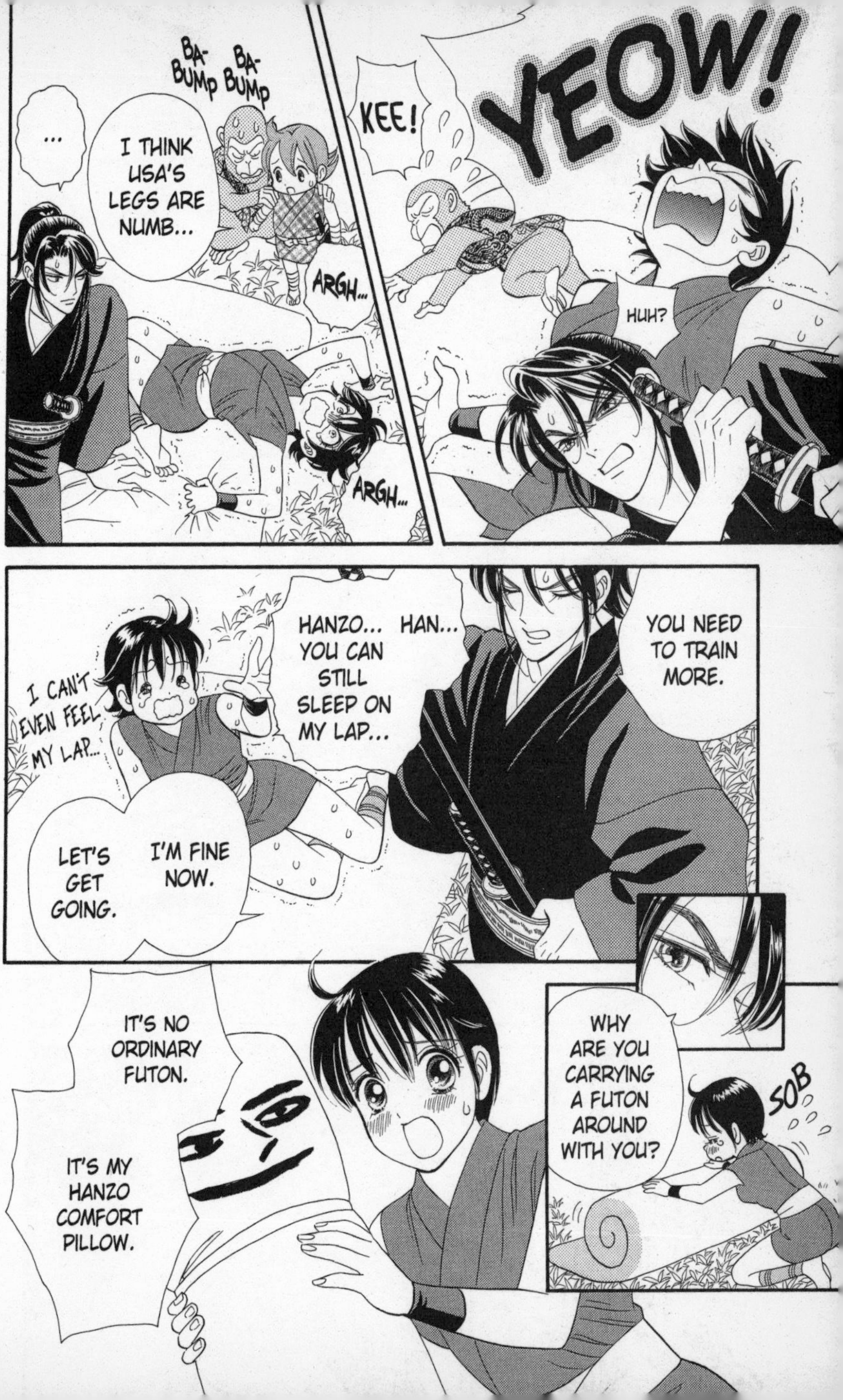
YEOW!
KEE!
HUH?
BA-BUMP BA-BUMP
I THINK USA'S LEGS ARE NUMB...
...
ARGH...
ARGH...
YOU NEED TO TRAIN MORE.
HANZO... HAN... YOU CAN STILL SLEEP ON MY LAP...
I CAN'T EVEN FEEL MY LAP...
I'M FINE NOW.
LET'S GET GOING.
WHY ARE YOU CARRYING A FUTON AROUND WITH YOU?
SOB
IT'S NO ORDINARY FUTON.
IT'S MY HANZO COMFORT PILLOW.

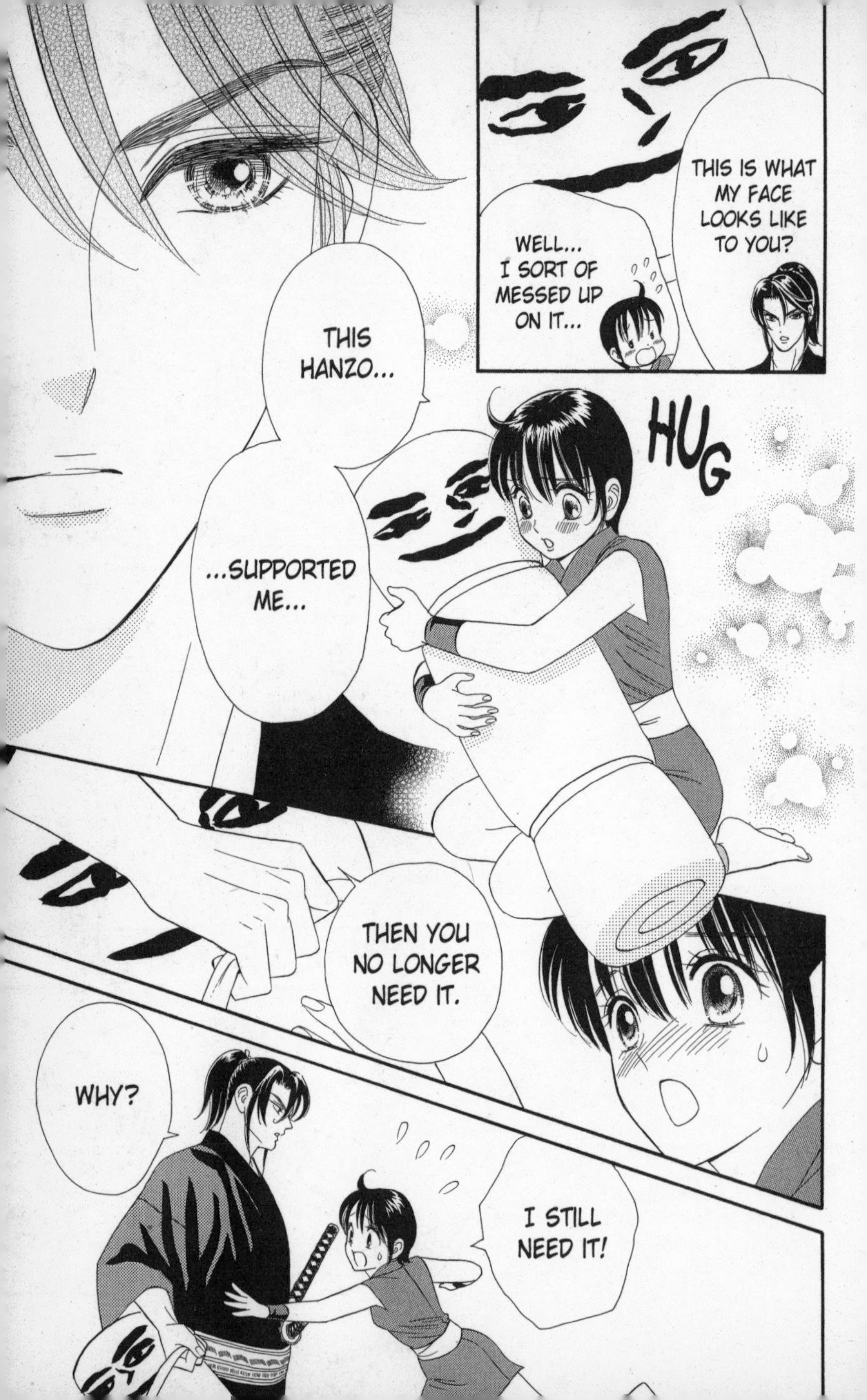
THIS IS WHAT MY FACE LOOKS LIKE TO YOU?
WELL... I SORT OF MESSED UP ON IT...
HUG
THIS HANZO...
...SUPPORTED ME...
THEN YOU NO LONGER NEED IT.
WHY?
I STILL NEED IT!

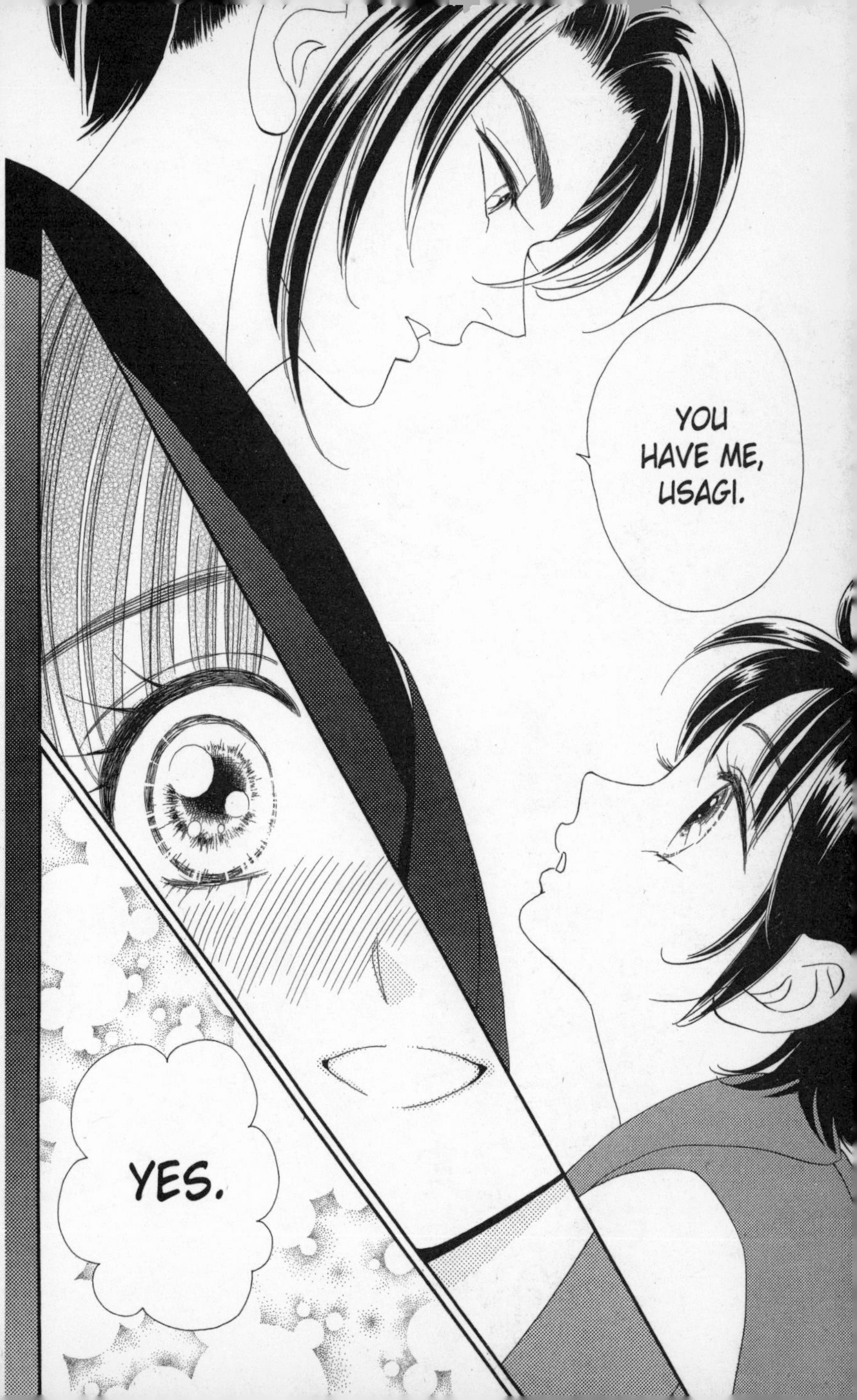
YOU HAVE ME, USAGI.
YES.

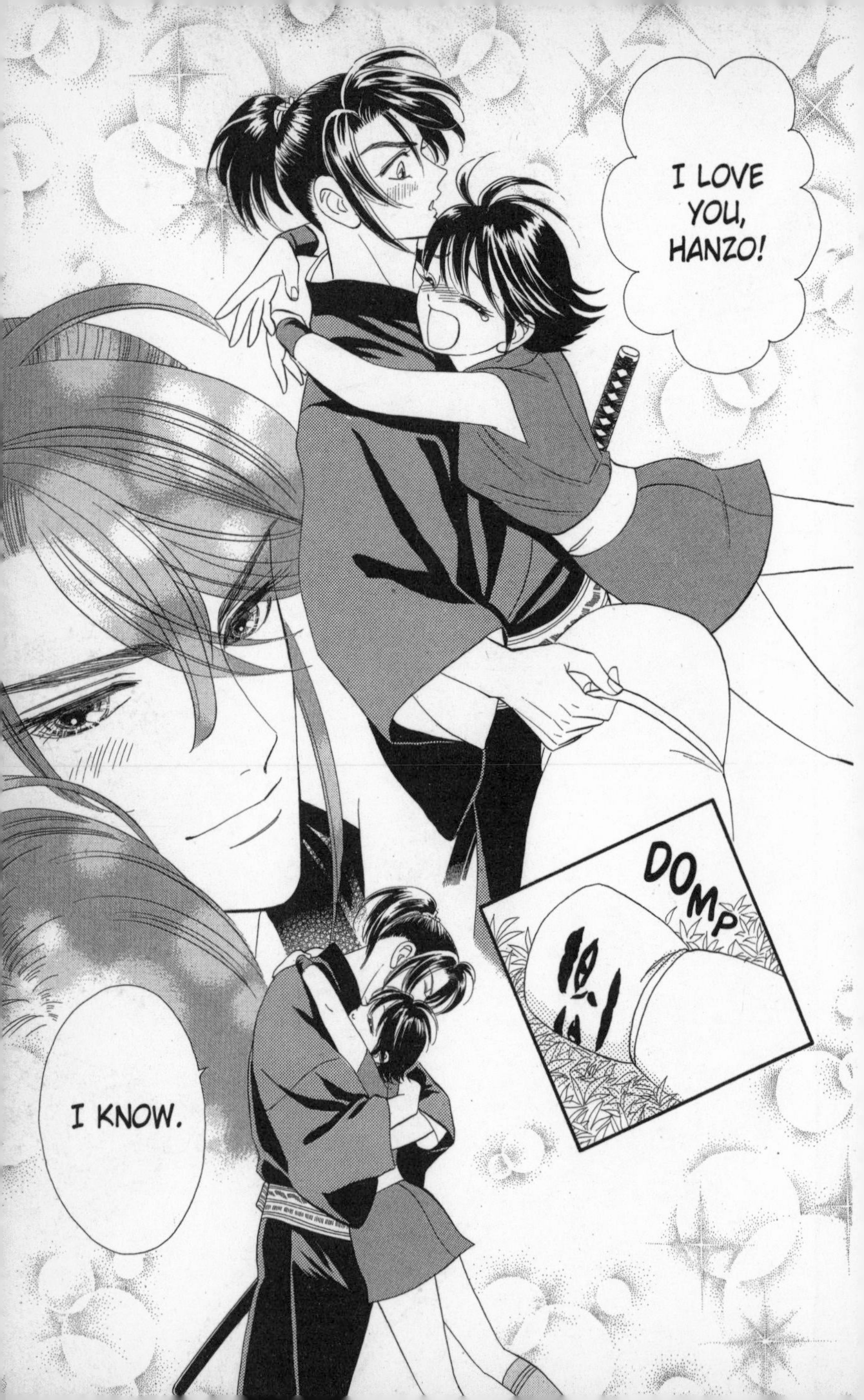
I LOVE YOU, HANZO!
DOMP
I KNOW.

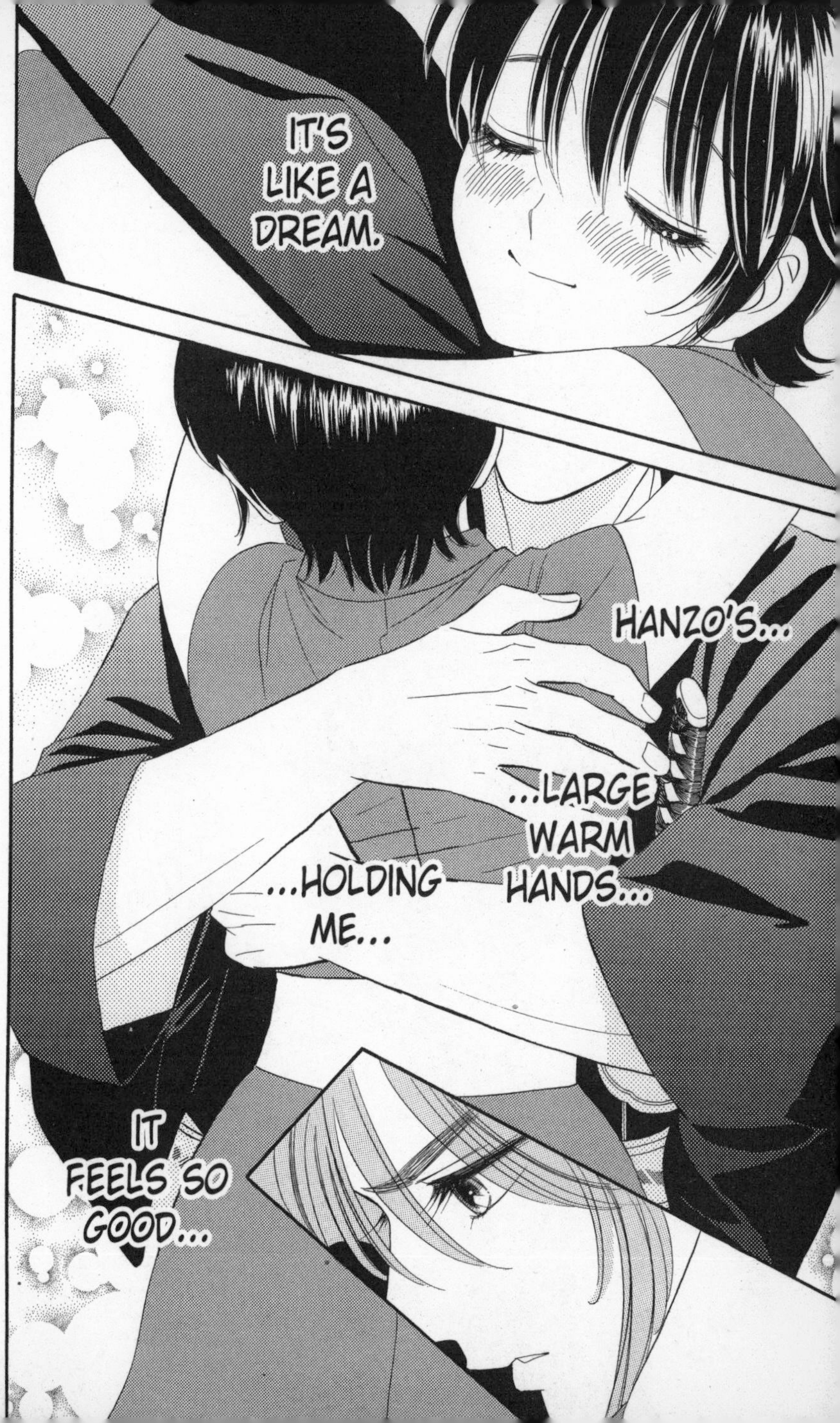
IT'S LIKE A DREAM.
HANZO'S...
...LARGE WARM HANDS...
...HOLDING ME...
IT FEELS SO GOOD...

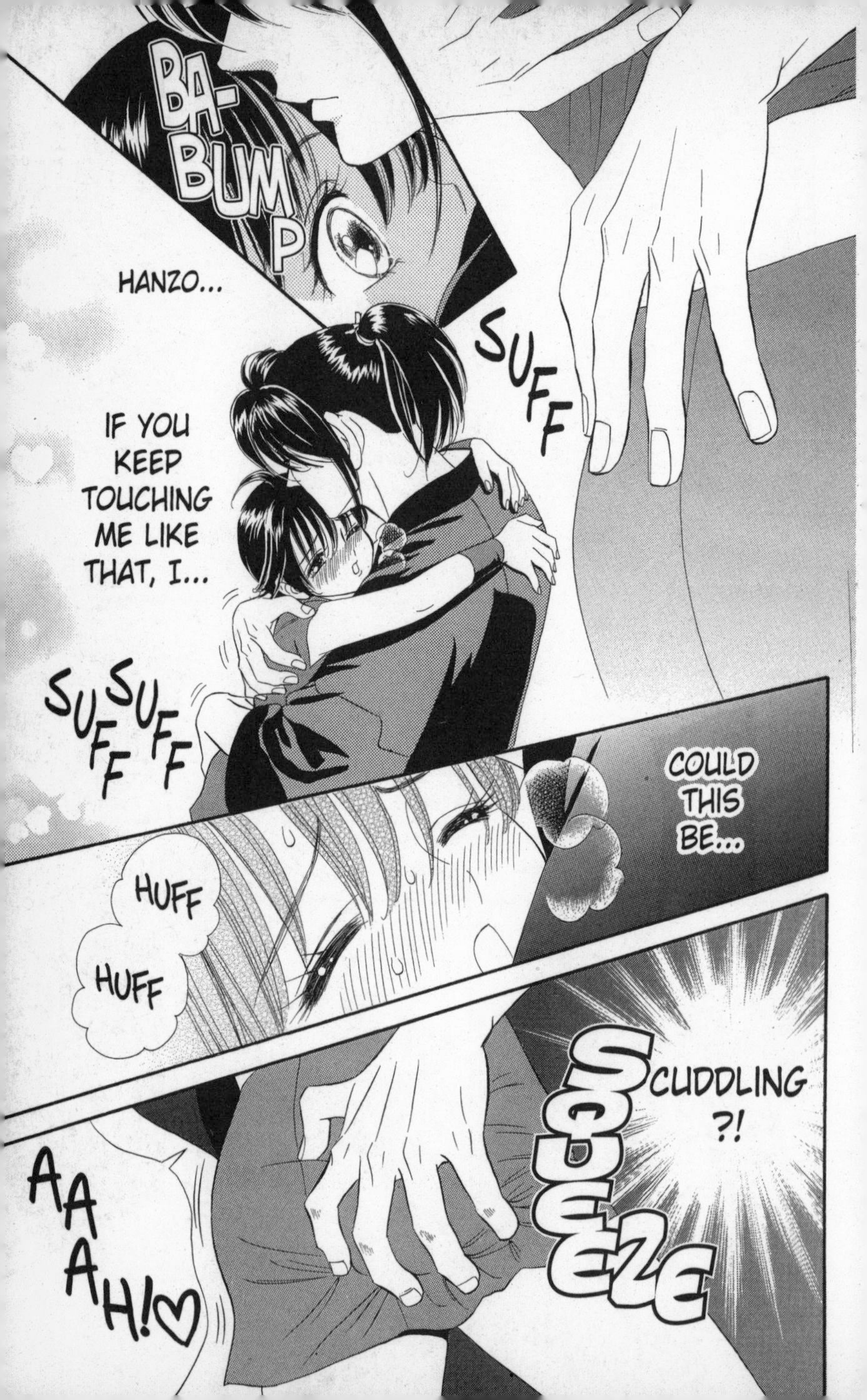
BA-BUMP
HANZO...
SUFF
IF YOU KEEP TOUCHING ME LIKE THAT, I...
SUFF SUFF
SUFF SUFF
COULD THIS BE...
HUFF
HUFF
CUDDLING ?!
SQUEEZE
AAAAH!♡

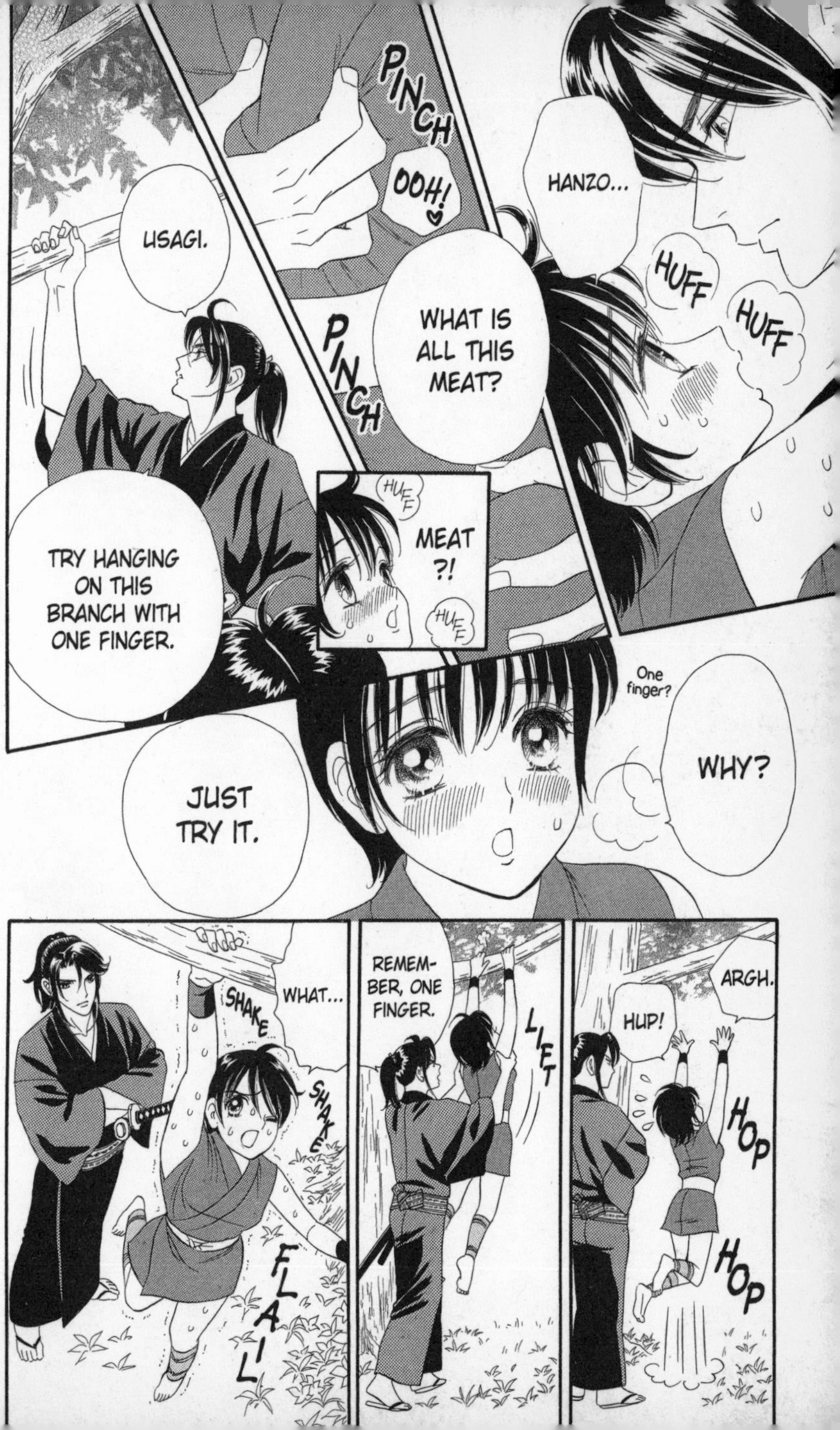
HANZO...
HUFF
HUFF
PINCH
OOH! ♥
PINCH
WHAT IS ALL THIS MEAT?
HUFF
MEAT ?!
HUFF
USAGI.
TRY HANGING ON THIS BRANCH WITH ONE FINGER.
One finger?
WHY?
JUST TRY IT.
ARGH.
HUP!
HOP
HOP
REMEM-BER, ONE FINGER.
LIFT
WHAT...
SHAKE...
SHAKE
FLAIL

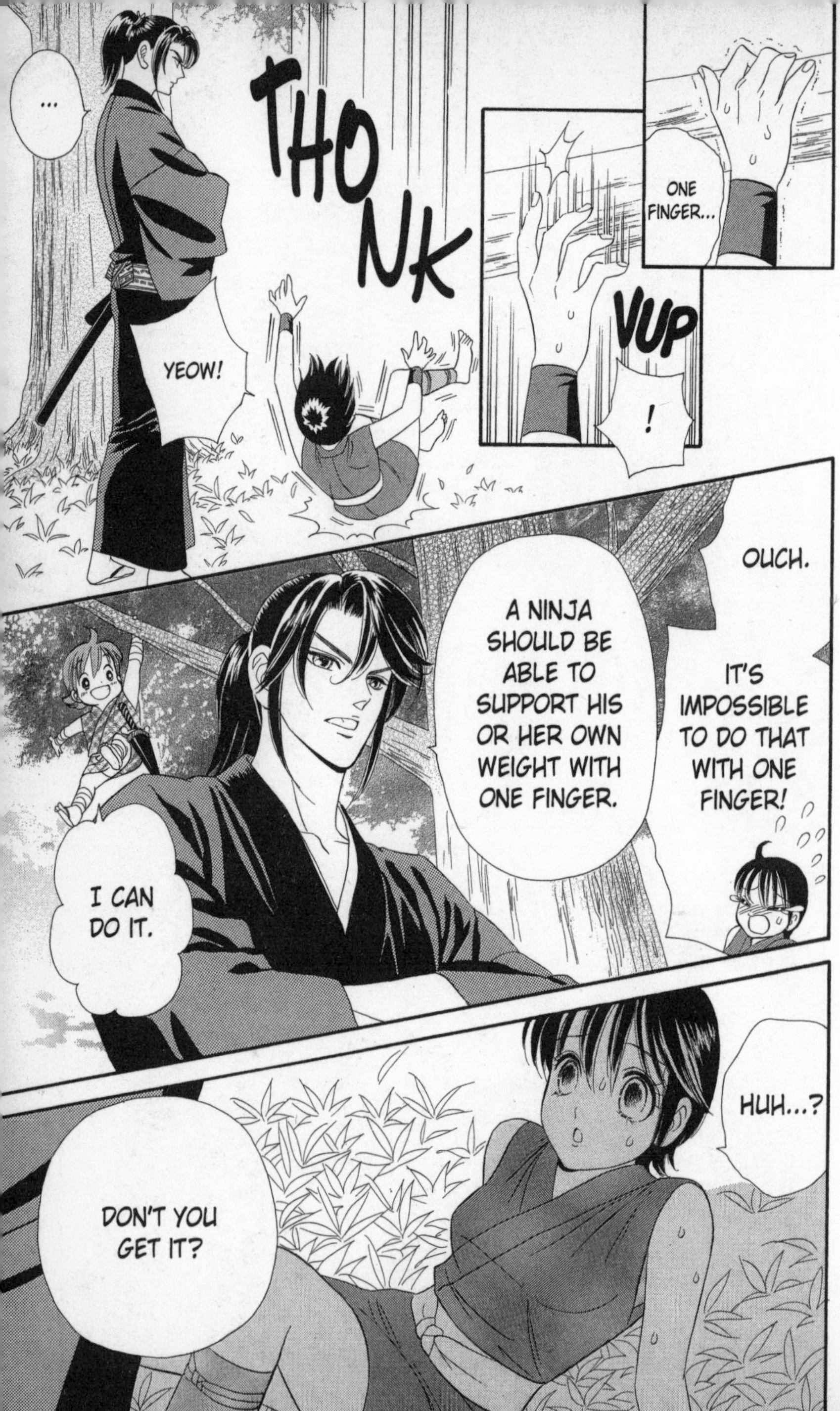
ONE FINGER...
VUP
!
THONK
YEOW!
...
OUCH.
IT'S IMPOSSIBLE TO DO THAT WITH ONE FINGER!
A NINJA SHOULD BE ABLE TO SUPPORT HIS OR HER OWN WEIGHT WITH ONE FINGER.
I CAN DO IT.
HUH...?
DON'T YOU GET IT?

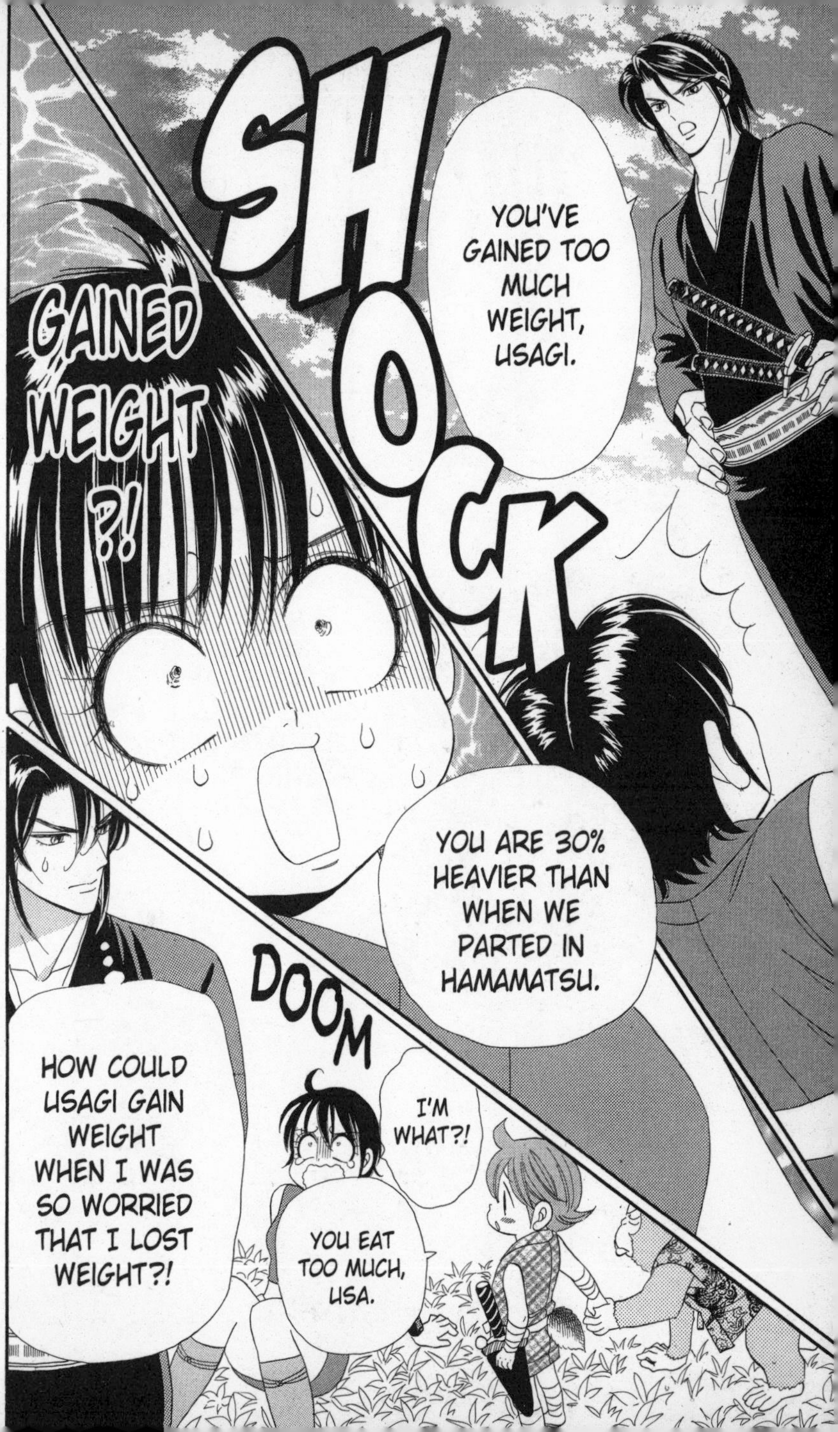
SHOCK
YOU'VE GAINED TOO MUCH WEIGHT, USAGI.
GAINED WEIGHT ?!
YOU ARE 30% HEAVIER THAN WHEN WE PARTED IN HAMAMATSU.
DOOM
I'M WHAT?!
YOU EAT TOO MUCH, USA.
HOW COULD USAGI GAIN WEIGHT WHEN I WAS SO WORRIED THAT I LOST WEIGHT?!

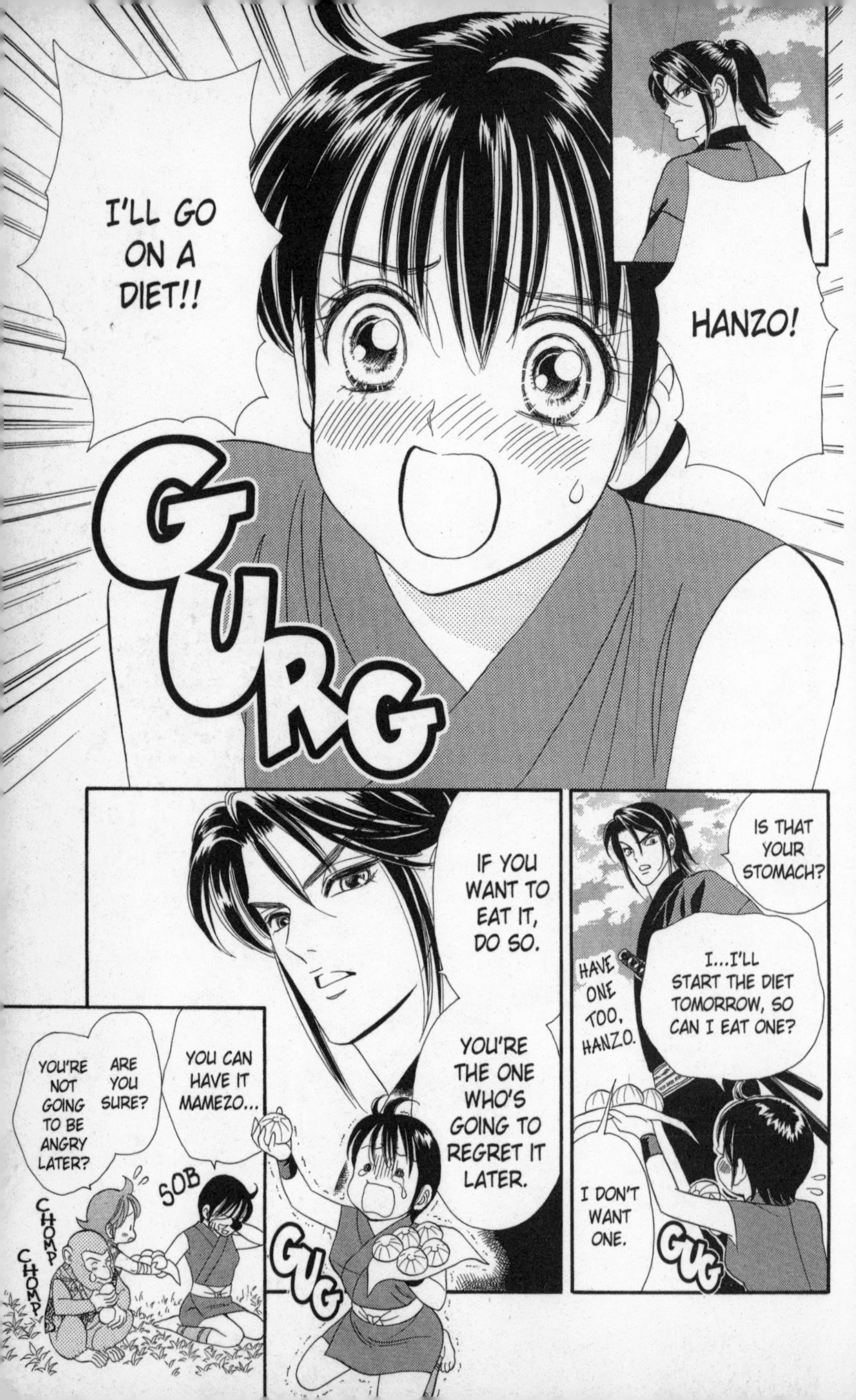
HANZO!
I'LL GO ON A DIET!!
GURG
IS THAT YOUR STOMACH?
I...I'LL START THE DIET TOMORROW, SO CAN I EAT ONE?
HAVE ONE TOO, HANZO.
I DON'T WANT ONE.
GUG
IF YOU WANT TO EAT IT, DO SO.
YOU'RE THE ONE WHO'S GOING TO REGRET IT LATER.
GUG
YOU CAN HAVE IT MAMEZO...
ARE YOU SURE?
YOU'RE NOT GOING TO BE ANGRY LATER?
SOB
CHOMP
CHOMP

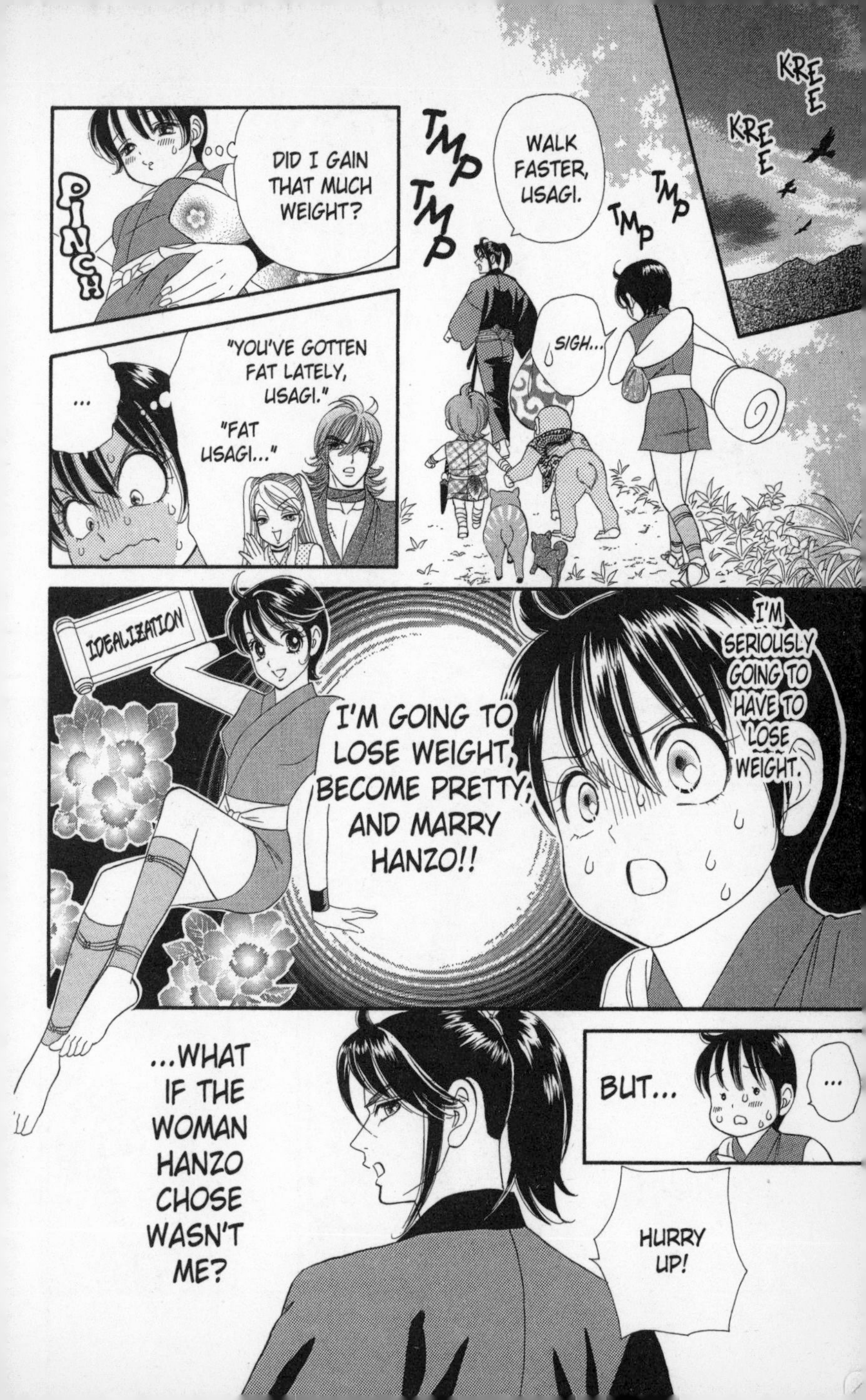
KREE
KREE
TMP TMP
WALK FASTER, USAGI.
TMP TMP
SIGH...
PINCH
DID I GAIN THAT MUCH WEIGHT?
...
"YOU'VE GOTTEN FAT LATELY, USAGI."
"FAT USAGI..."
I'M SERIOUSLY GOING TO HAVE TO LOSE WEIGHT.
I'M GOING TO LOSE WEIGHT, BECOME PRETTY, AND MARRY HANZO!!
IDEALIZATION
...
BUT...
HURRY UP!
...WHAT IF THE WOMAN HANZO CHOSE WASN'T ME?

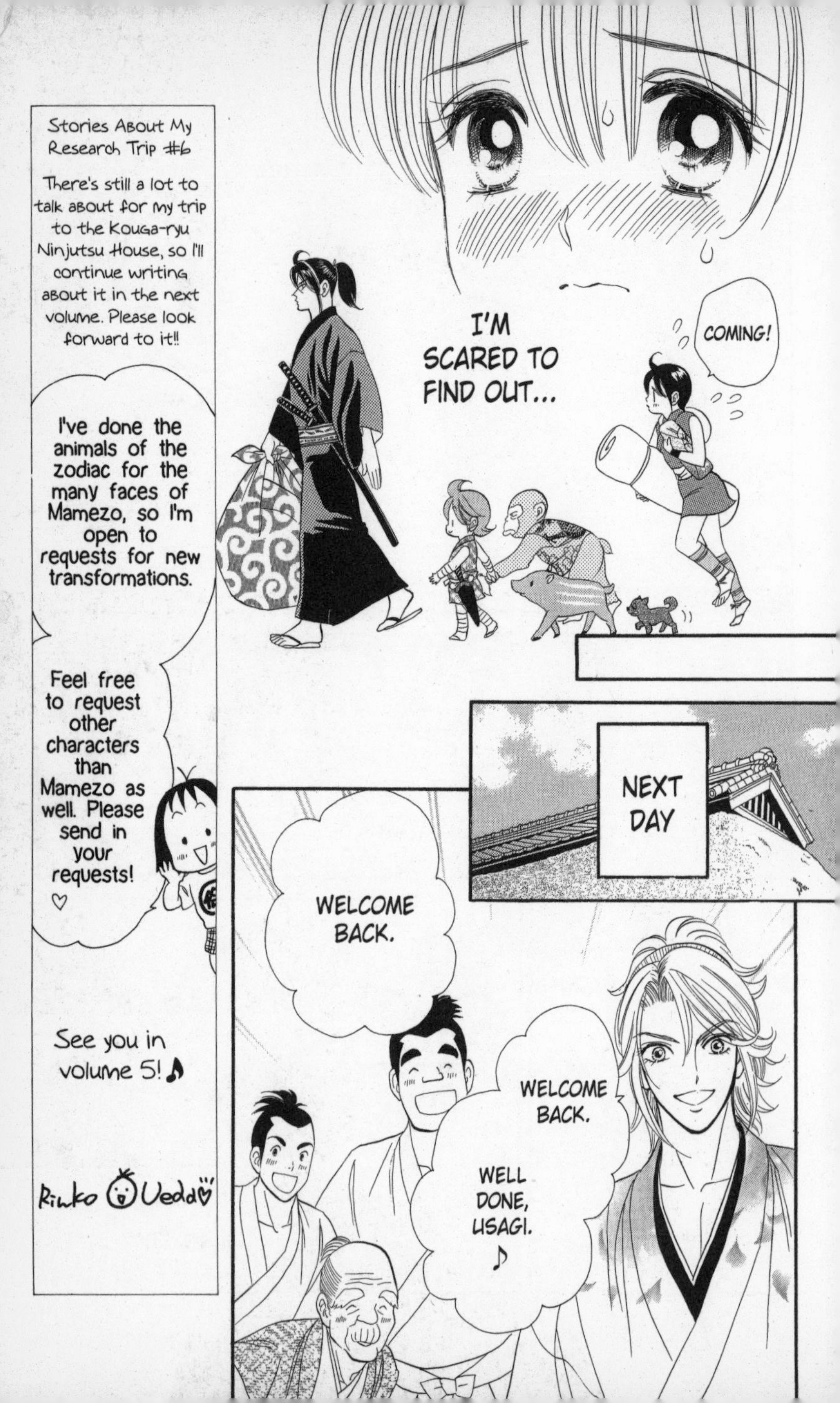
I'M SCARED TO FIND OUT...
COMING!
NEXT DAY
WELCOME BACK.
WELL DONE, USAGI. ♪
WELCOME BACK.

Stories About My Research Trip #6

There's still a lot to talk about for my trip to the Kouga-ryu Ninjutsu House, so I'll continue writing about it in the next volume. Please look forward to it!!

I've done the animals of the zodiac for the many faces of Mamezo, so I'm open to requests for new transformations.

Feel free to request other characters than Mamezo as well. Please send in your requests! ♡

See you in volume 5! ♪

Rinko Ueda ♡

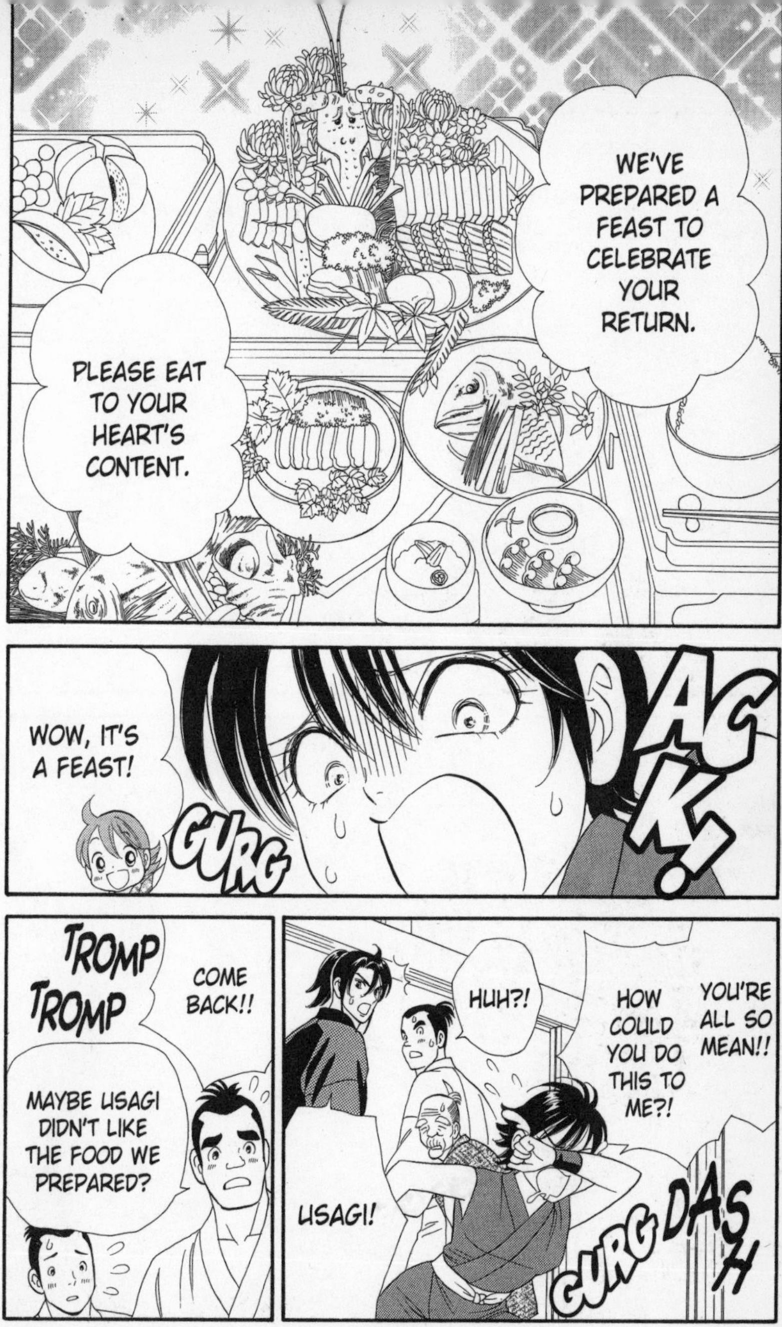
WE'VE PREPARED A FEAST TO CELEBRATE YOUR RETURN.
PLEASE EAT TO YOUR HEART'S CONTENT.
ACK!
WOW, IT'S A FEAST!
GURG
YOU'RE ALL SO MEAN!!
HOW COULD YOU DO THIS TO ME?!
HUH?!
USAGI!
GURG
DASH
COME BACK!!
TROMP TROMP
MAYBE USAGI DIDN'T LIKE THE FOOD WE PREPARED?

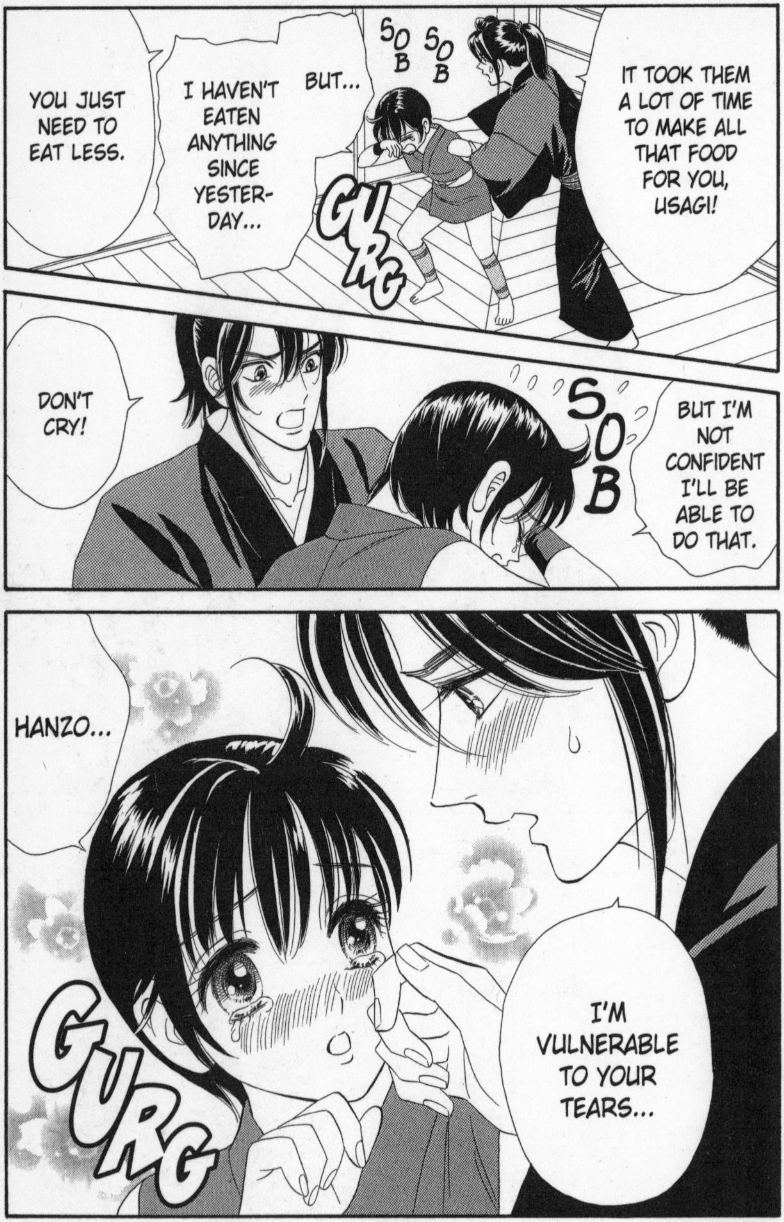
IT TOOK THEM A LOT OF TIME TO MAKE ALL THAT FOOD FOR YOU, USAGI!
SOB SOB
BUT...
I HAVEN'T EATEN ANYTHING SINCE YESTER-DAY...
GURG
YOU JUST NEED TO EAT LESS.
BUT I'M NOT CONFIDENT I'LL BE ABLE TO DO THAT.
SOB
DON'T CRY!
I'M VULNERABLE TO YOUR TEARS...
HANZO...
GURG

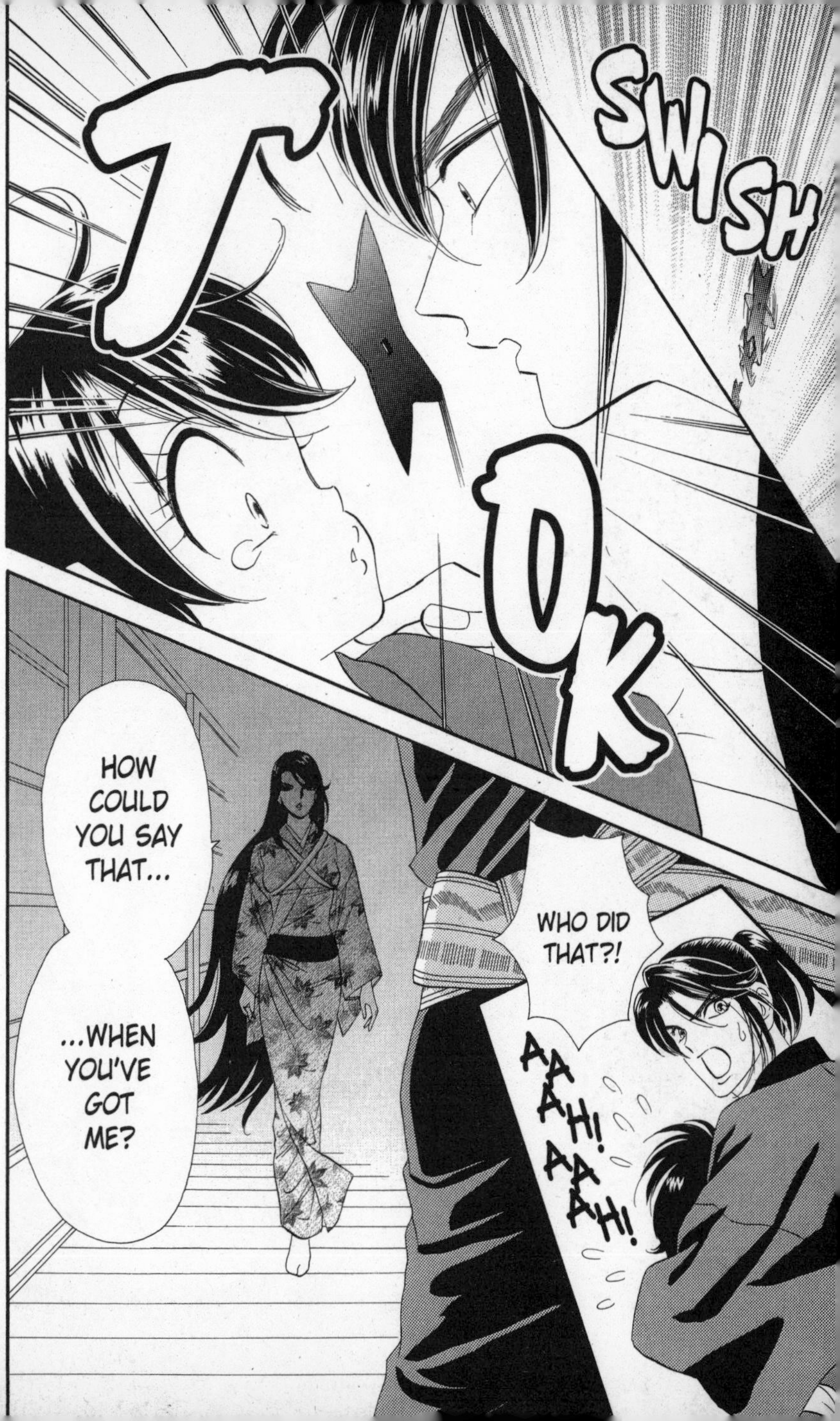
SWISH
TOK
WHO DID THAT?!
AAAH! AAAH!
HOW COULD YOU SAY THAT...
...WHEN YOU'VE GOT ME?

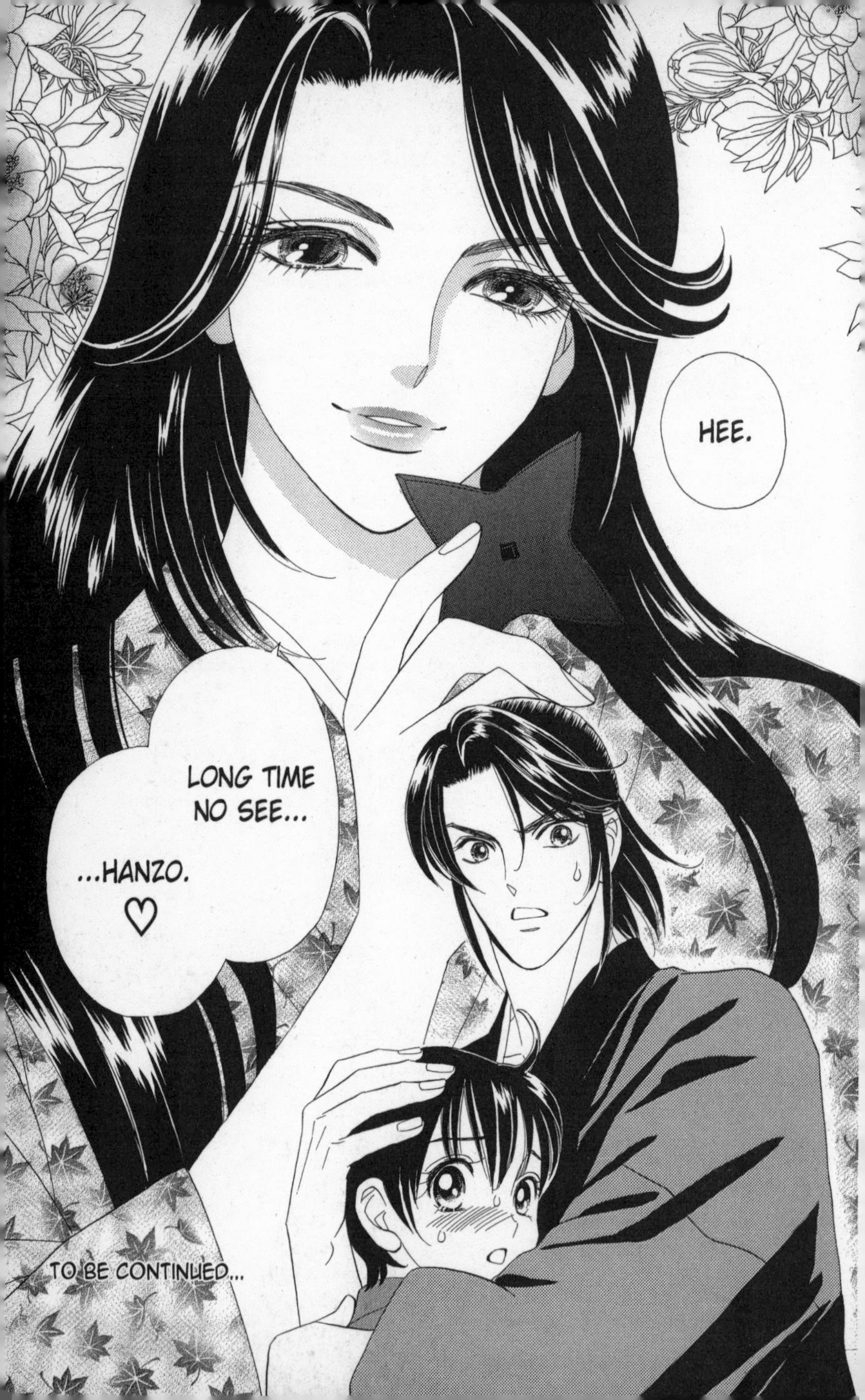
HEE.
LONG TIME NO SEE... ...HANZO. ♡
TO BE CONTINUED...

The ways of the ninja are mysterious indeed, so here is a glossary of terms to help you navigate the intricacies of their world.

Page 20: Ku
"Ku" is short for kuma, the Japanese word for "bear."

Page 29: Best Jeanist Award
The "Best Jeanist Award" is an annual Japanese Award given to those who look cool in jeans.

Page 35: Kuji finger weaving
In Buddhism, Kuji finger weaving dispels evil and bad influences.

Page 38: Rabbit
Usagi means "rabbit" in Japanese.

Page 136: Momotaro
Momotaro is usually translated in English as "Peach Boy," a folktale about a boy who is born from a giant peach. He defeats a demon to bring back treasure to his parents.

Page 2: Shimo no Hanzo
Shimo no means "the Lower," and in this case refers to Hanzo's geographic location rather than social status.

Page 2: Iga
Iga is a region on the island of Kyushu, and also the name of the famous ninja clan that originated there. Another area famous for its ninja is Koga, in the Shiga prefecture on Honshu. Many books claim that these two ninja clans were mortal enemies, but in reality inter-ninja relations were not as bad as stories paint them.

Page 4: Matsutake
Matsutake is a specific type of mushroom that can only be found at the foot of Japanese red pines. It is considered one of the greatest Japanese delicacies and it's unbelievably expensive.

Page 4: Zodiac
Usagi is referring to the oriental zodiac. It rotates according to a 12-year cycle: Mouse, Cow, Tiger, Rabbit, Dragon, Snake, Horse, Sheep, Monkey, Bird, Dog, Boar.

Page 7: Kouga
Kouga is another famous ninja area. Iga and Kouga are the two most famous places for ninja in Japan.

Ever since I started writing this series, I have begun to let go of my "hang-ups" even more than before. If I'm too fastidious about something, I limit my chances of finding new ideas. I intend to be fastidious about not being fastidious so that I can create fun stories about situations that seem impossible or outrageous.

–Rinko Ueda

Rinko Ueda is from Nara prefecture. She enjoys listening to the radio, drama CDs, and Rakugo comedy performances. Her works include *Ryo*, a series based on the legend of Gojo Bridge, *Home*, a story about love crossing national boundaries, and *Tail of the Moon (Tsuki no Shippo)*, a romantic ninja comedy.

TAIL OF THE MOON

Vol. 4

The Shojo Beat Manga Edition

STORY & ART BY

RINKO UEDA

Translation & Adaptation/Tetsuichiro Miyaki
Touch-up Art & Lettering/Mark McMurray
Design/Izumi Hirayama
Editor/Nancy Thistlethwaite

Editor in Chief, Books/Alvin Lu
Editor in Chief, Magazines/Marc Weidenbaum
VP of Publishing Licensing/Rika Inouye
VP of Sales/Gonzalo Ferreyra
Sr. VP of Marketing/Liza Coppola
Publisher/Hyoe Narita

Printed in Canada

Published by VIZ Media, LLC
P.O. Box 77064
San Francisco, CA 94107

Shojo Beat Manga Edition
10 9 8 7 6 5 4 3 2
First printing, April 2007
Second printing, November 2007

store.viz.com

RATED T+ FOR OLDER TEEN

PARENTAL ADVISORY

TAIL OF THE MOON is rated T+ for Older Teen and is recommended for ages 16 and up. This volume contains brief nudity and ninja violence

ratings.viz.com

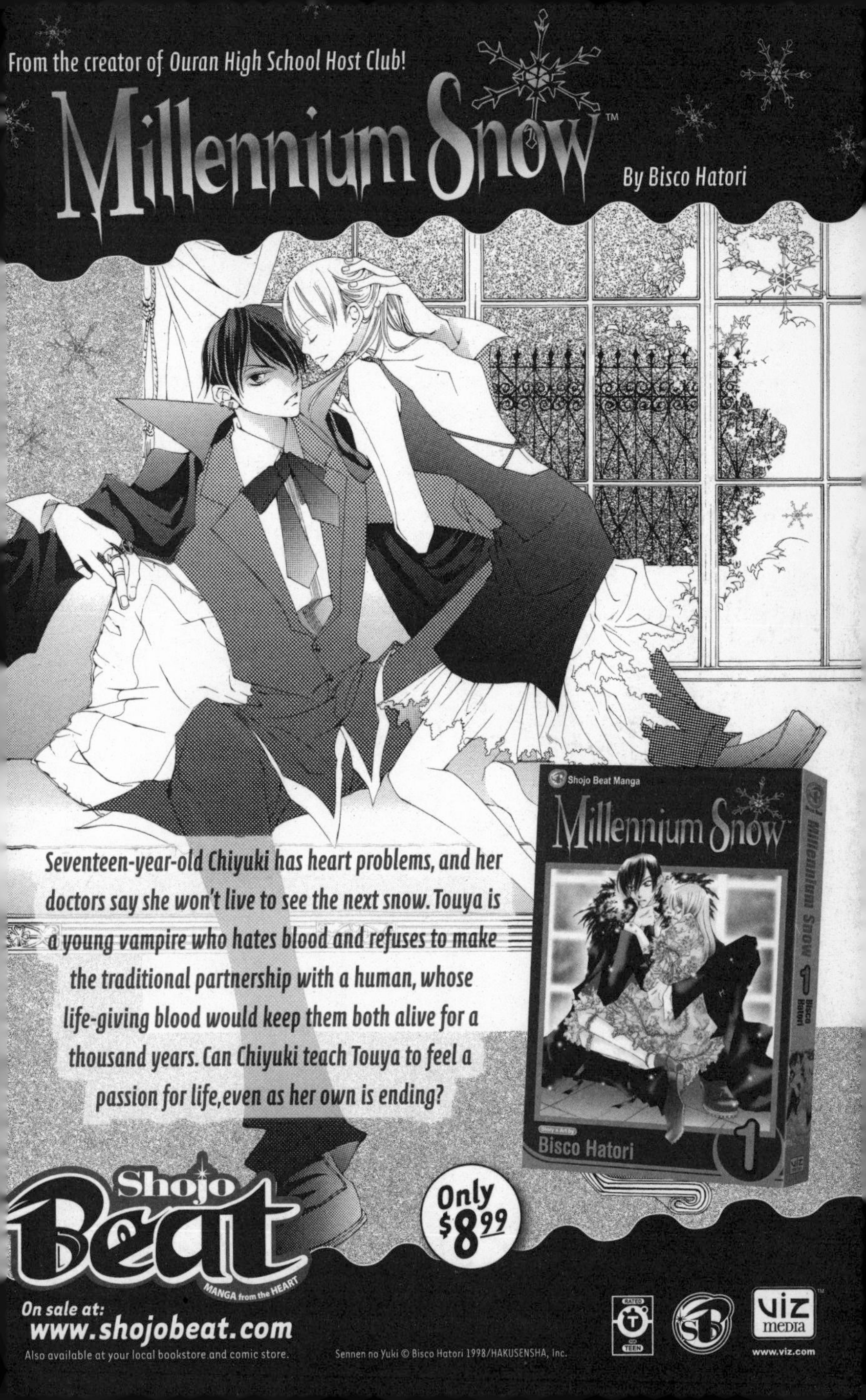

From the creator of Ouran High School Host Club!
Millennium Snow™
By Bisco Hatori
Seventeen-year-old Chiyuki has heart problems, and her doctors say she won't live to see the next snow. Touya is a young vampire who hates blood and refuses to make the traditional partnership with a human, whose life-giving blood would keep them both alive for a thousand years. Can Chiyuki teach Touya to feel a passion for life,even as her own is ending?
Shojo Beat Manga
Millennium Snow
Bisco Hatori
1
Only $8.99
Shojo Beat
MANGA from the HEART
On sale at:
www.shojobeat.com
Also available at your local bookstore and comic store.
Sennen no Yuki © Bisco Hatori 1998/HAKUSENSHA, Inc.
RATED T TEEN
viz media
www.viz.com

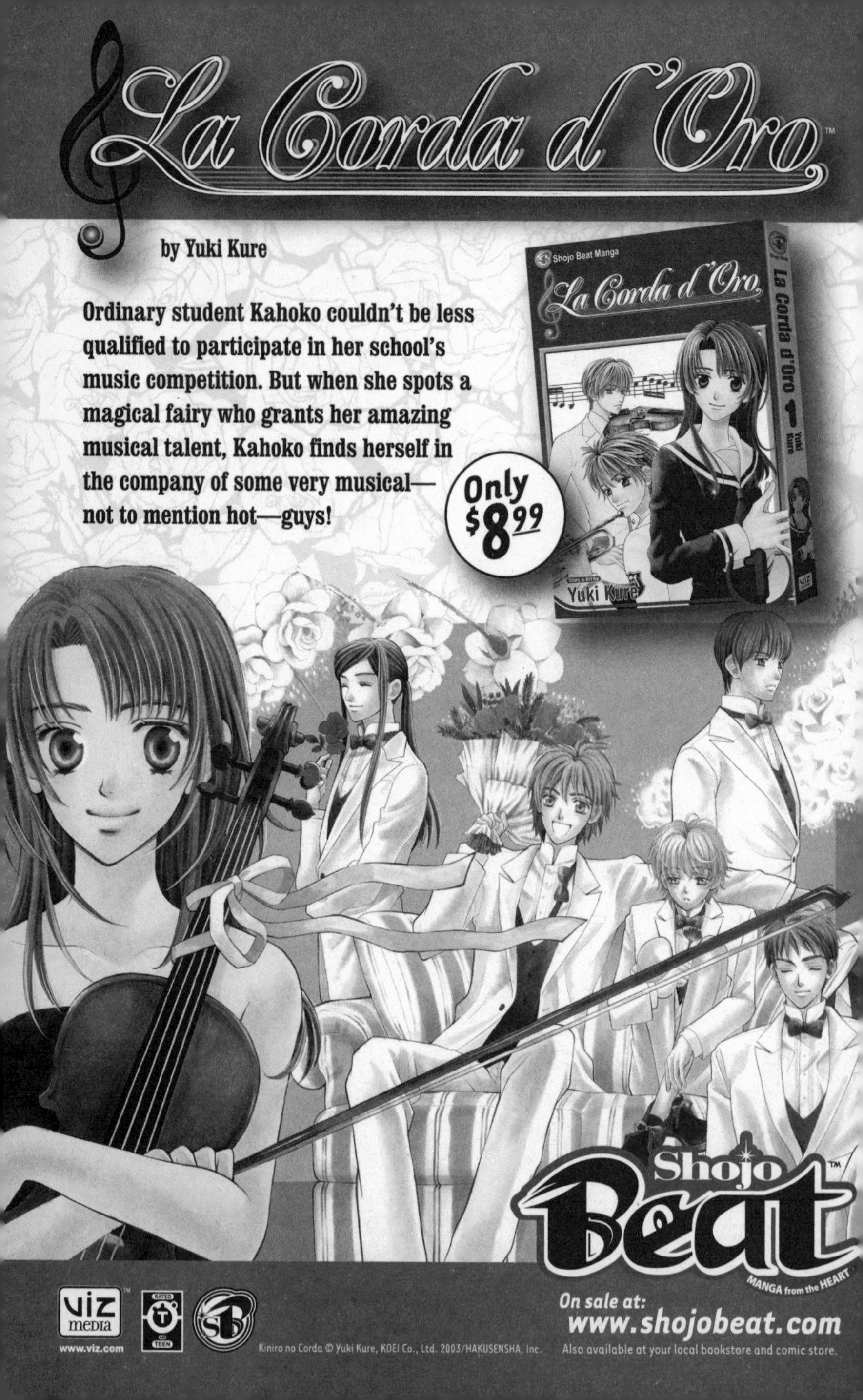

La Corda d'Oro™
by Yuki Kure
Ordinary student Kahoko couldn't be less qualified to participate in her school's music competition. But when she spots a magical fairy who grants her amazing musical talent, Kahoko finds herself in the company of some very musical—not to mention hot—guys!
Only $8.99
Shojo Beat Manga
La Corda d'Oro
Story & Art by Yuki Kure
Shojo Beat™
MANGA from the HEART
On sale at:
www.shojobeat.com
Also available at your local bookstore and comic store.
viz media
www.viz.com
RATED T TEEN
Kiniro no Corda © Yuki Kure, KOEI Co., Ltd. 2003/HAKUSENSHA, Inc.

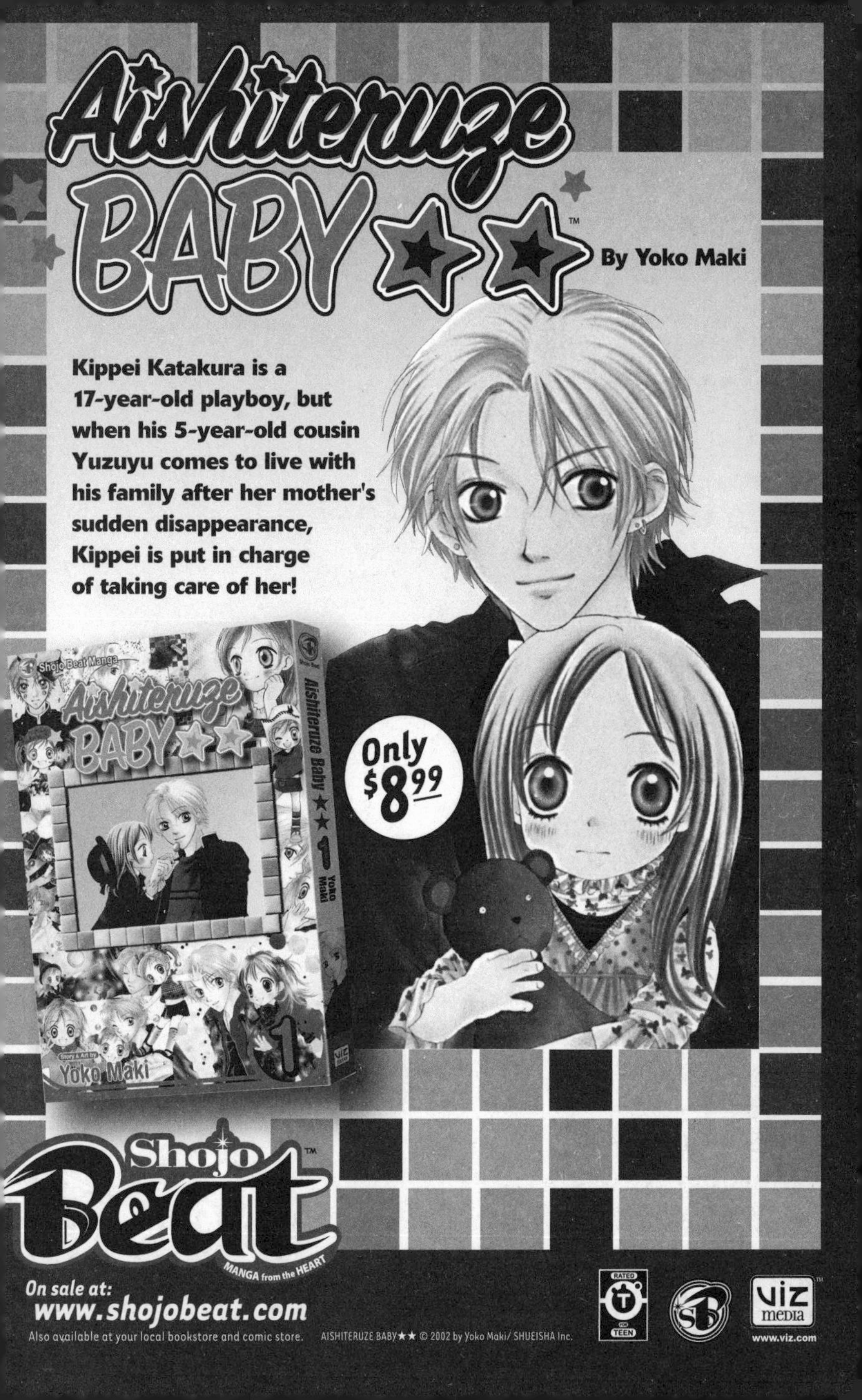
Aishiteruze BABY★★™
By Yoko Maki
Kippei Katakura is a 17-year-old playboy, but when his 5-year-old cousin Yuzuyu comes to live with his family after her mother's sudden disappearance, Kippei is put in charge of taking care of her!
Only $8.99
Shojo Beat Manga
Aishiteruze BABY★★
Aishiteruze Baby★★ 1 Yoko Maki
Story & Art by Yoko Maki
Shojo Beat™
MANGA from the HEART
On sale at:
www.shojobeat.com
Also available at your local bookstore and comic store.
AISHITERUZE BABY★★ © 2002 by Yoko Maki/ SHUEISHA Inc.
RATED T FOR TEEN
viz media
www.viz.com

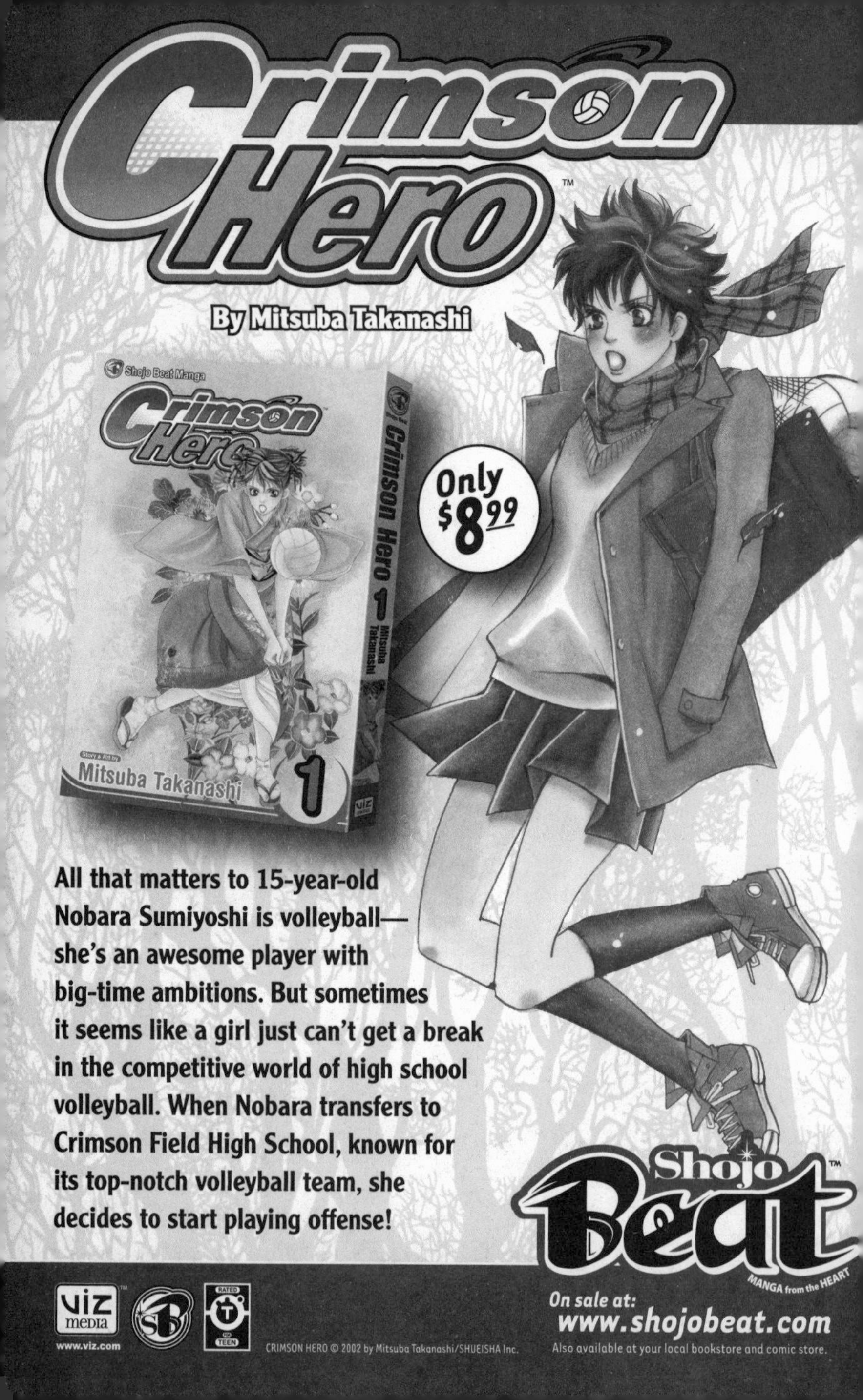
Crimson Hero™
By Mitsuba Takanashi
Shojo Beat Manga
Crimson Hero
Story & Art by
Mitsuba Takanashi
1
Only $8.99
All that matters to 15-year-old Nobara Sumiyoshi is volleyball—she's an awesome player with big-time ambitions. But sometimes it seems like a girl just can't get a break in the competitive world of high school volleyball. When Nobara transfers to Crimson Field High School, known for its top-notch volleyball team, she decides to start playing offense!
Shojo Beat™
MANGA from the HEART
On sale at:
www.shojobeat.com
Also available at your local bookstore and comic store.
viz media
www.viz.com
RATED T TEEN
CRIMSON HERO © 2002 by Mitsuba Takanashi/SHUEISHA Inc.

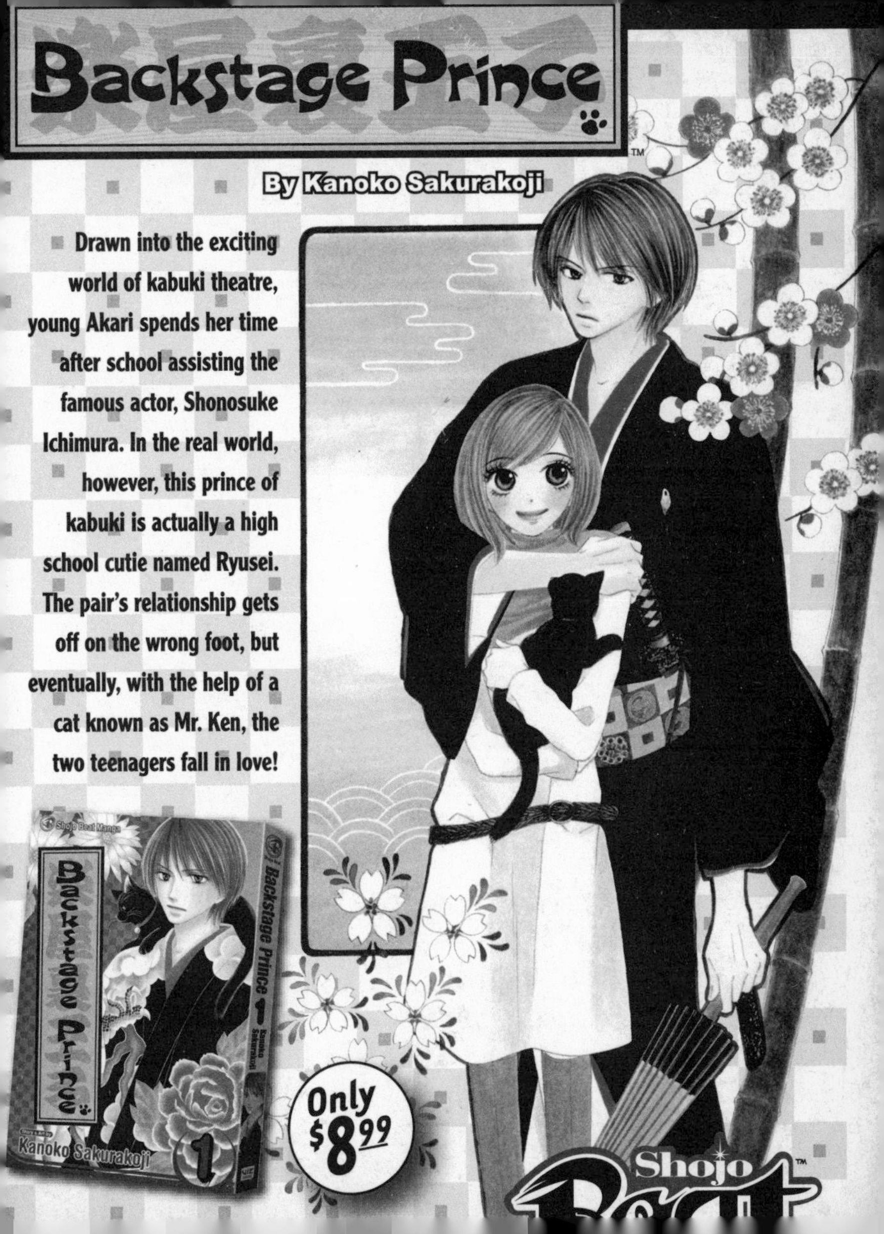
Backstage Prince
By Kanoko Sakurakoji
Drawn into the exciting world of kabuki theatre, young Akari spends her time after school assisting the famous actor, Shonosuke Ichimura. In the real world, however, this prince of kabuki is actually a high school cutie named Ryusei. The pair's relationship gets off on the wrong foot, but eventually, with the help of a cat known as Mr. Ken, the two teenagers fall in love!
Shojo Beat Manga
Backstage Prince
1
Kanoko Sakurakoji
Only $8.99
Shojo Beat

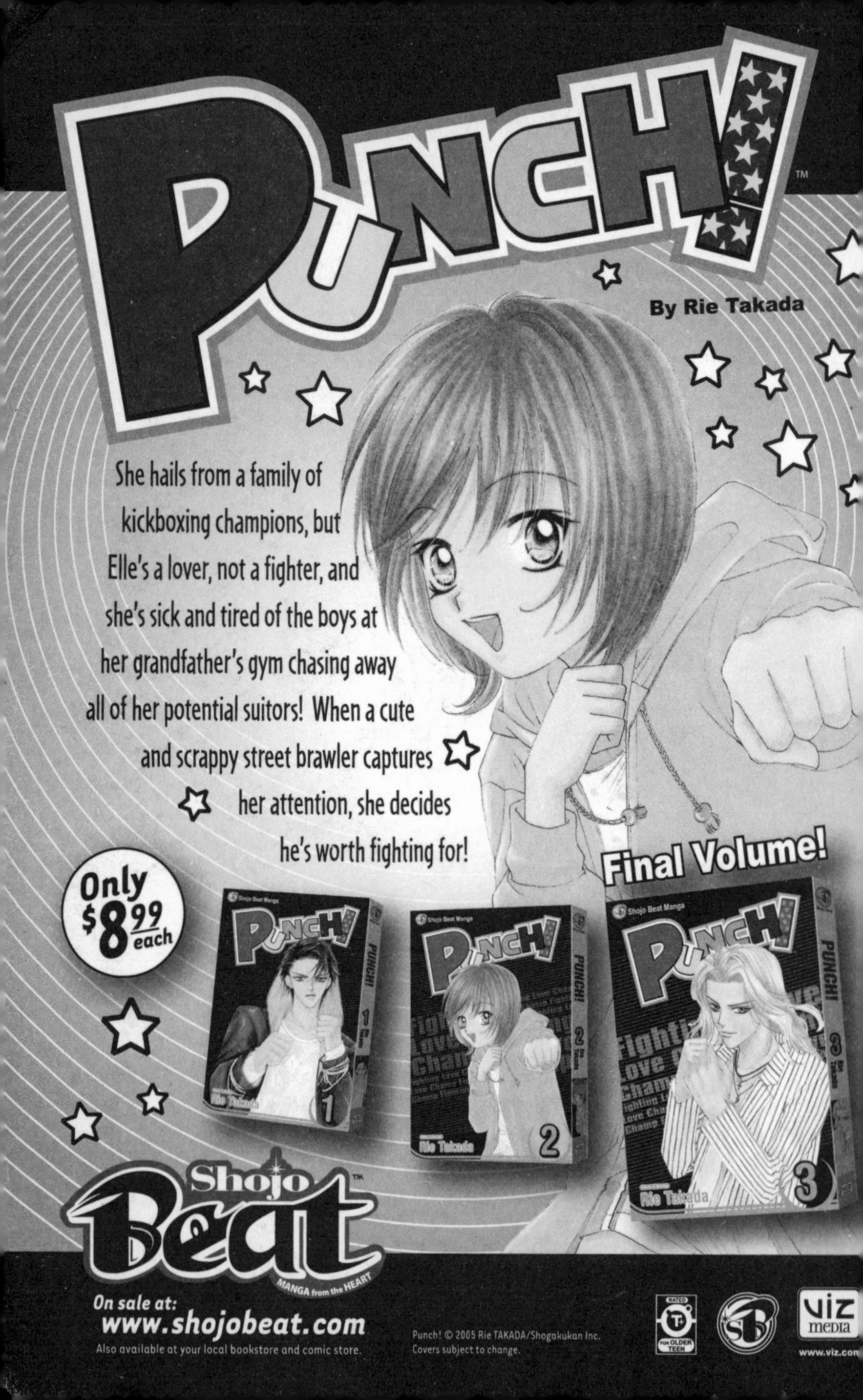
PUNCH!™
By Rie Takada
She hails from a family of kickboxing champions, but Elle's a lover, not a fighter, and she's sick and tired of the boys at her grandfather's gym chasing away all of her potential suitors! When a cute and scrappy street brawler captures her attention, she decides he's worth fighting for!
Only $8.99 each
Final Volume!
Shojo Beat™
MANGA from the HEART
On sale at:
www.shojobeat.com
Also available at your local bookstore and comic store.
Punch! © 2005 Rie TAKADA/Shogakukan Inc.
Covers subject to change.
RATED T+ FOR OLDER TEEN
viz media
www.viz.com

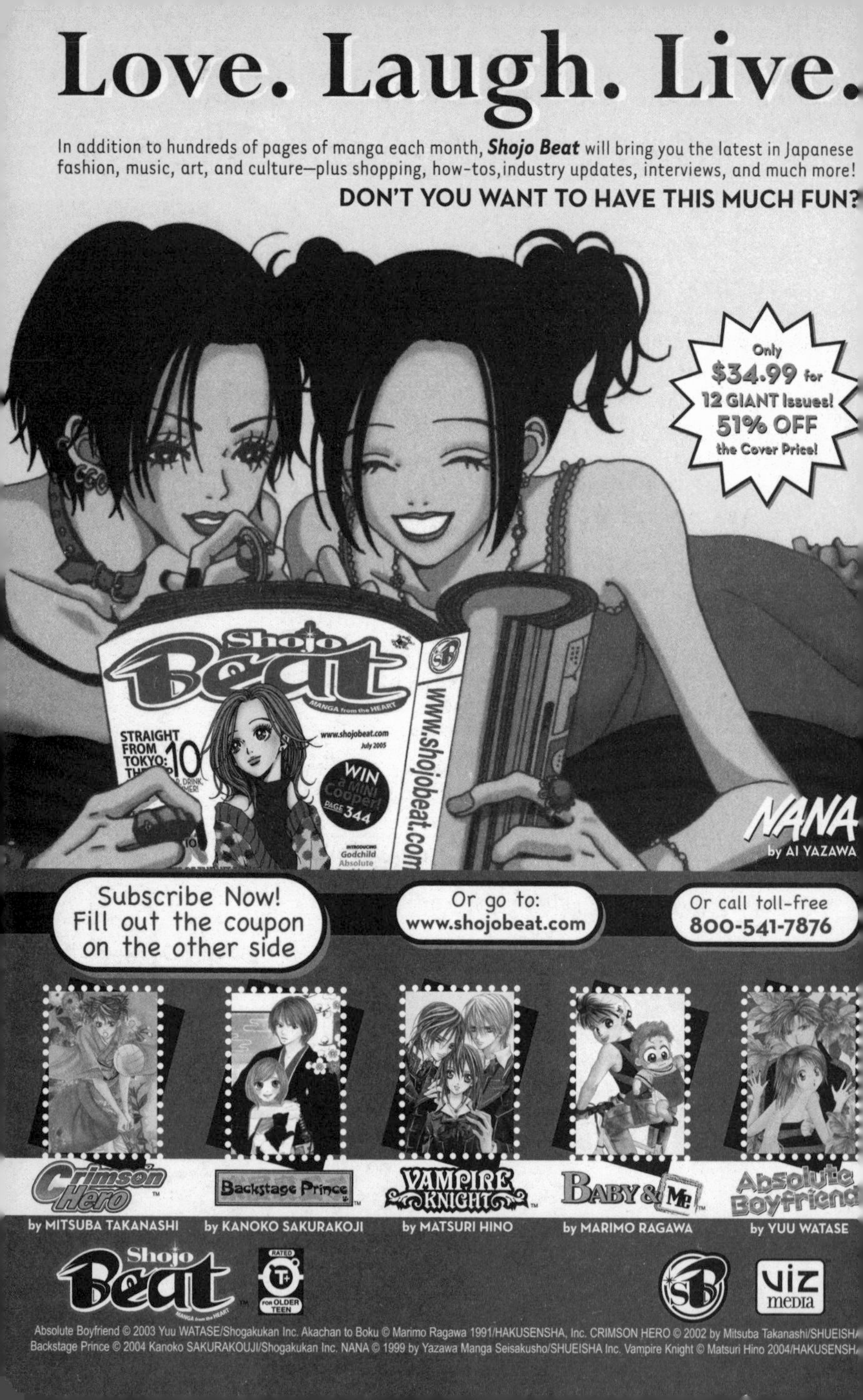
Love. Laugh. Live.
In addition to hundreds of pages of manga each month, Shojo Beat will bring you the latest in Japanese fashion, music, art, and culture—plus shopping, how-tos, industry updates, interviews, and much more!
DON'T YOU WANT TO HAVE THIS MUCH FUN?
Only $34.99 for 12 GIANT Issues! 51% OFF the Cover Price!
Shojo Beat
MANGA from the HEART
www.shojobeat.com
July 2005
STRAIGHT FROM TOKYO:
WIN a MINI Cooper! PAGE 344
www.shojobeat.com
NANA
by AI YAZAWA
Subscribe Now! Fill out the coupon on the other side
Or go to: www.shojobeat.com
Or call toll-free 800-541-7876
Crimson Hero
by MITSUBA TAKANASHI
Backstage Prince
by KANOKO SAKURAKOJI
VAMPIRE KNIGHT
by MATSURI HINO
BABY & ME
by MARIMO RAGAWA
Absolute Boyfriend
by YUU WATASE
Shojo Beat
MANGA from the HEART
RATED T+ FOR OLDER TEEN
viz media
Absolute Boyfriend © 2003 Yuu WATASE/Shogakukan Inc. Akachan to Boku © Marimo Ragawa 1991/HAKUSENSHA, Inc. CRIMSON HERO © 2002 by Mitsuba Takanashi/SHUEISHA
Backstage Prince © 2004 Kanoko SAKURAKOUJI/Shogakukan Inc. NANA © 1999 by Yazawa Manga Seisakusho/SHUEISHA Inc. Vampire Knight © Matsuri Hino 2004/HAKUSENSHA